Educating the Romantic Poets

Life and Learning in the Anglo-Classical Academy, 1770–1850

Romantic Reconfigurations:
Studies in Literature and Culture 1780–1850

Series Editors:
Professor Tim Fulford, De Montfort University
Professor Alan Vardy, Hunter College and the Graduate Center, CUNY

As befits a series published in the city of Roscoe and Rushton, a city that linked Britain to the transatlantic trade in cotton, in sugar, and in people, *Romantic Reconfigurations* reconfigures the literary and cultural geographies and histories of Romanticism. Topics featured include, but are by no means confined to, provincial and labouring-class writing, diasporic and colonial writing, natural history and other scientific discourse, journalism, popular culture, music and theatre, landscape and nature, cosmopolitanism and travel, poetics and form.

Educating the Romantic Poets

Life and Learning in the Anglo-Classical Academy, 1770–1850

Catherine E. Ross

LIVERPOOL UNIVERSITY PRESS

First published 2023 by
Liverpool University Press
4 Cambridge Street
Liverpool
L69 7ZU

Copyright © 2023 Catherine E. Ross

Catherine E. Ross has asserted the right to be identified as the author of this book in accordance with the Copyright, Designs and Patents Act 1988.

All rights reserved. No part of this book may be reproduced, stored in a retrieval system, or transmitted, in any form or by any means, electronic, mechanical, photocopying, recording, or otherwise, without the prior written permission of the publisher.

British Library Cataloguing-in-Publication data
A British Library CIP record is available

ISBN 978-1-83764-445-2 cased

Typeset by Carnegie Book Production, Lancaster
Printed and bound by CPI Group (UK) Ltd, Croydon CR0 4YY

Dedication

This book has been a long time in the making and could not have been completed without the help and encouragement of many people, above all those to whom it is now dedicated: My parents, Col. Charles C. Ross, U.S. Army Retired and Mrs Julia Moore Ross; my friend and research librarian, Ms Vandy Dubre; a leader whose ethics and courage inspired me along the way, Adm. William H. McRaven, U.S. Navy Retired; and my unstintingly supportive and beloved husband, Calvin 'Bud' Allen.

Contents

List of Illustrations		ix
List of Abbreviations		xi
Preface		xiii
1	Introduction	1
2	England's Public and Grammar Schools: First Lessons	27
3	England's Public and Grammar Schools: Lessons in Grammar, Memory, and Composition	49
4	England's Public and Grammar Schools: Lessons in Classical Literature, Rhetoric, Oratory, and Composition Training	71
5	Religious Instruction and Worship in the Anglo-Classical Academy	97
6	Oxford and Cambridge in the Romantic Period: 'Operose ignorance' or 'Good habits, and the principles of virtue and wisdom'?	131
7	University Life	161
8	The Curriculum of the English 'Confessional' University: Heroes, Shepherds, and 'Holding acquaintance with the stars'	183
9	Pedagogies of Oxford and Cambridge in the Georgian Period	203

10	The Educators of Oxford and Cambridge in the Georgian Period	223
11	Leadership at Oxford and Cambridge	241
12	Conclusions	273

Works Cited 279
Index 293

Illustrations

Figures

1	Winchester School House	28
2	Westminster birch rod and cane	42
3	Title page of a teaching text of *Aesop's Fables* in Greek and Latin, 1807	52
4	Title page of *Introduction to the Latin Tongue for the Use of Youth*, 1804	59
5	Speech Day Programme, Eton College, 1810	76
6	Percy Shelley's *Gradus*	80
7	Sydney Smith's English Prose Essay Prize book	85
8	Photograph of the bookplate for John Gillies' *History of Ancient Greece*	87
9	The Westminster Challenge	91
10	Interior, Eton College Chapel	100
11	Christ's Hospital, London	101
12	St Mary the Virgin church portico, Oxford	103
13	Title page of the Eton prayer book, *Preces Quotidianæ*	105
14	Fellow Commoner, Emmanuel College, Cambridge	154

15	Nobleman, Trinity College, Cambridge	155
16	Roll book of students at St John's College, Cambridge	157
17	The Geological Lecture Room, Oxford	185
18	George Canning's Collections List	196
19	Trinity College examination	209
20	Table of Contents of Banks, Hodson or Challis Papers XVIIIth Century	216
21	Samuel Vince in his rooms at Sidney Sussex College, Cambridge	237
22	All Souls College, Oxford: cloisters and chapel	261

Tables

1	Estimated cost of degrees at Oxford University	147
2	Estimated cost of degrees at Cambridge University	148

Abbreviations

'Biographia'	Samuel Taylor Coleridge. 'Biographia Literaria'. *Samuel Taylor Coleridge*, edited by H. J. Jackson, Oxford University Press, 1985, pp. 155–482
CLRS	Lynda Pratt, et al. *The Collected Letters of Robert Southey*. 2009. https://romantic-circles.org/editions/southey_letters
CLSTC	E. L. Griggs, ed. *Collected Letters of Samuel Taylor Coleridge*, vol. 1, 1785–1800. Clarendon, 1956
DNB	*Dictionary of National Biography*. England, Smith Elder, 1903
Graham	*Cambridge University Commission Report*
Hinds	*Oxford University Commission Report*
Prelude	Jonathan Wordsworth, M. H. Abrams, and Stephen Gill, eds. *The Prelude 1799, 1805, 1850*. W. W. Norton, 1979
WWMW	Stephen Gill, ed. *William Wordsworth: The Major Works*. Oxford University Press, 1984
WWPW	Thomas Hutchinson, ed., revised by Ernest De Selincourt. *The Poetical Works of Wordsworth: With Introduction and Notes*. Oxford University Press, 1974

Preface

The research supporting this project has been broad and interdisciplinary. Besides the Romantic texts and the work of many scholars of the period cited, this book drew upon biographies, memoirs, and various primary sources, such as the founding statutes of schools and colleges, the universities' official historical registers, the Royal Commission reports on the universities of 1852, the *Report of the Schools Inquiry Commission* of 1868, and various contemporaneous statutes and standard works of the Church of England. Schoolboys' letters, award-winning poems, and school magazines in the archives at Rugby, Winchester, Westminster, and Eton, were important resources. So too, were schoolmasters' letters, sermons, and memoirs; as were eighteenth- and nineteenth-century textbooks, periodical articles, and monographs on education. For details about teaching and learning in the university colleges, the Collections Books of Christ Church, the examination and enrollment registers of Balliol and St John's College, Cambridge, old examination papers from Trinity College, Cambridge, and the colleges' archival holdings of the papers, publications, sermons, and letters of university students, college tutors, and deans were used. While I recognise that there will be bias in what institutions choose to house in their archives, these documents are, nevertheless, informative, particularly about the educational values of the schools and colleges.

Site visits to the schools and colleges, with their gothic halls and chapels, manicured lawns and gardens, and, in many cases, surrounding countryside, were reminders of the power of place upon the minds of young people. Additionally, conversations with modern-day students at the schools and universities and attendance at school and college classes and events in their ancient buildings contributed to this account of how students in the Georgian

Educating the Romantic Poets

and early Victorian periods probably experienced their days at these institutions. Contemporary research on cognitive development, learning, and how college affects students was consulted, as were my own experiences and observations from several decades of attending and teaching in both secondary boarding schools and universities. In addition, clergymen and educators specialising in classics, English literature, and composition at Rugby, Winchester, Eton, and Westminster, and at Balliol, Christ Church, and King's College, Oxford, and St John's and Trinity Colleges, Cambridge were interviewed. I send my thanks over the ocean to each of them.

CHAPTER ONE

Introduction

> Several years ago, when the Author retired to his native mountains, with the hope of being enabled to construct a literary Work that might live, it was a reasonable thing that he should take a review of his own mind and examine how far Nature and Education has qualified him for such employment.
>
> William Wordsworth, *The Excursion*,
> Preface to the edition of 1814

> The history of training provides a new and largely unexplored route to understanding the mathematical physicist's way of knowing.
>
> Andrew Warwick, *Masters of Theory: Cambridge and the Rise of Mathematical Physics*

Marilyn Butler's influential volume *Romantics, Rebels and Reactionaries: English Literature and Its Background 1760–1830* opens with the observation that 'no other period has yielded so many poets, novelists, essayists and critics of true importance and individuality, writers who are not followers of greater names nor part of a school, but themselves distinctive voices'.[1] While scholars specialising in other periods might disagree with her statement, Butler follows it with a provocative question: What 'common factors' caused writers in the Romantic period 'to develop so richly and variously at the same time'? Or,

---

[1] Butler, p. 1.

as Wordsworth phrased it—how far have 'Nature and Education' qualified them for the employment of writing a 'literary Work that might live'? Over the years, many scholars have circled around these questions. Butler and others have examined ideas and attitudes generated by the revolutions in America and France and the long Napoleonic war. Alternative responses to this question have focused on factors such as economics, political economy and the public sphere, periodicals and the advent of cheap publication, celebrity culture, gender, and the emergence of various modern scientific disciplines. *Educating the Romantic Poets: Life and Learning in the Anglo-Classical Academy, 1770–1850* offers yet another way to think about Butler's—and Wordsworth's—questions by closely examining how the classical grammar schools and the colleges of Oxford and Cambridge trained many of the writers and readers in the Romantic period to read, write, and think. While it is difficult to measure precisely where learning starts and how it will 'take', it is universally accepted that schools and universities impart the foundational skills that enable students to continue to learn and function as adults. It is where they develop verbal, quantitative, and subject matter competence. During school years youngsters experience significant cognitive and intellectual development and start noticing and responding to contemporaneous expectations and models of social behaviour. They explore and negotiate their own positions regarding the cultural values, political arguments, and aesthetic tastes that circulate in their time. It is also clear that school and college years are when students begin recognising and developing their personal interests and talents. It was no accident that Wordsworth, Coleridge, Southey, Byron, and Percy Shelley all began to think of themselves as poets and to publish verse while at school or university. So, the project of this book has been to study how the worlds of the public and endowed grammar schools and Oxford and Cambridge operated to train them for the writer's life. This book is meant to open the subject of the Romantics' education up for further study.

I have been encouraged in this project by the example of Andrew Warwick's award-winning study of mathematics education at Cambridge, *Masters of Theory: Cambridge and the Rise of Mathematical Physics*. Beginning with the question 'In what ways do specific kinds of pedagogical regime have the power to produce or respecify the content and operation of a technical discipline',[2] he tracks how Cambridge's instruction in mathematics and theory during the early Victorian period differed significantly from Continental teaching, and yet those students and their teachers, including James Clerk Maxwell and William Thomson, created what specialists now call 'classical physics'. Warwick claims the foundation for these students was training in certain craft-like skills, ones that are often taken for granted, such as notation. He also shows how close

[2] Warwick, p. 39.

relationships between students and teachers and the competitive atmosphere at the university, in sports as well as intellectual pursuits, influenced students' 'ways of knowing' and their subsequent efforts as scientists. *Educating the Romantic Poets* begins with a pair of research questions similar to Warwick's: How did the Romantics' education foster their writing careers, and how did their early training in language and literature help to produce and respecify the content and operation of their writing? This question is particularly apt considering how the later poetry of the Lake Poets became increasingly formal and religiously orthodox. This project is also informed by my own years of learning and teaching, where I have seen how students' and educators' work is shaped not just by assigned texts and tasks but also by relationships, the institutional environment, and the daily news. This book does two things: it details *how* as well as *what* technical skills, literary knowledge, and cultural beliefs were taught in the Romantic academy, and it explains and shows how this data can be of service in understanding, writing about, and teaching Romantic texts. The research reported here also explains attitudes of the Romantics' readers, publishers, and critics, many of whom were similarly trained.

Wordsworth implicitly invites a study of this sort not only in his Preface to the 1814 *Excursion*, but even earlier, in the 'Advertisement' to *Lyrical Ballads*, where he appeals to those 'Readers of superior judgment' and those who are 'conversant' with 'our elder writers', noting, along with Sir Joshua Reynolds, that 'taste in poetry, and in all other arts' can only be 'produced by severe thought, and a long continued intercourse with the best models of composition'.[3] There can be little doubt that he is referring to readers who had been trained, as he and his peers had been, using the Greek, Roman, and Christian texts that the scholars in his day believed to be the 'best models' and with which they had experienced 'long continued intercourse' when they were at school and university. Wordsworth's statement also signals how important such training was to his own literary judgement, which many critics—contemporaneous and modern—have questioned, particularly with regard to his later works.

By focusing on these elite institutions only, this book appears to slight those authors who were excluded from the Anglican academies for religious or gender reasons, those who were educated in Scotland or the Dissenting Academies, and those who had little or no formal schooling. Among these groups number all the female writers of the period as well as Godwin, Blake, Burns, Equiano, Thelwall, Clare, Hazlitt, and Keats. Similar pedagogically focused studies of girls' boarding schools, dissenting academies, private academies and tutoring, dame schools, Sunday schools, and apprenticeships are needed. The Anglo-classical schools and universities are treated here as a starting place, in the hopes

[3] WWMW, p. 591.

Educating the Romantic Poets

that other modes of education in the period will be studied in the same way in the future. Anglican classical institutions are a good starting place because they were older, more numerous, more widely available around the country, and better organised than most other teaching enterprises of the period. The students trained in these institutions were often socially prominent, so they exerted influence on both the shape of contemporary literary taste and what rolled off the presses of publishers of the day. Added to this, contemporaneous reception of those writers who were not trained in this tradition often depended on the literary knowledge and expectations of those who were.

What distinguishes this book from others is its pedagogical approach. *Educating the Romantic Poets* not only details the Anglo-classical programme's curriculum but also investigates the teaching methods, expected learning outcomes, and formative experiences outside the classroom. It outlines the methods of classical language training, which included close reading, translation, interpretation, memorisation, recitation, discussion, imitation, daily practice, and constant writing and review. It explains how students were taught the rules of prosody, the conventions of various literary genres, writerly work habits, and contemporaneous aesthetic standards. It also considers the effects of environment and community on schoolboys and college men.

Another innovation of this study is that it examines instruction at both the grammar schools and the universities. Most discussions of education in the Romantic period concentrate on only the schools or the universities, and they regularly criticise the former for rigidity and the latter for laxity. This book explains that, unlike school and university educators today, who rarely meet or interact, Romantic period schoolmasters and college tutors were classmates and friends with the same level of academic training. They communicated often, worked intentionally as partners, and considered themselves colleagues. Their curriculum and methods were conceived as a continuum, shaped by eighteenth-century understandings of the intellectual and social development of boys and young men, and they are better understood by viewing them as such. For these educators, the rigour and discipline of the schools followed by the remarkable freedom of university instruction were intentional and grew out of their understanding of human development. They believed that keeping students focused primarily on only three fields of study—classics, mathematics, and 'divinity'—was the best preparation for adulthood. The upshot of the schools' and colleges' emphasis upon close reading and constant, daily and/or weekly writing practice meant that Wordsworth's and Byron's generations received close to a decade of training in how to read and write verse before they ever entered the public arena. Moreover, these institutions had much to do with why England was a 'reading nation' in the Romantic period.[4]

---

[4] St Clair.

Introduction

The story about Anglo-classical education told here invites revision of certain long-held opinions about these schools, colleges, and educators that can, thereby, lead to new ways of thinking about the literary culture of that age and to new tools for interpreting the lives and literary works of certain Romantic writers. As will be explained in later chapters, this educational regime was, in many ways, ideal training in the poet's craft. It built rich vocabularies that emphasised appreciation of the sounds and rhythms of words and the rules of prosody. It acquainted youngsters quite intimately with literary genres and their conventions, starting with fables, colloquies, and psalms, and moving on to pastorals, epics, epistles, odes, drama, biography, history, and philosophy. Pupils at these schools read, *memorised*, talked about, and composed verse in Latin, Greek, or English *every week*. They memorised and were taught to practise the rules of grammar *daily*. As students at the university, these same young people had a certain amount of freedom to choose which of the texts in the universities' canon they would study and upon which they would be examined. Instruction almost always took the form of dialogue and practice with their college tutor; the time they spent sitting silently in lecture halls was minimal, and they continued to be required to write compositions—much longer ones—in verse or prose in three languages almost every week.

The evidence reported in this book shows that the Anglo-classical programme did not discourage learning, energy, and imagination, as has sometimes been charged. Quite the opposite. Data is presented here of schoolboys' sophisticated content knowledge and writing skills, of the affection they had for their schools and colleges, and of their energetic and imaginative efforts as both fledgling writers and citizens. Examples include the substance and quality of the writing in student papers preserved in the school and college archives and the essays and poems they published in their literary magazines. Other examples of the benefits of this education are their self-organised debating and literary societies, boys' efforts such as 'Helps to the Challenge' at Westminster, and college men's work as study partners or 'Fathers' for the Senate House exams. The hard academic work required in the Anglo-classical academy did not dim students' energy and imagination when they played, and examples are included below of students' enthusiastic invention and management of cross-country games and foot races, intercollegiate cricket matches, boating adventures, sock puddings and bucket brews, fetes for their fag masters, festive country picnics, and dramatic and musical entertainments. My research also shows that, despite their reputations for elitism, brutality, or ineptitude, the clergymen who taught at both the grammar schools and university colleges were often youthful and broad-minded individuals who were respected by their students. Some—such as William Frend of Jesus College and Thomas Jones of

Educating the Romantic Poets

Trinity—were courageous and outspoken supporters of reform. Many were excellent classicists, mathematicians, and theologians who published widely. Not a few were polymaths who could and did teach in disparate fields, a feat of interdisciplinarity that is rarely possible in the modern academy.

Included in the chapters that follow are selected examples from the writing of Romantic poets that make it clear that, while they complained rather predictably about school or college as students, they also recognised the benefits of their educational experiences. Byron was forever grateful for Dr Drury's help with his public speaking at Harrow, and he admired the witty Master of Trinity College, Dr Mansel. Coleridge told his brother he was happy as a lark reading Greek at Jesus College and bragged about how he used his college writing to impress the Evans girls. In Book Fifth of the 1850 *Prelude* Wordsworth recalls that it was at Hawkshead Grammar School that he first became conscious of the pleasure and charm 'Of words in tuneful order' and felt the 'passion and power' of poetry.[5] 'Words themselves', he writes in both the 1805 and 1850 editions, moved him and his companions 'with conscious pleasure'.[6] In Book Sixth he records that 'The poet's soul' was with him in his college days and that it was then that he first felt a 'fellowship/ Of modest sympathy' with the 'mighty names' of the literary world and was 'emboldened' to trust in his talents as a writer.[7]

Educating the Romantic Poets also highlights the uniqueness of the Romantics' moment in educational and national history. The Romantic era intelligentsia were the last to experience the orthodox Anglo-classical programme, and they did so in a transitional and often radically disruptive moment in European and English political history. After 1850, formal education in England changed forever—it became nationalised, technical, and specialised, and weekly verse themes became a thing of the past. When Wordsworth and Byron were in school, however, bright and/or privileged male youngsters still lived in semi-monastic communities where learning focused upon classical and biblical literature and mathematics. At the same time, governmental and social reform, personal freedom, and national security were on every thinking person's mind. Both revolutionary and traditional beliefs about human nature and society were circulating and facing off. Feudalism was giving way to respect for the rights of many more people and to new hopes of what the modern world calls 'upward mobility'. The beginnings of modern science and industrialisation were catching popular and scholarly attention and challenging long-held religious

---

[5] *Prelude*, p. 183, ll. 554–556. Reed's chronology of the early years speculates that this consciousness could have developed as early as the spring of Wordsworth's tenth year. See Reed, p. 50.

[6] *Prelude*, 1805, pp. 180–181, ll. 567–568; 1850, p. 183, ll. 544–545.

[7] *Prelude*, 1850, p. 189, ll. 42, 53. In the 1805 edition he uses the word 'encouraged', p. 188, l. 65, instead of 'emboldened'.

Introduction

beliefs. However, students in the Anglo-classical academies continued to learn grammar, to write verse exercises, and to do math problems and memory work much as their fathers and grandfathers had done.

It was not, however, a curriculum without relevance to what was going on in the outside world. Using the original Latin or Greek texts, schoolboys and college men read about city states and empires, leaders and tyrants, love of country and love of the countryside. Students were required to attend Anglican Church services daily and to study classical texts full of references to pagan deities; but they also heard or took part in debates about subscription to the 39 Articles, religious toleration, Unitarianism, deism, and atheism. At the same time some university fellows, along with gentleman amateurs, Scots, and dissenters, were helping to invent and beginning to teach the emerging disciplines of modern chemistry, geology, and anatomy, and to reform—albeit slowly and sometimes reluctantly—the curriculum, examination practices, and religious tests at Oxford and Cambridge. Circulating in the minds of the generations of schoolboys and college men that included Coleridge, Byron, and Tennyson was the language of Homer, Pindar, Hesiod, Thucydides, Demosthenes, and the Greek dramatists, as well as Virgil, Horace, Ovid, Julius Caesar, and the Roman satirists. But so too was the language of Paine, Burke, Price, Godwin, Wollstonecraft, Clarkson, and Wilberforce. Many of these students were also reading and discussing (and eventually publishing) articles in *The Morning Post*, *The Morning Chronicle*, *The Times*, *Monthly Magazine*, *The Analytic Review*, *The British Critic*, *The Critical Review*, *The Anti-Jacobin*, *The Edinburgh Annual Register*, *The London Magazine, or Gentleman's Monthly Intelligencer*, and the many pamphlets inspired by current events and debates. Their letters also reference their reading and discussion of the works of Shakespeare, Spenser, Milton, Thomson, Bowles, Scott, and Chatterton. Days that began and ended with readings from the King James Bible and the liturgies of the *Book of Common Prayer* might also be spent reading Euclid, Newton, and Paley. There can be little doubt that when these young men became members of the English republic of letters, thanks to the universally recognised credential of having spent time in the Anglo-classical academy, they entered that public space with minds teeming with the news and ways of thinking about the paradoxical challenges of their day. Moreover, their writing skills were at the ready.

Calling attention to how youngsters of the Romantic period experienced a very traditional religious and classical education while living in such unsettled times helps to explain not a few of the puzzling utterances and literary or life choices of certain Romantic poets. These include Southey's, Coleridge's, and Wordsworth's swing from embracing the 'new dawn' of the French Revolution, questioning the English establishment, and exploring Unitarianism to works such as Wordsworth's *Ecclesiastical Sketches* (1822), Coleridge's *Aids to Reflection*

(1825) and *Constitution of Church and State* (1829), and Southey's *Book of the Church* (1828) and *Sir Thomas More: Or, Colloquies on the Progress of Society* (1829). The nature of this education clarifies, as well, why early on Wordsworth had the audacity to declare in the Preface to *Lyrical Ballads* that poets in his generation could bind 'together by passion and knowledge the vast empire of human society as it is spread over the whole earth, and over all time'.[8] The physical and temporal scope of this statement reflects both contemporaneous and ancient sensibilities, the latter of which were made possible by Wordsworth's studies in the Anglo-classical academy. Moreover, we must assume that Wordsworth was recalling his experience at Hawkshead Grammar School with his schoolmasters William Taylor and Thomas Bowman when he told Lady Beaumont in 1807 that the role of the poet is 'to teach the young and the gracious of every age to see, to think, and feel, and therefore to become more actively and securely virtuous'.[9] The constancy of religious practice in school also helps to explain why, as Robert Ryan argues persuasively in *The Romantic Reformation*, that Wordsworth's career, taken all together, was 'essentially that of a religious teacher'.[10] Ryan's observation squares with another comment in the poet's same letter to Lady Beaumont where he declares that 'to be incapable of a feeling of Poetry … is to be without love of human nature and reverence for God'.[11]

The precise ways in which lessons register in the hearts and minds of students is difficult to tease out or measure, but, given the Romantics' rich vocabulary, reliance on classical and biblical allusions, and embrace of forms such as the ode, elegy, pastoral, epic, psalm, epistle, and hymn, there can be little doubt that their classical training helped to shape at the very least their generic conceptions. Stuart Curran has cited these conceptions as part of 'the culture of Romanticism'.[12] The Romantics' training also explains 'the most eccentric feature of the entire culture', the fact that it was 'simply mad for poetry'.[13] This madness began with their first lesson in school, which was to compose metrical verse. This remarkably 'writing-intensive' programme also helps to clarify why Wordsworth, Coleridge, and Southey were competent enough, when challenged by the spirit of their age, to use that training in innovative and distinctively individual ways and then, in later life, could turn and also produce carefully structured traditional forms that were familiar to their educated audience. Evidence about the nature of the Romantics' Anglo-classical education helps to explain not only the nature and changes of the older

[8] WWMW, p. 606.
[9] WWLMY, p. 46.
[10] Ryan, p. 82.
[11] WWLMY, p. 146.
[12] Curran, p. 4.
[13] Curran, p. 15.

Introduction

Romantics' careers but also Byron's and Shelley's adoption of classical settings for some of their most politically radical statements, the mystical spirituality of Shelley's irreligion, and both Byron's preference for wit and satire over lyrical verse and his playful balancing of the twin impulses of doubt and belief.[14]

Many of the details provided here—not only about the curriculum and educational practices of the schools and colleges but also about how these institutions worked together to manage students' transition from childhood to early adulthood—are not widely known among scholars. Readers may be surprised or possibly impressed by some of the educational practices and routines that this book reports. The school week included Saturdays, most days started early—usually at 6 a.m.—and every day began and ended with Anglican prayer services. By the age of ten or 11 most boys could read, speak, and write Latin. By the age of 14 many could do the same with Greek. It was not unusual for pupils aged 14 or 15 to be assigned to write three themes in several languages each week, two of which would be in verse. Pupils' motivations to do such work included curiosity, competition, family and personal honour, hero-worship, and fear of their schoolmasters' or parents' rod. With virtually no adult supervision, youngsters also organised their own sporting events and games and created their own literary magazines and debating societies. Spirited contests of content knowledge and speaking and debating skills as well as public recitations of classical literary works—often before distinguished or even royal visitors—were traditional at many schools as well.

Assuming that youngsters had learned most of their lessons and how to focus and work hard as schoolboys, English university tutors and deans accorded older students the freedom due them as 'gentlemen' to make their own choices about how hard they would study the classical poetry and drama, ancient history and philosophy, rhetoric, logic, scripture, church history, mathematics, astronomy, and physics that were offered at the universities and in which they would be examined each term. College tutors, not the universities' professors, shouldered most of the teaching. In many cases, tutors were younger fellows known to be excellent scholars (and sometimes athletes). Well acquainted with the curriculum and with collegians' behaviour, these educators customised their teaching to the talents and aspirations of the individuals assigned to them and recommended or warned against certain professors' lectures. Tutors were responsible not only for students' learning but also for their behaviour, finances, and spiritual formation. At the larger colleges, along with reading

---

[14] Ryan characterises Byron's religion stance as 'oscillation, a regular, predictable, harmonic motion between two opposing intellectual tendencies whose mutual correction resulted in something much closer to equipoise than to turmoil. Since neither skepticism nor uncritical belief seemed to him an adequate response to the condition of the universe, he deliberately adopted a strategic position between the two alternatives', p. 124. Ryan also notes that the Christian Socialist F. D. Maurice considered Byron 'a true friend of religion', p. 120.

Educating the Romantic Poets

and twice-weekly tutorials, a weekly essay was usually required, as were formal disputations or declamations in Latin at least once a year.

Not all students chose to complete a degree. In that period, simply attending Oxford or Cambridge for several terms, especially after having spent years at a public school, was considered an acceptable choice. Students such as Coleridge and Southey, who took this path, nevertheless referred to and were accorded respect for having once been members of university colleges. The process of completing a degree by undergoing university examinations was a much anticipated and very public annual inter-collegiate contest. Both oral and written university exams stretched over several weeks. Students' scores were published daily, and seniors were cheered through the ordeal by their classmates. Wranglers and winners of 'double firsts' were recognised for this honour for the rest of their lives. All of these experiences—memorising Latin as little boys, writing verses every week in several languages, close reading of classical and biblical literature, debating, competing on examinations, daily chapel—were some of the 'common factors' that help to explain why 'so many poets, novelist, essayists, and critics of true importance and individuality' emerged in the Romantic period.

It is worth recalling that schools such as Hawkshead, Westminster, Christ's Hospital, Harrow, and Eton and the great colleges of Oxford and Cambridge trained a long list of important literary and public men living in England during the eighteenth and early nineteenth centuries. Not only were Wordsworth, Coleridge, Southey, Byron, and Shelley trained at one or both of these levels, but so too were Thomas Warton, Thomas Percy, William Cowper, Erasmus Darwin, George Crabbe, George Dyer, William Lisle Bowles, Charles Lamb, and Leigh Hunt. In addition to these poets, important musicians, composers, and writers or editors of hymns, such as Charles Wesley, John Clarke Whitfield, and Thomas Cotterill, also attended these schools and colleges. Many influential literary editors, publishers, and critics of the period were trained in the Anglo-classical tradition as well, though some also attended Scottish schools and universities. Among these men were Francis Jeffrey, Henry Brougham, and Sydney Smith, of the *Edinburgh Review*; William Gifford and John Taylor Coleridge, of *The Quarterly Review*; George Canning, the founder of the *Anti-Jacobin, or, Weekly Examiner*; and John Wilson and John Gibson Lockhart, editors of *Blackwood's*. The list of other important prose writers, moral and natural philosophers, mathematicians, and historians educated in the classical grammar or public schools and at Oxford or Cambridge is long as well. Among them number Adam Smith, Horace Walpole, Matthew 'Monk' Lewis, Thomas De Quincey, William Gilpin, Jeremy Bentham, William Paley, William Wilberforce, John Herschel, and Thomas Babington Macaulay.[15]

---

[15] This group also includes John Wesley, David Hartley, Samuel Johnson, Henry Cavendish, John Horne Took, Edward Gibbon, Joseph Banks, Vicesimus Knox, Thomas

The influence of the Anglo-classical academy does not end with literary men. Most Church of England clergy and virtually all bishops were graduates of one of the universities; and, as Sara Slinn makes very clear, 'the literate [and literary] clergyman was a cultural norm'.[16] Many of these churchmen stayed in close contact with their university colleges throughout their lives or served as masters or headmasters at schools, and they played meaningful roles elsewhere in the public, private, and literary life of Hanoverian England. The list of legal scholars, barristers, justices, members of parliament, privy councillors, chancellors of the exchequer, foreign secretaries, and prime ministers who received training in the Anglo-classical academy in the Hanoverian period is also quite lengthy.[17]

While various modern socio-political and humanitarian criticisms of these schools and of Georgian Oxbridge are apt, in this study I have chosen to set these aside for the most part and simply to focus as explicitly as possible on what texts, subjects, and methods were used at these institutions to teach students to read, write, and get along and how this information might be used by literary scholars. Throughout the book the terms 'Anglo-classical academy' or 'Anglo-classical tradition' are used to refer collectively to both the Latin grammar schools and the colleges of Oxford and Cambridge because the programmes of both were largely classical, staffed by Anglican clergy, and closely linked.[18] Moreover, because educators at both levels were well acquainted with each other and the curricula, methods, and traditions they used, there was more consistency in what and how the educators at the schools and colleges taught in that period than there is today.

What has been said about these institutions

The Anglo-classical academy, with its reputation for being conservative, brutal, and boring, seems hardly likely to inspire imaginative writing, much less the free-wheeling spirit usually associated with the Romantic Age. Originally called 'public' schools because they were founded to educate poor children, by

---

Malthus, Charles Lamb, Henry Hallam, Mark Peter Roget, Richard Whately, William Hamilton, Charles Babbage, George Peacock, and Thomas Beddoes.

[16] Slinn, p. 76.

[17] Among the prime ministers who attended the great schools and Oxford or Cambridge during this period were Rockingham, North, Grafton, Shelburne, Portland, Addington, Pitt, Grenville, Perceval, Grey, Jenkinson, Liverpool, Canning, and Peel. Added to this group are Blackstone and Fox. The so-called 'Ministry of All the Talents' (1806 to 1807) was trained in the classical academy as well.

[18] Four of the earliest public schools and university colleges were explicitly founded as sister institutions, and boys from the schools almost always matriculated at their sister college. Eton and King's College were founded in this way by Henry VI, as were Winchester and New College by William of Wykeham.

the Georgian period the 'great schools'—such as Winchester and Eton—had become the training grounds for privileged youngsters who were expected to attend university and become public servants in the church, the courts, and parliament. They had many provincial imitators in smaller endowed grammar schools, which were attended by the sons of the 'better' families in expectation of being properly prepared for Oxford or Cambridge. These institutions excluded girls and dissenters, and their expense put them beyond the means of most working-class families. Operating as confessional rather than research institutions, the universities explicitly valorised the national church, patriarchy, social hierarchy, and models of 'gentlemanly' behaviour that are now questioned or contested. In contrast to educators in the more liberal and 'modern' alternatives, such as the dissenting academies, the universities on the Continent and in Scotland, and, after 1826, University College London, the schoolmasters and college dons at these Anglo-classical institutions are often represented as antiquated in their methods and uninterested in or hostile to the rising democratic hopes and increasingly enlightened social beliefs that emerged in response to the American and French Revolutions. Contributing to the Anglo-classical institutions' bad reputation are the well-known stories of school floggings, sinecures, and university wall lectures.

Other reasons for the bad reputation of the Anglo-classical academy include Byron's 'impatience' with 'The drill'd dull lesson, forced down word by word' at Harrow[19] and Southey's passionate condemnation of the 'brutality and absurdity of flogging',[20] which caused him to be expelled from Westminster and deprived of a place at Christ Church. In *The Prelude* Wordsworth writes about feeling out of place at St John's. Equally well known is Shelley's expulsion from University College, Oxford, for publishing opinions hardly considered radical today. Added to this, though both Coleridge and Byron were at times quite serious 'readers' at Jesus College and Trinity, most scholars are far more familiar with their days of drinking, debauchery, and indebtedness at Cambridge.

In 1809 and 1810 the *Edinburgh Review* ran a series of articles that 'calumniated' the Anglo-classical academy.[21] Schoolboys' minds, the critics wrote, were numbed and their spirits dampened by rote learning of dead languages. Critics charged that college students and fellows were apathetic, melancholy, and dissolute and that university faculty were 'gloomy bigots', 'lazy monks', or 'ignorant pretenders to learning and science'.[22] Other typical complaints

---

[19] McGann, *Lord Byron: The Major Works*, p. 170, Canto IV, ll. 680, 674.
[20] Southey, 'No. V', p. 78.
[21] *Edinburgh Review*, 'Art. I'; 'Art. III. *Essays on Professional Education*'; 'Art. VII. A Reply to the Calumnies'; 'Article III'; 'Art. X'.
[22] Qtd in Edward Copleston, p. 10.

Introduction

about the classical academy in the period included disapproval of the use of pagan texts and schoolboy games on Sundays and disgust at rumours of vice of various sorts at both the schools and university colleges.[23] Public discussion and criticism of the cost, curriculum, and exclusivity of English classical education rarely abated in the Romantic period. In the 1830s the *Edinburgh Review* piled on with more critical articles.[24] The concerns that were generated by such public discussion led to the appointments of two royal commissions, which convened in the early 1850s in order to 'inquire into the State, Discipline, Studies, and Revenues' of both Cambridge and Oxford.[25] A series of Schools Inquiry Commissions, starting in 1858 and lasting several decades, also looked into the classical grammar schools.[26]

Reformers in late Georgian England, including Henry Brougham, dismissed the curricula and traditions of the public and grammar schools and the two English universities as unenlightened relics of social attitudes, religious beliefs, and thought systems that were or should soon be things of the past. Impressed by the work of dissenting academies and Scottish universities, they founded the secular University College in London, along with its own grammar school.[27] They sponsored Mechanics Institutes and advocated broadly for the democratisation of education. Other responses to this need were the charity and Sunday schools of Sarah Trimmer and Hannah More and the monitorial schools of Joseph Lancaster and Dr Andrew Bell. It should not be forgotten that, while he was a Cambridge fellow and tutor at Jesus College, William Frend also founded two Sunday schools for the poor children in the two parishes he served.[28] Eventually a series of national education acts was passed that provided compulsory primary education for all English children. In the second half of the nineteenth century new civic universities were established in Manchester (1851), Bristol (1873), and Liverpool (1881)[29] and five women's colleges were opened at Cambridge and Oxford.[30]

---

[23] See Chandos; Midgley.
[24] *Edinburgh Review*, 'Art. III. The Public Schools of England—Westminster and Eton'; 'Art. VI '.
[25] Graham.
[26] Taunton *et al.*
[27] The teachers at the grammar school were, however, Anglican clergy.
[28] Kenneth Johnston notes not only that these schools' teaching of reading was 'transformative' but also that the children so enjoyed their lessons that 'not one could be persuaded to keep away but for some very urgent reasons' (*Usual Suspects*, p. 81).
[29] Other civic universities were established at Birmingham, Leeds, and Sheffield in the early twentieth century.
[30] These were Girton (1869) and Newnham (1871) at Cambridge and Lady Margaret Hall (1879), Somerville (1879), St Anne's (1879), St Hugh's (1886), and St Hilda's (1893) at Oxford.

Despite their critics and exclusivity, the Anglo-classical academies were the longest-standing sites of organised secondary and higher education in England; and, significantly, most English men and women thought that the classical training they provided was the only sure sign of an educated person. Unrest in Europe in the Romantic period kept many of those interested in a more scientific university education away from the more modern research universities on the Continent. Some families turned to private secondary instruction, the dissenting academies, or the Scottish universities, but the Anglo-classical academy continued to be the choice of most parents of means or of those who hoped to advance their sons in English society. Moreover, enrolments at the schools and the universities rose after 1800 above what might have been expected due to population increase.

The two royal commissions on the universities made a number of recommendations about examinations, inclusivity, and more modern subjects, but neither called for the end of the classical curriculum and both expressed the wish, as the Oxford commissioners put it, to raise the university 'to a still higher position than that which it now occupies in the opinion of the world at large'.[31] *The Report of the Schools Inquiry Commission* of 1868 makes it clear that while many middle- and upper-class parents wanted more and better education for their daughters and hoped that their sons' schools and colleges might provide more 'useful' subjects, especially in the emerging natural sciences, they did not want to dispense with traditional instruction in Latin, mathematics, and religion.[32] Considered a 'touchstone of class', a classical education appealed to 'the new capitalists and plutocrats of City and trading Empire'.[33]

Given this chequered history, it is no surprise that little has been written in the twenty-first century about how English education operated in the years between 1770 and 1850. The studies that are available usually cite the curriculum but do not consider teaching methods, learning outcomes, or the social effects of life in these communities. There are, however, many general sources, dating from as early as 1818, that offer information about the Georgian schools. Nicholas Carlisle's *A Concise Description of the Endowed Grammar Schools in England and Wales* (1818), in two volumes, is one of the earliest. This series provides information about selected schools' histories, size, and enrolment, and in some cases brief notes about what was taught. Carlisle's book is especially useful because it reflects common attitudes about education in that time. It includes, for example, comments that the free school at Aylesbury 'is more of a Commercial than Classical description, [so] it's very nature has precluded it

---

[31] Hinds, pp. 2–3.
[32] Taunton *et al.*, vol. 1, pp. 17–18.
[33] Tyerman, p. 99.

Introduction

from producing many men of great literary attainments'.[34] In contrast, Carlisle concludes his entry about Eton by claiming it would take 'many volumes' to contain the list of Etonians 'who have attained superior Learning, or have distinguished themselves as Divines, as Statesmen and Benefactors of Mankind'.[35]

Two of the most reliable general accounts of late Hanoverian education written in the twentieth century are Nicholas Hann's *New Trends in Education in the Eighteenth Century* (1951) and John Lawson and Harold Silver's *A Social History of Education in England* (1976). Hans offers a broad survey of the range of educational opportunities available at that time, including not only the denominational institutions such as the Anglo-classical and dissenting academies but also private and technical schools, home and private tutors, education of women, and adult education. Regarding the Anglo-classical academy, Hans rightly asserts that the mathematical training there promoted the advance of modern science, that the universities were 'not as moribund in the eighteenth century as general opinion affirms', and that good, hard work was often done at both levels.[36] These are themes this book will explore. Lawson and Silver's *Social History of Education in England* provides four chapters about schooling between the years 1660 and 1900. These survey the charity schools, grammar schools, private academies, tutors, Sunday Schools, monitorial schools, and the universities, as well as various movements to educate the poor. It is an excellent overview but tells us nothing about *how* education took place at any of these sites. However, the book rightly takes note of how interested the English were in education and how changes in late Hanoverian society led to reforms that finally included females and the poor and that integrated more 'modern' languages, science, and technology into the existing curriculum. Lawson and Silver confirm that the endowed grammar schools, public schools, Oxford, and Cambridge, continued to be the favoured sites of education in England.

Individual school histories, such as Sargeaunt's *Annals of Westminster School* (1898), Maxwell-Lyte's *A History of Eton College, 1440–1884* (1889), Allan's *Christ's Hospital* (1949), and Christopher Tyerman's *A History of Harrow School* (2000) are helpful resources. They name educators, describe traditions and typical student pastimes, and provide anecdotes about pupils and schoolmasters. These books do not, however, supply many details about the content of lessons, the methods used, or the work that was asked of students. Tyerman notes that Harrow demonstrated 'the very English combination of aristocratic egalitarianism and elitism'[37] and that boyish rowdiness and

---

[34] Carlisle, p. 46.
[35] Carlisle, p. 89.
[36] Hans, p. 41.
[37] Tyerman, p. 155.

irreligion were part of the culture. He notes that some of the worst actors at Harrow during these years went on to distinguished careers in the church or government and many 'remembered their schooldays with intense almost elegiac affection'.[38]

John Chandos's *Boys Together: English Public Schools 1800–1864* (1984) is the most carefully detailed account of the public schools' daily life. Chandos says little, however, about the curriculum or teaching methods, focusing more on the darker aspects of school life, such as bullying, 'vice', and bad teachers. While reprehensible, these problems were not new in 1800, and they continue to be a part of the messy business of growing up, going to school, and teaching even today; so, it is unfortunate that Chandos's book does not include this caveat. Nevertheless, Chandos rightly asserts that the 'mystic' of a school—the lived experience of being a member of a historic institutional—is a mirror of its times. To this I add that the schools tell us a good deal about what the parents of the Romantic writers hoped and feared for their children.

James Bowen's paper 'Education, ideology and the ruling class: Hellenism and English public schools in the nineteenth century' argues that the primary work of the Anglo-classical academy was to promote the Tory patriarch, 'class identity', and a gentlemanly ideal of the liberal arts.[39] Bowen's portrait of the public schools as 'debased' and his pronouncement that the educational skills and principles of schoolmasters of the period were 'limited' do not square, however, with the evidence unearthed in my research. Moreover, Bowen does not recognise the rising interest in the natural sciences, which was underway in this period thanks to mathematicians at Cambridge and gentleman amateurs around the country, many of whom were educated in these schools and university colleges.

Matthew Adams's *Teaching Classics in English Schools, 1500–1840* (2015) is one of the few books about the Anglo-classical tradition that is written by a practising classics teacher. His book offers an authoritative account of the medieval education programme and how English schoolmasters began to modify it in the seventeenth century. He catalogues the classical texts that were most often used and notes the use of commonplace books and language aids such as Erasmus's *De Copia Verborum* and *De Copia Rerum*.[40] He mentions writing assignments and claims that forced verse composition and translation exercises were disliked by parents and students alike. My research contests this generalisation, however. For example, I have found examples of pupils' letters home that express real pride in their verses and recitation. In *The Prelude*,

---

[38] Tyerman, p. 171.
[39] Bowen, p. 164.
[40] Adams, p. 83.

Introduction

Wordsworth notes that 'for the better part/ Of two delightful hours' he and John Fleming, a friend and classmate at Hawkshead

> ... strolled along
> By the still borders of the misty lake
> Repeating favoured verses in one voice
> Or conning more, as happy as the birds
> That round us chaunted. Well might we be glad,
> Lifted above the ground by airy fancies,
> More bright than madness or the dreams of wine;[41]

Similarly, in their self-published literary magazines pupils proudly included their poems and essays and voiced their pleasure in classical and biblical language studies.

Adams reports on student riots and flogging, news no school history should neglect, but he does not remind readers that the reason these episodes are so famous is because they were not the norm at the schools. Chapter 2 of this book explains that, while corporal punishment was accepted by most families, beating pupils was usually the schoolmasters' last resort, after lines, exercise, social pressure, and embarrassment failed to correct a boy. Adams is right, however, to point out that, because of the flogging stories, classics became associated with brutal teaching. Paradoxically, the classical schools were also associated with gentility or 'the quality', one reason they continued to be popular with parents.

Help in understanding the effects of religious life and learning at these schools and colleges is provided by David Newsome's *Godliness and Good Learning* (1961) and more recently by Sarah Slinn's book, *The Education of the Anglican Clergy, 1780–1839* (2017). Newsome's profiles of representative educators and pupils in the Victorian period illustrate religious attitudes and practices that were also typical in the Georgian years. He emphasises the kindly humanity of many of the teachers at the great schools and claims that the 'most formative influences' on the lives of intellectuals and scholars at that time were 'the teaching and personality of their headmasters' and the friendships they made in what he depicts as a generally benign environment.[42] While Slinn complains that Anglican education at the universities did not do enough to prepare young clergymen for the realities of daily labour in their profession, she confirms, as does Newsome, that Anglican worship and theological or biblical study were a major part of daily life and learning at both the schools

---

[41] *Prelude* 1850, p. 183, ll. 561–568.
[42] Newsome, p. 9.

Educating the Romantic Poets

and universities, a circumstance that originally surprised me, but which now seems quite significant.

Essential to any study of Hanoverian education in the Anglo-classical tradition are the university histories published by the Oxford and Cambridge University Presses.[43] These volumes provide many of the 'see also' references used throughout this book. They cover some of the same topics that this book does, such as administration, political and religious matters, curriculum, headmasters, deans, and fellows. They do not, however, offer many details about how teaching and learning took place day by day. Some of this sort of information is available in Christopher Wordsworth's rambling and anecdotal *Scholae Academicae* (1877). Many of the practices that Wordsworth reports, such as exams and 'hard reading', were still an important part of life in the colleges in the nineteenth century. George Dyer's *History of the University and Colleges of Cambridge* (1814) is also useful, especially given his friendships with Romantic writers, William Frend, and others in London's dissenting circle.

Brian Simon's authoritative four-volume series *Studies in the History of Education*, published between 1960 and 1974, probably helped to limit modern scholarly interest in the Anglo-classical academy in the Romantic period. The volume covering the years 1780 to 1870 dismisses English university education in that time as having 'fallen on evil days' and asserts that 'such teaching as there was [at the grammar schools] was often of the lowest standard'.[44] Both opinions are revised in *Educating the Romantic Poets*. Sheldon Rothblatt's volumes on the universities[45] are more positive about Georgian Oxford and Cambridge. Rothblatt asserts that the style of life at the universities 'was tangible proof of liberality and civility', but he adds that the universities 'were composed of an odd mixture of melancholic monks and fashionable dons, of official old subjects and marginal new ones'.[46] He says little about the daily practices of collegiate teaching at that time.

Graham Midgley's *University Life in Eighteenth-Century Oxford* (1996) also presents a more positive account of the college experience, though his focus is primarily on what took place outside of tutorial rooms and lecture halls. Richly detailed and amusing, this book describes an important aspect of college life—the learning derived from the pleasures we know most of the Romantic poets also enjoyed at university: walking, swimming, riding,

---

[43] These include Sutherland and Mitchell; Brock and Curthoys Parts 1 and 2; Brockliss; Morgan *et al.*; and Searby.

[44] Simon, pp. 85, 95. Simon's volumes were written from the perspective of a twentieth-century education reformer whose interest was in fostering comprehensive and useful training for all citizens.

[45] *Revolution of the Dons* (1968) and *Tradition and Change in English Liberal Education* (1976).

[46] Rothblatt, *Tradition*, p. 100.

Introduction

sports, wine and tea parties, and, above all, college friendships. Gambling, chasing women, and pranks are also part of the story Midgley tells. Though the students'-eye view of life in the university that he offers says little about pedagogy or literary instruction, it does make it clear that Anglican worship was an accepted part of daily life, that life in Georgian Oxford was livelier than other accounts typically maintain, and that most students were generally quite happy at the university.[47] My research suggests that the same can be said about Cambridge at that time, though hotter debates about contemporaneous political and religious matters made it a less peaceful place.

Among the few books that explicitly connect collegiate experience to Romantic literature is Ben Ross Schneider's *Wordsworth's Cambridge Education* (1957). Schneider's work has been called a 'prosy version of *The Prelude*',[48] and it certainly rehearses *The Prelude*'s widely accepted mythos of Wordsworth, the innocent country lad who was embarrassed to be a sizar and who was shocked and disgusted by the worldly ambitions, careerism, competition, and impiety of faculty and students at the university. Schneider contends that it was these feelings that caused Wordsworth to reject the world of the university and what his parsimonious family assumed would be the beginning of a brilliant clerical career. These feelings, Schneider claims, were the root of a 'dialectic' the poet would stand by the rest of his life: 'country against city, nature against man, imagination against reason, and organism against mechanism'.[49] *Educating the Romantic Poets* responds to Schneider's work, pointing out, for example, that Wordsworth was not entirely miserable when he was at Cambridge and that other sizars from the north country found it possible to excel academically. I also note that, in later life, Wordsworth revised his judgements of academic life. He kept in touch with many of the leading Hellenists of the day and was pleased when Oxford's professor of poetry from 1831 to 1841, John Keble, dedicated *Praelectiones Academicae* to him.[50] When his brother Christopher became master of Trinity Wordsworth made a number of visits back to Cambridge. Staying in style at the Master's Lodge, he often held court with admiring undergraduates, and he dedicated *The River Duddon* (1820) to his scholarly brother.[51] Wordsworth also made a point of urging Clarkson's son to contend for honours at the university, something he was himself unwilling to do, and he advised one of his nephews, while an undergraduate, not to trouble himself 'reading *modern* authors *at present*' but to 'confine your attention to

---

[47] See also Darwall-Smith and Horder.
[48] Douglas, p. 302.
[49] Schneider, pp. 49–50.
[50] This is the volume of his lectures on poetry, which he delivered as Professor of Poetry at Oxford from 1832 to 1841.
[51] William Knight, p. 296. In that poem, he says that he 'reveres the choice' that took his brother from his 'native hills': p. 296, ll. 19–20.

ancient classical writers; make yourself master of them: and when you have done that, you will come down to us; and then you will be able to judge us according to our deserts'.[52]

The relationship of Wordsworth's schoolboy education to his literary accomplishments is explored by Richard Clancey's *Wordsworth's Classical Undersong: Education, Rhetoric, and Poetic Truth* (2000). Clancey maintains that the study of classics at Hawkshead, particularly of Aristotle and Horace, was central to Wordsworth' moral and ethical education. He argues that Wordsworth's self-portrait in *The Prelude* is a product of his understanding of Horace's concept of *ethos*. Paul Elledge's *Speaking Up, Talking Back, Acting Up, and Bowing Out* (2000) discusses how Byron's rhetorical training, coaching by his headmaster, and social experiences at Harrow contributed to the performative style of his mature writing (2000). Elledge's 'unapologetically inferential criticism' (15) analyses the mind and work of Byron the schoolboy in order to read Byron the adult poet. He claims that the passages Byron chose to perform for Speech Days were early efforts to solace himself and to experiment with his public persona. The strategies young Byron devised, Elledge maintains, were replicated and polished in his mature poetry. One other scholar has noted how the Romantics' education, particularly training in classical ecphrasis provided by the *progymnasmata*, shaped their depictions of the natural world. In *The Poetics of Description Imagined Places in European Literature* (2006) Janice Hewlett Koelb asserts that Wordsworth's descriptions of home that enact 'nontranscendent imaginative participation in a self-transforming natural world' owe much to Aphthonius' writing exercises. She further argues that Byron's locodescriptive passages in *Don Juan* are similarly shaped by his knowledge of classical ecphrasis and by his reaction to Wordsworth's use of it in *The Excursion*.[53] *Educating the Romantic Poets* is designed to give interested scholars the tools to pursue studies similar to these.

Alan Richardson has aptly observed that education is a promising site for 're-thinking Romantic-era culture' and the writings and endeavours of Rousseau, the Edgeworths, and Sarah Trimmer.[54] Focusing upon the politics of children's books and their representations of childhood, he claims that 'changes in educational methods, institutions, and ideologies in the Romantic period not only transformed the concept of childhood but also the definition and status of literature'.[55] I agree that educational theories of the period had an impact on the definition of literature at that time and that they affected

---

[52] Christopher Wordsworth, *Memoirs*, vol. 1, p. 48.
[53] Koelb, pp. 155–156.
[54] Richardson, p. 2; he also devotes chapters to attitudes about and movements to advance the education of girls and children of the working classes.
[55] Richardson, p. xiv.

Introduction

the themes and forms chosen by some writers in the period. No doubt *Emile*, *Practical Education*, and Sara Trimmer's spelling books and *Fabulous Histories* also had some effect; but, as this book details, the reach and the influence of the Anglo-classical educators and programme surpassed them. *Educating the Romantic Poets* does, however, share Richardson's belief that '[i]n its wider sense of mental growth, education might be taken as defining the Romantic ethos'.[56]

A very useful catalogue of the range of Wordsworth's thoughts about education is Hongxiau Xu's unpublished PhD dissertation, 'Poet as Teacher: Wordsworth's Practical and Poetic Engagement with Education'. Xu points out that much of what the poet said about education was not a critique of his own Anglo-classical education but an expression of concern that poor children were not receiving enough religious and ethical training. Xu argues convincingly that Wordsworth did not always prefer education by nature over that which was accomplished by books and human teachers.[57] While noting that Wordsworth was anxious about the negative uses of 'emulation' or competition in schools, she also cites his belief that education has power to 'regulate the mind's disordered frame' and to vitalise the mind and trigger the imagination.[58] Throughout her dissertation, Xu highlights a phenomenon that I take up in Chapter 5, which is how closely Wordsworth associates teaching, imagination, and religion with the role of the poet.

It is worthwhile recalling Dinah Birch's *Our Victorian Education* (2008), where she reminds modern readers of a belief common in Victorian England that education is 'more than a matter of social or economic advantage, or even the transmission of knowledge', that it 'changes lives' and 'enlarges what a person sees and reverences'.[59] *Educating the Romantic Poets* demonstrates that a similar set of beliefs circulated in the Romantic period and shows some of the ways that Romantic-era teachers enlarged what their students saw and reverenced.

One last group of sources needs to be mentioned. Many modern scholars of English literature, especially in the US, have not studied Latin, much less Greek, and this lack makes it harder to appreciate the curriculum and methods of Anglo-classical academy. Without training in the classical languages and literature, it is also difficult for a reader to recognise how certain metrical schemes, grammatical arrangements, idioms, or distinctive styles would have been instructive to writing students in the Georgian period. Helping to overcome these limitations are *The Oxford History of Classical Reception in*

---

[56] Richardson, p. 6.
[57] Xu, p. 46.
[58] 'Lines written as a School Exercise at Hawkshead, *Anno Aetatis* 14' in Wordsworth, *The Complete Poetical Works of William Wordsworth, in Ten Volumes*. Vol. 1: Early Poems, p. 3.
[59] Birch, pp. 124, 128, 135.

Educating the Romantic Poets

English Literature, vol. 3, 1660–1790 (2012), edited by David Hopkins and Charles Martindale, and *The Oxford History of Classical Reception in English Literature*, vol. 4, 1790–1890 (2015), edited by Norman Vance and Jennifer Wallace. These works include chapters focusing on the legacies of Homer, Ovid, Virgil, and Lucan, and on topics such as satire, epic, pastoral, georgics, class, politics, myth, religion, and gender. Also helpful for those without classical backgrounds are the writings of Bruce Graver[60] and various contributions by Yopi Prins and Simon Goldhill on Victorian culture and classical antiquity.[61]

What this book offers

While this book does not categorically endorse the traditional humanistic teaching programme of the Anglo-classical academy, it does make clear how useful it was to fledgling poets. The academy's painstaking methods of textual study and imitative composition, which emphasised careful word choice, prosody, and generic conventions, are of particular interest. Given a willing and talented student, the outcomes of this programme include sizeable vocabularies, well-honed sentence skills, awareness of the rhythm and music of language, well-trained and richly stocked memories, and knowledge of diverse literary forms and their conventions. The benefits of so many weeks and years spent facing a blank page and a deadline cannot be discounted. In *Outliers: The Story of Success* (2011), Malcolm Gladwell outlines his now well-known 10,000 Hours Rule. He argues that it takes 10,000 hours of practice to achieve mastery of a skill such as playing the piano. We cannot be sure exactly how long it would have taken schoolboys in the Romantic period to do all of their 'literary' assignments, but given the long hours and six-day work week, the fact that two-thirds of the curriculum focused on in-class reading, translation, construal, and discussion of classical and biblical texts, and the amount of writing and memory work that was routinely assigned, it is safe to assume that these youngsters logged many thousands of hours of 'literary' practice before they entered the larger world.

---

[60] Among Graver's contributions are 'Classical Inheritances'; 'Wordsworth's Translations from Latin Poetry'; 'Wordsworth and the Language of Epic'; 'Wordsworth's Georgic Beginnings'; and '"Honourable Toil", the Georgic Ethic of "Prelude I"'.

[61] For a brief look into classical reception theory, see dueling articles by Martindale and Goldhill in Hall and Harrop. They debate aestheticist and historicist models of reception study. Hiscock has characterised this debate as 'between reception study as a mutually transformative, transhistorical, aesthetic encounter (allied, not opposed, to a rich sensitivity to historical relativity); and as a discipline that must be rooted in close engagement with the historical and cultural contexts of the reception of antiquity's alterity' (p. 323). See also Yopie Prins, 'Metrical Translation' and 'Historical Poetics'. Also Goldhill, *Victorian Culture and Classical Antiquity* and *The Poet's Voice*.

Introduction

The programme of the grammar schools also fostered skills that are especially helpful to writers, such as focus, resilience, and grit. The universities promoted self-discipline, free inquiry, and lively public discourse, also of great value to writers. Training of this sort helps to explain why Wordsworth claimed that he and the other poets in his acquaintance have 'acquired a greater readiness and power in expressing' what they think and feel than other men.[62] This book will explain why such early intellectual confidence is not entirely unmerited. It will show how the lessons of this classical education can be tracked in their mature writing and recognised in their audience's reception of their work. Men trained in these schools were familiar with Homer's heroes but also with his didacticism; they knew that Hesiod believed in the necessity of labour and prudential piety, that Callimachus used homely detail and personal reminiscence, and that Horace and Quintilian both believed that the good character of the rhetor is his most persuasive appeal. They had also read and memorised so much classical verse that they knew what a carefully constructed poem sounded like. Information such as this can be used comparatively to assess the Romantic poets' success in pursuing similar ends, beliefs, styles, aural effects, or arguments in their work and in interpreting Romantic readers' response to these matters. Scholars working on prosody can be assisted by the news that poets trained in these schools had been carefully schooled in the complicated rules of stress-rhythms and had been taught what speech-conditions allow for elision. They were also accustomed to extrametrical syllables, understood how to use moraic trochees, and knew that there were laws of harmony and general custom in poetry. As schoolboys they had also been taught to use hexameter for solemnity, to alternate hexameter with pentameter to effect tenderness, and to use sapphics or alcaics to elevate their lyrics.

Another contribution of this book is the attention it gives to the dailiness of Anglican religious practice at both schools and colleges. This circumstance serves as a reminder that the spirit of this age, which Hazlitt calls out for its 'preposterous rage for novelty',[63] still dictated that promising youngsters and those destined for leadership were expected to be entirely familiar with scripture and fully prepared as communicants of the Church of England. Modern scholars should not ignore the effects of young people gathering every day in consecrated spaces to hear prayers and sacred music. Georgian

---

[62] WWMW, p. 604. His education may also help to explain the origin of his claim that they are possessed of 'a more lively sensibility … and a more comprehensive soul' (p. 603). Given what he writes in *The Prelude*, it would seem that young Wordsworth exercised his lively sensibilities during his school days at Hawkshead; Byron might say the same thing about his time at Harrow. Wordsworth's reference to comprehensive souls elsewhere in this passage may have its roots in the religious training that both the schools and university colleges provided.

[63] Hazlitt, paragraph 2.

educators acknowledged that they could not make boys or young men pious; and they recognised that required chapel sometimes aroused resentment and protest or merely habituated conformity to established authority. However, it is hard to criticise educators' desire to provide young people space and time for private mental processes that might lead willing souls to some personal sense of a metaphysical other. The recent publication of *The Cambridge Companion to British Romanticism and Religion* (2021) has announced a 'new era of study' that calls for 'reliable introductions to the ways in which religious beliefs and perceptions shaped the history of the period'. This book contributes to such study. It also supports another trend in Romantic studies that calls attention to the later writing of the Romantic poets—see here especially recent work by Fulford, Pratt, and Robinson.[64] Many of the later works by Southey, Coleridge, and Wordsworth that these scholars discuss demonstrate the maturation of linguistic and poetic skills that were laid down and refined by schoolmasters and college tutors working in the Anglo-classical tradition. The poets' later works also manifest a return to certain beliefs about Christian duty, moral leadership, faith, and English manhood that were part of the ethos of institutions such as Westminster, Christ's Hospital, Hawkshead, Oxford, and Cambridge. Thus, while this book offers fresh insights into the early, better-known works of certain Romantic-period writers by offering new information about what they had quite recently studied, memorised, and/or imitated in writing assignments at school or college, it also provides information to assist critical studies of later Romantic texts in which the writers employ forms or explore themes that echo or rehearse the conservative Anglican beliefs and the classical literary tastes recalled from their lessons at school and university.

Educating the Romantic Poets also invites scholars to revisit Richardson's claim that education was part of the Romantic ethos. The Romantics are universally heralded for being radicals, revolutionaries, and iconoclasts, not schoolmasters. Yet many showed life-long interest not only in learning but also in teaching. Some devised educational or utopian schemes, such as Godwin's plan for a seminary at Epsom, Southey's and Coleridge's scheme of Pantisocracy, and the reading programme Percy Shelley shared with Mary Godwin, which she continued to expand and pursue throughout her life. Southey championed Dr Andrew Bell's monitorial system.[65] In 1811 Wordsworth became so interested in monitorial education that he began assisting the master of the village school in Grasmere every day.[66] In the Preface to *Lyrical Ballads* Wordsworth emphasises the translating and knowledge-bearing tasks

---

[64] Fulford, *Late Poetry* and *Wordsworth's Poetry*; Fulford and Pratt; Robinson.
[65] In point of fact, he carried on quite a hostile campaign against Bell's rival, Lancaster.
[66] Moorman, *William Wordsworth: A Biography: Later Years 1803–1850*, p. 178.

Introduction

of the poet.[67] A decade later he told his friend George Beaumont that 'Every great Poet is a Teacher.'[68] In a letter of 4 January 1810 to John Miller, he writes that his poems 'are fitted to communicate knowledge, to awaken kindly or noble dispositions, or to strengthen the intellectual powers'.[69] These are precisely the same tasks and goals pursued by the Anglo-classical educators studied here.

When Coleridge and Southey left their universities in 1795, they turned to teaching, partly to support themselves but also because both had come to believe it was important to be of 'service to society'.[70] Southey's reviews, his histories and biographies, the *Book of the Church* (1824), and *Sir Thomas More, Or Colloquies on the Progress and Prospects of Society* (1829) were written to support his family, but all were also educative.[71] Coleridge's body of prose works—including lectures, journalistic gambits, political pamphlets, and Christian apologetics—also demonstrate the impulse to teach. His notion of the clerisy was based on his belief that a class of educated, reading people was needed to guide and teach the nation. Though he did not have the focus to maintain a lecturing career, for five years from 1822 to 1827 he conducted informal weekly seminars for young thinkers in a room in Lincoln's Inn Field. Other intellectuals of the age, including Joseph Banks, Humphry Davy, and Sydney Smith, provided adult education by founding or lecturing at places such as the Royal, British, and Philomathic Institutions. It can be argued that the motivations for these Romantics' educational impulses drew from the intellectual energies generated by the Enlightenment, the beginnings of the rise of modern science, and the political and social unrest of the time; but the evidence in this book suggests that it was also assisted by the curriculum, pedagogies, educational communities, and teachers they knew, and the duty of learning and dedication to public service that were sanctioned by these institutions. Added to this, Georgian schoolmasters and college tutors often modelled imitation-worthy lives devoted to the life of the mind, to teaching, learning, and writing, or at least to a life spent in a quiet place where intelligence and rational thought mattered—a model that both Wordsworth and Southey embraced. They imparted this ethos at a critical moment in their students' lives, and in so doing they contributed to the shape and sound and meaning of Romantic literature.

---

[67] The poet, he says, is 'in the situation of a translator' and he binds society together by 'passion and knowledge' (WWMW, p. 604).
[68] WWLMY, p. 195.
[69] WWLMY, p. 383.
[70] Charles Cuthbert Southey, vol. 1, p. 190.
[71] According to his earliest biographer, Southey wrote *The Book of the Church* for 'reverent' Anglicans to 'put in the hands of their children': qtd in Charles Cuthbert Southey, vol. 2, pp. 356, 201, n. *.

Educating the Romantic Poets

Finally, this account of teaching and learning in the Anglo-classical academy offers contemporary educators the opportunity to view their profession, curriculum, and practices historically, and to compare the outcomes of their work with those of the Georgian educators. Though our cultures are very different, my research suggests that the hearts and minds of the students and educators in the Anglo-classical academy were not terribly different from those of male students and educators in modern schools and universities. Much of what students learned then depended as it does today upon the willingness, talent, and ambition of each individual learner and the skill and humanity of teachers. Students in the Georgian academies discussed here could be just as energetic or lazy, silly or serious, arrogant or anxious as modern students can be. Many of their teachers manifested the same range of characteristics, but most appear to have taken their work and reputations seriously, and even the worst of them believed they were acting within the bounds of acceptable or even prescribed practice. A few of these educators were truly excellent; a few were terrible; most were good enough. The Anglo-classical curriculum, with its unique pedagogies and traditions, was the constant in this arena, and, while interest in adding modern science and languages, English literature and modern history to the curriculum was growing, most English citizens at that time still assumed that a classical programme in an Anglican community provided the best possible foundation and the most useful knowledge and skills upon which a youngster could build a life. As this book shows, it was also remarkably effective at educating the Romantic poets.

Chapter Two

England's Public and Grammar Schools

First Lessons

I believe that England would not be what she is without her system of public education; and that no other country can become what England is, without the advantages of such a system.

George Canning

… we cannot think public schools favourable to the cultivation of knowledge; and we have equally strong doubts if they be so to the cultivation of morals.

The Edinburgh Review

Pupils at the Romantic era Anglo-classical schools found themselves initiated at a tender age into a unique and carefully observed culture, one specifically chosen for them by their parents or guardians. Each of these 'little worlds' had its local lore and vocabulary, characterising names for the forms ('Nonsense' boys), terms for teachers ('beaks'), special privileges for older boys (town visits and the fagging services of junior boys), dedicated walks or gathering places (Winchester's St Catherine's Hill and Rugby's King's Oak), yearly events (Eton's *Montem* or Winchester's *Ad Portas*), and founders' prayers written and recited only for and by them. According to Byron, he found something more important at school: 'kindred hearts … a home, a world, a paradise'.[1]

---

[1] Byron, 'Childish Recollections', *Hours of Idleness*, p. 75, ll. 214–218.

Educating the Romantic Poets

Figure 1. Winchester School House.

The little worlds of the schools

Thomas Arnold quipped that 'Education goes on out of school as well as in school, and very often far more vigorously.' The memories of many of his pupils underscore this statement. One lad recalled that the highlight of his days at Rugby were 'speeches, sports, rows, fagging and shirking, form privileges, praeposters, boarding houses, and protégés'.[2] Pupils at the other schools told similar stories, recalling skirmishes with friends, games, and play-at-fours. Added to these memorable and formative experiences, the spartan living conditions and long school days inured youngsters to hard work and taught them self-discipline. Old boys commented that in school they learned courage, hatred of tyrants, humility, responsibility, imagination, wit, and tenacity. They also said that they learned how to get along with others, when to obey and when to protest, and how to look out for their friends and the littler ones. The actor William Macready (1793–1873) said that life at Eton taught him 'FORTITUDE'.[3] Shelley averred in the Dedication to 'Laon and Cythna' that his experiences at school, which included 'suffering' and tyrannical classmates, caused him to resolve always to 'be wise,/And just, and free,

[2] *Rugby Magazine*, 'School a Little World', p. 99.
[3] Toynbee, vol. 1, p. vii.

and mild'.[4] Southey commented on the inequality that station produces at a public school and railed against this in *The Flagellant*. He also claimed that the public schools 'generated that kind of spirit', which is 'liable to explode upon' occasions of 'injustice'.[5] Christ's Hospital provided a more egalitarian but equally spirited community, for, along with a small class of 'Grecians' bound for university, it prepared close to 600 youngsters for apprenticeships, trade, or clerkships. While local details varied, all of these schools guided pupils' and poets' first steps toward their adult lives and careers in similar ways.

Founding principles

The men who established the great public schools—typically bishops and kings[6]—made it very clear that the Anglican Church and its values should be the foundation of all higher learning. This circumstance conferred on the schools an aura of ancient seriousness and helped to instil students' respect for, or at least compliance with, the schools' pedagogies, curriculum, and traditions. The statutes of the oldest school, Winchester, declared that the course of study at the school was to focus on Holy Scriptures, classical languages, philosophy, and civil and canon law to the ends that 'the praise of God may be spread, the church ruled, the strength and fervour of the Christian religion grow hotter, and all knowledge and virtue be increased in strength'.[7] Westminster's statutes call for 'the liberal education of youths' and the molding of their 'morals and manners' through 'instruction in the tongues, in the poets and the orators'.[8] In his *Essays, Moral and Literary*, Vicesimus Knox (1752–1821), the headmaster of Tonbridge School, writes that the 'two principal objects in a well-conducted education, are to cultivate a good heart, and to give the understanding such additional strength and information, as may safely direct the heart in the various events of life,

---

[4] Reiman and Powers, p. 96.

[5] CLRS, Pt 5, #3225.

[6] William of Wykeham (1320–1404), bishop of Winchester and chancellor of England, founded both Winchester and New College, Oxford, as partners in 1393. Eton and King's College were similarly established as sister institutions in 1440 by King Henry VI. John Colet (1467–1519), the Dean of St Paul's Cathedral in London, worked closely with Erasmus to establish the grammar school at St Paul's in 1509. Christ's Hospital was a joint project of Edward VII, the bishop of London, the lord mayor, and philanthropists of the city. Edwin Sandys, the archbishop of York, founded the school at Hawkshead in 1585. These circumstances conferred on them a certain aura and helped to instil students' respect for or at least compliance with whatever went on there.

[7] Leach, pp. 69–70.

[8] Sargeaunt, p. 4. The school was also charged quite specifically with the enforcement of 'cleanliness of skin and neatness of dress, hair, and nails' and to make sure no boys had lice (p. 13).

Educating the Romantic Poets

and teach the possessor of it to act up to the dignity of human nature'.[9] These values, expressed and modelled in pupils' early days, contributed to Romantic era notions of the duties and value of poets to society, ranging from Wordsworth's claim that poets are the 'rock of defence of human nature' who 'bind together by passion and knowledge the vast empire of human society'[10] to Shelley's claim that poets are

> not only the authors of language and music ... they are the institutors of laws, and the founders of civil society ... and the teachers, who draw into a certain propinquity with the beautiful and the true that partial apprehension of the agencies of the invisible world which is called religion.[11]

Parents in Georgian England regularly sent their sons away to the classical boarding schools at a very young age. *A Plan of Education Delineated and Vindicated* (1784)[12] suggests that boys start school at the age of eight, arguing that valuable learning time is lost if parents wait until boys are 12 or 13. Shelley was sent to Syon Academy at the age of ten and two years later to Eton, where he boarded for six years. Horace Walpole and Monk Lewis resided at their schools for seven years. Wordsworth spent eight years at Hawkshead Grammar; he was nine when he started there. Both Erasmus Darwin and Coleridge were at their schools for nine years. Given the impressionability of youngsters in these early school years, it is little wonder that after almost a decade of learning classical vocabularies and grammar, closely reading classical literature, memorising passages from these texts, and being required to write weekly imitative themes in three languages (most often in verse), that they were primed for a literary life or at least to be very skilled readers.

Anyone who has attended or taught at a boarding school can testify that communal living away from home also has important socialising and maturing effect on youngsters. Identity formation, relationship skills, and learning about and testing boundaries are part of the experience at all schools, but especially at boarding schools. Robert Southey told his friend John May that the purpose of public schools was to help boys acquire knowledge of both the world and 'his contemporaries who will be auspicious in it from their rank fortune &

---

[9] Knox, 'Classical Learning Vindicated'. *Essays, Moral and Literary*, pp. 15–24.
[10] WWMW, p. 606.
[11] Reiman and Powers, p. 482.
[12] The full title of the book is *A Plan of Education Delineated and Vindicated: To Which Are Added a Letter to a Young Gentleman Designed for the University and for Holy Orders. And a Short Dissertation Upon the Stated Provision and Reasonable Expectations of Publick Teachers.*

stations'.[13] Elledge argues that the culture of Harrow and especially the Speech Days played an important part in Byron's self-formation and performative way of being in the world as an adult. As is well known, Wordsworth's love of English poetry was powerfully fostered by the love his Hawkshead schoolmaster, William Taylor, had for the poets.

School routines

The public-school year lasted 40 weeks. Holidays were taken at Christmas (about a month), Easter (a fortnight), and during the summer (one month). Boys went to class six days a week. When school was in session the daily routine was rigorous, but masters intentionally varied the order of classes, prayers, and free time to make sure boys never had three days in a row with the same lesson schedule. Planning such variety, called 'interleaving', typically has the effect of promoting pupils' ability to see relationships between different subjects and helping them form more lasting connections between new and old learning. The routine of a typical day at Eton, circa 1800, is characteristic of what went on at many of the schools during the Georgian period. Weekdays started at 6 a.m. with a dash outside to wash up at the cold-water pump, then room clean-up and morning prayer. At 7 a.m. an assistant master reviewed boys' memory work; an hour later the headmaster arrived and began the official school day, which consisted of six more hours of lessons, recitation, or guided study. When or if pupils got breakfast before class varied from school to school. Instruction was interrupted by the midday meal and by chapel at three. Pupils had an hour of free time after chapel, during which time they were free to visit local shops, to ramble into the nearby countryside, and to organise pick-up games of cricket, soccer, or handball. It should be noted that official school teams and inter-school sports competitions were not a regular part of school life until the Victorian period. An additional lesson was taught from 5 p.m. to 6 p.m., though twice each week masters called 'play-at-fours' and cancelled the late afternoon class.

At 6 p.m. Etonians either ate school-provided leftovers or made their own supper in dorms or private rooms, which were rented for them in town. Evening study time, which was monitored by senior boys, lasted from 7 p.m. to 8 p.m. Then all pupils assembled for evening prayer, after which they were locked into their dormitories for the night. From lockup until 10 or 11 p.m., pupils finished preparing their lessons for the next school day under the eye of prefects, and then did the rowdy things boys—young and old—rarely resist doing. Edward Coleridge commented that evenings in Eton's Long Chamber were 'neither moral, decent, nor cleanly'.[14] Thring describes nightly leaping matches and other

[13] CLRS, Pt 5, #3210.
[14] Edward Coleridge.

Educating the Romantic Poets

semi-Olympic adventures in the dormitory.[15] Once, as a prank, the Eton pupils carried a live donkey into the Long Chamber. Saturdays began just as weekdays did, with pupils rising at 6 a.m. for prayers. The morning continued with classes until the midday meal, after which pupils had more classes until chapel at 3 p.m. Saturday sessions focused on reviewing the past week's lessons—one of Georgian educators' most beneficial teaching strategies. Along with academic review on Saturdays, pupils' behaviour over the past week was inventoried and punishments were publicly meted out by the headmaster.[16] The school work week was finally over at around 4 p.m. on Saturday afternoons.

Boarding pupils in the Romantic period complained, just as they do today, about school food. Shrewsbury's headmaster Samuel Butler asked the right question, though: 'Who could ever hope to satisfy the real or fancied cravings of a hungry schoolboy?'[17] Records show that Eton employed cooks, a butcher, a cutler, a Purveyor of Oysters, and a Coffee Housekeeper; yet, according to Edward Coleridge, they could not collectively provide an 'eatable dinner'. Some schools handed out penny rolls, butter, and milk for breakfast. More often boys were left to scrounge and prepare their own breakfasts—boiled eggs, bread, butter, and coffee. The fare at the communal midday meal in the hall was bread, mutton or beef, and weak beer brewed on the premises. Shrewsbury pupils were certain that the initials of their headmaster Samuel Butler stood for Stale Bread, Sour Beer, Salt Butter, and Stinking Beef. The evening meal—if offered—consisted of leftovers. At some schools, the sixth form had the privilege of a hot evening meal served by younger pupils. Elsewhere, because the evening meal was cold leftovers, pupils preferred to send out to local inns for hot meals, which typically included meat and fruit pies. Alternatively, they cooked for themselves over the fireplaces in their dormitories, where they roasted sausages or potatoes and made toast. Some concocted 'puddings', which they boiled in socks; others made whiskey punch, which they mixed in washbasins. Provisions for these meals arrived in 'home hampers'—which could be richly stocked with items such as ham, pheasant, oysters, fruit, cheese, and sweets. At Harrow pupils were known to get into debt from the habit of creating sumptuous breakfasts, called 'Finds', with food they ordered in town.[18] Senior pupils with means and an enthusiastic fag might put together rather impressive meals. A young Rugby pupil proudly described a spread he put together for his fag-master and five seniors: lobster, salad, a dozen duck

---

[15] Parkin, pp. 22–23.

[16] At some schools, punishments took place on Fridays. Pupils at these schools called them 'flogging Fridays'.

[17] Qtd in Chandos, p. 123, n. ‡.

[18] Tyerman, p. 210.

eggs, and hot chocolate.[19] Boys living in boarding houses with 'dames' report meals of meat and fish, fruit pies, cheese, and bread.

On Sundays, pupils were expected at church services in the morning and at afternoon devotional sessions in which their schoolmasters guided younger pupils through the catechism and older ones through readings of sermons, works such as *The Whole Duty of Man* (1682), or texts such as Rev. George Pretyman's *Elements of Christian Theology: Containing Proofs of the Authenticity and Inspiration of the Holy Scriptures, a Summary of the History of the Jews, a Brief Statement of the Contents of the Several Books of the Old and New Testaments, a Short Account of the English Translations of the Bible, and of the Liturgy of the Church of England, and Scriptural Exposition of the 39 Articles of Religion* (1799). The title of this work accurately summarises the religious training provided at most of the schools, a topic taken up in greater detail in Chapter 5. Wordsworth's school day and week were similar, beginning at 6 or 6.30 a.m. with prayers. Classes were held until 11 a.m., after which pupils walked to their boarding houses for lunch; lessons resumed at 1 p.m. and lasted until 5 p.m. Hawkshead pupils had Saturday classes and were expected to join their headmaster in the parish church on Sundays and holy days, sitting in pews set aside specifically for them.[20]

Schoolmasters worried that the long vacations would interfere with boys' learning. For this reason, they regularly gave boys assignments to be completed during their time away from school. When Shelley was at Eton the headmaster assigned boys to read, translate, construe, and memorise 200 lines in Latin and 200 lines in Greek over Christmas vacation. A similar request was made for the Easter holiday, when Etonians were instructed to turn a short chapter of the book of Jeremiah into elegiacs, asclepiads, alcaics, or iambics. The 'Easter Task' at Winchester in 1828 involved writing a reply to Cowper's 'Tirocinium', a long poem that roundly criticises public schools. A typical summer work assignment at Eton was to prepare 400 lines from Homer and another 400 from Virgil. All of these exercises helped to prevent what modern educators call 'summer slide', when children can lose as much as two or three months of learning. They also accustomed children to reading, writing, and memorising in their private worlds.

Play and amusements

Georgian schoolmasters left the invention and conduct of play up to the pupils, a circumstance that resulted in various 'self-educating' pleasures. Rugby boys invented an annual coach race in which teams of juniors were harnessed to

---

[19] Falkus, p. 68.
[20] Thompson, pp. 104–105, 118, 269.

Educating the Romantic Poets

light curricles and were driven by seniors.[21] Harrow boys chased a classmate called the 'Jack-o'-lantern' through the dark over hill and dale, while he did his best to tease, taunt, and keep his pursuers in the chase. Boys arranged team sports competitions for themselves. They invented a form of handball called 'fives', and practised the classical sports of archery and wrestling. Cricket was probably the most popular sport among pupils at the schools. For many years, cricket team competitions were strictly intramural and scheduling, refereeing, and carrying injured players to the matron were the jobs of the players. Masters rarely supervised these games. The first extramural cricket match between Eton and Westminster, which took place in 1796, was organised by the players. Later, in the 1820s, Wordsworth's nephews Christopher and Charles would become famed cricketers for Winchester and Eton.

During the war years pupils organised a school rifle corps and conducted bayonet exercises. Boys at Winchester, Eton, and Rugby were allowed to and often did spend free time rambling, swimming, fishing, hunting birds' nests, and riding horses in the countryside around schools. After lessons were over, the young Wordsworths often sojourned in the Hawkshead churchyard or rambled about before they walked to the Tysons' home. Fortunate in their boarding house mistress, Ann Tyson, the brothers and their friends were free to take in what Mary Moorman calls 'the two great sights [of the local countryside]—water and sky'.[22] In *The Prelude* Wordsworth famously describes skating, rowing, and riding ponies with his Hawkshead classmates, as well as wandering late into the evenings over the fells of High Furness. In those days he 'communed with all I saw as something not apart from but inherent in my own immaterial nature'.[23] 'This,' writes Mary Moorman, 'was the marvellous gift of his schooldays.'[24] Among the sites of his rambling were his 'native hills', through which flowed the River Duddon. Some of Wordsworth's sonnets published in 1820 recall scenes he first visited during his school days fishing with a local angler, or later during his college vacations.[25] More than once he rambled past Seathwaite Chapel, the plain of Donnerdale, and the kirk of Ulpha with its 'pastoral graves'.[26] Sonnet XXVI in *The River Duddon* appears to describe memories from his teenage years, either in school or university, when he and his classmates were 'men growing out of boys'.[27] As he and his friends wandered, through the 'tangled woods' tracking the course of mountain streams, their rambles taught them 'random cares and truant joys', shielded

---

[21] R. J. Mackenzie, p. 497.
[22] *William Wordsworth: A Biography: Early Years 1770–1803*, p. 42.
[23] Note on 'Ode: Intimations of Immortality', Jared Curtis, *The Fenwick Notes*, p. 61.
[24] *William Wordsworth: A Biography: Early Years 1770–1803*, p. 41.
[25] Curtis, p. 31.
[26] WWPW, *The River Duddon*, Sonnets XVIII, XX, and XXI, pp. 300–301.
[27] WWPW, p. 302, l. 12.

them from 'from mischief and preserve[d] from stains [their] Vague minds'.[28] Shelley's country walks around Eton usually ended up at a pond that bears his name to this day. One of his school friends, Walter Halliday, reported that they often wandered 'for hours about Clewer, Frogmore, the Park at Windsor, [and] the Terrace'.[29] During these romps he was the 'delighted and willing listener to [Shelley's] marvellous stories of fairyland, and apparitions, and spirits, and haunted ground'.[30] Shelley's visits in town with Dr James Lind encouraged a parallel interest in natural science. It was Lind who counselled the youngster to be more 'systematic in his reading and speculation', advice he sometimes followed later when he directed young Mary Godwin's reading.[31]

Other 'self-educating' experiences that contributed to Romantic era pupils' early literary knowledge and skills were provided by the schools' debating societies and literary magazines. Aspiring orators belonging to the Rugby Debating Society met every Saturday in the fifth form school room, where they studied the subjects of their debates and practised the proper 'outward form and manner of debating'.[32] Boys reported that in these meetings they learned to 'listen with deference to reason and to abstain from uttering absurd propositions'.[33] The self-directed learning and interaction with peers that are involved in activities such as these usually have the effect of making new skills and new knowledge 'stick'.[34] Young debaters at Rugby commented with a certain amount of pride about such learning. One of the Rugby debaters wrote in the school magazine that together he and his team learned to focus on 'abstract truth'[35] and that along with 'fellowship', debating 'insinuated … a degree of civilization, of courtesy, of delicacy … into [our] manners'.[36] Byron's schoolboy oratorical experiences preparing for the Speech Days at Harrow School have been insightfully discussed by Elledge, who claims that these 'performances encoded and reflected a host of anxieties, conflicts, rivalries, and ambitions which they also helped him to manage'.[37] Moreover, as Elledge explains, these learning experiences were part of Byron's identity formation as he created 'the text' that he so 'famously became'.[38]

Pupils in the Georgian period also found time and evidently took great pleasure in founding and publishing school magazines. Eton pupils worked on

---

[28] WWPW, pp. 301–302, ll. 3, 10–12.
[29] Qtd in Holmes, p. 24.
[30] Holmes, p. 24.
[31] Holmes, p. 26.
[32] *Rugby Magazine*, 'The Rugby Debating Society', pp. 14–15.
[33] *Rugby Magazine*, 'The Rugby Debating Society', p. 15.
[34] See Brown *et al.*
[35] *Rugby Magazine*, 'The Rugby Debating Society', p. 13.
[36] *Rugby Magazine*, 'The Rugby Debating Society', p. 15.
[37] Elledge, p. 1.
[38] Elledge, p. 2.

Educating the Romantic Poets

three different magazines in the Georgian period: *The Microcosm* (f. 1787),[39] *The Miniature* (f. 1802), and *The Etonian* (f. 1820). Westminster's *Trifler* was founded in 1789 to rival the *Microcosm*. Christ's Hospital pupils published the *Album*. Rugby pupils founded their magazine in 1835 and dedicated it to headmaster Thomas Arnold. Reflecting contemporaneous anxieties about political speech, the young editors of several of these schools banned politics and religion as subjects for their publication.[40] The writing that pupils published in these magazines included essays, verses, humorous columns, and letters to the editor. Together they provide a remarkable record of what youngsters in these school were learning and thinking, particularly about contemporary literature. In the pages of the *Rugby Magazine* were articles on national and local prejudice. *The Miniature*'s first edition published articles titled

I. Remarks on Novels and Romances.—Receipt for a Modern Romance

V. The Restlessness of the Human Mind

VI. Plagiarism—Laws against that offence.—Various Trials.—That of Solomon Grildrig [the *nom de plume* of one of *The Miniature*'s writers]

VIII. Description of the state of modern poetry—Advertisement of *Peter Poeticus*—Ode to the Rainbow

XIV. Death.—The effects of its consideration on a young mind.—The opinions of the Ancient Philosophers.—Superiority of Revelation

XVIII. Newspapers, Reviews, and Magazines

XXXIII. The Holy Scriptures, independent of their moral tendency, superior to all other human productions.[41]

In October 1820 *The Etonian* published a series of loco-descriptive sonnets—one about Dunster Hermitage and another about Barle-Edge Abbey, juvenile

---

[39] The young men who created this magazine were George Canning, John Hookham Frere, John and Robert 'Bobus' Smith; as adults they all went on to create magazines as well.

[40] See Bylaws of *The Etonian*, vol. 1, no. 1, October 1820, pp. 21–22. The editors of *The Etonian* allowed 'bashful' classmates to submit their writings privately; they did not, however, allow pupils to publish anonymously, as was the practice of the magazines and reviews published in the larger world. Some magazines, such as *The Flagellant*, used pen names. *The Etonian* staff reported that drinking pots of beer and smoking numerous cigars while editing the magazine were often necessary (Anonymous, 'The King of Clubs', pp. 21–22).

[41] Grildrig, vol. 1, issue 1, 1802, p. 1.

efforts that paralleled the sonnet-writing interests manifest at this time by Wordsworth. The volume also included essays on 'Rhyme and Reason' and 'Juvenile Friendship'. The November and December 1820 issues ran a pair of articles 'On Wordsworth's Poetry', followed in February 1821 with a poem entitled 'I was a boy (*in imitation of Wordsworth*)'.[42] This poem both honours and parodies the Lucy poems. Later in the volume is an essay 'On Coleridge's Poetry' in which the young writer concludes that

> to Coleridge and Wordsworth, the poetry, the philosophy, and the criticism of the present day does actually owe its peculiar character, and its distinguishing excellence over that of the last century, those who would trace the origin of the present opinions back for thirty years would find no difficulty in believing. These two men, essentially different as they are in many respects have been copied, imitated, and parodied by every poet who now lives. Lord Byron has owned his obligations to Mr. Coleridge, and the third Canto of 'Childe Harold' could not have been written unless Wordsworth had lived before it.[43]

Pupils published articles on Horace's poetry, Shakespeare's sonnets, the state of modern poetry, and Coleridge's 'Kubla Khan'. On occasion the articles and poems these magazines published were discussed in the *Gentlemen's Magazine*, the *Universal Magazine*, *St. James Magazine*, the *Classical Journal*, *The Quarterly Review*, and the *Annual Register*.[44] The educational value of the experience of composing, editing, and publishing while still at school was detailed by one of the *Rugby Magazine*'s young contributors. He wrote that these periodical endeavours, along with similar efforts by boys in the school Debating Society, 'were an instrument of good', for they raised 'the stakes' for student writers and speakers and gave them 'practice with skills they [would] need as men'.[45] Southey dramatically claimed that he was 'born into the world as a writer' when he and his classmates published the first number of *The Flagellant*.[46]

Long before George Canning launched *The Anti-Jacobin, or, Weekly Examiner* in 1797, he had experience with two student magazines at Eton. He was one of the founders of *The Microcosm*, cited above, which began with an explanatory essay citing 'the Heroes of Wit and Literature' in the *Spectator*,

---

[42] *The Etonian*, no. 4, 1821, pp. 273–274.

[43] *The Etonian*, no. 4, 1821, pp. 307–317. The Eton students' familiarity with the works of these poets is testimony of the popularity of the two older poets at the schools and, probably, in their families.

[44] The plays and prologues that boys performed annually at Westminster and Eton were also topics for some of these journals as well.

[45] *Rugby Magazine*, 'The Rugby Debating Society', p. 17.

[46] CLRS, Pt 5, #3210. They modelled the magazine on Eton's *Microcosm*.

Educating the Romantic Poets

the *Guardian*, and the *Rambler* as his models and the wish that this project would be 'amusing and instructive'.[47] He adds that, though he is young, he is confident that he has 'acquired a fund of knowledge, language, and observation' at Eton 'sufficient' to the endeavour. Canning also expresses the belief that schoolboys' efforts as writers and editors prepare them for 'greater glory' in the larger world.[48] This prediction held true for him, the son of a disinherited Irish landowner and an actress, for, after distinguishing himself at Christ Church, he held numerous government jobs and served as foreign minister during the war with France. Between 1822 and 1827 he was a leader of the House of Commons and, briefly, prime minister. As noted in Chapter 1, quite a few graduates of these schools became statesmen. A number of them also went on to success in the periodical presses of their day. Pupils from St Paul's were especially distinguished as journalists; among this group numbered Stephen Jones, editor of the *European Magazine*; John Bowyer Nichols, editor of *Gentleman's Magazine*; Samuel Bentley, publisher of *Bentley's Miscellany*; John Hamilton Reynolds, proprietor of the *Athenaeum* and contributor to the *Edinburgh Review*; William Roberts, editor of the *Looker On* and *The British Review*; and Charles Coote, editor of the *Critical Review*. The fact that so many of the men who wielded power in the world of publishing and literary criticism were classically educated should not be ignored by modern scholars.

In 1788 one young journalist wrote in the Westminster *Trifler* that, though he and his classmates were 'Pent in our lonely College', they could, nevertheless, 'compose/Some measur'd numbers, some unfetter'd prose' that would 'hold the mirror up to Nature'.[49] Other examples not only of the Westminster pupils' writing skill but also of their evolving literary opinions are worthy of note. In the opening essay of Number 35 of *The Trifler*, dated 24 January 1789, Timothy Touchstone (a collective *nom de plume* for the editors) begins,

> Simplicity in poetry, like simplicity in dress, is secure of admiration from those possessed of true taste ... . Modern poetry (by *modern* I shall now confine myself to that which has appeared within the last twenty years) has degenerated into monotonous jingling of rhime, an artificial transposition of words, and an indiscriminate, and therefore false, use of figurative expressions.[50]

The youthful writer continues, noting with scorn the 'disgraceful prejudices' and 'false taste' of 'modern' critics, who admire poets who employ 'laboured

---

[47] *The Microcosm, a periodical Work*, no. 1, November 1786, p. 6.
[48] *The Microcosm*, no. 1, 6–7, p. 12.
[49] Touchstone, 'Prefatory Address', pp. 6–7.
[50] Touchstone, 'Simplicity in Poetry', pp. 447–448.

versification', 'superfluous epithets', and 'paroxysms of bombast'.[51] He honours, instead, a poet who exhibits 'neatness of expression, and a rural imagination'.[52] Homer, he says, is the ideal bard, for he is 'sometimes simple, generally easy, and when he rises on the wings of sublimity, always intelligible'.[53] Moving from his knowledge of classical texts to his appreciation of biblical ones, the boy asserts that 'passages will occur, in which the style must be elevated, but no sublimity in thought can [justify florid expression]; for let it be remembered that the sacred writings of Scripture lose none of their divine fire by a perspicuous and simple tenor of language'.[54] Touchstone concludes his essay with the statement that 'Ease and simplicity are the best ornaments of nature', a line that might have been penned by Wordsworth or Keats.[55] Winthrop Mackworth Praed's poem 'School and School-Fellows' (1829) calls attention to the lessons and skills he learned at Eton, such as writing 'delightful sapphics', knowing 'the streets of Rome and Troy', and supping with 'Fates and Furies'. What Praed and other schoolboy writers said about learning, literature, and the little worlds of their schools helps to contextualise the poets' emergence from this stage of their education. It adds as well to modern critical understanding of the foundational literary knowledge and tastes of the poets and of many of those in their audience.

The darker lessons of boarding school life

Alongside the many positive effects of life at Anglican grammar schools lay the potential for some distinctly dark and damaging 'out of school' lessons. This was the case at the great public schools especially, where early exposure to class hierarchy as well as cruelty and tyranny, both grand and small, were always part of the school experience. An older pupil in Southey's house was finally dismissed as 'mad' after episodes in which he beat young Southey with a poker, hit him with a porter pot, and dangled him out of a window by his legs.[56] Boys stole upon Byron when he was sleeping and put his lame leg in a tub of water. Shelley was repeatedly taunted by older boys. These young poets were not entirely innocent themselves, however. Despite his righteous arguments against flagellation, Southey is reported to have lost his temper and beaten his fag. Though he typically protected younger pupils, Byron was known on occasion to be a brute and bully with his peers. Shelley, who behaved bizarrely by schoolboy standards, set himself apart by refusing the traditional junior boys' fag duties. In one of

---

[51] Touchstone, 'Simplicity in Poetry', p. 449.
[52] Touchstone, 'Simplicity in Poetry', p. 449.
[53] Touchstone, 'Simplicity in Poetry', p. 449.
[54] Touchstone, 'Simplicity in Poetry', pp. 455–456.
[55] The attitudes expressed in this essay are further evidence of the popularity of Wordsworth's early poetry and poetic theory in the Anglo-classical academy.
[56] Sargeaunt, p. 264.

Educating the Romantic Poets

many fits of temper he stabbed a classmate in the hand with a fork. Even at the provincial schools, few boys escaped some sort of ill treatment by classmates. In the eighteenth and nineteenth centuries these incidents, along with scraps or rows, were tacitly approved or at least tolerated as a part of school life, and they were usually viewed as a way for boys to prove their courage and earn respect.[57] Byron bragged about and was honoured for winning six out of seven battles at Harrow.[58] Some schools were proud that their students were battlers. At Harrow 'fists were honourable weapons'; old boys reported that they rarely held grudges after their battles. Most appeared (or pretended) to believe that fighting bred strength and led to a long and successful life. The bishop of Adelaide proudly boasted that 'we [Westminster] boys ... were ready to fight *everybody*'.[59]

Participating in some sort of warfare even (or especially) with adults seemed to be a point of honour at the public schools. A rebellion took place at Winchester in the spring of 1793, when the warden denied pupils a usual privilege, that of observing the Buckinghamshire militia's exercises. On 1 February France had declared war on England and Holland, so this ceremony had particular significance for the students, many of whom would soon be of age to join the army. One student went to see the militia anyway and, as a punishment, the warden cancelled Easter leave for the whole school. The English traditions of public demonstration and pamphlet wars probably added to these pupils' readiness to stand up against his tyranny. The senior boys twice petitioned more or less respectfully—*in Latin*—for a reprieve, but the warden refused. Students responded by boycotting classes. As the standoff continued, they pelted the usher with marbles, stole the porter's keys, and finally imprisoned the warden and two schoolmasters in the dining hall overnight. The students released their prisoners the next day but locked the school gates behind them. Eventually the high sheriff was summoned to the college to try to persuade the students to submit. The boys barricaded the outer gate and pulled up cobblestones from an interior courtyard, ready to rain them down upon the law from the top of the tower. They also pillaged swords and bludgeons from the school's armoury and hoisted 'the red cap of liberty'. Seeing this, the sheriff backed down. The students held the school for another day, but eventually the rebellion collapsed and 35 youngsters were sacked.[60]

Harrow had rebellions in 1771, 1805, and 1808.[61] Byron led the one in 1805 to protest the appointment of the new headmaster, Dr George Butler. He

[57] Chandos, p. 167.
[58] Marchand, *Byron: A Biography*, vol. 1, pp. 66–67.
[59] Qtd in Sargeaunt, p. 215.
[60] Leach, pp. 403–406.
[61] Henry Drury, who was visiting Byron at Newstead Abbey at the time, laughed and suggested that the insurrectionists had been reading Byron's poetry, Marchand, *Byron: A Biography*, vol. 2, p. 162.

and his classmates preferred another candidate, Dr Drury's younger brother, a popular undermaster. A plot to blow up one of the school buildings was stopped, but the new headmaster's desk was dragged outside and burned, and signs were posted around the school calling boys to rise up. For the rest of Byron's final term at the school he feuded with Butler and encouraged others to join in ridiculing him.[62] Byron's readiness to act during this period according to his beliefs or to his perceptions of injustice is an early indicator of the poet's later willingness to take such stands and to disrupt the status quo, behaviours he later explores in works such as *The Giaour*, *Manfred*, *Cain*, and *The Bride of Abydos*, and which he demonstrated at the end of his life by taking up the cause of Greek independence.

Not infrequently, the rod was used to curb schoolboy behaviours ranging from poor classwork or bad hygiene to rebellion. While more than one headmaster averred that the rod was usually the last resort, the number of different terms for corporal punishment at the schools—flogging, birching, swishing, tanning, caning, tunding, or bibling[63]—indicates how often this method superseded lesser punishments such as chores, lines, or demotion in class rank. No matter the term, few boys left school without at least one appointment with a rod of some sort. At Winchester tunding took place every day at breakfast, before the midday meal, and at the end of the school day. Typically, the tunding prefect toasted his victims at the next meal.[64] While corporal punishment of children at school or home seems quite barbaric today, for centuries before the Georgian period and, in fact, well into the twentieth century it was a widely accepted part of child raising. Usually more embarrassing than painful, the practice appears to have been generally accepted by most parents, teachers, and pupils in the Georgian period. Headmasters of the age viewed pupils as 'droves of shaggy Shetland ponies, freshly caught and impounded'.[65] 'The best teachers,' one old boy claimed, 'compelled industry first by force, and then worked by love.'[66] Taking their punishment 'like men' was a lesson Georgian fathers hoped their sons would learn at school, where the example of spartan boys who withstood beating without flinching or tears was well known.

---

[62] Butler, who had been senior wrangler at Cambridge in 1794 and Fellow of Sidney Sussex College, continued as headmaster until 1829. Despite Byron's disapproval, Butler was well liked, admired for his tact, skill, and athletic abilities.
[63] Tunding is from the Latin word *tundere*, to buffet or bruise; tunding referred to strokes on the back. Bibling referred to strokes on the bottom.
[64] Up until 1920, Winchester had specific rules about who might beat whom. The *Aulae Praefectus*—the prefect of the hall—had permission to punish anyone at the headmaster's instruction. A limit was set at ten strokes. Even though middle-class boys might be chosen as prefects, it appears that they were not allowed to beat a boy with a title.
[65] Mackenzie, p. 500.
[66] Mackenzie, p. 500.

Educating the Romantic Poets

Figure 2. Westminster birch rod and cane, modern facsimiles on show at Westminster School. Reproduced with kind permission of the Governing Body, Westminster School.

Young Southey cites spartan boys who were 'flagellated for hours, without mercy' and underwent this 'ceremony without a tear, without shrinking', in 'No. V' of *The Flagellant*, before famously trumpeting that flogging of English boys in a Christian school is an invention of 'the DEVIL!!!'[67] Southey urges classmates to think for themselves and to speak out against such tyranny and illegal authority. He adds that the practice of flogging is ineffective as well as evil, for it inculcates 'passive obedience ... sour tempers', and breaks 'the spirit

---

[67] Southey, 'No. V', p. 80.

of their unfortunate subjects, who in their turn, exercise the same tyranny over their inferiors, till the hall of learning becomes only a seminary for brutality!'[68] Citing Herodotus, Plutarch, Cicero, Seneca, and Lucian, Southey explains that flogging originated among the Greeks and Romans as an act of piety before their pagan gods. He scoffs at Roman Catholic monks who were driven by the 'fiend' of 'superstition' to flagellate themselves and notes that flogging was used by Protestant Christians only to exorcise the devil from demoniacs. Perhaps forgetting that he himself had been known to beat his fag, young Southey sagely quotes Grotius (whose text was used for Westminster's famous 'sacred Lesson'), Milton, St Athanasius, Jerome, and Moses to condemn the 'impiety and abomination of flogging'.[69] He concludes by calling for 'all doctors, reverends, and plain masters, to cease, without delay or repining, from the beastly and idolatrous custom of flogging'.[70]

Southey's headmaster, William Vincent, who was not amused by the article, immediately launched an angry investigation into the identity of the writer and even considered prosecuting the publisher for libel. Southey eventually admitted to being the culprit and apologised, but Vincent expelled the lad anyway.[71] Worse yet, he informed the dean of Christ Church, where Southey and most of his Westminster classmates were headed in the fall. The college withdrew its offer of admission to the youngster. In the following weeks, adding insult to injury, Vincent preached and published 'A Discourse addressed to the People of Great Britain' (1792), which was advertised 'to promote peace, subordination, brotherly love, and Christian charity', but which was a cruel piece of paternalistic double talk that Southey believed was aimed at him personally.[72] Prior to expelling Southey, Vincent had made a number of references to Southey's family's relative poverty. In the sermon, the headmaster proclaimed that 'society cannot exist without a class of poor', and that the poor must simply accept their lot 'in patience and content'[73] and count themselves fortunate to have poor laws and workhouses. Vincent praises Anglican schools, saying that 'education is necessary for the lowest, as well as the highest', so the lowest will know 'their religion or their duty', have 'virtuous habits', and be 'useful members to the community'.[74] Southey responded by writing angry

---

[68] Southey, 'No. V', pp. 76–77.
[69] Southey, 'No. V', p. 86.
[70] Southey, 'No. V', p. 88.
[71] Southey had already annoyed the head by writing an essay condemning Burke's *Reflections on the Revolution in France* and a romance in prose praising democratic kings. See Storey, p. 9. Southey later told friends that he thought Vincent was also prejudiced against him because his father was in trade.
[72] Vincent, 'Discourse', p. 7.
[73] Vincent, 'Discourse', p. 13.
[74] Vincent, 'Discourse', p. 17.

letters about tyranny and religious hypocrisy to his friends. Eventually he directed his efforts to arranging admission to Balliol, where he matriculated in the fall of 1792. Once at Oxford, Southey made new friends, reconnected with his old ones who were at Christ Church, participated in college discussions about the war and reform, sympathised with Unitarians, and began composing *Joan of Arc*. By midlife he came to believe that Vincent had, in fact, done him a favour. In 1819 he wrote Bedford that

> I have long, & with good reason, looked upon my expulsion from Westminster as having been in its consequences the luckiest event of my life. And for many years I should have been glad to have met the old man, in full persuasion that he would not have been sorry to have met with me.[75]

A year later, in May of 1820, Southey accepted the invitation of the new headmaster of Westminster, Edmund Goodenough, to be included in the list of the school stewards.

Forced service

In the seventeenth century the English public schools began to require the youngest boys to do forced service—called fagging or sweating—for the oldest students. Two of the great day schools, St Paul's and Merchant Taylors', and many of the smaller provincial schools did not permit fagging. Southey's, Byron's, and Shelley's schools did. The practice was different at each school, and most of what is known is based on anecdotes, gossip, and old boys' memories. This much is clear: at participating schools, boys in the two lowest forms were required to be servants and errand boys for the upper two forms. Enduring time as a 'fag', 'sweat', or 'doul' was considered a rite of passage that earned the youngest boys their place in the school and the right to have such a service done for them when they were seniors. Not incidentally, the system supplied free household labour. Apologists for the practice claim it tested boys' character and taught the older boys the responsible use of authority and the younger ones self-discipline and obedience. The fag system may have taught these lessons, and there is evidence that mistreating smaller and weaker students was considered cowardly and in bad taste at most schools; but the practice was wide open for abuse. Older boys could be quite cruel to their fags—taunting, baiting, or teasing them and keeping them busy at tedious chores when they needed to study, eat, or sleep. In 1830 the *Edinburgh Review* described fagging at the public schools as 'the only regular institution of slave-labour, enforced

---

[75] CLRS, Pt 6, #3280.

by brute violence' in the kingdom.[76] A Harrow headmaster in that period observed that the seniors' selection of new fags resembled the purchase of slave girls in the Middle East.[77]

Typically, every senior had a fag, and cricket or rowing captains and the head prefect might have several. Fags were expected to drop whatever they were doing at the first call of a senior boy. In some houses, records were kept of how many times a fag did duty; at one school, if a youngster did fewer than twenty errands in a week he might be thrashed.[78] Fags performed various jobs similar to those of household servants. Younger boys tapped as 'valets' brushed hats and jackets, repaired split seams, reattached buttons, polished shoes and boots, and carried messages. Some served as housemaids—making beds, fetching water for morning wash-up, supplying clean towels, sweeping and dusting the hall. At schools where students were responsible for their own breakfast and evening meals, fags often served as cooks or butlers. They made coffee, tea, or toast, boiled eggs, roasted potatoes and chestnuts, ran into town to buy cooked lobsters or sausages, set tables for the seniors' meals, and afterwards cleared and cleaned cutlery, dishes, and cookware. At Eton, however, seniors were expressly forbidden to order fags to cook, wait at the table, or clean shoes.[79] The worst job was 'Fire Fag'. On cold mornings, usually in pairs, these youngsters hoisted huge coal buckets or wood logs and dashed from one fireplace to the next, building or stoking fires. They were expected to keep these fires going all day.[80] 'Field Fags' assisted at games—chasing footballs and tennis balls, attending the wickets at cricket games, announcing time, and being generally useful to the players.

Apparently, most boys accepted the situation with 'cheerful stoicism', understanding that, by doing so, they were earning the right to have their own little servants when they were in the upper fifth and sixth forms.[81] Some of the small boys boasted of their toughness, and not all seniors were bullies. A good-hearted, self-disciplined fag-master could be a boon to a new boy—keeping an eye on him, standing up for him when necessary, and helping him with his studies. A young Etonian wrote home to say that he'd become 'quite accomplished' after just a few weeks of fagging for an 'awfully jolly' fag-master and had learned to cook eggs and lay a table.[82] Another youngster had the honour of fagging for a famed rower and member of the Eton Society, or Pop, the school's exclusive club for senior prefects. He was thrilled that he

[76] *Edinburgh Review*, 'Art. III. The Public Schools of England—Eton', p. 75.
[77] Fraser, p. 145.
[78] Falkus, p. 67.
[79] *Edinburgh Review*, 'Art. III. The Public Schools of England—Eton', p. 76.
[80] Falkus, pp. 67–72.
[81] Falkus, p. 67.
[82] Falkus, p. 67.

Educating the Romantic Poets

was, on occasion, admitted to the older student's room and into the presence of some of the school's most revered senior boys.[83]

In general, schoolmasters tolerated the system and even designated an adult manservant to rouse sleeping fags for their early morning duties. Shrewsbury's headmaster Samuel Butler (1774–1839) and several other headmasters set limits on what services might be asked of little boys and specified how the fags were to be treated. At some schools, individual housemasters banned fagging. In 1811 Dr Russell, the headmaster at Charterhouse, attempted to ban the tradition for the entire school and was met with a student rebellion.[84] Southey accepted the service of a fag when he was a senior. At Harrow Byron served as a fag, and as a senior he was known to be a benevolent fag-master. Shelley refused to fag and thereby lost respect among the pupils and, worse for him, the protection of seniors. In 1848 Winchester's Moberly wrote that this system of 'graduated subordination' and service was favoured by most schoolmasters, because it taught students 'skills in taking and keeping their position in life' and helped them learn how to curb 'absurd pretension'.[85] He added that the practice helped pupils to develop 'a general practical modesty' and their sense of their place—their 'boy-rank'—in the little world of the school.[86] With the notable exception of Percy Shelley, most students did not openly object to the practice, though they did express concern that they should only be assigned to serve seniors who were their equals or 'superiors' in social rank. Ten-year-old baronets were willing to serve other baronets or viscounts, but they found it degrading to serve anyone below their family's social station.

Moberly admitted that some fagging duties were 'irksome or painful' or even 'ridiculous', but he believed that this experience taught the older boys 'the limits of authority' and taught the young ones 'to submit cheerfully and readily to … *legitimate*, [authority, but] to grumble and complain at *everything* which [they understood to be] *undue*'.[87] The 'good sense' and 'early maturity of practical judgment' boys acquired from these experiences, Moberly said, was 'of unspeakable value in all the conduct of their lives' both in school and thereafter.[88] But it must be said that the system also naturalised or reinforced a social system based on class hierarchy and servitude and provided opportunities for boorish cruelty and victimisation of weaker youngsters. 'A boy begins as a slave and ends as a despot' was the judgement of *The Edinburgh Review*.[89] When the fag system worked, it did so in part because younger boys usually respect,

[83] Falkus, p. 68.
[84] Falkus, p. 61.
[85] Moberly, pp. viii, v.
[86] Moberly, p. v.
[87] Moberly, pp. x, xiii. Italics his.
[88] Moberly, p. v.
[89] *Edinburgh Review*, 'Art. III. The Public Schools of England—Eton', p. 77.

even worship, older boys as heroes. Even its critics admitted that friendships, kindness, and boys' senses of both of honour and humour often mitigated the wrongs of the system. Nevertheless, fagging legitimised occasions of rigid, frightening, and sometimes brutal hierarchy. Arnold wrote that he counted on the better outcomes of the practice and on the hope that boys' personal pride as young gentlemen and their duty and conscience as Christians would motivate them to avoid or try to prevent the cruel ones. But even Arnold's students could and did disappoint him in this regard. In one of his school sermons Arnold lamented that many boys do not care about 'the evil of sin' nor do they think there is anything 'very alarming in the condition of a sinner'.[90] He added, probably for its shaming effect, that 'Public schools are the very seats and nurseries of vice', where a boy who was once 'pure and honest' becomes 'utterly low, and base, and mischievous—where he loses his modesty, his respect for truth, and his affectionateness, and becomes coarse, and false, and unfeeling'.[91]

The usual 'sins' of schoolboys were not so base; more often they amounted to oversleeping, poor personal hygiene, and insufficient effort on their themes or memory work. More serious offences such as drinking, fighting, plagiarising, and lying of course occurred. Older pupils were found drunk in local pubs or in their rooms, sometimes on washtub whisky they had concocted themselves. Boys paid or forced classmates to write their themes for them. Southey was sometimes impressed for this duty, with the instruction that the themes he wrote were not to be too perfect in order to fool the master. Some pupils purchased old papers from willing servants who collected themes at the end of each school year. Arnold recorded concern about students' gambling, borrowing, idleness, and 'sensual wickedness'.[92] Though never explicitly stated, it appears that Arnold was aware that boarding school life and the fag system lent themselves to sexual experimentation and abuse. Various critics have asserted that bullying and the regular practice of corporal punishment by prefects (and some schoolmasters) was a sanctioned form of displaced sexual pleasure. Given that a strong sexual undercurrent cannot be avoided at any gathering of pubescent youngsters, there can be no doubt that some schoolboys in the Romantic period engaged in 'sensual wickedness'. The secrecy that is a typical part of these behaviours and the reluctance of students and adults to discuss the issue make it difficult to collect reliable data or to draw conclusions about the issue. The Public Schools Commission of 1861 did not address the issue of the sexual behaviours of students at all. It should, of course, be noted that schools cannot make youngsters gay or straight, and most children's gender identities are formed long before they go to boarding school. However,

[90] Arnold, Sermon XII, p. 106.
[91] Arnold, Sermon XII, pp. 110–111.
[92] Qtd in Chandos, p. 284.

Educating the Romantic Poets

boarding schools are places where early sexual experiences with partners of any gender and age can take place, and some will turn out to be terribly damaging. Until a more comprehensive survey of the letters and diaries of pupils at these schools has been made with attention focused on this issue, the only certain statement that can be made from this vantage point is that, along with the many shaping experiences gleaned from class, chapel, hall, and fields, boarding school pupils at the great public schools also found more opportunities than day pupils did to explore their gender identities and sexual interests, and this sometimes included unsought recruitment or coercion.[93]

Headmasters in the Georgian period noted that any sort of weakness, timidity, eccentricity, or unsociability, as well as obvious poverty, might bring out the meanness of schoolboys. Headmaster Moberly of Winchester marvelled at 'the natural tendency to cruelty among boys … . Not great boys only, but quite little ones, will molest, ill-treat, and give wanton pain to one another to an extent which is quite wonderful.'[94] Just as they left boys to themselves in sports, schoolmasters rarely intervened when boys were taunting or bullying each other. These behaviours were labelled by Moberly as part of the flow of school politics and were best dealt with by student prefects or monitors.[95] Schoolmasters operated on the principle that the push and pull of school life taught youngsters about 'their own position, the position of others, their mutual claims and rights, the ways of behaving to one another, [and] the propriety of different ranks in a school', for all of these negotiations have their counterparts in the 'relations, proprieties, delicacies, and usages of real life'.[96] Headmasters did, however, use Sunday sermons to remind students that they were expected to act as gentlemen and 'Christians, not heathens'.[97]

---

[93] Storr, pp. 103, 99.
[94] Moberly, p. xv.
[95] See the Prefects' unpublished notebook at Winchester.
[96] Moberly, p. xi.
[97] See also Eton headmaster Hawtrey's *Sermons and Lectures* (1849), where he delivers several lessons on boy behaviour.

Chapter Three

England's Public and Grammar Schools
Lessons in Grammar, Memory, and Composition

In *The Idea of the University* John Henry Newman, who was trained at the Anglo-classical school at Great Ealing, in West London, and at Trinity College, Oxford, details what he, as a college tutor, expected of students who arrived at Oxford fresh from their grammar schools. Students should have had 'intellectual training' of a sort that has brought 'the mind into form'.[1] The first step in that training, he explains, is

> to impress upon a boy's mind the idea of science, method, order, principle, and system, of rule and exception, of richness and harmony … . Let him once gain this habit of method, of starting from fixed points, of making his ground good as he goes, of distinguishing what he knows from what he does not know, and I conceive he will be gradually initiated into the largest and truest philosophical views.[2]

The poet James Beattie (1735–1803) explained why the era's educators were so dedicated to methodical grammatical studies.[3] He starts by saying that one must be 'something of a grammarian to be able thoroughly to understand a well-written book … [for] the complicated inflexions and syntax of these elegant tongues [give] rise to innumerable subtleties of connection, and minute varieties of meaning, whereof the superficial reader, who thinks grammar below

---

[1] Newman took a degree at Oxford in 1820 and became a Fellow at Oriel in 1822. For at least a decade he was a college tutor.
[2] Newman, pp. xliv–xlv.
[3] *Essays on Poetry and Music*. Beattie was trained in classical grammar in Scotland. Wordsworth read Beattie during his days at Hawkshead.

Educating the Romantic Poets

his notice can have no idea'.[4] He continues, saying that a properly trained student will show

> that he not only knows the general meaning, and the import of the particular words, but also [that he] can instantly refer each word to its class; enumerate all its terminations, specifying every change of sense, however minute, that may be produced by a change of inflexion or arrangement; explain its several dependencies, distinguish the literal meaning from the figurative, one species of figure from another, and even the philosophical use of words from the idiomatical, and the vulgar from the elegant; recollecting occasionally other words and phrases that are synonymous, or contrary, or of different though familiar signification; and accounting for what he says, either from the reason of the thing, or by quoting a rule of art, or a classical authority.[5]

Beattie concludes with the assertion that

> by such an exercise, the memory is likely to be more improved in strength and readiness, the attention better fixed, the judgment and taste more successfully exerted, and a habit of reflection and subtle discrimination more easily acquired, than it could be by any other employment equally suited to the capacity of childhood.[6]

This is an astonishing set of learning objectives, and it is difficult to believe that students in the Georgian period regularly achieved them. However, examples of pupils' verses and essays, their publications in their school magazines, and letters that are quoted throughout this book provide evidence that the Anglo-classical programme went a long way towards realising many of them.

The 'habit of method' for which Newman calls began seriously when pupils at the Anglo-classical schools were as young as eight, with a rigorous sequence of daily lessons in Latin grammar. Georgian schoolmasters defined the study of grammar very broadly. The *Appendix to the Eton Latin Grammar* (1796) explains that 'grammar' includes:

> *Orthography*[, which is] the art of spelling; *Etymology*, treats of the several kinds of words or parts of speech, with their accidents and formations; *Syntax* teaches the construction of words into sentences, according to their several relations to each other, and consists of two parts, Concord

---

[4] Beattie, pp. 508–509.
[5] Beattie, pp. 510–511.
[6] Beattie, p. 511.

Lessons in Grammar, Memory, and Composition

and Government; and *Prosody* instructs us in the quantity of syllables and their arrangement in versification.[7]

Schoolmasters launched boys' grammar studies by helping them build a functional Latin vocabulary, word by word. Teachers paid particular attention to proper pronunciation and to the quantities of the long and short vowels. When pupils learned enough nouns and verbs, they began reading short passages of Latin verse. Masters translated these passages and explained the pertinent grammar rules. Pupils were tasked each night with translating and memorising new verses along with related grammar rules and their exceptions (usually printed in Latin and often in hexameter). The job of translating was an important part of this training; here's what a Rugby student said about it:

> Coleridge, in his *Table Talk*, very justly observes, that good translation is far more difficult than original composition, and requires if not higher, at least far more rare qualities of mind. I have long amused myself by observing the errors into which various translators, from the youngest to the oldest, usually fall, and the instances of bad taste by which they disfigure at once their own language, and the author whom they profess to represent.[8]

According to Vicesimus Knox, the outcome of this sequence of assignments was that by the end of their first year youngsters were reading, understanding, and reciting simple classical fables (see Figure 3), epigrams, and colloquies, as well as passages from the Latin Bible.

Schoolmasters depended upon the receptivity of young children's brains to language acquisition, and they were careful to vary the ways in which boys were asked to engage with words. While these educators could not have explained their methods in this way, their early vocabulary lessons laid down foundational neuropathways for all subsequent language acquisition. Repeated daily, such instruction about word forms, meanings, roots, endings, and the rules governing their usage added additional, patterned knowledge and strengthened existing neural pathways in pupil's developing brains. Memorising the words and the rules—usually in verse—reinforced these lessons. Reciting or hearing their classmates recite the previous night's memory work added another layer of practice that helped to solidify new learning. Teachers linked the lessons, day by day, challenging pupils to recall words and linguistic patterns from the previous lesson to apply to new ones. This process also provokes what cognitive scientists call the prediction response and the

---

[7] Anonymous, *Appendix to the Eton Latin Grammar*, p. 3.
[8] *Rugby Magazine*, 'Some Remarks', p. 358.

Figure 3. Title page of a teaching text of *Aesop's Fables* in Greek and Latin, 1807. Reproduced by permission of the Provost and Fellows of Eton College.

Lessons in Grammar, Memory, and Composition

expectancy effect.[9] In children, the mental exercise of prediction followed by the fulfilment of expectations has been proven to release dopamine, a chemical neurotransmitter closely associated with pleasure and intrinsic motivation.[10] When pupils were subsequently tasked with composing imitations of the passages they were reading and memorising, yet another form of learning reinforcement and a more complicated mental process was put in play. This routine of reading, translating, memorising, reciting, and imitating was typical at all of the Anglo-classical schools, and it was capped at the end of each week with a summative review. After several years learning Latin in this way, teachers at some schools—including those that Wordsworth, Coleridge, Southey, Byron, and Shelley attended—added Greek (with its unique metres). The advantage to writers of knowing Greek was explained by Thomas De Quincey: Greek 'ben[ds] to the purposes of him who use[s] it beyond the material of other languages; it [is] an instrument for a larger compass of modulations'.[11] Westminster School added studies of Hebrew, using Old Testament texts for pupils' reading lessons.[12] From time to time, St Paul's taught Arabic. Modern European languages were not taught, but families could arrange for their sons to study French or Italian with a paid tutor.

Much of the early language instruction in the schools involved what educators call 'boring but important work'; these tasks are fundamental to students' progress, but usually require self-transcendent motivation, perseverance, and/or grit. To keep boys on track—and thereby to instil grit and teach them perseverance—schoolmasters relied on several motivators. The first was the simple willingness of children to do what is asked of them and to please their teachers. Masters also appealed to boys' self-respect and desire to do what their parents (or England or God) expected of them. Two more powerful motivators were competition and 'emulation', which were 'purposely excited by the masters'.[13] These were especially helpful in keeping boys on tasks that they might have otherwise been tempted to abandon. Finally, of course, punishments ranging from shaming to caning were also used. While cause and effect cannot be unequivocally demonstrated, it is nevertheless reasonable to suggest that the tenacity that Wordsworth, Southey, Byron, and Shelley demonstrated as adults in the sometimes boring but

---

[9] Cozolino, p. 154.

[10] See Willis and Willis, pp. 67–68. A simple example of this process that many will recognise is the way young children love to 'read' or hear the same bedtime stories over and over again.

[11] Masson, p. 64.

[12] While there is considerable disagreement on what might be considered the typical conventions of Hebrew poetry, most scholars agree that parallelism or cadenced balancing of parts is common in the Old Testament. Pupils who went from Westminster to Christ Church were expected to continue their studies of Hebrew at college.

[13] 'Art. III. The Public Schools of England—Westminster and Eton', *Edinburgh Review*, p. 66.

Educating the Romantic Poets

nevertheless important tasks of their writing careers was one of the effects of their grammar schools' programme that trained them to do the boring but important work without too much complaint. It seems likely that such training also came to the aid of these men later in life when they faced personal challenges ranging from bad reviews and poor sales to scandal, domestic turmoil, illness, and the early deaths of loved ones.

Vicesimus Knox recommended that boys study grammar 'daily and hourly' and that, as soon as they learned nouns, pronouns, and verbs, they should read 'an entertaining Latin author'.[14] The first Latin texts teachers usually assigned to young boys were Ovid's *Metamorphoses*, *Cordery's Colloquies*, and Phaedrus's fables.[15] The simple conversational Latin in Terence's plays made them another popular classroom text, as were the dialogues that Erasmus composed for schoolchildren. Younger boys also read Cornelius Nepos's short biographies of figures such as Miltiades, the wily hero of the Battle of Marathon, and Hannibal, whose crossing of the Alps with elephants no doubt enthralled little boys. Schoolmasters used Cicero's letters to his son and Martial's witty epigrams that make fun of city life and the bad behaviour of the people who live there. Surviving schoolboy letters and magazine articles of the period make it clear that pupils prided themselves on their growing knowledge of classical languages and their proper use; one even took it upon himself to point out to his mother the grammatical errors in one of her letters.[16]

At Eton and many other schools the first lesson on Monday mornings for the younger pupils came from the Latin New Testament. After reading eight or ten lines of scripture with his pupils, the schoolmaster would parse the passage for them. The pronunciation, quantities of the vowels, meanings, and grammatical relationships of every word in every line were explained. Because most schoolmasters were also clergymen, we can assume that they elaborated on the simpler theological messages of these texts. Just as with the pagan texts, pupils were expected to memorise these passages and the relevant grammar rules.[17] These lessons not only taught Latin words and grammar but also gave youngsters early and intimate familiarity with scripture. On Tuesday selected pupils were called on to recite the verses they had memorised or to

---

[14] Knox, *Liberal Education*, p. 47.

[15] Thompson reports that Wordsworth was 'strongly attached to Ovid' after reading his *Metamorphoses* at school, p. 91.

[16] Grant.

[17] At Eton, boys were instructed to compose short phrases called 'vulgaria', which illustrated the grammar rules they were expected to know. An English grammar text used in the Georgian period offers the following example of the kinds of rule the students were expected to memorise: 'A Noun is the Name of a Thing that may be seen, felt, heard, or understood: As the Name of my Hand in Latin, is *manus*; the Name of an House, is *domus*; the Name of Goodness, is *bonitas*'. Lily, p. 12.

Lessons in Grammar, Memory, and Composition

answer questions about meanings, word forms, and syntax. Coleridge's nephew Edward, who was a King's Scholar at Eton, reported that, due to the number of boys in his form, in some years he was called to recite only twice in a term. However, because he never knew when he might be 'called up' to recite or answer grammar questions, and feared the shame of doing poorly, he rarely shirked his memory work.[18] This routine of translating, parsing, memorising, reciting, and questioning was repeated several times each week, with breaks at midweek and on Saturdays.

At Eton the younger boys were expected to learn and conjugate at least three new verbs and to learn and decline three new nouns each week. One early exercise asked the boys to translate 'I teach, you read, he hears' and 'I did love; you did laugh; he did sleep' into Latin. Teachers used *Exempla Minora: or, New English Examples to be Rendered into Latin adapted to the Rules of the Latin Grammar*, by Thomas Morell (1703–1784).[19] Pupils read and compared their translations in class the next day. By the end of a typical week, pupils had worked closely on at least fifty lines from various texts in Latin and had learned between six and 12 new verbs and the same number of new nouns. One typical assignment was to translate selections from Corderius's Latin *Colloquies* into English. For example:

What are you doing?
I am repeating by myself.
What are you repeating?
The task, which the master hath set us today.
Do you retain it in memory?
So I think.
Let us repeat together; thus each of us will say the better before the master.
Begin you then, who have challenged me.
Come on, be attentive, that you do not suffer me to go wrong.

The schools' encouragement of partner or group study referenced in this exercise was also an effective practice, and it was often necessary in the periods when enrolments were so high that a single schoolmaster might be responsible for as many as 70 boys in a form.[20]

In addition to translations and recitations of dialogues, each week young Etonians memorised at least three new pages of rules in their Latin grammar and wrote sentences using those rules. Many of the grammar textbooks were

---

[18] Edward Coleridge.
[19] Numerous editions of the *Exempla* were in use in the eighteenth and nineteenth centuries.
[20] Maxwell-Lyte, p. 359.

Educating the Romantic Poets

written in Latin, and often in verse. A writer in the 1831 *Edinburgh Review* bitterly complained that

> these grammatical rules, with their various exceptions or limitations, [had] been violently tortured into doggerel Latin verses; while the unhappy boy toiling through these wilds of poetical grammar, bewildered and unconscious of any object, is told, as if in mockery: *visum est grammaticae metricis lenire laborem Praeceptis*! (Translation: 'learning grammar metrically is soothing work').[21]

Nevertheless, Hanoverian schoolmasters preferred the method. Because young boys memorise so easily and verse assists the memory, teachers viewed this exercise as a reasonable one. In fact, Arnold observed that his pupils had an easier time remembering grammar rules in Latin verse than they did in English.[22]

The text used for grammar instruction at most of the schools was some form of the *Lily Latin Grammar*, also titled *A short introduction of grammar generally to be used ... for the bringing up all those that intend to attain to the knowledge of the Latin tongue*. This is the book that Henry VIII decreed to be used in all classical schools, and it was used to teach Queen Elizabeth I, Shakespeare, Cromwell, and Milton. Composed by William Lily (1468–1522), the headmaster of St Paul's School, with input from Dean Colet and Erasmus, it was entirely in Latin. Eton revised it in 1758, and thereafter the *Eton Grammar* was the standard school grammar at many schools. Eton published a revised English version in 1804, *An English Introduction to the Latin Tongue for the Use of Youth* (see Figure 4).[23] Pupils were supplied with dictionaries. Entick's abridged Latin dictionary was recommended for the younger boys

---

[21] *Edinburgh Review*, 'Art. III. A Latin Grammar for Use at Westminster School', p. 67.
[22] Stanley, vol. 1, p. 122.
[23] Eton supplemented its grammar with *The Accidence, or, First Rudiments of the Latin Tongue, for the Use of Youth*. Charles Lamb refers to this text in 'The Old and the New Schoolmaster' in *Essays of Elia*. From time to time headmasters at Eton and other schools published revisions of the grammar, usually adding allusions to their schools and traditions. Westminster published a Latin grammar in English, *An English Introduction to the Latin Tongue, for the Use of the Lower Forms in Westminster-School* (1732). One of the most blistering critiques of the English public schools, published by the *Edinburgh Review* in 1830, tore apart the grammars that the schools were using, saying they were inaccurate, imprecise, and 'marked by almost every fault under which such treatises can labour', 'Art III. The Public Schools of England—Eton', p. 68. The criticisms in this article, however, should be read with caution, for at the end of the piece the author reveals that he and others at the journal were bristling over the news that the English government had recently 'thought itself called upon to institute a Commission of Inquiry and Reform for the more remote, and we will venture to say, the far more pure and perfect Universities of Scotland' (p. 80).

Lessons in Grammar, Memory, and Composition

and Ainsworth's more scholarly and 'copious' dictionary for older ones.[24] *Schrevelius's Lexicon* was commonly used for the study of Greek because schoolmasters believed it was particularly well adapted for teaching the Greek Testament and Homer.

Many boys quickly and rather easily became proficient in Latin and had little trouble translating and memorising new lines each night. The preface of an auxiliary textbook, *An Introduction to Construing and Parsing of Latin Adapted to the Eton Grammar*, which circulated when Shelley was at school, explains that 'many of the Principal Rules will be firmly fixed in memory, and their application perfectly understood' by the time a boy had 'advanced as far as the 53rd page'.[25] According to the schedule at Eton, this would have been done by the ninth week of a boy's first term at school. In *A Short Introduction of Grammar Compiled and Set Forth for the Bringing up of All Those That Intend to Attain the Knowledge of the Latin Tongue* (1728), an English edition based on *Lily's Grammar*, the authors state that most young scholars can learn 'every Part [of grammar] not by Rote, but by Reason' with little more than 'a quarter of a Year's Diligence'.[26] Besides the expected information about declensions and conjugations, these books discuss the rules and practices of classical prosody and include examples of figures such as synthesis, synecdoche, and prolepsis.

Teachers expressed their hope that boys would 'understand what [was]committed to Memory', so they created supplemental handbooks, exercise books, and lists of study questions. Two such texts were the *Greek Examiner* and *Grammaticae Quaestiones: Or a Grammatical Examination by Questions Only*. The author of one such Latin 'question book', Nathaniel Morgan, an Etonian who taught at Bath Grammar School, advertised his textbook by reporting that, while using these questions, his scholars had 'improved more in Grammatical knowledge in one quarter, than they had before in twice that time … [because his method] obliges Children to use their reasoning Powers, and leads them pleasantly on to the Pursuit of real fundamental Knowledge'.[27] Among Morgan's 'pleasant' questions were:

How do you distinguish the numbers of nouns?
What question does the Nominative Case answer?
How many degrees of Comparison do Adjectives admit of?
What Distinction do you make between a Verb Transitive and a Verb Intransitive?[28]

---

[24] Knox, *Liberal Education*, p. 52.
[25] Anonymous, *An Introduction to Construing*, p. vii.
[26] Anonymous, *An Introduction to Construing*, p. iii.
[27] Morgan, p. vii.
[28] Morgan, pp. 9, 10, 15, 20; capitalisation his.

Educating the Romantic Poets

The textbook was well reviewed and required three editions. Vicesimus Knox, however, eschewed the use of question books, handbooks, 'Nomenclators or parsing indexes', asserting that 'the dictionary, the grammar, and the LIVING INSTRUCTOR, constantly near, are the only allowable auxiliaries'.[29]

Weekly review was another essential part of the grammar lessons. As *Lily's Grammar* explains, boys were to be 'occupied in a continual rehearsing and looking back again to those things they have learned'.[30] Friday afternoons and Saturday mornings were review sessions. At these times, boys rehearsed their memory work and grammar rules and some read their best verses aloud. This sequence of lessons, with its reliance on close reading, memory, practice, writing, and review was standard at schools of the period. Georgian educators cautioned against moving on to new lessons if the current week's lesson had not been carefully reviewed and firmly grasped. As noted above, modern neuroscientists advocate frequent review, small stakes testing, and practice.[31] Indeed, many of the language pedagogies of the Anglo-classical schoolmasters are in line with the best practices suggested for school-age children by modern research and were more rigorously and regularly practised than they typically are today.[32] Thomas Arnold claimed that 'The study of language ... was given for the very purpose of forming the human mind in youth; and the Greek and Latin languages ... seem the very instruments by which this is to be effected.'[33]

Memory work

It should be no surprise, given the examples of how Anglo-classical schoolmasters taught grammar, that Georgian educators agreed with Aeschylus's maxim that 'memory is the mother of all wisdom'. Teachers of the period firmly believed that 'the instruction of childhood depends more on memory than intellect'.[34] Even the critics of English public schools at *The Edinburgh Review* maintained that 'the practice of learning by heart ... when properly regulated, tends both to improve the taste and strengthen the memory.'[35] Arnold agreed, commenting on the tendency of foreign texts to stay in boys' memories better than English ones did. In his *Essays on Poetry and Music*, Beattie argues that literature 'when taught in a foreign dialect will perhaps be found to leave a deeper impression upon the memory, than when explained in

[29] Knox, *Liberal Education*, p. 54.
[30] Lily, p. iv.
[31] Lang, p. 20.
[32] Vincent, *Defence*, p. 188.
[33] Stanley, vol. 1, pp. 121–120.
[34] Sargeaunt, p. 30.
[35] *Edinburgh Review*, 'Art. III. The Public Schools of England—Westminster and Eton', p. 71.

Lessons in Grammar, Memory, and Composition

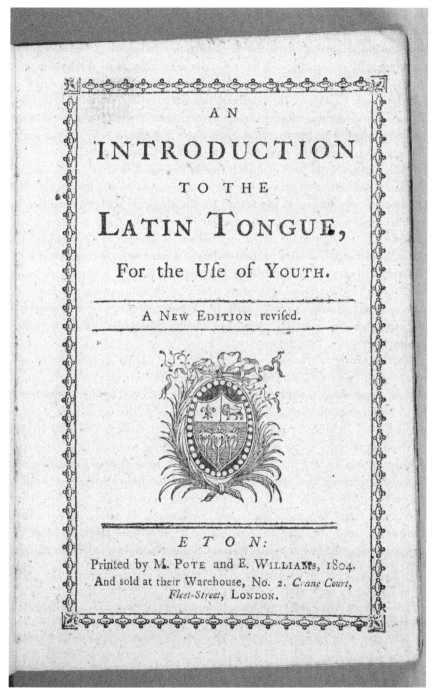

Figure 4. Title page of *Introduction to the Latin Tongue for the Use of Youth*, 1804. Reproduced by permission of the Provost and Fellows of Eton College.

Educating the Romantic Poets

the mother tongue'; and, indeed, powerful memories were an invaluable tool for the Romantic poets. In the *Biographia Literaria* Coleridge comments on the wisdom of 'storing the memory, during the period when the memory is the predominant faculty, with facts for the after exercise of the judgment'.[36] In *A Treatise on Education, with a Sketch of the Author's Method* (1773, 1784), George Chapman, the headmaster of the grammar school at Dumfries, Scotland, voiced the opinion that memorised texts make a deeper and more lasting impression on pupils' minds than those they simply read and put aside. Knox agreed, explaining that it was not enough just to read classics: a boy, he said, benefits from having a great number of words and phrases 'enforced upon the sensorium' and 'laid up in the storehouse of his memory'.[37] The emphasis on memory work is founded on the classical rhetorical tradition, in which memory is one of the five canons. The Pythagoreans were especially dedicated to using memory training, for they considered the possession of a powerful memory necessary to their endeavours to recollect the immortal soul. In later Christian times, cultivating the memory became a part of salvation theology.[38] Teachers also hastened to remind boys and parents that memory exercises were designed to help pupils become accustomed to public speaking in preparation for the days when they might address parliament or preach before an Anglican congregation.

At the Georgian classical schools, young boys' first memory work was words, grammar rules, and Latin verse. Assisted by their growing appreciation of 'longs and shorts' and their natural sense of rhythm and rhyming sounds, many youngsters memorised hundreds of lines easily. This practice gave pupils an early and intimate acquaintance with musical phrasing and well-crafted metrical verse. Moreover, as anyone who has been required to do memory work in youth knows, many of these passages are still easy to recall years later. Schoolmasters also appealed to youngsters' natural competitiveness when assigning memory work. Battles over who could memorise the most lines were not uncommon. When Arnold was at Winchester, he was reputed to have memorised three thousand lines of Homer.[39] Boys from several schools are reputed to have recited the entire *Aeneid*. Charles Merivale, a student at Harrow

---

[36] 'Biographia', p. 162.

[37] Knox, *Liberal Education*, p. 101. Knox rather dramatically asserts that 'by committing to memory the thoughts and words of heroes, and of worthies, who eminently shone in every species of excellence' students will acquire 'honour, spirit, [and] liberality', p. 497.

[38] The importance of memory is not unprecedented in other cultures. Rabbinical students are trained to memorise the Torah; in the Middle Ages Chinese students were expected to memorise works by Confucius and the commentaries by Zhu Xi (1130–1200). The Brahmin tradition of India even today depends on students having highly trained memories.

[39] Clarke, p. 54. The *Iliad* is approximately 15,500 lines.

Lessons in Grammar, Memory, and Composition

in 1824, was famous for having memorised Virgil's *Eclogues* and *Georgics*, and most of Catullus, Juvenal, and Lucan.[40] Coleridge's nephew Edward memorised and recited nearly all of the satires of Juvenal, the whole of Euripides's *Alcestis*, and Aeschylus's *Prometheus Vinctus*. Some students, such as Leigh Hunt and Charles Darwin, complained later in life that their memory work meant little to them at the time;[41] yet it cannot be denied that copious memory work in youth acquaints youths quite intimately with aesthetically pleasing rhythms and sounds and provides them with retrievable literary references in later life. Thomas Arnold, who was no friend of meaningless busywork marvelled at the vigor of youthful memory and defended the schools' use of memorisation exercises. Knox asserted that a boy 'habituated to the task [of memory work] will learn thirty or forty lines, as an evening exercise, with great ease, and with apparent pleasure. This is really done', he said, 'three or four nights in a week, in our best schools'.[42]

Having a good memory may not seem as important in modern times, when information can be easily retrieved electronically from portable devices, but in Georgian England it was especially valuable. Eton's Winthrop Mackworth Praed (1802–1839)[43] commented that the effect of reading and memorising classical poetry, drama, and satire gave him a 'copious and splendid command of language' and an 'ear tuned up … to the "noiseless music of the spheres"'.[44] He added that the experience of memorising great literature gave poets 'prototypes' to 'impregnate with the living soul and breath of [their own] Imagination'.[45] Coleridge comments in the *Biographia* that this process awakened for him 'the fond and unmixed LOVE and ADMIRATION' of literature.[46] During Wordsworth's 1820 European trip, while visiting Helen Maria Williams in Paris, he complimented her with a recitation of her sonnet 'To Hope'. This was a poem that he memorised as a schoolboy and that inspired his first published sonnet 'On Seeing Miss Helen Maria Williams Weep at a Tale of Distress' (1787). The memory training that Wordsworth, Coleridge, George Dyer, Lamb, Leigh Hunt, Southey, Byron, Monk Lewis,

---

[40] Charles Merivale (1808–1893) was an English historian and churchman who for many years served as dean of Ely Cathedral. His father was the *Quarterly Reviewer* J. H. Merivale, and his maternal grandfather was Byron's headmaster at Harrow, James Drury.

[41] Clarke, p. 58.

[42] Knox, *Liberal Education*, p. 99.

[43] At Trinity College, Cambridge Praed was the winner of multiple Greek and English poetry medals. He is the author of the poem 'school and School Fellows', quoted elsewhere in this book. The Praed Society is a poetry society currently existing at Eton, one of over 20 societies that meet to discuss students' interests. Membership is by invitation.

[44] *The Etonian*, 1787, no. 2, p. 102.

[45] *The Etonian*, 1787, no. 2, p. 102.

[46] Halmi *et al.*, p. 383.

Educating the Romantic Poets

and Percy Shelley all received in school was an essential asset to them in their writing careers. Lucy Newlyn discusses how important shared memories were to William and Dorothy Wordsworth and their literary partnership.[47] Fulford has called scholarly attention to Wordsworth's 'layered assemblage of poetic fragments from his past manuscripts', his invention of memorial verse, and his use of the memories of the women in his family.[48] He argues, in fact, that 'recollection [is a] part of Wordsworth's poetics'.[49] Critics and writers themselves may never be entirely certain of when and where the words, images, themes, or rhythms of a text originate. Nor can anyone be sure if works of imagination are invented, recalled, borrowed, or—as is most likely—a commingling of all three. But there can be no doubt that among the most common subjects or references in Romantic poetry are memories, past lives, lost youth, passing away, and loss. Credit for the importance of this theme and the skills that were needed to express it must go, at least in part, to the mnemonic training provided by the Anglo-classical academy; hence, understanding the memory training that was a daily part of Anglo-classical education can be useful to scholars, particularly those interested in the composition process and influence studies. Other issues or moments in poets' careers, such as charges of plagiarism against the often drug-addled Coleridge or Wordsworth's reliance upon 'sublime' memories that allowed him to 'see into the life of things', might also be profitably revisited in the context of this memory training.

Memory work was important with the youngest boys; schoolmasters claimed that 'all the instruction of childhood depends more on memory than intellect'.[50] But when their pupils began to grow up and develop higher order cognitive skills, they adjusted their pedagogies. Dr Vincent of Westminster commented that once boys reach the 'age of comprehension, from twelve or fourteen to sixteen or eighteen', 'if the master teaches only words [and relies on boys' memories alone], he is a blockhead.'[51] In language studies with the upper forms, Vincent was interested in training boys to notice 'the composition of the Poet' and to appreciate 'the order, connexion, and relation of part to part'.[52] He also expected boys to recall and make connections to 'allusion[s] to History, Mythology, and Geography'.[53]

[47] Newlyn, pp. 30–31.
[48] Fulford, *Wordsworth's Poetry*, pp. 95–96. See especially Fulford's discussion of Wordsworth's 'lateness' in Chapter 8.
[49] Fulford, *Wordsworth's Poetry*, p. 94.
[50] Vincent, *Defence*, p. 190.
[51] Vincent, *Defence*, p. 190.
[52] Vincent, *Defence*, p. 190.
[53] Vincent, *Defence*, p. 191.

Lessons in prosody

Perhaps the most interesting facet of the grammar schools' programme and how it trained youngsters for the writing life is the attention these schools gave to prosody. Almost all assigned readings for younger boys were in Latin verse; so, along with word meanings and grammar rules, from a very early age, pupils were trained to hear the rhythm and music of language, and they were tutored in the basics of classical prosody. Classics teachers operate with the understanding that

> every line in classical Latin poetry is constructed with reference to a recognizable difference, in time, between long and short vowels, as are many of the sentences and periods of the masters of Latin prose, and we lose much of the music and rhythm of all good Latin style if we ourselves ignore those subtle and alternating differences to which the Roman ear was so sensitive.[54]

Students in the schools learned, therefore, that metre in Latin poetry depends on the length or 'quantity' as well as the stress of syllables, and that patterns of 'longs' and 'shorts' are the basis of the metrical feet out of which Latin verse is built. So, for example, a Latin iambic foot is composed of a short syllable followed by a long syllable, not just a soft syllable and a stressed or accented one. Once pupils started learning Greek, they were taught that, while Greek metre also depends upon longs and shorts, accents in Greek are based on pitch, not stress, and that certain substitutions—such as a spondee for a dactyl—were permissible.[55]

Prosody was so much a part of Anglo-classical education that the first written assignment given to the youngest boys at Eton, and at several other schools as well, was to write strings of Latin words—'nonsense verses'—that were arranged according to a prescribed metre. The words of these 'verses' did not have to make sense; they simply had to scan properly.[56] The purpose was to help boys practice proper pronunciation and to make them aware of the quantities—the longs and

---

[54] Peck, pp. 51–52.
[55] In his history of Cambridge, George Dyer calls attention to *Metronariston*, a work by the Trinity College scholar John Warner, who argues that classical authors 'wrote with regard both to *syllabic* and *accentual* quantity', a method Dyer believes 'formed the harmony of their verse' and some of their prose (vol. 2, p. 319, n. a). Dyer comments that this 'delightful combination seems lost among us' and recommends the book to the public schools' (vol. 2, p. 319, n. a). Dyer notes that Mathew Raine, who was named a Fellow at Trinity in 1794, later used Warner as a master at Charterhouse.
[56] Because of this particular practice, at some schools first-year students were called 'Nonsense Boys'.

Educating the Romantic Poets

shorts—of certain vowels or syllables. As soon as boys had large enough Latin vocabularies, schoolmasters asked them to write Latin verses that made sense. Southey reported doing the nonsense verse exercise at the preparatory school he attended prior to enrolling at Westminster. With every subsequent lesson Georgian schoolmasters took pains to make sure pupils became accustomed to listening to the sound of language and to considering pace, pitch, and accents in written and spoken language. One schoolmaster is supposed to have blurted out to a tone-deaf boy, 'How can you possibly be a gentleman if you cannot get your longs and shorts right?' Training in prosody at the schools was constant and extensive. Pupils memorised the names and common uses of metrical feet—not only the typical ones with which most students are familiar today, but also amphibrachs, molossi, and choriambs. The grammar textbook Morgan used at Bath Grammar School asked pupils to answer questions such as 'What is the use of Prosody?' and 'What is Synaloepha?'[57] Three metrical conventions standard in classical Latin—the accentuation of the final foot, an extrametrical final syllable, and the common use of moraic trochees[58]—also became part of the schoolboy's standard literary knowledge base.[59] As John Milner explains in *An Abstract of Latin Syntax; … to which is Added, Prosody, Or, The Art of Latin Poetry … for the Use of Schools* (1743), pupils in Georgian schools learned that 'the Variety of [the Ancients'] Measures [were] answerable to the several Kinds of Poetry'.[60] They were taught, for example, that

> the Majestic Gravity of Hexameter agrees with the Solemnity of the Epic. The Softness of the Pentameter, alternately added to the Hexameter, fits that to the Sweetness and Tenderness of the Elegy. The Sapphic, Alcaic, and Phaleucian Measures, &c. mixed together, best suit the musical and sublime Spirit of the Lyric; whilst the Simplicity of the Iambic, more nearly resembling Prose, is peculiarly proper for the Stage.[61]

Remarkable as it may seem to modern educators, by the time most pupils at these schools were 16 they could not only identify the metre and generic conventions of a wide range of classical works but had written scores of lines of iambic pentameter or dactylic hexameter arranged in elegiac couplets, blank verse (with internal rhymes), or Sapphic strophes in *three* languages. The 'Horace Lesson' at Westminster, which was imitated at other schools, required

---

[57] Morgan, pp. 120–121.

[58] A *mora* is a measurement of time in phonology; in Latin, some long syllables will consist of two mora, a short syllable will have only one; hence, the moraic trochee is a fuller or longer foot than other trochees.

[59] Parsons, p. 120.

[60] Milner, p. 49.

[61] Milner, p. 49.

fifth-form boys to recast Horatian odes in different metres. One of the many verse exercises at Westminster, the 'sacred Exercise', required senior students to produce 20 Latin hexameters on a biblical subject. Composition exercises such as these gave credence to the generally held opinion of the grammar schools, and of Westminster in particular, that these schools were 'the most favoured cradle of the Muses'.

The Romantic critics and classical prosody

The schoolmasters' painstaking instruction in prosody is not only an index of how well trained their students were in the knowledge and skills needed for poetic composition. It is also an explanation for why the critics were so hard on the early writing of the 'brotherhood of poets, who have haunted for some years about the Lakes of Cumberland'.[62] The critics and editors of eighteenth- and nineteenth-century journals and their audience were, as Jeffrey says, a 'more instructed class of readers'.[63] Their 'ordinary judgment in poetry' was based upon respect for the 'established systems of poetry and criticism'.[64] In poetry they expected to see 'recognizable and venerated' patterns of metre and the 'fine propriety' of elegant and dignified diction. These, Jeffrey explains, arise from 'judicious or happy applications of expressions which have been sanctified by the use of famous writers, or which bear the stamp of a simple or venerable antiquity'.[65] Jeffrey laments that Southey and Wordsworth 'borrow their phrases from a different and a scantier *gradus ad Parnassus*' and compares at least one of the poems in Wordsworth's *Poems in Two Volumes* (1807) to a 'theme of an unpractised schoolboy'.[66]

To emphasise the seriousness of critical and public distaste for the metrical innovation of the Lake poets, Jeffrey opens the review of Southey's *Thalaba the Destroyer* by invoking the religious controversies of the day, ones that were and would continue to be hotly debated in the Anglo-classical academy:

> Poetry has this much, at least, in common with religion, and its standards were fixed long ago, by certain inspired writers, whose authority it is no longer lawful to call in question; and that many profess to be entirely devoted to it, who have no *good works* to produce in support of their pretensions. The catholic poetical church, too, has worked but few miracles since the first ages of its establishment; and has been more

---

[62] Jeffrey, 'Art. XIV. *Poems, in Two Volumes*', p. 214.
[63] Jeffrey, 'Art. XIV. *Poems, in Two Volumes*', p. 217.
[64] Jeffrey, 'Art. I. *The Excursion*', p. 4 and 'Art. VIII. *Thalaba, the Destroyer*', p. 63.
[65] Jeffrey, 'Art. XIV. *Poems, in Two Volumes*', pp. 216–217.
[66] Jeffrey, 'Art. XIV. *Poems, in Two Volumes*', p. 218.

prolific, for a long time of doctors than of saints; It has had its corruptions and reformation also, and has given birth to an infinite variety of heresies and errors, the follower of which have hated and persecuted each other as cordially as other bigots.[67]

Jeffrey continues in this vein, claiming that Southey and Wordsworth are a 'sect ... [that] abandoned old models ... [but has not] yet created any [pleasing] models of their own'.[68] He calls them 'dissenters from the established systems of poetry and criticism'.[69] While his review allows that *Thalaba* is 'the fruit of much reading' and that Southey has taken care (like a good schoolboy) to be 'scrupulously correct in the citation of his authorities',[70] he laments that the poem is composed of a sorry, sophomoric mess of 'scraps, borrowed from the oriental tale-books, and travels into the Mahometan countries, seasoned up for the English reader with some fragments of our own ballads, and shreds of our older sermons'.[71] He implies, with the possible exception of sermons, that these sources have none of the authority and appeal that classical ones do. By the end of the article, even though Jeffrey admits that Southey demonstrates 'a very considerable portion of poetical talent' and a 'richness of poetical conception that would do honour to more faultless compositions'[72]—all of which should be credited to his training at Westminster School—he denounces *Thalaba* as a product of 'perverted taste' that has 'but little acquaintance with those chaster and severer graces, by whom the epic muse would be most suitably attended'.[73]

[67] Jeffrey, 'Art. VIII. *Thalaba, the Destroyer*', p. 63.
[68] Jeffrey, 'Art. VIII. *Thalaba, the Destroyer*', pp. 63–64.
[69] Jeffrey, 'Art. VIII. *Thalaba, the Destroyer*', p. 63. Elsewhere in the review Jeffrey explains, 'we are never reconciled to a stanza of a new structure, till we have accustomed our era to it by two or three repetitions. This is the case, even where we have the assistance of rhyme to direct us in our search after regularity, and where the definite form and appearance of a stanza assures us that regularity is to be found. Where both of these are wanting, it may be imagined that our condition will be still more deplorable ... . In reading verse, in general, we are guided to the discovery of its melody, by a sort of preconception of its cadence and compass; without which, it might often fail to be suggested by the mere articulation of the syllables ... [this is even the case with] the unusual measures of the ancient authors. We have never known any one who fell in, at the first trial, with the proper rhythm and cadence of the *pervigilium Veneris*, or the choral lyrics of the Greek dramatists' (pp. 72–73).
[70] Jeffrey, 'Art. VIII. *Thalaba, the Destroyer*', p. 77.
[71] Jeffrey, 'Art. VIII. *Thalaba, the Destroyer*', p. 77.
[72] In his review of *Madoc*, Jeffrey comments that for all the flaws in the poem (chief among them are length and unengaging characters), Southey is 'gifted with an unusual copiousness of diction and facility of smooth versification'. Jeffrey, 'Art. I. *Madoc, a Poem*', p. 4.
[73] Jeffrey, 'Art. VIII. *Thalaba, the Destroyer*', pp. 64, 77, 79–80, 83.

Lessons in Grammar, Memory, and Composition

As already noted, the tone of Jeffrey's review of Wordsworth's *Poems in Two Volumes* is that of a schoolmaster shaming and correcting an unruly pupil. He repeats the 'namby pamby' complaint he made about Southey, noting that Wordsworth 'can write good verses when he pleases', but that the lad is 'a bad imitator' and needs to make an 'end of this folly'.[74] The rebellious youngster should reclaim his allegiance to the proper and 'established laws of poetry' and restore to 'that ancient and venerable code its due honour and authority'.[75] Years later, when reviewing *The Excursion* (1814), Jeffrey calls attention to Wordsworth's age—he's been at this now for twenty years and should be 'sufficiently matured' and past boyish 'affectation and mysticism and prolixity' as well as 'moral and devotional raving'.[76] He notes that educated readers have an expectation of 'common poetical phraseology' and 'fine or dignified expressions',[77] and decries the poet's word choices, which 'dilute the harmony', and his blank verse, which 'weakens the whole structure'.[78] Wordsworth's intentional experiments with rhythms and language in *Lyrical Ballads* (made possible by his training in classical forms as a student), had seemed amusing and interesting when the volume first came out. However, his 'childishness and affectation' in *Poems in Two Volumes* (1807) and insistence upon using informal language, loose metre without end rhyme or other patterning and at such length in *The Excursion* (1814) were too much for Jeffrey and many in Wordsworth's classically trained audience. 'Men of literature and ordinary judgment in poetry' don't want to see repeated 'the mystical verbiage of the methodist pulpit'; they expect dialogues patterned after the classical ones, not those between an '*old Scotch Pedlar*' and an aged vicar.[79] Above all, they expect verse based on the 'established systems of poetry and criticism'.[80]

The lessons of the Georgian grammar schools in vocabulary and syntax, which Jeffrey and others so valued, seem terribly tedious to modern scholars and teachers, but they trained students to write grammatically correct sentences and imparted lasting, sophisticated knowledge of the metrical complexities of sophisticated poetry. Having spent thousands of hours of reading and writing poetry, boys left school with commonplace books full of notes and quotations, a well-thumbed *Gradus ad Parnassus*, and sheaves of old themes in verse and prose. This regimen explains why the Romantic intelligentsia were, as Stuart Curran has aptly observed, 'simply mad for poetry'.[81] They loved poetry

---

[74] Jeffrey, 'Art. XIV. *Poems, in Two Volumes*', p. 231.
[75] Jeffrey, 'Art. XIV. *Poems, in Two Volumes*', pp. 228, 231.
[76] Jeffrey, 'Art. I. *The Excursion*', pp. 3, 4.
[77] Jeffrey, 'Art. VIII. *Thalaba, the Destroyer*', p. 64.
[78] Jeffrey, 'Art. I. *The Excursion*', p. 1.
[79] Jeffrey, 'Art. I. *The Excursion*', pp. 4, 5.
[80] Jeffrey, 'Art. VIII. *Thalaba, the Destroyer*', p. 63.
[81] Curran, p. 15.

because they had been thoroughly taught to read it, appreciate, it, and write it themselves. They had been trained to think carefully about words and to hear their rhythms. As the next chapter about the literature they read in school explains, they were also taught that intelligent adults took literature and the republic of letters seriously and believed that citizens in that republic had a duty of service to society.

An interesting and pertinent example of the effectiveness of the language and metrical instruction boys received in the Anglo-classical schools is Wordsworth's earliest known poem, 'Written as a School Exercise at Hawkshead'. Composed when Wordsworth was 14, it demonstrates skill in prosody and knowledge of classical and Augustan lore and style. The poem is also an indicator of how he responded to the learning environment of his school. The headnote, written years later, recalls that he composed the verses from the 'impulse of my own mind', but that he was also attempting an imitation of Pope's style and versification.[82] The poem is a framed narrative of 112 lines of iambic pentameter arranged in rhyming couplets, in which 'The Power of EDUCATION'[83] rises as if in a dream or vision. This is not, however, the education of 'rigid precepts' but 'she who trains the generous British youth' in 'the bright paths of fair majestic Truth'.[84] Young Wordsworth's figure of English Education is stern, but also smiling and attended by 'all the powers, design'd/ To curb, exalt, reform the tender mind'.[85] The schoolboy depicted in the poem responds with eager, 'panting breast', driven by 'Emulation', but also by 'shame', until he responds with 'Industry', which—of course—brings a smile to Education's 'pensive face'.[86]

The poem reflects the religious mission of the Anglo-classical schools and is, perhaps, a foreshadowing of Wordsworth's later arguments in *Ecclesiastical Sonnets*, for he explains how 'Religion' replaces 'superstition', lulls 'the warring passions', drives away 'savage thoughts', enlivens 'Hope', and beams 'on Britain's sons a bright day'.[87] Hawkshead School itself is depicted as Education's happy home, where she

> ... loved to show the tender age
> The golden precepts of the classic page;
> To lead the mind to those Elysian plains
> Where, throned in gold, immortal Science reigns;
> Fair to the view is sacred Truth display'd

---

[82] WWPW, p. 482.
[83] WWPW, p. 482, l. 6. Italics mine.
[84] WWPW, p. 482, ll. 7–12.
[85] WWPW, p. 482, ll. 12–18.
[86] WWPW, p. 482, ll. 19–24.
[87] WWPW, p. 483, ll. 31–36.

Lessons in Grammar, Memory, and Composition

In all the majesty of light array'd,
To teach, on rapid wings, the curious soul
To roam from heaven to heaven, from pole to pole,
From thence to search the mystic cause of things
And follow Nature to her secret springs;[88]

Elsewhere in the poem, young Wordsworth writes that Education turns boys from vice to virtue. She also teaches them to 'peruse the book of man', to be 'severely honest', to emulate the 'rigors of the Sires of Rome', but not to forget the 'gentler manners' of the private world.[89] Education, he says, encourages boys to have tender hearts and to weep without shame. In a move that William Taylor, his poetry-loving schoolmaster, no doubt appreciated, young Wordsworth ends his composition by having Education exhort the pupil to 'snatch the slumbering lyre' and to get busy writing *another* poem.[90]

---

[88] WWPW, p. 483, ll. 67–76.
[89] WWPW, p. 483, ll. 85, 87, 89, 90.
[90] Taylor died the next year, in 1786.

Chapter Four

England's Public and Grammar Schools
Lessons in Classical Literature, Rhetoric, Oratory, and Composition Training

> The habits of criticism learned in studying the classics give us the capacity for close attention, [and] the awareness of meanings and phrasing, that would otherwise be lost in translation.
>
> A Rugby student, *Rugby Magazine* (1835)

The earliest literary works that little boys read in school were 'amusive fables', with beautiful descriptions, that Beattie says could 'soothe or awaken the human passions'.[1] Knox urged schoolmasters to choose books with beautiful 'type and paper … for these allure and please the eye'.[2] Works by Ovid, Terence, and Phaedrus were also popular because they offered moral stories that were easy to read. With regard to literary instruction, Westminster's Vincent commented that 'time is required as well as teaching … [and] No man can teach faster than a boy can learn'.[3] Knox was confident that, by the fifth form, a pupil could 'discover the meanings of his lessons by his own efforts and the use of dictionaries' and had developed the self-discipline to do this work with little correction by his teacher.[4] This, he admitted, 'will be difficult at first', but boys 'must be accustomed to solitary study, and habits must be formed of literary labour'.[5]

---

[1] Beattie, p. 497.
[2] Knox, *Liberal Education*, p. 57.
[3] Vincent, *Defence*, p. 190.
[4] Knox, *Liberal Education*, p. 57.
[5] Knox, *Liberal Education*, pp. 57–58.

Educating the Romantic Poets

The first complex text boys read was the *Aeneid*. Beyond its literary excellence and cultural significance, the epic gave youngsters the occasion to consider issues that became very important in the Romantic public sphere and to them personally, such as national pride, free will, the different forms of power, and love of home and family. It also afforded them one of the classical world's finest examples of sustained dactylic hexameter. Schoolboys read Virgil's *Georgics* as well. Written in an unsettled time, not unlike that of the Romantics, these poems are recognised models of descriptive imagery, and they praise themes that were also important to Romantic poets—the beauty of nature and the virtues of country life and rural labour.[6] Kenneth Johnston has commented that these texts also rehearse an idea that was especially concerning in Wordsworth's day, the notion of 'rural republican virtue checking urban imperial excess'.[7]

Along with Virgil, boys at Eton and many other schools used *Scriptores Romani*, which was an anthology of texts that offered them, as one teacher noted, a lot of 'fine, hard Latin' by Cicero, Quintilian, and Livy. Other texts assigned included the later chapters of *Metamorphoses* and Ovid's *Tristia*. The *Tristia* may have been chosen to caution boys during the dark days when men such as Thelwall, Frend, and Thomas Fysshe Palmer were being prosecuted, expelled, or transported for controversial public utterances. Praised by classicists for his shrewd word choice, Ovid's survey of classical myth in *Metamorphoses* probably provided schoolboys some of their earliest opportunities to think critically about human character and motivations and to compare the Anglican God with the cruel and arbitrary behaviour of the inhabitants of the pagan pantheon. In addition to Ovid, pupils at the schools read almost all of Horace's verse epistles about love, friendship, and poetry. These poems accustomed youngsters to the tempo of heroic couplets, rhythmically smooth hexameter, and the adroit use of alcaics and sapphics. Additionally, many of Horace's works represent a figure that loomed large in the culture of the Anglo-classical academy and the Georgian public sphere: the ideal gentleman, a wise and humane man who endeavours to see the world with humour rather than bitterness and who advocates moderation and the moral health of the state.[8]

Other Latin texts popular at the schools were Cicero's *de Officiis* and *De Amicitia*, chosen by educators for his fatherly advice on moral duty and friendship.[9] Older pupils read both Cicero's and Sallust's accounts of the Catiline conspiracy. To appeal to boys' sense of humour, or their adolescent cynicism,

---

[6] For more on the *Georgics*, see Graver, 'Wordsworth's Georgic Beginnings', and Heinzelman.

[7] Johnston, *The Hidden Wordsworth*, p. 72.

[8] Ogilvie, pp. 49–50. See also Clancey.

[9] Knox particularly favoured Cicero's style, which, he says, 'abounds with "Sweets from which the industrious bee may collect much honey"', *Liberal Education*, p. 84.

Lessons in Classical Literature, Rhetoric, Oratory, and Composition Training

schoolmasters had them read Terence's comedies of manners. Pupils also read Juvenal's and Persius's satires on human folly and the corruption of Roman society. Military history was always popular with schoolboys and had special relevance in the late Georgian period. Among the war stories most often assigned during the years of the French Revolution and war with Napoleon were Caesar's commentaries on the Gallic and civil wars and Livy's and Tacitus's cautionary tales about the decline and fall of Rome. A significant aspect of learning history from Livy was his tendency to interpret historical events as the products of individual personality and morality. He credited the rise and fall of Roman power to moral decline, which began—he says—when the old teaching was allowed to lapse.

Other histories popular at the schools in the Georgian and early Victorian periods were Herodotus's account of the Greco-Persian wars and Xenophon's and Thucydides' chronicles of Peloponnesian War. Thomas Arnold, who published a translation of Thucydides, said that he used Thucydides' work at Rugby because it was no mere 'idle inquiry about remote ages and forgotten institutions but a living picture of things present, fitted not so much for the curiosity of the scholar as for the instruction of the statesman and the citizen'.[10] Arnold also explained that he chose classical histories that raised familiar civil or metaphysical questions in order to help his pupils consider these issues with 'abstraction' and unbiased judgement when they occurred in their own times.[11] Many of the classical histories youngsters at these schools were assigned to read tell stories that had relevance in the Romantic period—the tyranny registered in Demosthenes, the heroising of farmer-republicans in Plutarch, Tacitus, Livy, and Cicero, and their famous challenges to Caesarism.

Greek texts that were popular at the schools were, of course, the *Iliad* and the *Odyssey*, plays by Aeschylus and Euripides, Lucian's comic dialogues, Epictetus's discourses on stoicism, Longinus's literary criticism, and the Septuagint. Other Greek texts assigned at the schools were Hesiod's *Works and Days*, Theocritus's bucolic poetry, Callimachus's epigrams and elegies, Sappho's lyrics, and Pindar's irregular odes. From this wide range of texts schoolboys became familiar with Greek ideas about honour and heroism and the military virtues of courage, strategy, comradeship, and loyalty. They learned as well how important freedom and the countryside were to those classical writers. We know that Wordsworth had advanced to Greek studies at Hawkshead by the time he was 14. He used Hendricks's Greek lexicon and owned (and presumably read) a copy of Demosthenes. In 1785 his father bought him a copy of Euclid in Greek and an exercise book. Coleridge remarks in the *Biographia Literaria* that he learned in school to prefer the Greeks—Demosthenes and

---

[10] Qtd in Ogilvie, p. 105.
[11] Stanley, vol. 1, p. 122.

Educating the Romantic Poets

Homer—over Cicero and Virgil.[12] Moreover, he credits his study of classical literature at Christ's Hospital School for his 'sense of beauty in forms and sounds'.[13] It is fair to assume that many other pupils in these schools became similarly accustomed to the forms and sounds of classical verse and carried this knowledge with them when, as adults, they read contemporary English verse. Coleridge's headmaster, Dr Boyer, trained him to compare writers such as Lucretius, Terence, and Catullus to those from other ages and he introduced the Grecians to Shakespeare and Milton. Using both classical and English texts, Boyer taught his pupils that 'poetry ... had a logic of its own, as severe as that of science; and more difficult, because more subtle, more complex, and dependent on more, and more fugitive causes'; moreover, every word has 'a reason assignable' as does its placement in a line.[14] The headmaster of Westminster, William Vincent, explained that schoolmasters believed that 'the style, the diction, the manner, the sublimity, [and] the perfection' of classical literature 'stimulate pupils to aspire to equal excellence' in their writing.[15] Pupils not only read, translated, and parsed such texts every day, they also memorised them. As explained more fully in Chapter 5, the most carefully studied books at school were the four Gospels and the book of Acts. These studies, along with daily readings of the psalms and passages from the Old and New Testaments in morning and evening prayers, meant that the vocabulary, stories, ideas, and style of scripture became blended in schoolboys' thought world with those of 'pagan' culture.

Rhetoric and oratory

In addition to studying language and literature, public and grammar school pupils were also trained in rhetoric, oratory, and not incidentally citizenship, because most often these lessons were framed as preparation for leadership in the state. Schoolmasters used *Farnaby's Rhetoric*, which introduces the rhetorical theories of Isocrates and Aristotle and explores the canons of invention, arrangement, style, memory, and delivery. Quintilian's *Institutes of Oratory*, with its advice on how to become 'a good man speaking well', was also a standard text. Evidence of how effective instruction in argument was at the public schools can be seen in the essays published in the school magazines. Schoolboys wrote critical essays about poems that were carefully supported with evidence. They made persuasive claims about the value of learning and writing in Latin, and famously campaigned against traditions of the schools

---

[12] 'Biographia', p. 59.
[13] 'Biographia', p. 164.
[14] 'Biographia', p. 159.
[15] Vincent, *Defence*, p. 188.

such as flogging. Southey's essay for No. V of *The Flagellant* should have been admired by his headmaster for its structure, research, use of evidence, and correctness. The essay attends to ethos, kairos, logos, and quite emphatically to pathos. Young Southey builds his ethos by citing throughout his knowledge of the classical world, the Old Testament, the history of Christianity, and the primitive fathers, including St Athanasius and Jerome. The essay refers to contemporary unrest in the country, the violence against Priestley, and ongoing debates about the trinity. It demonstrates his understanding of the principles of Christian faith, recalled from Westminster's Sacred Lesson using Grotius (whom he cites), and England's claim to be a Christian country. Sneering at how pagans, 'Catholicks', and tyrants of the ancient world used flogging, he doubts 'not but that every schoolmaster will be ready to let the uplifted rod drop from his hand, when he hears that flogging was invented by the DEVIL!!!'[16] He even appeals to practicality, noting that flogging pupils turns them against their teachers. Had he stopped there, perhaps his headmaster might have had a different response. But, caught up in the thrill of his argument and his own ringing words, Southey closes with not only a Unitarian claim but also with the charge that all teachers who flog 'performeth the will of Satan' and 'commiteth an abomination'.[17] Though the consequences of publishing this essay were unfortunate, the language, well-chosen examples, structure, and confident bombast it demonstrates are evidence of the sort of rhetorical training Westminster and other public schools offered in the Romantic period.

As for instruction in oratory, the schools took Quintilian's best advice, which is for students to have plenty of practice. Speech training at school began with weekly recitations of memory work in class and prayers and the liturgy in chapel. Formal declamations, debates, recitations of classical or original verse at public occasions, and performances in school plays followed. Often these activities were framed as preparation for the boys' future lives in the Church or parliament. At Winchester, boys were required to declaim before the assembled pupils and faculty each year. The routine for these declamations required two boys to write opposing theses in Latin and to debate each other (in Latin) with a third student serving as questioner. Some of these events at Winchester and elsewhere were also attended by parents, and local, university, and government dignitaries. St Paul's School held open disputations in the churchyard of St Bartholomew's and annual orations at the end of each academic year. At Christ's Hospital, orations took place in the great hall; in the centre of the room was the lord mayor's table, where he and the speakers sat. The headmaster, in wig and gown, stood behind the mayor, ready to prompt the speakers. The Christ's Hospital orations and those at St Paul's were quite often noted in the London press.

[16] Southey, 'No. V', p. 80.
[17] Southey, 'No. V', p. 89.

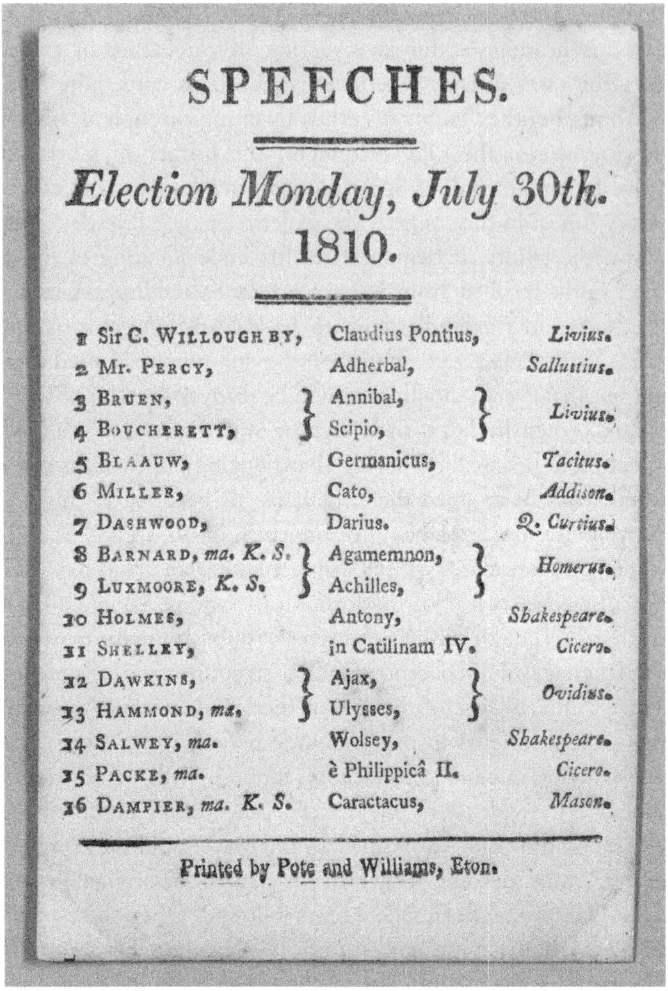

Educating the Romantic Poets

SPEECHES.

Election Monday, July 30th. 1810.

1 Sir C. Willoughby,	Claudius Pontius,	Livius.
2 Mr. Percy,	Adherbal,	Sallustius.
3 Bruen,	Annibal,	Livius.
4 Boucherett,	Scipio,	
5 Blaauw,	Germanicus,	Tacitus.
6 Miller,	Cato,	Addison.
7 Dashwood,	Darius.	Q. Curtius.
8 Barnard, ma. K. S.	Agamemnon,	Homerus.
9 Luxmoore, K. S.	Achilles,	
10 Holmes,	Antony,	Shakespeare.
11 Shelley,	in Catilinam IV.	Cicero.
12 Dawkins,	Ajax,	Ovidius.
13 Hammond, ma.	Ulysses,	
14 Salwey, ma.	Wolsey,	Shakespeare.
15 Packe, ma.	è Philippicâ II.	Cicero.
16 Dampier, ma. K. S.	Caractacus,	Mason.

Printed by Pote and Williams, Eton.

Figure 5. Speech Day Programme, Eton College, 1810.
Number 11 is Percy Shelley's speech. Reproduced by permission of
the Provost and Fellows of Eton College.

Speech day at Harrow was a festive holiday. Throngs of parents gathered to hear 'monologues in many tongues', prize compositions, and dramatic scenes in Greek, English, French, or German. The school corps band played, as did a larger military band. The time-honoured traditions of 'cheering on the steps' and house-singing closed the day.[18] 'Salmon and claret cup', one headmaster declared, were 'essential' parts of the festivities.[19] Elledge notes how fervently

---

[18] Elledge, p. 6.
[19] Elledge, p. 6.

Lessons in Classical Literature, Rhetoric, Oratory, and Composition Training

Byron prepared for and delivered his speeches. His Zanga oration was spoken so passionately that he almost passed out at its conclusion. Elledge's exploration of how these experiences shaped Byron's emotional and intellectual development is a model for other similar studies.

Other schools' speech days were similar to Harrow's, combining public speaking exercises, dramatic performances, and readings of pupils' original poems. St Paul's pupils delivered original elegiac verses before successive sovereigns on the occasions of royal births, marriages, or coronations. 'Medal Speaking' at Winchester gave boys the occasion to earn royal medals for Latin and English verse, prose, and orations. The winners of the medals recited their compositions in evening dress before the monarch. Similar competitions for headmasters' prizes and for universities' fellows' prizes were established. The Westminster faculty required pupils to deliver 'declamations' on topics that might serve them should they become MPs. During the Romantic period these included speeches praising the great men of the school, naval victories, and fallen heroes. These occasions were open to the public. At Eton, the school year always ended with Election Monday. Wearing coats and tails, selected pupils delivered classical orations and pieces by Shakespeare, Addison, and Mason[20] before the entire school and representatives of the universities who had come to 'elect' students for their colleges. Shelley was one of the students honoured to speak in 1810 (see Figure 5). He chose Cicero's fourth oration denouncing the Catiline conspiracy. The power of such moments in the lives of young learners, but especially in those of young poets, should not be underestimated.[21]

Writing instruction: translation and imitation, verse and prose

Composition pedagogies were strikingly consistent from school to school in the Romantic period. After pupils mastered 'nonsense verse', the first serious writing assignment they received was translation, which allowed them to work on their vocabulary, grammar, and sentence skills without also having to invent what to say. Producing translations that accurately reflect nuances of meaning in a source text is not, however, an easy mental task. Schoolboys in Wordsworth's and Byron's lifetimes were asked to do this every day. Various sorts of translation exercise were used in the schools. In class the master would question pupils orally about a text's general meaning and about word choices and sentence structure. In their private study time, pupils would produce written translations of the passages read in class. Teachers asked pupils to mimic the style and feeling of the original in correct, idiomatic English. Sometimes pupils were instructed to take their freshly written English translations, translate them back into Latin,

---

[20] They used Mason's *Caractacus*, which is modelled on Greek tragedy.
[21] See Heath and Heath.

and then compare their version to the original. When the source text was in verse, boys were instructed to produce translations in both prose and verse. By the time most pupils were 14, they were doing this sort of work every week using texts by Homer, Thucydides, Virgil, and Livy. This traditional series of writing exercises, practised week after week, however, was slowly watered down and then largely discontinued after Wordsworth's and Byron's generations left school, for the natural sciences began displacing language studies from the 1830s and there simply was not enough time for the same sort of work in both disciplines.

When translating prose, the Westminster grammar advised pupils to start with the verb—the action at the centre of each sentence—then to seek the subject and object. The case of these nouns would help them differentiate between these two. Pupils in the period described the work of translating as an exercise in locating the main ideas of a passage and as a 'trial of taste and memory'.[22] Citing Coleridge's observation in *Table Talk* that translation requires high and rare qualities of mind, the student author of *On the Method of Translating employed at in Rugby School* explains that

> Translating is as good or better training in writing than mere English exercises because if you get into a spot of difficulty, a writer is inclined to shape ideas to words instead of allowing the ideas to shape the words. If you are tasked with translation, you have to stick to the ideas first.[23]

The emphasis in the schools upon translation explains why a large part of Byron's first published volume of verse, *Hours of Idleness*, is devoted to translations and imitation of classical verse, particularly Anacreon and Catullus.

The effects of language study and translating practice show up throughout the careers of the classically educated writers. In the Preface to *Lyrical Ballads* Wordsworth says that the poet should consider himself as 'in the situation of a translator', who deems himself justified when he substitutes 'excellences of another kind for those which are unattainable by him'.[24] One of the goals of Wordsworth's and Coleridge's trip to Germany in 1798 was to gain language skills they could use to earn money writing translations. Coleridge made good on this plan in 1800 with his translation of Schiller's *Wallenstein*. Wordsworth's translation of the *Aeneid* in 1823—though much later—is another example of the effects of learning translation skills in school and college. According to Graver, Wordsworth's 'rendering of Virgil's Latin is remarkably subtle and complex', and it is not only 'literally accurate' but also preserves the 'essential qualities of the language of [the] original', including Virgil's 'patterns of sound,

---

[22] *Rugby Magazine*, 'On the Method of Translation', pp. 33–34.
[23] *Rugby Magazine*, 'On the Method of Translation', p. 34.
[24] WWMW, p. 604.

Lessons in Classical Literature, Rhetoric, Oratory, and Composition Training

syntax, cadence, and idea'.[25] In the 1820s, when Southey and Wordsworth were working on *The Book of the Church* and *Ecclesiastical Sketches*, both men put these skills to use translating the works of Bede.

Along with translations, verses in imitation of classical models were the most common writing assignment given to public and grammar schoolboys. Knox explained that one reason for this exercise was to teach boys to recognise the quantities of Latin syllables, 'without knowledge of which [they] will not be able to read Latin with propriety'.[26] Second-year pupils at the schools were typically required each week to produce ten to 12 lines of meaningful Latin in specified metres. The purpose of this practice, teachers explained, was to help tune pupils' 'ears to harmony' and to afford them 'greater pleasure in reading poetry'.[27] In *Biographia Literaria*, Coleridge remarks that his contemporaries' admirable ability to 'translate … prose thoughts into poetic language had been kept up by, if it did not wholly arise from, the custom of writing Latin verses, and [by] the great importance attached to these exercises in our public schools'.[28]

To assist with their verse-writing, pupils used poetical dictionaries. At Eton they used the *Gradus ad Parnassus*—the steps to Parnassus—which includes definitions of Latin words, markings of each word's accents and quantities, synonyms, and examples of poetic phrases that use the word. Shelley's *Gradus* is in the archives at Eton, inscribed on the cover page with his name and the date 1806 (see Figure 6). Georgian schoolmasters suggested that boys refer to books such as John Newbery's *Poetry made Familiar and Easy* (1770), which explains that poetry should 'borrow from Nature everything that is gay and delightful' and that it should 'please and instruct'.[29] Newbery defines the 'true Poet' as one who is

> distinguished by a fruitfulness of Invention, a lively Imagination tempered by solid judgment, and Nobleness of Sentiments and Ideas, and bold, lofty, and figurative Manner of Expression. He thoroughly understands the Nature of his Subject; and [regardless of the length of his poem], he forms a Design or Plan, by which every Verse is directed to a certain End, and each has a just Dependance on the other.[30]

When boys were assigned to compose imitations of classical verse, they were instructed to use the styles and metres of the original texts. Etonians were

---

[25] Graver, 'Wordsworth's Translations from Latin Poetry', p. 261.
[26] Knox, *Liberal Education*, p. 60.
[27] Sargeaunt, p. 31.
[28] 'Biographia', p. 166.
[29] Newbery, pp. v–vi.
[30] Newbery, p. 8.

Educating the Romantic Poets

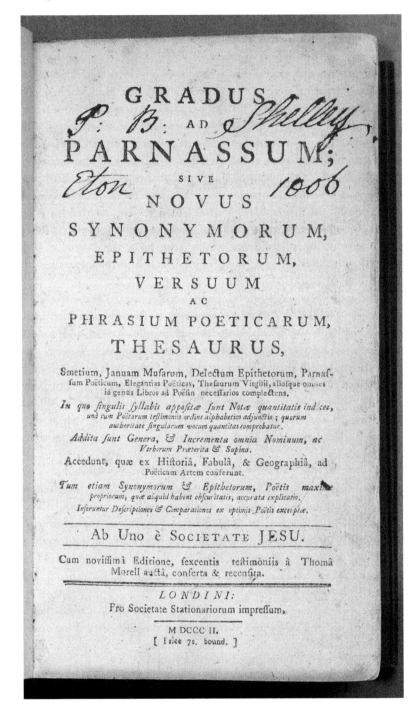

Figure 6. Percy Shelley's *Gradus*. Reproduced by permission of the Provost and Fellows of Eton College.

most often asked to imitate classical lyrics using elegiac couplets and iambic pentameter. Older boys at Eton and Winchester would typically be asked each week to write 20 to 40 lines of Latin or Greek verse and a second, long lyric in English. Boys got good at this fairly quickly. In 1811, when asked to write an inscription for a monument, Southey recalls how easily he composed epitaphs and inscriptions when a schoolboy: 'little time is required for composing ten or fifteen lines, when the matter is once ready', as it was with school assignments.[31] Byron refers in his letters to his exercises in Greek hexameter at Harrow and brags that he could write 30 or 40 Greek hexameters with little trouble.[32] Wordsworth reports that he first began writing his 'earliest songs' at 'the command' of his favourite schoolmaster, William Taylor.[33]

Dr Arnold tasked the sixth form at Rugby to write verses describing 'two shepherds praising in alternating stanzas the sea and a river' and giving voice to 'Christian's thanks, after crossing the river, for his successful conquest of life's danger'. Other verse topics used at Rugby included the telegraph, balloons, university, and Westminster men, the last of which probably gave pupils the opportunity to compose invective, satire, or mock-heroic verse. For the annual prize competitions one year, Rugby pupils were asked to translate ten lines of poetry from Dryden into Latin hexameters and 15 lines from Milton's *Samson Agonistes* into Greek iambics. Arnold also asked seniors to make Latin translations of Book IV of Cowper's *The Task* and Pope's *Third Moral Epistle*. Knox found it useful to ask pupils to write epigrams, with the direction that they could include only one thought. In another exercise, he scrambled the words of selected epigrams by Martial and asked pupils to restore them to their original metrical order.

While *The Edinburgh Review* and others ridiculed the Anglo-classical tradition of verse-writing, Oxford's professor of poetry Edward Copleston staunchly defended the practice: 'It is not that we seek to stock the world with new poems, but to give play in the most effectual manner to the poetic faculty, which exists to a certain degree in all minds, and which, like every other faculty, ought to lie wholly uncultivated in none.'[34] Copleston adds that writing verse is 'useful' because it teaches

> a habit of compression without obscurity; a habit of selecting the fittest materials, and of setting them in the nicest order; and a command of

---

[31] CLRS, Pt 4, #1988. He says writing first drafts took less than an hour.
[32] Marchand, *Byron: A Biography*, vol. 1, p. 67.
[33] *Prelude*, 1850, p. 387, ll. 551–552.
[34] Edward Copleston, p. 129.

Educating the Romantic Poets

pure, terse, and polished diction, which cannot long be practiced without imparting a salutary tincture to all other kinds of composition.[35]

Pupils relied on their *gradus* and were known on occasion to use old copies of former pupils' poetic endeavours (peddled to them by school employees) to produce their required verses. From time to time, however, excellent, original verses resulted from these assignments, many of which were published in school magazines such as *The Etonian* and *The Rugby Magazine* or collected in bound volumes and housed in places of honour at the schools.[36] As noted above, versifying skill was honoured at the schools' end of year events and in the prize competitions. For each prize, a common topic was given to the pupils; the judges were usually fellows at one of the school's affiliated colleges at Oxford or Cambridge. This exercise gave pupils an opportunity to see a variety of responses to the same writing assignment. Often these prize-winning compositions helped boys earn exhibitions—or scholarships—to university, and they readied them for similar collegiate endeavours, such as competing for the coveted Browne Medal for Greek verse at Cambridge, an honour which Coleridge and two Romantic-era headmasters, Goddard and Keate, each earned.

The shift to teaching prose composition at most of these schools came only after pupils had served an apprenticeship in Latin translation and verse composition. Knox advised teachers not to give prose writing assignments until pupils were at least 13. The particulars of these assignments appear to be derived, at least in part, from the sequence outlined in the Greek *progymnasmata*, which starts with pleasant, even playful, tasks matched to children's cognitive development.[37] For a boy's first English prose theme, Knox asked boys to retell one of Aesop's fables in English; a second prose assignment was to write a letter on a familiar subject to a parent or sibling. Schoolmasters' theme assignments included descriptive pieces. Two that Arnold assigned were 'Describe the era in which Isaiah delivered his prophecies' and 'What state of affairs would a person touring Europe during the summer of 1815 find

---

[35] Edward Copleston, p. 131. Copleston was a prize-winning poet in school and university himself. He earned one of his many academic prizes for an essay in English on a topic that the faculty at Christ Church described as being 'a subject of national interest'. The topic was 'Agriculture', and, for this essay, he was personally thanked on behalf of the Agricultural Society by Sir John Sinclair, the society's president. See William James Copleston, p. 5.

[36] See, for example, *Musae Etonensis* (1755), *Anthologia Wintoniensis*, and the Rugby Honours books, which are beautifully bound leather volumes. Some are housed in the schools' archives, others in the headmasters' offices.

[37] The *progymnasmata* offers the following sequence of writing assignments: fable, tale, *chreia*, proverb, confirmation/refutation, amplification, or elaboration of a commonly held belief, encomium/invective, comparison, character pieces (*ethopoeia*, *prosopopoeia*, and *eidolopoeia*), description, thesis or argument, and finally persuasive pieces advocating action.

Lessons in Classical Literature, Rhetoric, Oratory, and Composition Training

among the various peoples he happened upon'—an assignment that makes it clear that boys were aware of life outside the schools' 'little world'. As Koelb reminds us, classical teaching of ecphrasis, the 12th exercise of the 14 in Aphthonius' *progymnasmata*, included 'psychologically sensitive descriptions' that included persons, things, time, place, brute animals, and plants. She asserts that Wordsworth adapted classical examples of ecphrasis when he described 'the fit between the human mind and the external world',[38] which Graver has called 'his most important subject'.[39] Yet another of Arnold's assignments borrowed from classical textbooks was to ask sixth form pupils to define eight words: *honour, duty, faith, philosophy, art, beauty, romantic*, and *the sublime*. The first prose 'essay' assignments were simply to rehearse received arguments rather than to invent new ones. This sequencing allowed pupils to practise correctness, fluency, and arrangement before performing the far more difficult task of invention. Indeed, schoolmasters were not particularly concerned with originality in these compositions.

The schools routinely required the writing of least two compositions a week; at Knox's school pupils wrote or revised almost every day. Most of his pupils' prose assignments in English were imitations of writers they were reading at the time, such as Virgil, Cicero, Pope, and Addison. He asserted that the 'habit of accuracy and care in the collocation of words, which is required in Latin works, will insensibly extend its good effects to [pupils' writing in English]'.[40] Though he conceded the demanding nature of the writing programme, Knox clung to his belief that 'Much practice and long habit are necessary, to give excellence and facility [to writing]'.[41] He added that he knew many boys who experienced the 'natural pleasure of invention, and the consciousness of increasing strength of mind' from writing.[42] The author of *A Plan of Education Delineated and Vindicated* (1784) spoke for many teachers of the time in saying that 'taste and elegance in Composition … can only be acquired by long practice and the perusal of good Authors, joined to a competent share of natural Abilities.'[43] Though schoolmasters in Wordsworth's day had no control over their pupils' native talents, they did at least see to it that the boys had plenty of practice. Arnold attached great importance to prose composition in Latin on the grounds that this sort of writing was not only 'the best means of acquiring a sound knowledge of the ancient authors, but [also] of attaining a mastery over the English language'.[44]

---

[38] Koelb, p. 14.
[39] Qtd in Koelb, p. 14, from Graver, 'Wordsworth's Georgic Beginnings', p. 156.
[40] Knox, *Liberal Education*, p. 82.
[41] Knox, *Liberal Education*, p. 83.
[42] Knox, *Liberal Education*, p. 65.
[43] Croft, p. 30.
[44] Stanley, vol. 1, p. 131.

Educating the Romantic Poets

The archive at Winchester has piles of the 'task essays' that boys wrote for the annual prose prize. In 1788 Sydney Smith won the prize for his English prose essay entitled 'Not only every Age of human Life but every Station and Profession has Vices and Imperfections which are almost peculiar to itself'.[45] Mathematicians are too attached to exact numbers, he said; lawyers to making clever arguments; military men to being brave and active. The chief vice of the poet, he claimed, is selfishness. To this observation he added that for some people 'there can hardly be a more troublesome or insipid being than a Poet'. Ironically, the prize book for this essay was a collection of the poems of Apollonius of Rhodes. As evidence of Smith's pride in receiving this award, he had the volume elegantly (and expensively) bound in leather and ivory (see Figure 7). Besides the 'task essays', Winchester masters also assigned a Latin prose paper that required research and allowed boys to investigate and express their own tastes and interests. A student quoted in Leach reports that most boys truly enjoyed this assignment.[46]

Expatiating on the importance of such composition work, one Rugby student counselled his classmates that they could never learn the 'niceties' of language just by reading; they must also write early and often. Moreover, he adds, 'It is better to write in another language than one's own because this helps keep language in bounds.'[47] Another student wrote that 'one of the greatest reasons for studying the classics … is that till very lately … our literature had not advanced so far as that of the Greeks and Romans; so that we had to study their writings as models … when the art was in a greater degree of perfection.'[48] The student's awareness of differences in style is notable. He observes that the old English ballads are similar in style to Homer, Milton's style is similar to that of Aeschylus, Addison's works are similar to the writings of Cicero, and 'the old chronicles' are similar to the work of Herodotus. He adds, however, that there are simply no equals in 'modern garb' to the writings of Demosthenes, Tacitus, and Thucydides.[49] For a youth to be capable of such literary judgements is surprising; that the schoolboys reading this magazine were likely to have been interested in the topic is even more impressive.

The number of writing assignments and how regularly they were assigned to pupils in the Romantic period are noteworthy. At Rugby 14-year-old boys received at least three weekly writing assignments. St Paul's senior boys composed 'moral themes or declamations' in prose or verse three afternoons a

---

[45] The essay is unpublished; it can be found in the archives of Winchester College.
[46] Leach, pp. 426–427. I am puzzled about where students did this research, for the library collections at most of the schools were reserved for the masters, and students were not allowed to use them.
[47] *Rugby Magazine*, 'On Composition', pp. 66–67.
[48] *Rugby Magazine*, 'Some Remarks', p. 35.
[49] *Rugby Magazine*, 'Some Remarks', p. 35.

Lessons in Classical Literature, Rhetoric, Oratory, and Composition Training

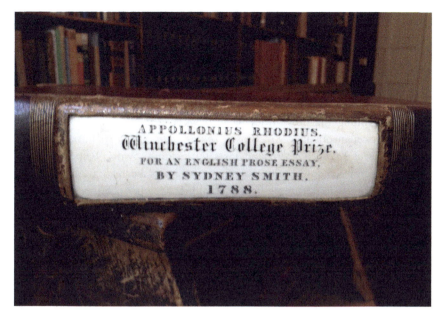

Figure 7. Sydney Smith's English Prose Essay Prize book, plate in ivory. Winchester College Archive.

week and a 'Divine theme' in prose or verse on Saturdays. Knox enforced one of the most rigorous writing programmes at Tonbridge Grammar: on Monday evening boys were asked to write Latin themes; on Tuesday evening, Latin verses; on Wednesday evening, an English letter; on Thursday evening, English verses; on Friday evening, Latin verses; and in the interval from Saturday to Monday, a Latin and an English theme.[50] Clarke reckons that in this era during one year at Rugby a boy would have been assigned to write translations of 1,000 lines of Latin or Greek prose and 800 lines of Latin or Greek verse, to write 15 prose essays (mostly in Latin) and 700 lines of original verse in Latin, Greek, and English. If a student stayed in school four to eight years, as many of the Romantics did, the amount of writing he would have produced was impressive: 4,000 to 8,000 lines of Latin or Greek prose translation; 3,200 to 6,400 lines of Latin or Greek verse translation; 60 to 120 prose essays; and 2,800 to 5,600 lines (the equivalent of 200 to 400 sonnets) of original verse.

Apparently, the rigours of the school curriculum neither cooled pupils' interest in reading nor dulled their interest in the life of the mind. School historians such as Maxwell-Lyte, Archer, and Sargeaunt all cite examples of pupils' descriptions of real pleasure in reading Thucydides, Herodotus, Juvenal, Livy, Tacitus, Sophocles, and Ovid. Boys also wrote home enthusiastically about

---

[50] Knox, *Liberal Education*, p. 62.

Educating the Romantic Poets

reading Milton, Pope, Chaucer, Spenser, Chesterfield's letters, *The Spectator*, and newspaper articles about the war on the Continent and the political state of the kingdom.[51] William Grant wrote to his parents that he was reading *Roderick Random* and asked them to send him copies of the *Iliad*, *Tom Jones*, a volume of Terence, and the orations of Lysias.

Thanks to Duncan Wu, we have a detailed catalogue of Wordsworth's reading.[52] Among the prose titles he read while a pupil at Hawkshead were Aikin's 'Miscellaneous Pieces in Prose', *The Arabian Nights*, Arthurian legends, *The Sorrows of Young Werther*, and texts by Fielding, Swift, Walpole, Francis Bacon, Newton, and Cervantes. Among the poets he read were Akenside, Beattie, Burns, Chatterton, Chaucer, Collins, Cowper, Dante, Goldsmith, Gray, Langhorne, Milton, Percy, Pope, Shakespeare, Charlotte Smith, Spenser, Thomson, Warton, and Helen Maria Williams. Periodicals such as the *Annual Register*, *European Magazine*, and *The Spectator* were on his list as well. Byron enjoyed having the reputation of being a lazy and mischievous schoolboy, but he also bragged that he 'read eating, read in bed, read when no one else was reading, and had read all sorts of reading since I was five years old'.[53] In 1807, two years after leaving Harrow, Byron recorded a remarkable reading list 'from memory', about half of which he claimed to have read as a schoolboy. It includes histories of 18 countries and numerous biographies, among them those of Sallust, Caesar, Czar Peter, Marlborough, Buonaparte, 'all the British poets', Kames, and Newton. Apparently, the poet's curiosity about the lived experiences and behaviour of powerful or passionate men, such as those he portrays in *Manfred*, *Beppo*, and *The Corsair*, started early on and was fostered in his school world.

Oddly enough, even though literature was the primary focus of education at these schools, and even though boys often reported their pleasure in reading as a pastime, some of the wealthiest schools did not provide lending libraries for their pupils. Eton's first schoolboy library, founded in 1842, was opened and maintained by the pupils themselves. They required subscription, and invited donations from parents, teachers, and alumni. The list of works in their collection tells much about what the pupils and donors believed was worth reading. The library contained 32 classical texts, 30 volumes of English poetry or prose, 25 books on Christian topics, and 18 books of English history or speeches.[54] Hawkshead School provided a library for the boys; it, too, was

---

[51] Probably some of the surviving letters were assigned by their schoolmasters, so the boys' enthusiasms may have been calculated at least in part to please their teachers.
[52] Wu, *Wordsworth's Reading 1770–1799* and *Wordsworth's Reading 1800–1815*.
[53] Qtd in Marchand, *Byron: A Biography*, vol. 1, p. 84.
[54] The collection included works by Byron, Campbell, Coleridge, Crabbe, Erasmus Darwin, Dryden, Ben Jonson, Samuel Johnson (including the *Dictionary*), Otway, Massenger, Milton, Pope (including his *Homer*), Roger, Scott, Shakespeare, Southey, Spenser, Swift,

Lessons in Classical Literature, Rhetoric, Oratory, and Composition Training

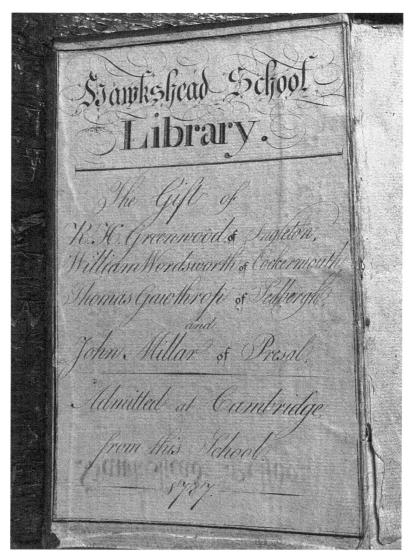

Figure 8. Photograph of the bookplate for John Gillies' *History of Ancient Greece*, presented to the Hawkshead School Library in 1787, including William Wordsworth's name. Reproduced by permission of the Trustees of Hawkshead Grammar School.

managed by pupils. Graduating seniors built the collection by contributing

and Wordsworth. Nonfiction texts in the collection were Bacon's *Works*, Bentley's *Dissertation on Phalaris*, Blackstone's *Commentaries*, Blair's *Lectures and Sermons*, Burke's *Works* (12 vols), Fox's speeches (6 vols), Franklin's *Works*, Gibbon's *Roman Empire* and *Miscellaneous Works*, Gladstone's *Church and State*, Goldsmith's *Natural History* (6 vols), Hume and Smollett's *History of England*, Sir William Jones's *Works and Life* (11 vols), Locke's *Works*, Newton's *On the Prophesies* (but not the *Principia*), Paley's *Evidences*, Pitt's speeches,

87

Educating the Romantic Poets

'leaving books'. Wordsworth and several of his classmates pooled their money and left the school a history of Greece and a translation of Tasso's *Jerusalem*.[55]

Several issues of the Rugby student magazine during Thomas Arnold's time demonstrate pupils' respect for classical studies. One Rugby pupil wrote that 'the principal end of [classical] education is to train and exercise the mind. It is not to teach facts, but the way to use facts.'[56] Another article explained that 'The habits of criticism learned in studying the classics give us the capacity for close attention, [and] the awareness of meanings and phrasing, that would otherwise be lost in translation.'[57] This student added that the 'principal ground on which … the importance of the study of the classics rests' is the degree to which it assists boys in the 'right understanding and appreciation of the Christian religion'.[58] A third Rugby pupil added that the 'great end of education of boys is to call forth and direct the affections aright'.[59] No doubt these pupils first heard these arguments from their schoolmasters, but the fact that they chose to voice them in their magazine, whose readers were most often other boys, is significant.

It should be noted that educators in the Georgian classical schools were not ignorant of the advances in science in their own day and were aware of arguments that the classical programme should move aside for these and other 'modern studies'. Derwent Coleridge, who taught at an Anglo-classical grammar school and was the founder of the first national school to prepare poor students to become schoolteachers, had this to say about replacing classics with more practical studies:

> When it is proposed to substitute calculation for grammar, that is for reading or literature, in the education of youth, I cannot but remember that the former thus left to itself supplies no examples of conduct, kindles no generous ardour, awakens no kindly sympathy; above all, that it leaves undeveloped the sense of beauty, shutting out a source of innocent enjoyment, open in rich abundance to the poorest man.[60]

The schools did not, however, rule out studies of arithmetic, algebra, geometry, geography, history, and astronomy. These subjects were often taught, however, in a way that supported boys' classical language studies. For example, at

Sir Walter Raleigh's *Works* (8 vols), Sir Joshua Reynolds' *Works* (3 vols), Adam Smith's *Wealth of Nations* (3 vols), and Wilberforce's *View of Christianity*.

[55] Moorman, *William Wordsworth: A Biography: Early Years 1770–1803*, pp. 86–87.
[56] *Rugby Magazine*, 'On the Method of Translation', p. 67.
[57] *Rugby Magazine*, 'Some Remarks', p. 363.
[58] *Rugby Magazine*, 'Some Remarks', p. 362.
[59] *Rugby Magazine*, 'School Society', p. 208.
[60] Hainton and Hainton, p. 197.

Lessons in Classical Literature, Rhetoric, Oratory, and Composition Training

some schools, pupils learned geometry by reading Euclid in Greek and world geography by reading Pomponius Mela in Latin. Pupils were typically assigned weekly map-drawing exercises, and these were often of the classical world. History lessons recounted the stories of Athens, Sparta, and Rome and might include biographies of emperors, senators, and generals. Knox responded to calls for more modern subjects by pointing out that classical studies give pupils 'knowledge of ourselves and our duty'.[61]

Assessment

Modern-day teachers and professors would balk at having to mark the number of student 'themes' that typically landed on Georgian schoolmasters' desks. Teachers found a variety of ways to minimise the job of assessment and to maximise feedback on their pupils' writing. For one thing, the assigned themes in prose and verse were relatively short, usually only two or three pages. Pupils were encouraged to submit their themes to prefects or private tutors for comments before bringing them to class, which minimised the masters' amount of correction (and frustration). The time-saving practice of reading the papers aloud and critiquing them on the spot in class was also common. Chapman reported that he followed this practice two or three times a week and usually invited comments from the class as well. Knox advised schoolmasters not to be overly critical of boys' early writing, for they make 'many and egregious mistakes' early on. He also warned that too much correction would encourage boys to plagiarise. Coleridge described a method Boyer used to critique his writing: the master saved four or five themes, lined them up on his desk, and asked pointed questions about each one. 'Why this or that sentence might not have found as appropriate a place under this or that other theme: and if no satisfying answer could be returned, and two faults of the same kind were found in one exercise', the offending papers were torn up.[62] All of this feedback on student writing had several effects: the obvious one of helping them correct their errors, and the less obvious ones of helping them experience the reactions of an audience and of demonstrating to them that writing is a public act with consequences.

Unfortunately, little written evidence of Georgian schoolboys' progress, such as course grades or teachers' comments, has survived. However, the Eton archives contain three finely scrawled pages dated 1823, on which headmaster John Keate recorded his impressions of the performance of a group of fifth-form boys in 'Latin language, Greek language, Themes, Verses, and Geography'. This document appears to be his comments on the pupils' 'removal examination', a biannual

---

[61] Knox, *Liberal Education*, p. 59.
[62] 'Biographia', p. 160.

event that determined if a student would be promoted to the next higher form. Keate used five descriptors of student achievement: 'performs well', 'middling', 'poor', 'bad', and 'very bad' with qualifiers such as 'rather' or 'almost'. Of the 94 boys whose Latin language skills were measured, 55 were ranked as having 'done well', nine as 'middling', 18 as 'poor', and the remaining 12 as 'bad'. Of 92 boys assessed in Greek, 35 performed well; the remaining pupils' performances were evenly distributed over the categories of middling, poor, and bad; a few stragglers were judged to be 'very bad'. In the other three areas—themes, verses, and geography—by far the strongest showings were in verse-composition: close to half of the fifth form produced good to middling verses. In the area of prose-writing, approximately 20 per cent of the class fell into each of the five assessment categories. The worst area of performance was geography, in which more than half the class's work was described as 'poor' or worse. Besides commenting on the pupils' skills, Keate also cited aspects of their behaviour, with descriptors such as 'well-behaved', 'painstaking', 'diligent', and 'great passion and industry'. One youngster was described as 'clever but uncertain', another 'does well, but [is] idle', and yet another 'does not so much as he might'.

Most of the Anglo-classical schools had 'removal' examinations such as these. Along with written exams, oral exams were also common, and these were usually quite public. Based on their performances, boys either 'advanced in glory or were kept back to their shame' for at least a half year. The exams were designed not only to assess skills but also to train pupils to think on their feet and to build or test their competitive and emulative spirits. The questions and tasks on removal exams referred to Latin, Greek, and New Testament works the boys had studied; and in most cases they also included both an original theme and a translation of a formerly unseen passage of Latin or Greek. The exam period might last as long as five days. During Arnold's headship at Rugby, on the first day of these exams, boys answered questions about the books of Matthew and Acts. The second, third, and fourth days were spent translating passages and answering written questions on Homer, Herodotus, Thucydides, Sophocles, Theocritus, Virgil, Horace, Livy, and Pliny. Student rankings from the top to the bottom of the class were posted for all to see. Finally, on the fifth day *viva voce* examinations were conducted on Xenophon and Cicero. Part of the exam was also to write a list of original compositions: a poem in Latin using elegiac couplets, a prose essay in Latin, a poem in Greek using hexameter, a number of iambics in Greek based upon a text from Shakespeare, a Greek prose translation, and Latin prose based upon a piece in *The Spectator*. Pupils were allowed to use dictionaries or lexicons for these original compositions. Many schoolmasters around the country used a similar examination process, including sessions that were oral and public.

Another example of the sort of assessment methods employed at these schools is the Westminster Challenge, the annual competition among

Lessons in Classical Literature, Rhetoric, Oratory, and Composition Training

Figure 9. The Westminster Challenge, document in the Westminster School Archives. Reproduced with kind permission of the Governing Body, Westminster School.

fourth-form boys for the honour and privileges of being King's Scholars. This ordeal lasted for six weeks and was a sort of verbal schoolboy duel. To prepare, pupils memorised a set list of Greek and Latin epigraphs and hired sixth-form King's Scholars, called 'Helps in the Challenge', to assist them in reviewing the grammar rules necessary to construe and parse each passage. The Helps also coached the competing pupils on winning strategies. The event began when the two lowest boys in the form stood up in front of a table around which were arrayed the headmaster and a small group of sixth-form Helps and moderators; beyond the table, in banked seats, sat the rest of their fourth-form classmates (see Figure 9). The first two challengers were given a passage randomly chosen by the headmaster from the set texts list. A third student, 'The Next in Turn', kept a scorecard of the proceedings.[63] The first student had to recite the passage and respond to questions put to him by his challenger about its meaning and grammar. Any question relating to the sense, words, or grammar of the passage was fair game. Questions went back and forth between pupils until one boy failed to answer three questions. He was excused, the Next in Turn came to the table, and the process started again. Sometimes the challenge could last late into the night. It would begin again the next day, and the next, until one boy finally triumphed. The exhausted but exultant youngster was carried around the school quad with great honour and rejoicing, before he and the top finishers (usually a total of ten in number) took their places on the Foundation as King's Scholars.[64]

---

[63] Copies of these are maintained in the Westminster School archives; they appear to be rather like today's baseball scorecards.

[64] In his second year at Westminster Southey took part in the Challenge, but did not advance.

Educating the Romantic Poets

The tradition of spirited academic competition epitomised by The Westminster Challenge was in place at many of the schools. At Winchester each year pupils participated in 'Standing Up'. This exercise took place in the last week of the long half, and pupils were required to learn many lines by heart and then to stand up, recite them, and be prepared to construe them. In 1838 older boys did 600 lines of Latin, the younger boys did 100 lines. All classes were halted for the week prior to 'Standing Up' to enable pupils to prepare for the competition. Boys' performances in these examinations led to their class rank and were an important factor in the decisions of fellows from Oxford and Cambridge about which boys would be invited to matriculate.

Other methods schools had of assessing pupils' writing and learning took the form of public appositions and 'supplications'. At Chapman's grammar school 'The Supplication' took place early in the year. Boys wrote Latin poems, and the best were presented to the town council with the request for holiday, if the poems were good enough. This practice gave students a real-world experience of the power of good writing. A former student described similar traditions at St Paul's and Christ's Hospital's—appositions and annual orations—as opportunities to 'show off', both for the pupils and the schools, but these events also made it clear to pupils that writing and public speaking skills were serious matters. At St Paul's the pupils' orations, which took place outside in Bartholomew Square, were followed up with a question-and-answer period. Parents and local dignitaries were invited to most of these events, and curious members of the public were also welcome. Besides giving youngsters the chance to firm up and demonstrate their learning, these events helped them develop poise in front of the audience. Accounts of the St Paul's appositions often appeared in the London newspapers. *The Universal Magazine of Knowledge and Pleasure* of 17 March 1768 described an apposition attended by the dukes of Wellington and Cumberland:

> Gentlemen on the foundation of St Paul's School were publicly examined in the different parts of literature; after which the eight senior youths made several speeches in Latin, Greek, and English before a numerous and polite assembly in the school; one speech in particular, which was received with great applause, on the following question, viz. 'Ought virtue to show itself most in prosperity or adversity?' At the same time Mr. Filmer, one of the senior scholars, was elected to Christ Church College, in Oxford, on the usual exhibition of that noble and well-endowed school.[65]

---

[65] Anonymous, 'St Paul's Appositions', p. 348.

Lessons in Classical Literature, Rhetoric, Oratory, and Composition Training

Modern-day schools are often judged by how many students are accepted at universities or colleges and by how prestigious those institutions are. It appears that most youngsters from public or endowed grammar schools who wanted to matriculate at a university college could find a place at one of them, as long as he could pay or earn a scholarship. College admissions were typically determined late in boys' senior year at the 'summer Election'. At Westminster, this was a four-day event during which pupils recited Latin verse competitions, epigrams, or essays they had prepared in advance before a board of electors, who also interrogated candidates individually. The board included the dean and a canon from the abbey, the dean and a fellow of Christ Church, the master and a fellow of Trinity, Cambridge, and the school's headmaster. If a youngster did not earn an 'election' to his first-choice college, he could take a place at an alternative college in the university and transfer later if a place came open. As already noted, some schools were partnered with colleges at the universities and could usually place several of their boys there, often with 'exhibitions' or scholarship tickets. Eton's Kings Scholars were bound for King's College, Cambridge, and New College always had openings for youngsters from Winchester. Westminster pupils usually found places at Christ Church,[66] and Hawkshead School could count on St John's to save places for northern boys. Founders' kin had automatic entry to most colleges as well.

Yet another way to assess the effectiveness of instruction at the public and grammar schools of the Georgian period is the quality of the pupils' prize compositions and of the essays and poems they published in their school magazines. I have read examples of these papers at several of the schools. Their essays are carefully structured, grammatically correct, and specifically detailed. The writers' voices are confident and often playful. Their poems show that these youngsters understood the conventions of pastoral and heroic verse, could compose long poems in iambic pentameter or common metre, knew to use strong verbs, and could handle figures such as synecdoche and personification. School boys also addressed rather sophisticated topics. The first number of Westminster's *Trifler* offered essays on morality, manners, poetry, satire, and 'characters'. The first number of the *Rugby Magazine* included pieces on the progress of nations from barbarism to civilisation, national and local prejudice, the decline of manners, Horace's poetry and Shakespeare's sonnets, the state of modern poetry, the state of English theatre, and essays with the following titles: 'Newspapers, Reviews, and Magazines', 'Restlessness of the Human Mind', and 'The Superiority of the Holy Scriptures over all other Compositions'.

---

[66] As an example of how closely related the schools and university colleges were at that time, Christ Church required all Westminster boys to continue studying Hebrew. Study of Hebrew was optional for students from the other schools.

Educating the Romantic Poets

Along with the example of Wordsworth's earliest poem, written at school and quoted in Chapter 3, the following excerpts from schoolboy verse, written at Winchester and Eton, complete the picture of what pupils at these schools learned to do with metrical language. In a poem composed for the Easter Task at Winchester in 1828, one student writes about the school that 'We love thy virtue, which severely mild,/Instructs the scholar and delights the child'. In *The Etonian* a series of sonnets begins with this quatrain from a poem entitled 'Written on the Last Leaf of Shakespeare':

> So now the charmed book is ended, Mary!
> The wand is broken, and the spell is o'er
> And thou hast mused or smiled o'er witch and faery,
> Till Fancy's imp familiar semblance wore.

The sonnet goes on to recommend that Mary return to reading 'Divinest SPENSER!' Following this sonnet, with its monastic imagery, is another one that suggests the student was quite familiar with contemporaneous verse.

> Barle-Edge Abbey
>
> And Time has spar'd no more! Those ruins gray
> Left the sole vouchers for the house of prayer.
> To tell the pensive truant from his way
> That voice of rapture one was breathing there!
> Strange! For the mountain rears its head as high,
> The river murmurs in its course as clear;—
> E'en yet methinks a spirit lingers here;
> And each lone fragment, as I wonder by,
> Speaks of a fall'n Religion. Awful thought!
> To those who know how frail all earthly power,
> When the dread summons of our latest hour
> Calls us away—to be as we have fought
> The fight of faith! But hark! the night-wind sings
> Farewell! Still record of forgotten things.

By the time young men such as these writers were ready to leave for Oxford or Cambridge, they clearly knew something about stress, longs, shorts, pitch, pattern, and genre in poetry and had learned to listen for the music of language. They had read very slowly and carefully an impressive range of texts, including epics, odes, pastorals, comedies, tragedies, psalms, proverbs, Gospels, epistles, histories, biographies, essays, dialogues, and orations in Latin and Greek. These lessons included instruction about the conventions of these literary forms,

Lessons in Classical Literature, Rhetoric, Oratory, and Composition Training

including structure, register, figures of speech, and common rhetorical figures. Students' memories were full of the sounds, words, phrasings, and stories of both the classical canon and the Bible. Perhaps most significantly, pupils had practised writing verse and prose almost daily for years.

CHAPTER FIVE

Religious Instruction and Worship in the Anglo-Classical Academy

> The principal ground on which ... the importance of the study of the classics rests is the degree to which it assists boys in the right understanding and appreciation of the Christian religion.
>
> A Rugby pupil, 1835

> There cannot be a good man without religion. Nor will he become a good senator, a good judge, a good commander, or fill the lower departments of civil and social life with integrity and honour, who disregards [the faith], and from principle seeks only self-interest and private gratification.
>
> Vicesimus Knox

Religion—in the form of daily Anglican worship, scriptural study, and instruction in theology and church history—was a through-line from boyhood to young manhood for those who were trained in the Anglo-classical academy. The emphasis upon religious life at the schools and universities helps to explain certain Romantic writers' religious, anti-religious, reforming or religiously ambivalent activities and writing when they were adults. In *On the Principles of English University Education* (1837), William Whewell (1794–1866), who was a student at Trinity College, Cambridge, and thereafter a Wrangler, Smith's prizeman, fellow, mathematics and natural philosophy tutor, and eventually master of the College,[1] explains that 'the

---

[1] The son of a master-carpenter, Whewell was noticed in his boyhood for his cleverness by an Anglican vicar, who trained him in grammar and arranged to send him to Heversham

religion taught in a young man's boyhood and college days is intended to form an unbroken part of the business of his life'.[2] While he acknowledges that boys and young men cannot be made 'pious by compulsion' and that religious services cannot 'control men's wandering minds, or drive the spirit of prayer to their hearts', they can at least provide structure to the day.[3] 'Regular habits of daily worship', he wrote, benefit a student's education because they are 'inconsistent with extreme listlessness, or frequent revelry, or wild extravagance of demeanour'.[4] He hazards the guess that even those who enter the chapel with resentment at the early hour or the requirement itself have 'their thoughts calmed and solemnized by [the] stillness and order [of the Anglican service]'.[5] He continues, expressing a belief shared by many Anglican educators that these practices helped to 'preserve the social sympathy of English worship' and that regular prayer and worship in youth produce 'a character of mind' that guides and supports a person 'in the wider and busier scenes of life'. He adds that the Anglican services impart a 'refined and elevated tone of thought [that prepares a person's soul for] its own future place in a higher region of purity and blessedness'.[6] Whewell dedicated his two-volume tome *Elements of Morality, including Polity* in 1845 to Wordsworth, whose *Ecclesiastical Sketches* (1822) appear to echo Whewell's thinking about the social and emotional roles the church played in England.

The Anglican Church

In the eighteenth and early nineteenth centuries the national Church was a mix of utilitarianism, Pelagianism, and eudaimonism. Anglican educators, all of whom trained at Oxford or Cambridge, tended to be practical and/or intellectual rather than emotional in their religious practice. Operating on the belief that humankind in general is fundamentally good and graciously endowed with free will, their teaching aimed to guide students toward human happiness based on personal virtue, practice of sound 'English' values, and good works. Some scholars have argued that the Oxford dons lacked philosophical originality, but all agree that the university was a

---

Grammar School in Westmorland. Thereafter he matriculated at Trinity. He was inducted into the Royal Society in 1820 and was ordained in 1825. He held various chaired professorships and while Master of Trinity he also served twice as the Vice Chancellor of the University.

[2] Whewell, p. 82.
[3] Whewell, pp. 112–113.
[4] Whewell, pp. 112, 114.
[5] Whewell, p. 112.
[6] Whewell, p. 119.

'bulwark of the established order in the church and state'.[7] The university's theological teaching, liturgies, sermons, and social views were a combination of Tudor apology, eighteenth-century moralism, biblical commentary, and latitudinarianism. At Cambridge, this middle way was also inflected by Newtonianism and the emerging natural sciences. William Paley's utilitarian notions about happiness, outlined in his *Principles of Moral and Political Philosophy* (1785), and his watch and watchmaker model, explained in the preface to *Natural Theology, or Evidences of the Existence and Attributes of the Deity* (1802), were widely embraced. More than Oxford, Cambridge allowed room for deist, Unitarian, and evangelical discourse and activities, as long as college members more or less behaved themselves and did not speak too publicly about their divergent views. However, even the more progressive natural philosophers at Georgian Cambridge, men who taught students to interpret material phenomena as the functioning of the laws of the natural world, rather than direct godly interventions, and those who argued for Unitarian principles, believed—or at least maintained publicly—that the world and its laws were the creation of a living, Judeo-Christian God.[8]

While practices varied from place to place, no pupil at the schools or student at the universities lived a day without some sort of encounter with the Church of England. Most of the larger grammar schools had chapels where pupils gathered several times a day. Eton's chapel is notable for its length, height, and fifteenth-century wall paintings in the Flemish style (see Figure 10).[9] At Westminster, the great abbey itself was (and still is) cleared of public visitors before student prayer services. On Sundays, Anglican schoolboys around the country heard their headmasters' sermons in their school chapel or were sent to nearby churches to hear local vicars preach. During his first three years as a boarding student, Wordsworth attended Sunday services at the 'snow white church' on the hill just above Hawkshead Grammar School.[10] This continued for five more years after the Tysons moved to the village of Colthouse. If the weather was bad, however, Ann Tyson might troop her boarders to the nearby Quaker meeting house. Coleridge and his schoolmates worshipped at Christ Church, Newgate Street, opposite St Paul's Cathedral. Rebuilt by Christopher Wren after the Great Fire, Christ Church was a dignified edifice, with a spire, buttresses, and exterior decorations of pineapples and pediments. On great occasions, such as those described in Blake's 'Holy Thursday', Christ's Hospital pupils were marched along with other charity children of London across the street to St Paul's Cathedral, where

---

[7] Green, 'Religion in the Colleges', p. 464.

[8] There were members of the colleges who were atheists, but they typically kept this belief to themselves.

[9] See Howe *et al.*

[10] *Prelude*, 1850, p. 127, l. 21.

Educating the Romantic Poets

Figure 10. Interior, Eton College Chapel.

a special booth was set up to house them in their distinctive blue coats (see Figure 11). During Byron's time at Harrow, boys were sent to the Church of St Mary, Harrow-on-the-Hill, for services. In 'Lines Written beneath an Elm in the Churchyard of Harrow', Byron recalls musing 'the twilight hours away' in that space.[11] He describes it as a place where he 'loved to dwell' and where 'all [his] hopes arose'.[12] As an adult Byron considered having his body laid to rest at the church. While this did not come to pass, Byron arranged, with the help of his former schoolmaster, Henry Drury, for his daughter Allegra to be buried there.[13]

The university colleges all had their own chapels as well. Most are solemnly beautiful spaces, some with exquisite stained-glass windows. The chapels of Emmanuel and Pembroke Colleges were designed by Christopher Wren to be acoustical masterpieces. The seating in these chapels is that of the intimate

---

[11] Byron, 'Harrow on the Hill', l. 10.
[12] Byron, 'Harrow on the Hill', ll. 22, 25.
[13] Byron wanted Allegra's tablet to include his name, something the church wardens and parishioners protested. The child was eventually buried inside the church door, under the present doormat, without a tablet (Marchand, *Byron: A Biography*, vol. 2, p. 1001, n.). Byron was buried in the family vault at St Mary Magdalen Church, Hucknall Torkard, after Westminster Abbey declined the request that he be buried there.

Religious Instruction and Worship in the Anglo-Classical Academy

Figure 11. Christ's Hospital, London: one of the boys standing beside a table, his hand on some books, the exterior of the New Hall behind. Colour lithograph after J. Cristall. Wellcome Collection. Public Domain Mark.

medieval *quire*; stalls face each other across the aisle and are raked to improve acoustics. In *Ecclesiastical Sketches*, Wordsworth describes the effects of the interior of King's College Chapel, Cambridge. It was, he says, an 'immense/ And glorious Work of fine intelligence!'[14]

---

[14] Jackson, *Sonnet Series*, pp. 201–202, Part III, 'XXIV', ll. 4–5.

Educating the Romantic Poets

>...fashioned for the sense
>These lofty pillars, spread that branching root
>Self-poised, and scooped into ten thousand cells,
>Where light and shade repose where music dwells
>Lingering—and wandering on as loth to die;
>Like thoughts whose very sweetness yieldeth proof
>That they were born for immortality.[15]

Daily worship in such spaces could not have been without some effect, even upon bored, sleepy, or grudging students. The churches used for the universities' large communal services—Great St Mary's in Cambridge and the Church of St Mary the Virgin in Oxford—are also historically significant. During the Reformation, Cranmer gave Martin Bucer sanctuary in Great St Mary's, and both he and Erasmus preached from its three-decker pulpit. Distinguished by its barley twist portico columns, St Mary the Virgin in Oxford was the site in 1555 of the trials of bishops Latimer, Ridley, and Cranmer. In 1828 and for the next fifteen years John Henry Newman was the vicar and most frequent preacher at the church. John Keble preached his 'National Apostasy' sermon there in 1833.

Along with the historical significance of these churches, the architectural elegance of the larger sanctuaries and the quiet beauty of the smaller ones, the interior decoration of these sites contributed to the experience of worship there. The walls of many are decorated with tablets inscribed with the Decalogue, the Lord's prayer, and the creeds. After the Restoration royal coats of arms were also hung prominently in most Anglican churches and college chapels. Busts and plaques memorialise masters, dons, other churchmen, and students, some of whom had given a lifetime of service and others who had died honourably in battle or tragically in youth. Under their aisles and in their churchyards are the graves of these and other souls. So, even if students in the period did not appreciate the religious services they attended every day, they could not ignore the importance and dignity of these spaces. When Wordsworth turned in the 1820s to writing about churches and church history in *Ecclesiastical Sketches*, he could look back on 50 years spent in such buildings—first with his mother, then with school and college classmates, and later, almost every Sunday, dating from the baptism of his first child and the churching of his wife Mary in July 1803.

Worship services and prayer

As prescribed by the *Book of Common Prayer*, schools and many of the colleges conducted three services on weekdays and Saturdays: morning prayer

---

[15] Jackson, *Sonnet Series*, p. 202, Part III, 'XXIV', ll. 8–14.

Figure 12. St Mary the Virgin church portico, Oxford.

or matins, afternoon chapel, and evening prayer or vespers. Not all institutions required attendance at all services, but all schoolboys and college men gathered for communal prayer at least once and usually twice every day. Matins started early, often before breakfast at the schools. Typical morning services consisted of brief scripture readings and prayers. On Wednesdays and Fridays, a hymn and the litany were usually added. When William and Christopher

Educating the Romantic Poets

Wordsworth were students at Cambridge (1787–1794) and Byron and George Chinnery were at Trinity and Christ Church (1805–1811), morning prayer started at 8 a.m. Lessons at the schools ended each day at 3 p.m. with afternoon chapel, no doubt a welcome break for the pupils. Services on saints' days, feast days, communion Sundays, or historic occasions were not to be missed; college students were required to wear white surplices to these events. George Chinnery described his first surplice service in Christ Church Cathedral:

> the ceremony is remarkably fine, the chapel is lighted up with wax candles. But it was still more imposing [as] all the young men are dressed in white; a band of little boys sing the psalms accompanied by the organ; they are dressed in white; the organ plays very often during the service ... [a clergyman] sings the responses ... and the creed at the end. The dean himself read the communion service.[16]

Often schoolboys prayed in Latin, which most understood by the end of their first term. The form of the Latin prayers used by pupils at St Paul's dated from the Middle Ages and was used well into the Victorian period. Even if boys recited their prayers mindlessly, praying in Latin tied the practice to the historical church and had an elevating effect. Bishop Thomas Ken's *Manual of Prayers for the Use of the Scholars of Winchester College* (1675) was used by William Collins, Thomas Wharton, William Lisle Bowles, Sydney Smith, and Thomas Arnold when they were at the school. The manual includes shortened Latin prayers, a collect, the *Pater Noster*, and the following prayer for the students:

> O Philotheus, you cannot enough thank God for the order of the place you live in, where there is so much care taken to make you a good Christian as well as a good scholar, where you go so frequently to prayers, every day in the chapel and in the school, and sing hymns and psalms to God so frequently in your chamber, and in the chapel, and in the hall, so that you are in a manner brought up in a perpetuity of prayer.

The prayers used at Eton in the eighteenth and nineteenth centuries are collected in a volume entitled *Preces quotidianae in usum Scholae Collegii Regalis apud Etonam*, 1760 (see Figure 13). The book begins with a section in Latin that reproduces the 64th and 122nd psalms. Psalm 64 takes note of the many crimes and the 'deep cunning' of the human heart and mind and reminds the 'righteous who take refuge in the Lord' that 'God will shoot his arrows at the wicked'. The 122nd Psalm begins with 'I was glad when they

---

[16] Chinnery, letter of 16 January 1808.

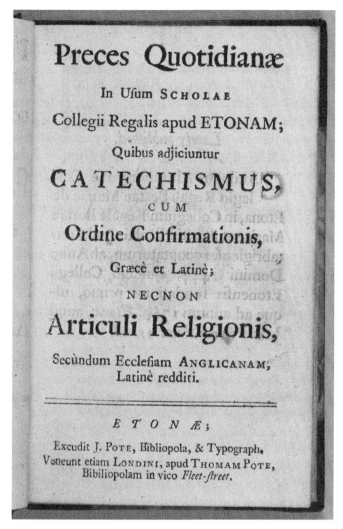

Figure 13. Title page of the Eton prayer book, *Preces Quotidianæ*.
Reproduced by permission of the Provost and Fellows of Eton College.

said to me, "Let us go into the House of the LORD!"' and concludes with three different calls for peace—in the land, in the city, and in one's heart. Following these psalms are responses in Latin, ante- and post-prandial graces, and the *Pater Noster*. A section entitled 'Private Devotions' explains how Eton students might pray in the morning, at midday, and when they go to bed at night, as well as when they travel, 'face temptation', or 'fall into sin'.[17] Eton's 'Directions for the Day Time' quotes Bishop Ken's Winchester prayer and

---

[17] Anonymous, *Preces Quotidianae*, pp. 26–34.

Educating the Romantic Poets

adds that Etonians must be accountable to God for their many opportunities and blessings. 'Prayer', the book continues, 'is the very Life of a Christian; and therefore, we are so frequently commanded to pray without ceasing: Not that we can be always on our Knees, but that we would accustom ourselves to frequent Thoughts of God, that wheresoever we are, he sees us.'[18] The Eton prayer book also counsels students to gather from the psalms those 'short Sentences which most affect' them, to memorise these lines, and then to say them from time to time through the day, for they are the 'short Breathings of the Soul of God'.[19] Evening prayer was almost always by candlelight. At Eton in Shelley's time, the service took place in the darkened Lower School and was read in Latin. The colleges at Oxford and Cambridge all held Evening Prayer services, usually around 9 p.m.; university students were expected to attend.

Sundays

The liturgy used for Sunday services was longer and included more readings and music. Wordsworth emphasises the historicity as well as the effects of this liturgy in *Ecclesiastical Sketches*, Part III, Sonnet 'XII The Liturgy':

> Yes, if the intensities of hope and fear
> Attract us still, and passionate exercise
> Of lofty thoughts, the way before us lies
> Distinct with signs, through which in set career
> As through a zodiac, moves the ritual year
> Of England's Church; stupendous mysteries!
> Which whoso travels in her bosom eyes,
> As he approaches them, with solemn cheer.
> Upon that circle traced from sacred story
> We only dare to cast a transient glance,
> Trusting in hope that Others may advance
> With mind intent upon the King of Glory,
> From his mild advent till his countenance
> Shall dissipate the seas and mountains hoary.[20]

Schoolboys and college men spent many hours participating in Sunday services and in afternoon or evening lessons or lectures. During services at schools, pupils chanted psalms; prefects or undermasters read scripture lessons; and the headmaster preached. The focus of the Sunday service was the

---

[18] Anonymous, *Preces Quotidianae*, p. 30.
[19] Anonymous, *Preces Quotidianae*, pp. 30–31.
[20] Jackson, *Sonnet Series*, pp. 194–195.

sermon, which was most often based upon the scripture readings appointed for the week by the Lectionary in the *Book of Common Prayer*. Predictably, headmasters also used their sermons to address current national events, issues at the schools, and the trials and temptations of boyhood. Dr Drury of Harrow left the preaching of sermons to undermasters, but most took this clerical duty quite seriously. The announced intent of the sermons of George Moberly, the headmaster of Winchester from 1835 to 1866, was to fill pupils with the 'reverent, and earnest, and dutiful desire to sanctify [their] boyish years to God's service in all innocent and devout living'.[21] Arnold's Rugby School sermons, each of which builds from a passage of scripture, constitute a remarkable inventory of the behaviours of late Romantic and early Victorian boyhood and what adults thought about them. Recurring topics were bad habits, idleness, recklessness, thoughtlessness, and extravagance. Each sermon works as an interlocking lesson, recalling and building from the previous Sunday's message, laying down a new theme, and preparing the ground for the coming week. These texts testify to Arnold's rhetorical training, knowledge of his audience, and ability to tie scripture to human nature. References are also frequently made to pupils' fathers and mothers, and their pride in and hopes or fears for their sons. In each sermon Arnold paused to address pupils directly in personal terms.

Sunday services at Cambridge and Oxford were large affairs and both university churches were packed. George Chinnery was impressed by his first all-university Sunday service at St Mary's, especially as the vice chancellor, proctors, heads of houses, and all the fellows filed in wearing their full academic regalia. At Oxford there was an early morning prayer service and a longer service with the litany and a sermon celebrated at 9 a.m. Sunday services at Cambridge usually started at 10 a.m. and might last until well after noon. The centrepieces of these services were long, scholarly sermons delivered in English by college preachers, tutors, university professors, college heads, or fellows on a rotating schedule. University sermons were accompanied by the scripture readings prescribed for the week. Observing the perspicacious style of the Royal Society, but not infrequently punctuated with decorous platitudes, these sermons were often published by the universities and reviewed in periodicals. In the Georgian period sermons were popular reading among the intelligentsia and 'sermon gadding'—taking notes and commenting on the style of sermons—was in vogue.[22] Often the first writing assignment on Monday morning was to discuss some aspect of the previous day's sermon. Modern commentators, used to much more colloquial and bombastic preaching, have judged Georgian sermons to be dry

---

[21] Moberly, p. 198.
[22] Gregory, p. 97.

Educating the Romantic Poets

and methodical, lacking in 'holy excitement', 'passionate pleading', 'heroic challenge', or 'winged imagination'.[23] They serve, nevertheless, as models of how men in that era were expected to speak before the educated classes on important public occasions. As such, they may also help to explain the register Wordsworth uses in his later sonnets.

A few examples of sermons from important Sundays at Cambridge include a discourse on the possible sins that can be committed in the name of utility, one that cautions against scientific scepticism, one on the efficacy of prayer, and another that urges young men to educate the heart as well as the head. At Oxford, sermon topics included the principles of the reformation, the need for repentance, and Christian redemption. George Chinnery wrote his mother about one of the first sermons he heard at the university, delivered by the Subdean of Christ Church, Dr Hall:

> I really think it was the best sermon I had ever heard both as to matter and delivery; it was deeply theological as it was written for a learned congregation consisting of all the members of our own college, of the Vice Chancellor & heads of all the other colleges; but this sermon was preceded by an Anthem, & a very long prayer; during these & during the sermon we were forced to stand, and had not Dr. Hall by his superior Oratory entirely captivated my attention, I think I should have found it too long.[24]

In Henry VIII's day, subjects who shirked Sunday services were fined, and this practice continued for college students in the Georgian period. Oxford not only fined students but sometimes required them to write themes as punishment.[25] At Cambridge the fine amounted to a little less than a pound (in 2020 money) for each missed chapel and twice that for missing services on surplice days and Sundays. Considering the number of services, these debts could mount up. In 1791 Coleridge told his brother that he and his classmates went to 'Chapel twice a day—every time we miss, we pay twopence, and fourpence on … Sundays, Saints' days, and the eves of Saints' days. I am remarkably religious upon an economical plan.'[26]

Southey's headmaster at Westminster reported that boys prayed as often as ten times a day. By my calculation, pupils in the schools attended close to 600 and college men probably attended at least 300 services each academic

---

[23] Davies, p. 73.
[24] Chinnery, letter of 31 January 1808.
[25] Green, 'Religion in the Colleges'. Green notes, however, that some fines were not imposed until a student missed chapel four times in a week (p. 431).
[26] CLSTC, I, p. 16.

year. Because these occasions always followed the liturgy of the 1662 *Book of Common Prayer* and its calendar of daily scripture reading, a person attending both Morning and Evening Prayer would have heard portions of all 150 psalms *each* month. He would have also heard the New Testament read through *twice* every year and most of the Old Testament once a year. There can be little doubt that such a regimen, practised consistently through a young person's school and college days, had effects. Several other points should be made about the prominence of the 1662 *Book of Common Prayer* in the academy. First, it bases the Anglican faith on words, verses, and texts—that is, on literature. Second, at times the prayer book was the only work in English that students were sure to read every day; as such, its 'elegantly ordinary' style furnished schoolboys and college men with a common standard of public discourse in their native tongue.[27] Third, two of the outstanding stylistic characteristics of the 1662 book are its intentional use of everyday language—closer than the scriptures are to the 'real language of men'—and a level of 'directness, simplicity, and harmony'[28] that C. S. Lewis called 'pithiness'.[29] Other stylistic markers of the prayers and responses in the book are parallel construction, doublets ('from lightning, and tempest ... from battle, and murder; Good Lord, deliver us'), and triplets ('may it please thee to succour, help, and comfort all that are in danger, necessity, and tribulation').[30] A quick scan of almost any book and any version of *The Prelude* reveals how often Wordsworth's blank verse relies upon these constructions. In 'Tintern Abbey' Wordsworth interrupts one of the most memorable doublets in the poem—the one describing 'nature and the language of the sense' as the 'anchor of my purest thoughts ... and soul of all my moral being' with the triplet describing nature as 'the nurse,/The guide, the guardian of my heart'.[31] The resounding conclusion of *The Prelude* is distinguished by phrases such as 'sanctified/ By reason and by truth'; 'what we have loved/Others will love', 'mid revolutions in the hopes/And fears of men', and, finally, the 'mind of man ... is itself/Of substance and of fabric more divine'.[32]

Schoolboys and college men were not finished with religious matters after the Sunday morning services. On Sunday afternoons, headmasters called pupils to attend lessons based on chapters from popular devotional works such as *The Whole Duty of Man* (1658). This book celebrates temperance, diligence, contentedness, consideration, meekness, and humility. The book

---

[27] Hefling and Shattuck, p. 3.
[28] Cummings, p. 211.
[29] Stanwood, p. 141.
[30] Stanwood, p. 141.
[31] WWMW, p. 134, ll. 109–112.
[32] *Prelude*; in the 1850 edition he revises line 443, adding a verb and changing 'truth' to 'faith': 'sanctified/By reason, blest by faith', p. 482, ll. 443–452; p. 483, ll. 447–446.

Educating the Romantic Poets

lists human duties in this order: first to God, charity, and prayer; then to family, friends, and also to servants, who—the book asserts—deserve to have good and just masters. Thomas Arnold delivered scripture lectures to the whole school on Sunday afternoons. At Charterhouse[33] there was an additional Sunday evening service that included music and lessons read by students. Sunday afternoons at both universities were often spent listening to fellows and college preachers discourse on the 39 Articles, the Greek Testament, and the writings of the Church fathers, and to various contemporaneous debates about moral duty.

The ritual of communal prayer was intended to strengthen students' faith, to give structure and a measure of moral earnestness to schoolboys' and college men's lives, and not incidentally to remind them that their studies were of high importance and should be taken seriously. The Anglican liturgies also reminded all members of the academy that they were Englishmen. The practice of mandatory church attendance was and is controversial; moreover, the extent to which these practices took effect in the lives of students is difficult to measure. Green reports that, at Oxford, not only undergraduates but also some fellows viewed chapel as a disagreeable or tedious chore, and on occasion they pointedly absented themselves from prayers. More privileged students, such as noblemen and gentleman commoners at some Oxford colleges, were only required to attend services on Thursdays.[34] Students who did attend sometimes put on airs of irreverence or were observed laughing, talking, sleeping, or sitting when they should be kneeling. While this news cannot be discounted, the fact that approximately a third of the students at the universities matriculated with the intention of becoming clergymen suggests that not all who attended chapel made a mockery of the occasions. Wordsworth complains in both the 1805 and 1850 *Preludes* about the folly of requiring chapel attendance for college students who have no interest in the services; and he begs 'Presidents and Deans' to 'spare the house of God' from such 'irreverence'.[35] In college both Coleridge and Southey turned away from Anglican trinitarian arguments and embraced Unitarianism. It seems clear, however, that Wordsworth's, Coleridge's, and Southey's later lives and writing about faith and the English Church are testimony to the long-term effects of their Anglican schooling.

---

[33] The Wordsworths' youngest son briefly attended Charterhouse.
[34] Green, 'Religion in the Colleges', pp. 431–432.
[35] *Prelude*, 1805, p. 112, ll. 421, 415, 428; 1850, p. 113, ll. 413, 408, 422. When his brother Christopher was Master of Trinity he enforced chapel attendance more than past masters had, a move that was not well received.

Religious Instruction and Worship in the Anglo-Classical Academy

Confirmation and communion

Along with conducting daily chapel and Sunday services, schoolmasters were charged with preparing students for confirmation. This process usually took place in a youngster's 13th year. Moberly wrote that 'making boys religious', 'catechizing them faithfully and painfully', preparing them 'carefully for Confirmation', and encouraging them in 'self-chosen vows of holy and faithful living' were the schools' most important jobs.[36] In addition to confirming pupils, most headmasters were charged with preparing them to celebrate the eucharist, which in that period was administered only four times a year. At least two of these occasions fell during the academic year and were treated as very formal events. The 1662 *Book of Common Prayer* warns that no 'notorious evil liver' who might have 'done any wrong to his neighbours by word or deed' might participate in the service until 'he hath openly declared himself to have truly repented and amended his former naughty life'.[37] Accordingly, headmasters capitalised on these instructions to use the weeks leading up to communion services to inventory their students' behaviour, to explain and discuss the meaning of the eucharist, and to remind students that they were expected to be 'sober, peaceable, and truly conscientious Sons of the Church of England'.[38]

At Oxford, communion was celebrated on the first Sunday of each month and on Church feast days.[39] The fellows of Oxford and Cambridge were charged, just as the headmasters of the schools were, with the duty of preparing students for these high liturgical services with special instructional and prayer sessions prior to the events. Jeremy Bentham, who experienced his first university eucharist at the age of 12, described how Queen's College, Oxford prepared him:

> we were lectured in the New Testament three days before and as many after that day: to prepare for which awful duty I read Nelson on the Sacrament … . I intended to fast that morning, but it would not do, for I began to grow sick for want of victuals: and was forced to eat a bit of breakfast … . We did St Paul's Epistle to the Hebrews for lecture in the Greek Testament.[40]

University students observed Lent and celebrated Easter and the springtime Eucharist with music and fanfare.

---

[36] Moberly, pp. xxvii–xxviii.
[37] Cummings, p. 389.
[38] Cummings, p. 211.
[39] Green, 'Religion in the Colleges', p. 426. Historically, the frequency of communion has been a charged issue in the Anglican Church. Roman Catholics celebrate it every Sunday; after the Reformation this practice was considered entirely improper by most Protestant groups.
[40] Qtd in Green, 'Religion in the Colleges', p. 429.

Educating the Romantic Poets

Informal religious gatherings

Perhaps inspired by the model of the Wesley's 'Holy Club' at Oxford, from time to time in the Romantic period college men at both universities gathered informally in their rooms or around town to discuss religious matters ranging from evangelism to Unitarianism. These occasions were often viewed by college authorities with suspicion. At Oxford evangelically inclined students from Christ Church, Lincoln, Magdalen, Queen's, Pembroke, Merton, and Brasenose met in the commons or their college rooms for religious discussion and prayer. Junior fellows were known to join these gatherings. The nineteenth-century evangelical movement, now called the Great Awakening, emerged at this time. When Thomas Arnold and John Keble were at Corpus Christi between 1811 and 1814 their classmate John Taylor Coleridge, the poet's nephew, described how the two men often wrangled in the common room over their differing religious ideas. 'These two', he recalled, 'held their opinions with a zeal and tenacity proportionate to their importance; each believed the other in error pernicious to the faith and dangerous to himself; and what they believed sincerely, each thought himself bound to state, and stated it openly, it may be with too much of warmth'.[41]

At Cambridge, evangelical students from St John's, Magdalene, and Queens' also gathered in their college rooms. William Wilberforce, who matriculated at St John's in 1776, associated with Cambridge evangelicals. This involvement led to his religious conversion in 1784. Isaac Milner (who later dealt mercilessly with William Frend's religious reformism) became lifelong friends with Wilberforce that same year. When Milner was named president of Queens' College in 1788 he made it a centre of evangelical thought. One of the Cambridge evangelicals, Charles Jerram, described his religious activities in the 1790s. Students formed among themselves, he said, 'two or three parties of religious persons, for the purpose of reading together some portion of the Greek Testament—discussing some topic given out at a previous Meeting for consideration—and concluding the whole with singing a hymn and prayer'.[42]

These practices, Jerram asserts, were 'useful and interesting', keeping 'alive the spark of personal religion', which the demanding studies of mathematics and classics could sometimes dim.[43] Some of the students who participated in these activities went on to join missionary efforts in Africa, India, and the South Pacific. Others, with very different ideas, assembled in local homes, halls, or chapels to contest Anglican trinitarianism.

---

[41] Stanley, vol. 1, p. 14. J. T. Coleridge also recorded that while he, Arnold, and Keble were at Corpus Christi, Samuel Taylor Coleridge sent them copies of *Lyrical Ballads* and *Poems in Two Volumes* and the students admired the 'truth and beauty' in WWPW, p. 16.
[42] Qtd in Searby, p. 323.
[43] Searby, p. 323.

The purposes of these prayer and conversation groups were not only to enrich members' personal experience of faith, but also to campaign for religious freedom and the civil rights of students, slaves, prisoners, the poor, the aged, and children. Some university men did charity work; others, like Wilberforce, became abolitionists.[44] Despite these students' earnestness, college heads typically disapproved of such extra-curricular endeavours and would sometimes balk at giving testimonials for ordinands who met in this way. Having witnessed the revolution in France and the toppling of the French church, university dons feared these activities would cause the universities to be seen as 'seed-beds of schism'.[45] This fear was certainly on the minds of senior members of Cambridge between 1788 and 1793, when their young Unitarian colleague, the Jesus College fellow and tutor William Frend, was campaigning against both the trinity and required subscription to the 39 Articles of Religion (see Chapter 11).

The presence of Charles Simeon (1759–1836) in the university community is worthy of note here. A fellow of King's College, Simeon was appointed vicar of Holy Trinity Church in Cambridge in 1783 at the age of 24. He remained a resident fellow of King's College his entire life. His preaching both in that church and when he took his turn as a preacher at the university was compelling and personal. It was not uncommon for him to close his sermons with genuine, racking tears or to cause his congregation to weep as well. Besides his preaching, Simeon also held Friday evening conversation parties in his rooms at King's. Discussion was frank and probing. He spoke with students about their personal faith, about the challenges of the clergyman's life, and about practical matters, such as homiletics. The young men who followed him were as numerous and enthusiastic as those who later followed Newman at Oxford. Wordsworth's brother Christopher attended at least one of his Sunday evening sermons.[46] Simeon's 21-volume *Horae Homileticae* (1819–1828) is a collection of his sermons and a guide to sermon-writing; it includes scholarly explications of scripture to assist young preachers. It sold well and earned him a rather astonishing £5,000. Searby contrasts Simeon's scholarly but narrow, literal readings of scripture negatively with Whewell's efforts, a bit later, to align his studies of natural philosophy with a broader Anglican faith. Simeon's work, however, was 'the most important single influence on many generations of Cambridge ordinands'.[47] In his long life, Simeon had a hand in training and encouraging close to a third of the men called to the Anglican ministry in the Romantic

---

[44] John Newton, a repentant former slave trader, became his spiritual advisor, and shortly thereafter Wilberforce began campaigning for abolition.
[45] Green, 'Religion in the Colleges', p. 466.
[46] Christopher Wordsworth, *Social Life*, p. 599.
[47] Searby, pp. 335, 328.

Educating the Romantic Poets

and early Victorian periods. He also helped to establish the Church Missionary Society and was involved in the Religious Tract Society and the British and Foreign Bible Society.

Church music in the Georgian period

Along with seriously devout university men such as Simeon and Frend, the architecture of the college churches and chapels, and the language of the Anglican liturgies, the music used in these services is worthy of attention. Church music at the schools and colleges in the period was usually performed by trained choirs of men and boys, and it was restrained and decorous. Low-church Anglican scholars considered congregational singing of the now well-known and admired hymns of Isaac Watts or the Wesleys undignified and 'enthusiastic' (a bad thing). Oxford's high church men also discouraged singing in church.[48] Hymns by Richard Baxter and the Olney hymns[49] by John Newton and William Cowper were sometimes sung, but the preferred religious music in the Georgian schools and colleges was heard, not sung, by communicants. Directed by professional musicians, these highly trained choirs were usually accompanied by organs and, sometimes, by strings and woodwinds. Three colleges at Oxford—Christ Church, New College, and Magdalen—were famous for their choral music and annual musical performances. Byron's college chapel had an excellent all-male choir; and, as is well known, the poet was especially fond of one of the choristers. Trinity also had one of the best organs available, constructed between 1694 and 1706 by the famous organ builder 'Father' Bernard Smith (c.1630–1708). In his second sonnet about King's College Chapel, in *Ecclesiastical Sketches*, Part III, 'XXV The Same' Wordsworth comments on the acoustics in King's College Chapel:

> But from the arms of silence—list! O list!
> The music burstest into second life;
> The notes luxuriate, every stone is kissed
> By sound, or ghost of sound, in mazy strife;
> Heart-thrilling strains, that cast, before the eye
> Of the devout, a veil of ecstasy![50]

---

[48] Brockliss, p. 219.

[49] The Olney Hymns, which were written for a poor country church and express early English evangelism, were originally published in February 1779. The most famous of these hymns is 'Amazing Grace'. During Wordsworth's and Coleridge's middle age, these hymns were widely published, though, as far as I can tell, they were not typically used in broad church services during their lifetimes.

[50] Jackson, *Sonnet Series*, p. 202, ll. 9–14.

Religious Instruction and Worship in the Anglo-Classical Academy

The composers that were popular in Georgian period included Henry Purcell (1659–1695), William Croft (1678–1727), George Frederick Handel (1685–1759), Benjamin Cooke (1734–1793), and Thomas Attwood (1765–1838). Selections from their work, along with canticles or chants, and the metrical psalms of Sternhold and Hopkins,[51] were the musical works most commonly performed by school and college choirs. Handel's *Messiah* was a staple of the Oxford *Encaenia* celebrations, which culminated in an enthusiastic performance of the Hallelujah Chorus. Metrical psalms used ballad or 'common metre' with alternating lines of tetrameter and trimeter. In services they were 'lined out', a process in which the music leader, deacon, or clergyman would sing the psalm one line at a time, and the congregation would repeat each phrase after him. The proliferation of the Sternhold and Hopkins Psalter directly influenced the popularity of poems and tunes in this metre.[52] Walker points out that, thanks to years of church attendance in their youth, the Romantic poets were well aware of common metre, and she points to Coleridge's use of it in 'Rime of the Ancient Mariner' and to Byron's use of Wesley's 'long metre' in 'She Walks in Beauty'. She asserts that, in both cases, the reading audience would have recognised these metres from mornings spent in church. Some in the period found metrical psalms monotonous and complained that their inversions were awkward and their progressions plodding. One eighteenth-century commentator cited by Temperley scoffed at 'the miserable scandalous doggerel of Hopkins and Sternhold' and cringed at the 'screaming of boys who bawl out what they neither feel nor understand'.[53] Others in the period, however, found this choral practice uplifting. An eighteenth-century clergyman quoted by Temperley encouraged his colleagues to teach their congregations, especially the youth, with psalmody, noting how 'inexpressibly elevating' it is to hear 'the voice of a great multitude, as the voice of many waters and of mighty thunders, to speak in the words of Scripture, making a joyful noise to the God of their salvation, and singing His praises with understanding'.[54]

---

[51] The first edition of the Sternhold and Hopkins psalms is dated 1547. By the eighteenth century the *Book of Common Prayer* also included metrical psalms produced in collaboration with the poet laureate Nahum Tate (1652–1715) and a royal chaplain, Nicholas Brady (1659–1726). Other hymns, including the Doxology of Thomas Ken (1637–1711), one of the great Anglican hynodists, were added to the *BCP* during the early Victorian period.

[52] Walker, p. 24.

[53] Temperley, p. 240.

[54] Temperley, p. 241.

Educating the Romantic Poets

Lessons in the faith

As already explained, the original purpose of teaching Latin, Greek, and Hebrew was to enable students to read the scriptures in their earliest forms and to interpret them accurately. For classroom instruction in religious matters schoolmasters used the *Book of Common Prayer*, Grotius's *De veritate religionis Christianae* (*On the Truth of the Christian Religion*), *The Whole Duty of Man*, and the scriptures themselves. Monday morning lessons for the little boys began with an assignment in the New Testament. The last lesson on Saturdays typically ended with recitation of the catechism and the school prayer. At Westminster in Vincent's time schoolboys translated psalms from the Hebrew and selections from the Gospels in Latin every day. Each week they were assigned a verse composition on a psalm or a sermon. Older pupils wrote themes on passages from the New Testament, the psalms, and events in biblical history. According to Vincent, the most important and intensive series of lessons at Westminster was the Sacred Exercise, which was based on Grotius's *De veritate religionis Christianae*. Typical of seventeenth-century European Protestant apologetics, this work influenced many Enlightenment thinkers and eighteenth-century deists, including Thomas Jefferson.[55] Grotius (1593–1645), who was a Dutch jurist, argues in lawyerly fashion that the beliefs and morals of the Christian church are reasonable and enlightened, and that the 'end of Man is Happiness *after* this Life'. In addition, he urges tolerance of Muslims, Jews, and 'pagans', and unity among the various denominations within the Church. Vincent claims that no other lesson received more time or eager attention from schoolmasters than the Sacred Exercise, the whole of which took two years to complete.[56] Schools also taught older boys church history and required them to read sermons of notable churchmen. Arnold lectured all students on the English Reformation, and each week he included two lessons on the Old or New Testament in the sixth form's schedule. He emphasised the language of texts and their historical context and included biographies of the characters mentioned in the readings. If Arnold discussed a psalm, he encouraged boys to do what he been taught to do as pupil at Winchester: commit the text to memory. Many of the assignments he gave to sixth-form students required them to address theological issues. One such prompt was: *valet rerum ipsarum scientia, nisi accedat ingenii vigor, quæ informem molem in veram doctrinam effingat* ('Little does knowledge of mere things advance us unless attended by a spiritual vigor capable of turning a shapeless mass into true doctrine').

The Georgian universities required all students, not just those bound for the clergy, to study scripture, particularly the four Gospels, theology,

---

[55] Thomas Jefferson is reputed to have given a copy of Grotius' work to his son-in-law.
[56] Vincent, *Defence*, p. 37.

sermons, and homiletics. College students reviewed Grotius and studied William Paley's *Natural Theology, or Evidences of the Existence and Attributes of the Deity* (1802). They read scriptural commentaries, the writings of the church fathers, and texts such as Pearson's explication of the Apostle's Creed. Between 1783 and 1823 all students at Corpus Christi were required to abridge Dr Randolph's Divinity Lectures and to attend the college president's lectures on the 39 Articles of Religion.[57] At Christ Church the catechist and theological lecturer James Chelsum (1740–1801), a vocal opponent of Gibbon, delivered *pro bono* weekly lectures on religious topics, including especially miracles. The university-wide exam that all Oxford students took after their second year covered Old Testament and Church history, the English Reformation, the four Gospels, Paley, and the 39 Articles. The Oxford Schools examination taken by seniors seeking high honours and fellowships included questions on Genesis and 50 psalms in Hebrew; on the Gospels of Matthew, Mark, Luke, and John in Greek; Grotius's theology; and the Apostle's Creed. University exams at Cambridge covered a similar range of religious texts. The Oxford royal commissioners reported that, because of the 'very large preponderance of the theological element' in the studies and religious practices at the universities, a 'man who can take a degree is already in point of attainments three-fourths of a Clerk in Orders'.[58] This is significant news for scholars.

University students also studied homiletics. The sermons of John Tillotson (1630–1694, archbishop of Canterbury) and Dr Robert South (1634–1716, prebendary of Westminster and Canon of Christ Church) were often used as exemplars and for explication exercises. Known for his broad-church approach to the faith, Tillotson's style has been described as 'simple, elegant, candid, clear, and rational'.[59] Recurring themes for Tillotson were man's duty to God and to his neighbour, the importance of education, and family religion.[60] According to Davies, Tillotson and his followers preferred a decidedly 'urbane' Jesus. 'The Virtues of his Life', Tillotson wrote

> are pure, without any Mixture of Infirmity and Imperfection. He had Humility without Meanness of Spirit; Innocency without Weakness; Wisdom without Cunning; and Constancy and Resolution in that which was good, without Stiffness of Conceit, and Peremptoriness of Humour: In a word, his Virtues were shining without Vanity, Heroical

---

[57] Green, 'Religion in the Colleges', p. 433.
[58] Hinds, p. x.
[59] Qtd in Davies, p. 7. Warburton was a literary critic and friend of Alexander Pope.
[60] See his *Sixteen Sermons*, published in 1694, especially Sermon VI.

without anything of Transport, and very extraordinary without being in the least extravagant.[61]

Among Dr South's topics were 'Wisdom', 'The Image of God in Man, and 'The Practice of Religion Enforced by Reason.[62] College men wrote critiques of these sermons and were directed to read 'moralistic' tomes and popular devotional works as well. No doubt these were the texts—'the works of our best moralists ... collections of the finest letters ... memoirs of characters of worth and suffering ... and the strongest examples of moral and religious endurance'—that Jane Austen's character Anne Elliot suggests to the sorrow-stricken Captain Benwick as substitutes for the poetry of Byron and Scott.[63]

Other religious texts studied by Romantic-period college men included Oxford's Bampton lectures on church doctrine,[64] which typically addressed topics such as the authority of scripture, the doctrine of atonement, religious enthusiasm, and challenges to the Church of England by atheists, Unitarians, and other nonconformists. The university sermons and Bampton lectures are collected in multivolume editions and provide a trove of texts worthy of further exploration by literary scholars of the period.[65] The Bampton preachers at Oxford whose sermons were most often admired in the Romantic period include James Ussher (1793), John Eveleigh (1794), Thomas Wirtle (1794), and Henry Matthew (1797); important sermons at Cambridge during the same

---

[61] Qtd in Davies, p. 56.
[62] See South.
[63] Austen, p. 73.
[64] The Bampton Lectures are eight lecture-sermons preached at the Oxford university church on Sundays in the Lent and Act terms. Established in 1780, they continue to this day and are considered to be Protestant Christendom's most distinguished lectureships. The discourses were designed to 'confirm and establish the Christian Faith, and to confute all heretics and schismatics', to support the authority of the scriptures and the writings of the church fathers, and to affirm the idea of the Trinity as 'comprehended in the Apostle's and Nicene creeds', as stated in the will of the Rev. John Bampton (1690–1751). Bampton lecturers included public orators, college chaplains, fellows, doctors of divinity, and college heads. Among them were Edward Tatham (1789, rector of Lincoln College; his lectures were entitled 'The Chart and Scale of Truth'), John Everleigh (1792, provost of Oriel College, his lectures endeavored to 'state regularly the substance of our religion from its earliest declarations in the Scriptures of both the Old and New Testaments to its complete publication after the resurrection of Christ'), and Richard Whately (1822, fellow of Oriel; his lectures were entitled 'The Use and Abuse of Party Feeling in Matter of Religion'). Other sermons were on 'Practical Faith' (1783); 'A Comparison of Mahometism and Christianity' (1784); 'The Use and Abuse of Reason' (1786); 'A view of the evidences of Christianity at the close of the pretended age of reason' (1805); and 'The truth and consistence of divine revelation; with some remarks on the contrary extremes of Infidelity and Enthusiasm' (1811).
[65] Sermons are available, sorted by the years they were preached, and can be accessed here: http://anglicanhistory.org/england/bampton/. Accessed 5 April 2023.

Religious Instruction and Worship in the Anglo-Classical Academy

period were those of William Craven (1783), Isaac Barrow (1788), Charles Simeon (1794), and James Fawcett (1794).[66]

Georgian opinions about the purpose and style of preaching can be discerned from various handbooks of the period. In 1783 the chaplain of Christ Church College, John Cooke, published *The Preacher's Assistant ... Containing A Series of the Texts of Sermons and Discourses published singly or in volumes by Divines of the Church of England ... from the Reformation to the Present*. In two volumes of over 1,000 pages, Cooke's collection includes sermons that were thought at that time to be of importance, including some by dissenters. Topics are arranged according to the books of the Old and New Testament and cover issues such as piety, friendship, faith, the duties of parents, blasphemy, murder, suicide, covetousness, slander, and adultery. John Napleton's *Advice to a Student in the University, Concerning the Qualifications and Duties of a Minister of the Gospel in the Church of England* (1795) seems to have been popular at the universities. A preacher is expected, Napleton claims, to have as 'melodious' a voice as possible, to read with 'judicious pauses, emphases, and change of voice as may help to open' the meaning of the psalms and lessons to the hearer and 'impress it upon his mind'.[67] To do this, the minister must have a full and 'correct knowledge of the sacred texts' from having studied them in their original languages.[68] Napleton's sermon-writing advice includes the suggestion that all compositions be perspicuous, easily understood, and presented in 'direct' language.[69] He counselled students to avoid figurative expressions, to speak in 'our Mother Tongue', and to avoid affectation or flourishes from foreign tongues, especially French.[70] He emphasises that sermons should be well organised, with statements, proofs, and illustrations offered in short, almost mathematically logical steps.[71] Students should also keep in mind, Napleton writes, that the clergyman's duty is to be a 'Rational Agent ... Spiritual Counsellor, and Charitable Friend'.[72]

As far as the content of sermons goes, Napleton reminds students that the clergyman's ultimate responsibility is 'to instruct and persuade in things pertaining to the eternal happiness of mankind'.[73] He urges university students not to 'disturb the minds of a Congregation with doubts' about their religion

---

[66] Dates refer to the years these men preached their most often cited sermons at the university.
[67] Napleton, pp. 46, 48.
[68] Napleton, p. 51.
[69] Napleton, p. 58.
[70] Napleton, p. 62.
[71] Napleton, p. 59.
[72] Napleton, p. 73.
[73] Napleton, p. 64.

Educating the Romantic Poets

that may not have ever occurred to them and to avoid reference to the complicated theological questions that they study at the university.[74] He also counsels students not to take on critics of the church or atheists.[75] Instead, Napleton asserts that the Anglican minister should focus upon teaching his flock the attributes of God, which Napleton lists as his power, love, patience, mercy, steadfastness, and his gift of a Saviour. Finally, the clergyman should remind communicants that God calls them to obedience and to have faith that they will meet their reward in Heaven.

Did the schools' religious instruction and discipline have real or lasting effects upon students? Perhaps it inflamed a few with an early love of God and religion. It is more likely that such instruction went above the pupils' heads, bored them, or gave them cause, as in the case of young Southey, to resent religious authority.[76] Westminster's Vincent admits, 'we cast our bread upon the waters ... we experience no instantaneous conviction or conversion, nor do we hope it; and if we asserted it, it might be justly replied it is easy to make boys as well as men hypocrites, but very difficult to make them religious.'[77] Noting that the age of reflection will arrive eventually for his students, Vincent continues: 'men, even young men, feel the want and consolation of religion: and it is when those thoughts present themselves, that memory will suggest the precepts and principles, proposed to them in their youth. It is to that period we look for word of success.'[78]

Even if a young man was willing and open to religious instruction, it is difficult to measure how chapel services, divinity studies, Anglican homiletics, private study or prayer groups, or beautiful chapels and church music, shaped what the Romantic poets felt, thought, or wrote. Wordsworth's question—who knows 'the individual hour in which/His habits were first sown, even as a seed?'[79]—is a fair one. Nevertheless, the story of the Romantics' religious training seems worthy of renewed or expanded study by twenty-first-century scholars.[80] A number of recent studies by scholars of education about how college affects students also seem to support such a line of inquiry. For example, some of these researchers have found that students' academic performance and leadership skills are impacted positively in institutions that encourage spiritual or religious discussion.[81] Other studies have

---

[74] Napleton, pp. 68–69.
[75] Napleton, p. 71.
[76] See Southey, 'No. V'.
[77] Vincent, *Defence*, p. 41.
[78] Vincent, *Defence*, pp. 41–42.
[79] *Prelude*, 1805, Bk 2, ll. 211–212.
[80] See Ryan; Deboo; Ulmer; Wright, *Samuel Taylor Coleridge*; Barbeau, *Religion in Romantic England* and *The Cambridge Companion to British Romanticism and Religion*.
[81] Mayhew, *et al.*, p. 239. Another of the studies surveyed finds that the higher the

Religious Instruction and Worship in the Anglo-Classical Academy

suggested that the institutional mission of a university 'plays an important role in fostering citizenship', civic values, and student behaviours.[82] Though using this data retrospectively to comment on students who were part of a very different academic environment and historical moment has its limitations, it seems safe to assume that students in the Georgian schools and universities were not entirely deaf or blind to what they heard and witnessed in the religious parts of their education. The turn in Wordsworth's, Coleridge's, and Southey's religious politics from the radicalism of their early days to the traditional Anglicanism of their maturity affirm this assumption.

Using the Romantics' religious education

The scope of this book does not allow for an extensive exploration of the diverse and changing religious writing of the Romantic poets trained in the Anglo-classical tradition. But it does make it clear that by the time college students in Wordsworth's, Byron's, and Tennyson's generations reached adulthood, they were entirely familiar with scripture, biblical language, Anglican liturgies, contemporaneous religious beliefs, and theological controversies. They were also well acquainted with and related to clergymen, and they understood the church hierarchy and the role it played in English history, politics, culture, and aesthetics. This information can be useful in critical interpretation of certain texts. It also helps to explain contemporaneous reception of those works. For example, the history of schoolboys' and college men's time spent in church explains why many in Wordsworth's audience after 1820 appreciated *The River Duddon* and *Ecclesiastical Sketches* more than most modern readers do. As Tim Fulford explains in *Wordsworth's Poetry, 1815–1845*, these sonnet sequences articulate 'spirituality as the product of a tradition' that many of Wordsworth's readers shared, and the verses employed a poetic form that they knew and appreciated.[83] Fulford argues quite convincingly, however, that these verses were not just expressions of faith but also 'a materialization of [Wordsworth's] own devotion to traditional poetics' and should be appreciated as 'a radical historicization and monumentalization of art'.[84]

The nature of the religious aspects of the Romantics' education also helps to explain Byron's religious thought and what Ryan aptly labels his 'metaphysical versatility'.[85] Reviewing Byron's comments on religion, ranging from deism

---

degree of 'religiousness of the student body', the more likely students will be individually charitable in later life, p. 322.
[82] Mayhew, *et al.*, p. 322.
[83] Fulford, *Wordsworth's Poetry*, p. 214.
[84] Fulford, *Wordsworth's Poetry*, pp. 215, 238.
[85] Ryan, p. 122.

to unquestioning belief, Ryan argues that Byron achieved a sort of religious 'oscillation': that is, a

> regular, predictable, harmonic motion between two opposing intellectual tendencies whose mutual correction resulted in something much closer to equipoise than to turmoil. Since neither scepticism nor uncritical belief seemed to him an adequate response to the condition of the universe, he deliberately adopted a strategic position between the two alternatives.[86]

Byron's cagey ambivalence about religious matters surfaces in *Manfred*, when, despite the hero's unhallowed studies, as he is dying, he asks for the abbot's hand and holds it as he passes away. Elsewhere, in *Don Juan*, when referring to sages and other good men, he compares them to one who is 'Diviner Still', with a note clarifying that he means 'CHRIST', adding that 'If ever God was man—or Man God—he was *both*. I never arraigned his creed, but the use—or abuse of it.'[87] Where, but in his Anglican school days at Harrow, where he lived a daily, settled routine that began and ended in prayer and where he was treated with kindness and respect by his clergyman teachers, could he have come to such notions?

Shelley's atheism was a hotter version of Byron's disdain for the corruptions of organised religion, which he began to express at Eton. While Shelley had little respect for religion at school, the quality of instruction in scripture, theology, and morality at Eton deserves some credit for the subtlety of Shelley's philosophical thought and his uncompromising hostility towards oppression, injustice, and deceit. His readiness to publish 'The Necessity of Atheism' at Oxford, where he knew leadership was fully committed to the established church, speaks as much about his intellectual confidence—gained from training at Eton—as it does about his theology. His rejection in that essay of the authority of others, his insistence that believers are simply intellectually lazy, and his declaration that 'An educated man ceases to be superstitious' are

---

[86] Ryan, p. 124. Ryan also notes that the Christian Socialist F. D. Maurice considered Byron 'a true friend of religion' (p. 120). Much to his disgust, Percy Shelley recognised that Byron had an abiding religious belief. Hobhouse insisted that his friend lived his entire life with an intimate sense of 'divinity, although he could not account for it' (p. 123). When Thomas Moore expressed his concern about the irreligious aspects of *Cain*, Byron wrote to him saying, 'I am no enemy of religion, but the contrary. As a proof I am educating my natural daughter a strict Catholic in a convent in Romagna; for I think people can never have *enough* of religion, if they have any' (qtd in Marchand, *Byron: A Biography*, vol. 3, p. 977). Though the reply drips with Byron's usual irony, the fact that he saw education as the route to religious belief is worth noting.

[87] McGann, *Lord Byron: The Major Works*, p. 823, *Don Juan*, Canto XI, Stanzas 17–18, ll. 131, 135–136, 138. Note for p. 823, p. 1067.

further evidence of the effects of an Eton education. We might also surmise that Shelley imbibed some metaphysical effects from his years in the Eton chapel, for throughout his writing he often expresses his sense of an eternal world spirit, 'The awful shadow of some unseen Power ... Spirit of BEAUTY' that visits 'each human heart'.[88] Moreover, the language and forms of his atheism are often informed by his schoolboy training in scripture. Obvious examples are his reference to Isaiah 29:11 in 'England in 1819' and the way he draws broadly from Christian millennial hopes in *Hellas* to imagine a new world order similar to that prophesied in the book of Matthew and an apocalypse like that portrayed in Revelations.

Of all the Romantics, Coleridge was the most religious, and the seeds of his lifelong engagement with spiritual and theological matters, what Holmes has called his 'religious, mystical conception of the world',[89] were planted in his earliest childhood, when he played in his father's church and churchyard, where he read the Bible (at the age of three) and heard the bells he later describes in 'Frost at Midnight'. These seeds began to sprout during his eight years as a Grecian at Christ's Hospital, where he was being prepared to follow his father to university and service in the Anglican church. Once at Cambridge, though he attended services twice a day, his maturing reason began to balk at some of the teachings of the established church. Fired by the events in France and reaction in England and by the writing, preaching, and controversial treatment of free thinkers such as the Jesus College tutor William Frend, Coleridge proclaimed himself a Unitarian. Believing he could no longer enter the Church in good conscience, and encouraged by the similarly disenchanted Robert Southey, the two friends left their colleges intent upon enacting their scheme of Pantisocracy. To earn money they did service of the sort expected of the clergyman–educators who had trained them both, they lectured and preached. Moreover, the dream of Pantisocracy appears to have been, among other things, an effort to recreate the semi-monastic life both had experienced in their boarding schools and with their college friends.

'Religious Musings' (1794–96), which was begun during his last term at Jesus College, exercises Coleridge's conflicted religious thoughts and questions and connects them with ongoing conversations begun at college about politics, utopian communities, the French Revolution, and English radicalism. If Coleridge's religious training is taken into consideration, 'The Eolian Harp', the first version of which was published in 1795 as 'Effusion XXXV', might be viewed not as a celebration of the Romantic imagination and rejection of religious dogma but as a cautionary tale to dissenters. Indeed, if read without the famous 'one life' passion, which was not added until 1816, the poem

---

[88] 'Hymn to Intellectual Beauty', Reiman and Powers, p. 93, ll. 1, 13, 7.
[89] Holmes, p. 19.

might also be understood as a homely revision of the Fall narrative, in which the beloved's 'mild reproof' of the speaker's 'Dim and unhallowed' thoughts, offered out of love and concern for his soul, moves him toward a sort of earthly resurrection and restores him to the couple's little garden paradise.[90]

Understanding the nature of Wordsworth's religious experiences in school and college helps to explain four phenomena to which Stephen Gill and Tim Fulford have called attention in their books *Wordsworth, A Life* (1990) and *Wordsworth's Poetry, 1815–1845* (2019). These are Wordsworth's embrace of religious and political orthodoxy, dating more or less from the publication of *The Excursion* in 1815; his focus upon churches and church history as the subjects of his later poems; his return to traditional forms such as odes, sonnets, inscriptions, and memorials; and the reception of his verse by his classically trained and nominally Anglican audience.

Both Hawkshead School and St John's College perpetuated religious traditions that were part of Wordsworth's (and his wife's) childhood and that became part of his life as a married man and father. Wordsworth's mother made sure her children attended services in the parish church. His house mother, Ann Tyson, continued this practice during his eight years at school, so his participation in daily prayer services and instruction in 'divinity' during his school and college days connected with his childhood experiences and lay in waiting as a resource in his later days as he began to raise a family. That family life was not without soul-shaking heartbreak—the drowning of his brother John in 1805 and the deaths of his daughter Catherine and favoured son Thomas in 1812. In his 30s and 40s, reviews of his poetry—particularly those out of Edinburgh—caused frustration and real professional and financial anxieties for him and his family. What he experienced in England after Peterloo—'political changes, political remedies, [and] political nostrums'—so worried Wordsworth that he came to believe that only 'virtue and religion' could bring relief to the 'great evils, sin, bondage, and misery' he beheld.[91] As Fulford rightly comments, much of his poetry after 1819 portrays the Lake District as a 'landscape where English spirituality could be discovered'.[92] The evidence of his education, his family experiences, his brother Christopher's leadership at Cambridge, his later letters and *Ecclesiastical Sketches* (1822) suggest that these sonnets were not only written for a national audience (and as a move to appeal to popular taste) but were also a genuine effort for himself—and his family—to recall, name, and confirm private experiences of faith—or

---

[90] Jackson, *Samuel Taylor Coleridge*. 'Coleridge's "Eolian Harp"', p. 29, ll. 49, 50, and Ross, '"Restore Me to Reality"'.

[91] Comments to the American Unitarian minister, Orville Dewey. Qtd in Gates, p. 129.

[92] Fulford, *Late Poetry*, p. 206.

lessons about the Church—that might sustain them. Indeed, such sustenance was necessary as the family faced the challenges of Dorothy's decline, Dora's death, and William and Mary's old age. The later years of Wordsworth's life appear to demonstrate the truth of the Westminster headmaster's observation that men will 'feel the want and consolation of religion'; and, when they do, their memories 'will suggest the [Anglican] precepts and principles proposed to them in their youth'.[93] Wordsworth's later, more religiously orthodox work, and that of Coleridge and Southey as well, might be considered the 'word of success' for which Vincent and other Anglican schoolmasters looked.

In midlife Wordsworth linked the church to education and the need to lift the nation out of its troubles. He spoke approvingly of the 'distinctly understood religious purposes' and 'moral influence' of the English grammar schools,[94] and he made sure his sons were educated in the tradition by clergymen. In *The Excursion*, Book IX, Wordsworth calls for education that might replace the 'ignorance' that breeds 'dark discontent' with 'moral and religious truth,/ Both understood and practiced' and that might thereby open a 'Vast circumference of hope' for the entire nation.[95] The poem itself is a remarkable review of four different approaches to religious faith that circulated in the Romantic period. The narrator expresses a more or less unexamined acceptance of Anglican orthodoxy; the Solitary is disillusioned with the failure of the Church to succour the poor; the Pastor discourses on the mysteries of faith and the meaning of suffering; and the Wanderer speaks for religion of nature. Written at the time when Catholic emancipation was being hotly debated and when momentum for both the Oxford Movement and the evangelicals' Great Awakening was growing, the poem tackles questions that were very much on his English audience's mind: what 'true religion should be … and what one must do to be saved'.[96] A decade later, in a letter to George Beaumont, the poet reflects upon 'the religion of gratitude' in a way that brings together all four religious discourses in *The Excursion* and suggests that at the very least the scriptural lessons that were so much a part of Wordsworth's Anglo-classical education stayed with him in later life. He wrote that

> the religion of gratitude cannot mislead us. Of that we are sure, and gratitude is the handmaid to hope, and hope the harbinger of faith. I look abroad upon Nature, I think of the best part of our species, I lean upon my friends, and I meditate upon the Scriptures, especially the

---

[93] Vincent, *Defence*, pp. 41–42.
[94] WWLMY, p. 23.
[95] WWPW, pp. 692–693, ll. 293–398.
[96] Ryan, p. 104.

Educating the Romantic Poets

Gospel of St. John; and my creed rises up of itself with the ease of an exhalation yet a fabric of adamant.[97]

In 1837 he wrote to his daughter Dora: 'You know how deeply I am interested in the education, above all the religious education of the people.'[98] In 1839 he wrote to Robinson that he wished to support a plan 'of Education in connection with and under the superintendence of the Church of England'.[99] Given Wordsworth's personal history and the place of the Church in his education and English culture, rather than dismissing his later, more religiously orthodox work as a desertion of 'songs consecrate to truth and liberty', as Shelley charges in 'To Wordsworth', it seems more accurate to read expressions in *The Excursion*, *The River Duddon*, and *Ecclesiastical Sketches* as mature efforts to deliver what Wordsworth had come to believe was a higher truth and a different, more traditionally English idea of liberty. The Church, to which so many of his later works refer, operated for him and many others in the trying times of the early nineteenth century as a reassuring and unifying local agent and a foundation of English nationhood.

A second phenomenon that the Anglo-classical schools' religious life helps to explain is Wordsworth's 'preoccupation' with Church history and church architecture in his sonnets.[100] In his biography of Wordsworth, Stephen Gill asserts that in the years after *Lyrical Ballads* and the 1799 *Prelude* Wordsworth wrote to explore 'what he knew and could trust'.[101] Fulford is even more specific, claiming that most of Wordsworth's later poems are 'profound explorations of the poet's task and searching meditations on the sources of power'.[102] In his earlier days, Wordsworth figures Nature as the source of that power. It is well known that as a schoolboy he rambled happily among and was inspired by the mountains and lakes of his native county, but during those days he also prayed almost every day in chapel and visited country churches and their churchyards. Fulford argues that Wordsworth came to believe that the English Church, with its history and its 'holy buildings', was the source of power for which he was looking, and his use of this figure in his later works was a 'materialization of his own devotion to traditional poetics'.[103] Given Wordsworth's experience at school, where he and so many others in his audience received their first training in poetics, where they learned to hear the music and to recognise the generic conventions of classical and biblical verse, and where they spent hours

---

[97] Qtd in Moorman, *William Wordsworth: A Biography: Later Years 1803–1850*, p. 107.
[98] De Selincourt, p. 489.
[99] De Selincourt, p. 709.
[100] Fulford, *Wordsworth's Poetry*, p. 214.
[101] Gill, *Wordsworth: A Life*, p. 152.
[102] Fulford, *Wordsworth's Poetry*, p. 4.
[103] Fulford, *Wordsworth's Poetry*, p. 215.

every week in Anglican spaces reciting Anglican prayers, this connection, or 'materialization', makes total sense. Wordsworth's use of church buildings to 'suggest how personal spirituality may take public shape'[104] harkened to positive memories he and many other similarly educated readers had of the Church and the cultural standard it represented. It should be noted as well that some of the *Ecclesiastical Sketches*, such as 'XXII Catechising', 'XXIII Confirmation', 'XXIV Confirmation Continued', and 'XXV Sacrament', attend quite specifically to the religious experiences of schoolchildren and their parents. The two sonnets on confirmation depict children as they seriously and self-consciously speak with 'their own lips ... the solemn promise' of the 'baptismal Vow'[105] and a mother's trembling and tearful joy as she witnesses the scene. 'Sacrament' depicts the first communion, that mysterious event for which many schoolboys had been carefully prepared by their headmasters.[106]

A third phenomenon in Wordsworth's career that has roots in both the religious and composition training of the Anglo-classical academy is his reclaiming the cultural authority of that training by more frequently alluding to scripture and Latin and Greek verse; by writing epistles and inscriptions, which are not only classical but also scriptural forms; and by his almost obsessive experimentation in the second half of his life with the tight, rhyming form of the sonnet.[107] As Fulford points out, between 1820 and the end of his life Wordsworth wrote more than 350 sonnets. He argues that Wordsworth developed the sonnet, and more specifically sonnets about church buildings and Church history, in order to articulate 'spirituality as the product of a tradition ... that had developed ... out of a distant [and shared] past'.[108] Noting that the sonnet form recalled for his audience the Protestant sonnets of Milton, Donne, and Herbert, Fulford also points out that the sonnet form gave Wordsworth the structure his oft-maligned blank verse could not.[109] As explained in Chapters 3 and 4, Wordsworth and other grammar schoolboys had been given remarkably regular and carefully structured practice in producing verse in specific traditional forms. A constant backdrop to the days when Wordsworth and his classmates were doing such work was unquestioned faith in the Anglican Church and echoes of the short metrical psalms used in services. Those days at school were also the ones in which Wordsworth first felt the passion and power of poetry and the pleasure and charm 'Of words in tuneful order'.[110] After the 'malevolence' and 'ignorance' expressed in the

---

[104] Fulford, *Wordsworth's Poetry*, p. 214.
[105] Jackson, *Sonnet Series*, p. 209, ll. 4–6.
[106] Jackson, *Sonnet Series*, p. 210.
[107] Fulford, *Wordsworth's Poetry*, p. 42.
[108] Fulford, *Wordsworth's Poetry*, p. 214.
[109] Fulford, *Wordsworth's Poetry*, p. 224.
[110] *Prelude*, 1850, p. 183, ll. 5554–5556.

Educating the Romantic Poets

searingly negative reviews of *Poems in Two Volumes* published in 1807[111] and the singeing comments that Jeffrey and others made about Wordsworth's blank verse in *The Excursion*, what better time for Wordsworth to call upon his schoolboy verse-writing talents, memories of psalmody, and his training in self-discipline by writing tightly constructed short poems, such as the rhymed couplets of the inscriptions and the rhymed octaves and sestets of sonnets?[112] It is also worth noting that the small space of retirement that is described in 'Nuns fret not' and that is the 'space' of all the sonnets is not too different from his room at St John's. Added to this, the participation of the nuns and hermits in church services parallels that of Anglican grammar schoolboys and college men in the Romantic period. The monastic influences in Wordsworth's poetry that have been discussed by scholars such as Fay and Fulford can also be attributed to his lived experience his Anglo-classical grammar school and university (see also Chapter 11).

A fourth phenomenon—Wordsworth's reception in his own time—also makes more sense when the nature of the religious as well as the linguistic training of the Anglo-classical academy is recognised. Gill catalogues and Fulford discusses how the early poems—those that modern scholars have long cited as Wordsworth's greatest works—were rejected by many of his contemporaries for their Jacobinism, their 'disrespect for established canons of taste', 'contempt for the conventional readership for poetry', and implicit disregard for traditional Anglican thought and practice.[113] Both scholars also point out how the later poems, such as the *River Duddon, Ecclesiastical Sketches*, and *Yarrow Revisited* (1835)—which have until recently been largely discounted by modern scholars—were considered by the nineteenth-century audience to be Wordsworth's best works. Some of these verses describe church buildings, memorialise churchgoing, or enact movements of the Anglican liturgy, as the 'Evening Voluntaries' do.[114] Still others recount English church history and religious traditions. These subjects were familiar and their terse, restrained, and impersonal style, as Fulford notes, was appealing to a reading audience that included literate church women and men who had been schooled in latitudinarian manners and who had been trained to appreciate (and compose) tightly controlled traditional verse forms. Fulford points out that these poems, which 'idealize the church's ideological role in ensuring local and national order', were also a 'self-defensive and self-interested act' for Wordsworth.[115]

[111] *WWLMY*, p. 145.
[112] Fulford points out that, after reading some of these bad reviews, Wordsworth sent Miltonic sonnets to the papers and started translating Michelangelo's Petrarchan sonnets. The latter exercise was a typical one for Anglican schoolboys.
[113] Fulford, *Wordsworth's Poetry*, p. 217.
[114] Fulford, *Wordsworth's Poetry*, p. 242.
[115] Fulford, *Wordsworth's Poetry*, p. 225.

They helped to scrub away his reputation as an egotistical Jacobin, which had plagued him since 1798. Fulford points out that these poems did much more, though, than redeem Wordsworth's reputation in the eyes of the nineteenth-century English establishment. He argues that they show Wordsworth to be a still-growing, still experimenting poet, for they 'dramatize the conflict between a recurrent concern to situate the self (writer and reader) in a larger whole within which it can find meaning (a historical institution or poetic tradition) and a restless need to reshape that whole or to preserve difference from it'.[116] The evidence of these later poems, and the diligence and determination of the aging poet to perfect them, are testimony of the long-term power of his training in school.

In sum, modern scholars would do well to take note of the Anglican boyhood and college days of the poets who attended services *every* day in consecrated, often beautiful spaces, accompanied by sacred music. Though sometimes students simply endured or even slept through these services, the Anglican liturgy, sacred readings, and prayers nevertheless invited them, repeatedly, to contemplate serious matters and to meditate upon unseen higher things in carefully crafted language. Putting aside the beliefs and politics of the Anglo-classical tradition and Romantic writers' theories and debates about the nature of the faculties of reason, fancy, passion, and imagination and the roles they play in composition, the act of thinking about and perhaps embracing some sort of religious faith in an abstract being or higher power, which is what Anglo-classical educators asked students to do *every* day, was a profound exercise of these students' reason, will, and imagination. In addition, the Anglo-classical academy's emphasis upon poetry, religious or classical, read in class or in church contributed to the age's respect for the genre and for poets. Recognising these students' daily study of the themes at the heart of Anglican practice also helps to explain why the poets often explored variations on the themes of suffering, sacrifice, sin, guilt, and forgiveness. Finally, early training and experience in the Anglo-classical tradition suggests why Wordsworth called himself a 'chosen son', why Coleridge invented the term 'clerisy' to refer to intellectuals, why Anglicans who read Blake labelled him a 'bardic prophet', and why even the atheist Percy Shelley claimed that poets are visionary legislators whose task is to access the 'eternal, the infinite, and the one'.[117]

---

[116] Fulford, *Wordsworth's Poetry*, p. 4.
[117] 'Defence of Poetry', in Reiman and Powers, p. 483.

Chapter Six

Oxford and Cambridge in the Romantic Period

'Operose ignorance' or 'Good habits, and the principles of virtue and wisdom'?

Questions about the universities' curriculum, exclusivity, and cost circulated widely in the Romantic public sphere, and some of the poets complained famously about their collegiate experiences. But they also wrote about the benefits of that training and the good friendships they made there. Coleridge called himself a 'proverb to the University for Idleness',[1] but he was an enthusiastic and competitive student at Jesus College for at least four terms. As a first-year student, he composed poetry 'like a mad dog', 'thanked God [he was] at Cambridge',[2] and wrote to his brother (in Latin) that 'I love classical studies more every day; they are my delight, in them I find both my serious and my lighter occupation.'[3] To Mrs Evans, Coleridge boasted that he had 'lately received the thanks of the College for a declamation I spoke in public; indeed, I meet with the most pointed remarks of respect'. Later that year he was selected by Cambridge's acclaimed classicist Porson to compete for the Craven Scholarship, and the following spring his work merited the renewal of his Rustat Scholarship.

Coleridge's days of achievement coincided with the period of controversy raised at the university by the activities of William Frend, a fellow in Coleridge's college. Frend's trial may have contributed to Coleridge's rash decision to enlist in the dragoons. However, when Coleridge's emotional confusion subsided, he wrote to George Coleridge contritely, saying 'Undoubtedly—my Brother! I would wish to return to College.'[4] Indeed, after his tutor and family extracted

---

[1] CLSTC, p. 67.
[2] CLSTC, p. 65.
[3] CLSTC, p. 27.
[4] CLSTC, p. 65.

Educating the Romantic Poets

him from the army he took care to be back at Cambridge in time to stand for (and win) yet another Rustat Scholarship examination in 1794.[5] Later that year, his friendship with Southey, their eagerness to build Pantisocracy (a classically informed utopian dream), and his growing doubts about Anglican trinitarian beliefs gave him reason enough to leave the university without completing a degree. However, outside the college walls he did not hesitate to identify himself as a university man. On the cover of the pamphlet for his Bristol public lectures he listed 'of Jesus College' after his name, and he included 'late of Jesus College' beneath his name on the title page of his *Poems on Various Subjects* (1796). Two decades later he referred to 'the glorious opportunities at Jesus College' on the flyleaf of a book intended for his sons.

Southey lost his place at Christ Church thanks to the vindictiveness of his Westminster headmaster after *The Flagellant* episode. He briefly entertained fantasies of assassinating Vincent; and when his last-minute admission to Balliol was arranged, he wondered if it were not disgraceful to 'sit and study Euclid' when 'Europe was on fire with freedom'.[6] But he soon rebounded and vowed to spend 'the prime of his life acquiring knowledge', and exercising 'philosophie' at Balliol.[7] Once he arrived at Oxford in December 1793 he wrote that 'over the pages of the philosophic Tacitus the hours of study pass rapidly as even those which are devoted to my friends & I have not found as yet one hour which I could wish to have [been] employed otherwise this is saying very much in praise of a collegiate life'.[8] He also describes reading ravenously and writing odes and prose inspired by classical satire. In his second year he described himself as 'once more among friends, alternately studying and philosophising, railing at college folly, and enjoying rational society'.[9] Though Southey entered college with disdain for the Tory patriarchy that ruled the schools, Oxford, and parliament, he recognised the role education could or should play in the campaign for social justice. He wrote to Bedford that 'an equal education would make any Lord & my shoemaker equally philosophic. Now I affirm that the first duty of [MS torn] where Liberty & Equality flourish is to regard the education of the people.'[10] Southey left the university without a degree, as others often did who no longer wished to join the Anglican ministry. But, upon his departure, Southey admitted that he had enjoyed 'democratizing gloriously' and that he 'did not quit Oxford without feeling something like regret'.[11] The words Southey put in

[5] Holmes, p. 58.
[6] CLRS, Pt 1, #30.
[7] CLRS, Pt 1, #30.
[8] CLRS, Pt 1, #42.
[9] Charles Cuthbert Southey, qtd on p. 203.
[10] CLRS, Pt 1, #38.
[11] Speck, p. 40.

the mouth of an imagined Cambridge student in *Letters from England: by Don Manuel Alvarez Espriella* (1808) probably sum up his judgement of his university: 'A knowledge of the world, that is to say of our world and of the men in it, is gained here, and that knowledge remains when Greek and Geometry are forgotten.'[12]

Wordsworth's comment about Cambridge in *The Prelude*—that he felt as though he was 'not for that hour or that place'—is well known, but his college classmates experienced him as 'gregarious and fully engaged with the society about him'.[13] Wordsworth took 'Presidents and Deans' to task for 'officious doings' that brought 'disgrace/ On the plain steeples of our English Church',[14] but he also expressed 'genuine admiration unimpaired' for that 'garden of great intellects' and 'spiritual men'.[15] Likewise, his scoffing at the anxious, competitive place-hunters at the university is outweighed by his approval of 'loyal students faithful to their books/ Half-and-half idlers, hardy recusants,/ And honest dunces'.[16] Elsewhere in *The Prelude* he characterises his days at St John's as a 'gladsome' and 'budding-time'.[17] In Book Ninth the poet exclaims,

> Oh sweet it is in academical groves
> To ruminate, with interchange of talk
> On rational liberty and hope in man,
> Justice and Peace.[18]

Perhaps Wordsworth's most significant and appreciative statement about his education and Cambridge comes earlier in Book Ninth, when he writes:

> Of many debts which afterwards I owed
> To Cambridge and an academic life,
> That something there was holden up to view
> Of a republic, where all stood thus far
> Upon equal ground, that they were brothers all
> In honour, as of one community—.[19]

A few lines later, the passage continues:

---

[12] Robert Southey, *Letters from England*, p. 23, Letter XLVI.
[13] Searby, p. 571.
[14] *Prelude*, 1805, p. 112, ll. 421, 424–425.
[15] *Prelude*, 1805, p. 104, ll. 275, 267, 269.
[16] *Prelude*, 1805, p. 94, ll. 62–64.
[17] *Prelude*, 1805, p. 102, ll. 217, 222.
[18] *Prelude*, 1805, p. 332, ll. 397, 401–403.
[19] *Prelude*, 1805, p. 324, ll. 227–232.

Educating the Romantic Poets

> Add unto this, subservience from the first
> To God and Nature's single sovereignty
> (Familiar presences of awful power),
> And fellowship with venerable books
> To sanction the proud workings of the soul,
> And mountain liberty. It could not be
> But that one tutored thus, who had been formed
> To thought and moral feeling in the way
> This story hath described, should look with awe
> Upon the faculties of man, receive
> Gladly the highest promises, and hail
> As best the government of equal rights
> And individual worth.[20]

Unlike Coleridge and Southey, Wordsworth stayed at university long enough to earn his BA. Moreover, both he and Southey saw to it that the boys in all three families had the opportunity to attend university.

Byron's accounts of his time at Cambridge should be reckoned in light of the universities' long tradition of requiring very little of the sons of noblemen, his lifelong delight in bragging about his own bad behaviour, and his frame of mind as his Trinity college career began. Byron told John Murray,

> When I went up to Trinity, in 1805, at the age of seventeen and a half, I was miserable ... I was wretched at leaving Harrow ... wretched at going to Cambridge instead of Oxford (there were no rooms vacant at Christ Church); wretched from some private domestic circumstances of different kinds, and consequently about as unsocial as a wolf taken from the troop.[21]

But he also told Murray that it was in the rooms of William Bankes, his 'collegiate pastor, and master, and patron' that he first read and was inspired by Sir Walter Scott.[22] In a letter he wrote from Cambridge to Elizabeth Pigot, he describes a 'villainous Chaos of Dice and Drunkenness ... Hunting, Mathematics ... Riot and Racing' and boasts about the 'Jockies, Gamblers, Boxers, Authors, parsons, and poets' that supped with him.[23] In the same letter, however, he proudly adds that he has 'written 214 pages of a novel, one poem of 380 Lines to be published (without my name) in a few weeks,

---

[20] *Prelude*, 1805, p. 324, ll. 237–249.
[21] Marchand, *Byron: A Biography*, vol. 1, p. 100.
[22] Marchand, *Byron: A Biography*, vol. 1, p. 100.
[23] Marchand, *Byron's Letters and Journals*, vol. 1, pp. 135–136.

with notes, 560 Lines of Bosworth Field, and 250 Lines of another poem in rhyme, besides half a dozen smaller pieces'.[24]

His friend Moore noted that, while Byron chose

> to satirise the mode of education in the university, he had yet a due discrimination in his respect for the individuals who belonged to it. I have always, indeed, heard him speak in high terms of praise of Hailstone [one of his tutors at Trinity], as well as of his master, Bishop Mansel ... and of others whose names I have now forgotten.[25]

Years after leaving Cambridge, in a notebook entry dated 12 January 1821, Byron writes that 'the happiest, perhaps days of my life (always excepting, here and there, a Harrow holiday)' were when he was 'living at Cambridge with Edward Noel Long'.[26] Byron had earlier described himself and Long as 'rival swimmers—fond of riding—reading—and conviviality'.[27] His use of the word *reading*, which at the English universities also means studying, is noteworthy.

In point of fact, Byron's reading as a student was impressive. In a journal begun in 1807, two years after he matriculated at Trinity, Byron offers a list of the texts that he claims he had 'perused' to date.[28] The list is probably inflated, and it includes reading at Harrow, but the catalogue is impressive, and his annotations suggest he did much more than just peruse many of these works. Among them are histories of 18 countries, scores of biographies (among them Sallust, Caesar, Czar Peter, Marlborough, Buonaparte, many British poets, Kames, and Newton), works by Blackstone and Montesquieu, nine philosophers (among them Paley, Locke, Bacon, Hume, and Berkeley), and five geographers (including Strabo in Latin). Additionally, he reports reading works on rhetoric and eloquence by Demosthenes, Cicero, Quintilian, and Sheridan; Austin's *Chironomia*; and a century of parliamentary debates. On the list were religious works by Blair, Tillotson, and Hooker, though he comments that these were 'all very tiresome. I abhor books of religion, though I reverence and love my God.'[29] The list of the poetry Byron read includes the British classics, works by 'most of the living poets, Scott, Southey, &c'., the Cid, and 'Greek and Latin [poets] without number'; and he adds that he had 'translated a good deal from both languages, verse as well as prose'.[30] All of the classical texts and many of the philosophical and religious texts he lists

---

[24] Marchand, *Byron's Letters and Journals*, vol. 1, p. 136.
[25] Moore, p. 106.
[26] Quennell, vol. 2, p. 563.
[27] Marchand, *Byron's Letters and Journals*, vol. 1, p. 104.
[28] Moore, pp. 46–49.
[29] Moore, p. 47.
[30] Moore, p. 47.

Educating the Romantic Poets

were standard readings at Harrow and/or Trinity; so, too, was the practice of translating them.

Despite the tradition that noblemen at university were playboys not scholars, Byron sheepishly confessed to being one of the 'steadiest' of the 'noble sons' of the university and admitted that he got into few 'scrapes and none of consequence' at Cambridge.[31] Indeed, for all his public sarcasm about school and college, Byron was one of the best read and most academically credentialled of the Romantic poets. He was eventually awarded not only the BA but also the MA degree, though the latter hinged more on his completion of minimal residence requirements than demonstrated scholarship. But the fact that he bothered to do this is noteworthy. *Fugitive Pieces* (1806), *Hours of Idleness* (1807), and *Poems on Various Occasions* (1807) were all written while Byron was enrolled at Cambridge, and all three volumes were published before he graduated. The frequency with which his poems refer to classical tales, settings, or figures that were standard readings of the curriculum is also significant. Added to this, we might assume that Byron's lifelong embrace of satiric humour was boosted and affirmed by the culture of wit that pervaded Trinity, by his and his classmates' admiration of Trinity's Master, William Lort Mansel, a celebrated wit and orator, and by reading Dryden and Pope with Hobhouse, a classmate, and Hodgson, a fellow, at Cambridge.

Criticisms of Oxford and Cambridge in the Georgian period

Despite these examples that portray the universities more positively, the universities' own members, particularly those at Cambridge, could be outspoken critics. One of these was John Jebb (1736–1786). A second wrangler, BA, MA, and fellow of Peterhouse, Jebb lectured and tutored in mathematics and the Greek Testament for nine years. His swerve to Unitarian beliefs moved him in 1771–72 to champion the Feathers Tavern Petition, which called for the abolition of subscription for all students and fellows. Between 1771 and 1775 Jebb and another Peterhouse fellow, Capel Lofft, proposed at least nine petitions to reform the university. Their call for public examinations for all undergraduates was supported by the utilitarian philosopher, fellow, and tutor of Christ's College, William Paley (1743–1805), whose *Principles of Moral and Political Philosophy* (1785), *View of the Evidence of Christianity* (1794), and *Natural Theology* (1802) would become standard texts at Cambridge in the nineteenth century. All of Jebb's ideas for reform, however, met with general resistance from the Senate. At least one account suggests that Jebb was so personally disliked that other college members were disinclined to support his ideas simply on those grounds. In 1775 he gave up on Cambridge and went

---

[31] Marchand, *Byron: A Biography*, vol. 1, p. 104.

to London, where he became a regular at the Essex Street Unitarian Chapel and began studying medicine.[32] Eleven years later a group of junior fellows at Trinity College, Cambridge, unhappy about the most recent fellows election, approached the master, John Hinchliffe, about reforms. The disgruntled group included Thomas Jones, who would one day be Byron's tutor. Hinchliffe resisted, so they took their complaint to the lord chancellor in London, an unprecedented move for junior fellows. The lord chancellor scolded them for insubordination but supported their cause.

Internal criticisms of the academy were sometimes delivered in Sunday sermons at the university churches. In 1782 among the topics addressed at Cambridge's Great St Mary's were 'the scandalous neglect of order and discipline throughout the University', 'the expensiveness' of attending university that 'made it almost impossible for common folk to do so without ruining themselves', and the waste of the colleges' 'great endowments' on fellows who 'spend their days idly in dissipation, dress and vanity'.[33] At about the same time, Vicesimus Knox, who had been educated at St John's College, Oxford, before becoming the headmaster of Tonbridge Grammar School, published *Liberal Education or a Practical Treatise on the Methods of Acquiring Useful and Polite Learning* (1785). In that volume, he delivers a blistering critique aimed at the universities' students and laments how quickly they become 'extravagant' and careless about 'their health, fortune, character and peace of mind'.[34]

Some of the internal criticisms of the curriculum at the universities reflected entirely antithetical concerns. One side, usually the younger fellows, wanted to make the curriculum more modern and 'useful' and to end religious tests and reliance upon Aristotelian logic. Older college members defended the classical and broad-church programme, citing the looming threats of attacks on the Catholic Church in France and challenges to the Church of England by Unitarians. In between these two camps fell the rector of Lincoln College, Edward Tatham (1749–1834). In a pamphlet entitled '*Oxonia Purgata*: A Series of Addresses on the New Discipline' (1807), he criticises Oxford's exams, approves of teaching Aristotle's rhetoric, but laments the continuing use of Aristotelian logic, claiming his methods of reasoning are 'not worth a louse'.[35] While Tatum supported Greek studies so students could more fully appreciate the Greek Testament, he expresses astonishment that the 'Youth of a Christian University in the nineteenth century, [are asked] to learn their

---

[32] He continued those studies at St Andrews in Scotland. After licensure by the London College of Physicians in 1777 he began a successful medical practice in that city. In 1779 he was made a Fellow of the Royal Society. See Roe, *Wordsworth and Coleridge*, p. 90 for more on Jebb's contribution to dissent at Cambridge.
[33] Qtd in Winstanley, p. 210.
[34] Knox, *Liberal Education*, pp. 45–46.
[35] Tatham, p. 6.

Educating the Romantic Poets

moral philosophy from Aristotle, that uncircumcised and unbaptized Philistine of the Schools'.[36] 'Is this not', he continues, 'to prefer the errors of Paganism to the oracles of Wisdom and Truth?'[37] Tatham kept hammering at members of the university about curricular reform, making himself and his arguments especially unwelcome with the three powerful college leaders—John Eveleigh (1748–1814), the provost of Oriel; Cyril Jackson (1746–1819), the dean of Christ Church; and John Parsons (1761–1819), the master of Balliol—who were already involved in the politically fraught business of reforming examinations. Another outspoken voice for reform at this time was that of William Frend (1757–1841), whose story is told in greater detail in Chapter 11. Frend complained about subscription on the grounds that college students were not yet wise enough to make the moral and philosophical decisions required for subscription. He also published calls for the university and the church to rethink the doctrine of the trinity.

While the university community was arguing internally about policies, doctrinal matters, and academic freedom, critics from outside the academy were also taking aim at them. These included educators, such as Joseph Priestley (1733–1804) and others at the dissenting academies, all of which offered a more 'modern' curriculum. Priestley's *Essay on a Course of Liberal Education, For Civil and Active Life* (1764, 1788) complained that the English universities did not properly prepare men to 'fill the principal stations of active life'.[38] The polymathic Priestley taught not only classical languages, grammar, and rhetoric but also English and European history, natural philosophy, and theology. He argued that 'grammar' studies as practised in the Anglican academy took too much time and were created by long-dead men who could not have 'imagined what … the true sources of wealth, power, and happiness' would be in England in the late eighteenth century.[39] His foundational beliefs about education were that 'the studies of youth should tend to fit them for the business of manhood [and] the employment of their riper years'.[40] To this end, he suggested that the subjects of 'civil history' and 'civil policy, such as the theory of laws, government, manufactures, commerce, naval force, &c'. should be added to programmes of higher education.[41]

Another critical voice in the educational debates was that of the Scottish Unitarian William Stevenson (1772–1829). An active man of letters in London, Stevenson wrote about education, agriculture, navigation, commerce, and chivalry for the *Edinburgh Encyclopaedia*, the *Edinburgh Review*, the

---

[36] Tatham, p. 7.
[37] Tatham, p. 7.
[38] Priestley, p. xvii.
[39] Priestley, p. xviii.
[40] Priestley, p. xix.
[41] Priestley, p. xxii.

Retrospective Review and The Society for the Diffusion of Useful Knowledge. He was also the chief compiler of data for the *Annual Register*. The son of a Royal Navy officer, Stevenson began his education at an English grammar school but moved to the dissenting academy at Daventry. After working as a classical tutor at Manchester Academy, Stevenson published his 'Remarks on the Very Inferior Utility of Classical Learning' (1796). In that text he argues 'The study of languages can strengthen only the memory, at the expense of much time, and commonly to the detriment of the judgment.'[42] It is nonsense, he writes, 'to suppose that Plato, Xenophon, Cicero, or Terence, must be studied, in order that we may be acquainted with the phrases and idioms of the English tongue; [or that] without a perfect acquaintance with them our style must be obscure and destitute of precision'.[43] While he agrees with the academy's belief that English education should be moral and religious, he asserts that, 'if the foundation of morals be the will and authority of the Deity, it is useless and absurd to have recourse to Epictetus, Xenophon, Seneca, or Cicero'.[44] Claiming that 'a mere classical scholar is not, by this knowledge connected with the world',[45] he argues that only the man who knows the natural sciences is truly in touch with the world and his fellow men, for he has 'knowledge of the laws and powers of nature, [which] … may either be applied to the advantage of man, or prevented from injuring him'.[46] Stevenson calls for more attention to the latest studies of chemistry, anatomy, and mechanics at the universities and, along with Priestley, for study of European history and the theories and practice of governments, law, and commerce. He advocates a 'systematic plan of education, in which every branch of knowledge, grammatical, natural, and moral, should have its appropriate and just rank'.[47] Stevenson clarifies his opinion about the appropriate rank of these branches by asserting that the 'primary object of good education is the knowledge of facts and habits of reasoning; the secondary object is the communication of ideas in the best manner'.[48]

The Edinburgh Review added similar criticisms of the universities' academic programme in a widely read series of articles published between 1808 and 1810. These articles have been attributed to Sydney Smith, John Playfair, and Richard Payne Knight, whose educations represented the three choices of higher education available to young men in the Georgian period: Smith had attended Winchester and Oxford; Playfair had studied at the more scientific

[42] Stevenson, p. 22.
[43] Stevenson, p. 18.
[44] Stevenson, p. 7.
[45] Stevenson, p. 28.
[46] Stevenson, p. 5.
[47] Stevenson, pp. 30–31.
[48] Stevenson, p. 35.

Educating the Romantic Poets

and 'modern' Scottish universities of Edinburgh and St Andrews; and Knight had been educated by private tutoring and travel. In one of its earliest salvos, published in January 1808, the *Edinburgh Review* used an article about La Place's *Traité de Méchanique Céleste* to criticise mathematical instruction at both of the universities, but especially at Oxford, for being grossly behind that of the Scottish and Continental academies. Taking on Tatham's argument from a less religious point of view, the article claims that Oxford's emphasis upon Aristotelian logic was sadly outdated and that the pedagogies at both universities did not rouse students' curiosity or awaken their 'spirit of discovery'.[49] In an 1809 review of Clarendon Press's new edition of Strabo's geography, the *Edinburgh Review* condemns Oxford's privileging of classical studies and its pedagogies over other more 'modern' subjects pursued on the Continent. The reviewer acerbically suggests that this curriculum and its methods of study are responsible—along with 'port and prejudice'—for impeding the industry and ambition of students in general and failing to serve the republic of letters.[50] The reviewer, Sydney Smith, ridicules the university press for publishing a text of 'operose ignorance', lazy schoolboy Latin, and shabby notes, and claims that the only improvements of this edition are its 'whiter paper, blacker ink, and neater type'.[51] Ironically, the specificity of Smith's criticisms of the translation betray how well Winchester and New College had trained him in Latin. Moreover, Smith grudgingly admits in the review that public leaders need a 'competent knowledge' of the Greek and Latin languages because such study 'is justly esteemed the most safe and effectual means of forming the taste, moulding the judgment, and directing the imaginations of those, whose stations or talents befit them for more active scenes of life and open to their dawning ambition the more brilliant prospects of political advancement'.[52]

In another article published in 1810 about Edgeworth's *Essays on Professional Education*, the *Edinburgh Review* complains that the emphasis of English university teaching on the classical languages, with its 'useless' attention to prosody, 'feeds [students] only with words' and risks their remaining 'narrow and limited being[s] to the end of [their] existence'.[53] The review also claims that 'The present state of classical education cultivates the imagination a great deal too much, and other habits of mind a great deal too little; and trains up many young men in a style of elegant imbecility, utterly unworthy of the talent with which nature has endowed them.'[54] While conceding that university education gives students 'quick feeling, lively fancy, and good taste', he claims

[49] *Edinburgh Review*, 'Art. I', p. 283.
[50] *Edinburgh Review*, 'Art. X', p. 441.
[51] *Edinburgh Review*, 'Art. X', pp. 441, 431.
[52] *Edinburgh Review*, 'Art. X', p. 430.
[53] *Edinburgh Review*, 'Art. III. *Essays on Professional Education*', pp. 42, 46.
[54] *Edinburgh Review*, 'Art. III. *Essays on Professional Education*', p. 48.

it leaves them with no 'talent for speculation and original inquiry ... . All the solid and masculine parts of [the college student's] understanding are left wholly without cultivation; he hates the pain of thinking and suspects every man whose boldness and or originality call upon him to defend his opinions and prove his assertions.'[55] In expressing his preference for 'professional' over classical education, the reviewer asks, 'what other measure is there of dignity in intellectual labour, but usefulness?'[56] This utilitarian attitude toward higher education grew during the nineteenth century, fuelled, ironically, by men whose university education in classics, mathematics, and religion prepared them to turn their reasoning and imagination to the invention of the modern sciences.

Articles debating the pros and cons of higher education appeared again in the *Edinburgh Review* in the 1820s and 1830s. Among them were reviews of 'Art. III. *The Proposals for Founding a University in London* Considered By an Oxonian' (1825), 'Article IX. *The Legality of the Present Academical System of the University of Oxford, Asserted against the New Calumnies of the Edinburgh Review*' (1831), and 'Article VI. 1. *Addenda ad Corpus Statutorum Universitatis Oxoniensis*' (1831). *The Quarterly Review* discussed issues in British universities at that time as well. A representative example is its article about Charles Babbage's *Reflections on the Decline of Science in England, and on Some of its Causes* (1830). Each of these claims that the nation is entering an age of improvement and progress and that England's classical academy needs to catch up with Europe and reclaim her international prominence.

Defenders of the universities

Despite these critics, the universities had staunch defenders. Two of these were Oxford's Edward Copleston (1776–1849) and Cambridge's William Whewell (1794–1866). Both men published widely read articles explaining the universities' practices and beliefs. When Copleston's 'A Reply to the Calumnies of the *Edinburgh Review* against Oxford Containing an Account of Studies Pursued in that University' came out in 1810, the entire university community took note. A tutor and fellow of Oriel and university professor of poetry from 1802 to 1812, Copleston defends Oxford's study of the classics, particularly Aristotle, claiming that Aristotle's rhetoric is 'a magazine of intellectual riches' that is not only 'a body of rules for good writing' but also 'a text-book of human feeling'.[57] Copleston explains that Oxford does not confine 'instruction to the grammatical niceties of a dead language' nor does it 'repress all attempts

---

[55] *Edinburgh Review*, 'Art. III. *Essays on Professional Education*', p. 49.
[56] *Edinburgh Review*, 'Art. III. *Essays on Professional Education*', p. 51.
[57] Edward Copleston, pp. 26–27.

Educating the Romantic Poets

at reasoning upon moral and political questions'.[58] Moreover, 'all the great topics, in which the mind of a public man should be well informed', are embraced at the university.[59] Copleston challenges the notion that usefulness should be the primary criterion by which an education is judged and asserts that making 'necessity the standard of what is praiseworthy or honourable is against the uniform judgment of mankind'.[60] He reminds critics of John Locke's pronouncement that the 'great work of a [teacher] is to … form the mind; to settle in his pupil good habits, and the principles of virtue and wisdom; to give him … a view of mankind … vigour, activity, and industry … [and finally] to teach him application and [to] accustom him to take pains'.[61] Noting that classical stories of love, loss, aspiration, and failure have lasted not only because they are part of England's common heritage and culture but also because they resonate with all human experience, Copleston claims that even students bound for work in business or trade need to be familiar with these stories. He reminds critics that students find in literature, as nowhere else, 'that common link, which, among the higher and middle departments of life, unites the jarring sections and subdivisions in one interest, which supplies common topics, and kindles common feelings'.[62] He further asserts that literary study

> expands and enlarges the mind, excites its faculties, and calls those limbs and muscles into freer exercise, which, by too constant use in one direction…are apt to lose somewhat of their native play and energy. And thus, without directly qualifying a person for any of the employments of life, literature enriches and ennobles all. Without teaching a student the peculiar business of any one office or calling, [the study of literature] enables that person to act his part in each of them with better judgment and fuller humanity … so that he will be fit, in the end, [as John Milton put it] to 'perform justly, skilfully, and magnanimously, all the offices, both private and public, of peace and war'.[63]

To bolster his claim that English university education is also 'useful' in practical ways, Copleston points out that loyal subjects and civil servants need the skills in rhetoric, logic, and civil discourse that the universities teach. He concludes that a citizenry without these skills is 'likely to be engrossed with petty views and interests, to under-rate the importance of all in which [they] are not concerned, to carry [their] partial notions into cases where they are

---

[58] Edward Copleston, pp. 162–163.
[59] Edward Copleston, p. 163.
[60] Edward Copleston, p. 166.
[61] Edward Copleston, qtd on p. 105.
[62] Edward Copleston, p. 111.
[63] Edward Copleston, pp. 111–112.

inapplicable, to act, in short, as so many unconnected units, displacing and repelling one another'.[64]

Twenty-six years later, writing from Trinity College, Cambridge, where he was a fellow and tutor, William Whewell offered a similarly spirited defence of his university in *On the Principles of English University Education* (1837). A natural philosopher and fellow of the Royal Society, Whewell argues that the study of mathematics and classics is both practical and permanent. He warns reformers that knowledge in many of the new fields of study, such as chemistry and political economy, while interesting, is rudimentary, tentative, and speculative.[65] Whewell explains that the tutorial method, whereby students learn mathematics and classics with hands-on problem-solving and constant writing, is 'practical' and personal. By contrast, he complains that the 'modern' curriculum was being delivered in large lectures without the opportunity for student questions or laboratory work. Whewell explains that because tutors work with students individually or in small groups several times every week, they know their students' talents and inclinations well. Hence, their correction of students' language, calculation, or understanding and their clarification of the 'principles of taste and criticism' arise out of the immediate teaching situation and are 'taught with the example before them'.[66] This mode of imparting information, he points out, is adapted to the occasion and the students; and therefore students assimilate knowledge more fully and learn to apply it.

Regarding mathematical studies specifically, Whewell explains that university-level algebra, geometry, and calculus were not taught simply as 'information, nor even as an instrument',[67] but as a means of developing students' 'habits of thought'.[68] In mathematics, Whewell notes, 'long chains of reasoning must be called up and used'.[69] 'Every person of mathematical cultivation', he asserts, 'is necessarily an analyst of conditions and connexions; and the analytical power awakened will commonly exercise itself upon language, as well as upon mathematical quantity.'[70] Whewell contends further that instruction in classics complements instruction in mathematics and works to achieve a 'general cultivation of all the best faculties' of the human mind.[71] He explains,

---

[64] Edward Copleston, p. 111.
[65] Whewell, pp. 9–10.
[66] Whewell, p. 147.
[67] Whewell, p. 43.
[68] Whewell, p. 34.
[69] Whewell, pp. 9–10, 12.
[70] Whewell, p. 40.
[71] Whewell, p. 41.

Educating the Romantic Poets

> The man of mathematical genius who, by the demands of his College or his University, is led to become familiar with the best Greek and Latin classics, becomes thus a man of liberal education, instead of being merely a powerful calculator. The elegant classical scholar, who is compelled, in the same way, to master the propositions of geometry and mechanics, acquires among them habits of rigour of thought and connexion of reasoning. He thus becomes fitted to deal with any subject with which reason can be concerned.[72]

The study of ancient literature, he adds, prepares a man for the future by furnishing him with a 'thorough acquaintance [and connection with] what has already been done ... in the way of extending our knowledge of earth, its elements, and its inhabitants'.[73]

The debate continues: the royal commissions

Despite the cases that Copleston and Whewell made for the theories and outcomes of teaching at their universities, the controversies over higher education in England continued in the nineteenth century. In a pointedly political effort to facilitate conversation about how to reform the universities, James Heywood FRS, a barrister of the Inner Temple who trained at Trinity College, Cambridge, personally commissioned G. R. M. Ward, a fellow of Trinity College, Oxford, and deputy high steward of that university, to produce an English translation of the Oxford University Statutes, so it would be easier to present a public case against them. Ward's translation was published in 1845 and registered a long and harsh catalogue of criticisms, starting with the assertion that the Hebdomadal Board is an oligarchy that is out of touch with the experiences of students and tutors.[74] He claimed that college heads are chosen most often because of their complaisance or inoffensiveness, rather than their academic skill,[75] adding that religious tests are 'pernicious'[76] and that the religious infighting at the university is 'repugnant to the nation'.[77] He further charged that the colleges' tutorial system had lost much of its vitality and that the university had given up teaching to become a mere 'market of degrees'.[78] He also complained that university professors, who as a group were

---

[72] Whewell, pp. 41–42.
[73] Whewell, p. 43.
[74] Heywood, pp. iv, viii.
[75] Heywood, p. xi.
[76] Heywood, pp. xiii–xiv.
[77] Heywood, pp. xiii, xxii.
[78] Heywood, pp. xxiv, xii.

becoming more scholarly than they had been in the past century, were excluded from decision-making at the university.[79]

Partly because of salvos such as this one, two parliamentary commissions were formed to inquire into the 'state, discipline, studies, and revenues' of the universities. While the royal commissions' studies began in 1850, after most of the college-educated Romantic writers were dead, their findings are not irrelevant to a study of the Romantics' educational experience, for the commissioners surveyed members of the generations to which the Romantics belonged. The members of the commissions included alumni, professors, and the heads of colleges. They gathered information according to the willingness of the university and college authorities and their graduates. The Oxford commissioners met 87 times from October 1850 to April 1852 and published their report in 1852. The Cambridge report did not include a calendar of meetings, but it appears that they were just as diligent in gathering to discharge their royal trust.

Both commission reports were careful to note their respect for the universities. The Oxford commissioners began by expressing their appreciation of 'the present excellences of the University' and their 'grateful sense of the benefits, moral and religious, as well as intellectual, which it has so long conferred on the country'.[80] Despite this conciliatory gesture, the Oxford commissioners' report is shaped as an explicitly corrective document, with sections in all capitals entitled 'PROPOSED REMEDIES' (to governance), 'PROPOSED IMPROVEMENTS' (to studies), 'CHANGES RECOMMENDED AS NECESSARY (relative to the colleges), and a Conclusion that lists 47 specific recommendations. These include reorganisation of the Hebdomadal Board to include chaired university professors and other 'Academical Teachers' as voting members and requiring an examination prior to matriculation— the latter a move that had a profound effect upon university admission, academic standards, the curriculum and pedagogies across the country when finally enacted by the universities. The Cambridge commissioners' report is less critical and is primarily descriptive. It does, however, embed several suggested reforms throughout the document, including 'Changes in the Statutes as necessary', noting with approval that a Cambridge committee had already undertaken a project to draft new governing guidelines.

Both commissions recommended reforming examinations and allowing students greater freedom in their choice of studies. While preserving classics and mathematics, they ask for the inclusion of more 'modern' courses of study such as civil engineering. Both groups call for integration of the professorial and tutorial systems, greater transparency with regard to awarding fellowships,

---

[79] Heywood, p. v.
[80] Hinds, pp. 2–3.

Educating the Romantic Poets

'extension'—that is, expansion—of the number of students, and the end of religious tests for admission. The Oxford commissioners took pains in their Preamble to explain that their project is not to destroy, in order to clear the ground for a new system, but to reform, in a right spirit, by improving, restoring, and enlarging. Their wish was to 'relieve the University from shackles which obstruct its progress, to root it more deeply in the affections of the nation, and to raise it to a still higher position than that which it now occupies in the opinion of the world at large'.[81]

Cost

A standard complaint about the universities in the Hanoverian period was cost. Finding entirely reliable information about college expenses in the era is difficult and comparing late Georgian college costs to those in the twenty-first century is complicated and inexact. The website MeasuringWorth.com offers one of the most reliable tools for calculating the relative value of costs, income, and purchasing power of money over time; it is used here to compare the price of higher education in the Romantic period with that of the twenty-first century.

De Quincey said that the cost of a year at Oxford, circa 1805, could be as high as £200; in 2020 this would be roughly equivalent to £16,600. In 1825 Copleston wrote to his brother that Oriel's charges for 'rooms, diet, and instruction' were usually less than £100 a year.[82] It was an amount he considered to be no more than 'what a gentleman must spend wherever he is, provided he wishes to live as other gentlemen do'.[83] The Oxford royal commissioners were unable to gather official numbers about costs from most of the college heads, but queries sent to individual members of colleges turned up plenty of information, and these numbers are similar to what De Quincey and Copleston reported earlier in the century. Using data gathered in the late 1840s, the commissioners reported that, after allowing for food, room rent, college and university fees, servants, books, groceries, furniture, and lights, a BA at Pembroke College, Oxford, would cost about £370. The cost of completing a degree at University College was reported to be £430. The commissioners added up all other expenses, such as travel, clothes, and normal student amusements, and reported that a family would have done well to spend no more than £600 on their son's university education. This total does not, however, include the cost of private tuition, which could cost between £30 and £50 a year. Elsewhere, in the Oxford report, Rev. J. D. Collis, MA,

---

[81] Hinds, pp. 2–3.
[82] William James Copleston, p. 9.
[83] William James Copleston, p. 9.

fellow of Worcester College and headmaster of the King Edward VI Grammar School, testified that he spent £725 2s 7d to complete his degree in the 1830s, an amount which he offset by winning a scholarship of £120.[84] Collis added, however, that this was low for Oxford and that the usual cost of a degree ranged between £800 and £1,000. An estimation of the relative equivalence of these sums is charted in Table 1.

Table 1. Estimated cost of degrees at Oxford University.

Source	College	Date	Cost to BA	Equiv. £ in 2020	Equiv. $ in 2020
De Quincey	Worcester	1805	£600	£49,800	$66,800
Copleston	Oriel	1825	£300	£25,200	$33,800
Collis	Worcester	1835	£725	£73,000	$97,300
Jeune	Pembroke	1849	£370	£39,200	$52,200
Stanley	University	1849	£515	£45,600	$60,800

The commissioners queried professors, fellows, and tutors in writing about these expenses; the consensus was that 'necessary College expenses are in most cases too moderate to admit of material reduction'.[85] Collis and others blamed the expense on students, who were extravagant, and on parents, who failed to deny or curb their sons' behaviour. One professor told the Oxford commissioners that the 'real causes of extravagance are the state of society in general, and the weakness of parents, who wish their sons to be like other young men'.[86] Three specific causes of student debt are mentioned: 'a growing taste for furniture and decorations, totally unsuitable', the expensive and 'excessive habit of smoking', and 'the habit of dining at inns, taverns, and clubs, in or about Oxford'.[87] Riding, hunting, and easy credit secured from willing tradesmen were also cited by college members as reasons for students' financial difficulties.

When queried by the royal commission about the cost of attending Cambridge, members of the colleges reported that 'the necessary expenses of a University Education cannot be materially reduced'[88] and listed the costs of a degree as within the range of or a little less than those posted by Oxford. Depending upon the college and the source, costs at Cambridge ranged from

[84] Hinds, p. 35.
[85] Hinds, 'Evidence', p. 19.
[86] Hinds, 'Evidence', p. 28.
[87] Hinds, 'Evidence', p. 24.
[88] Graham, p. 148.

£65 to £90 a year at Emmanuel, a little over £85 at Pembroke, and anywhere between £73 and £250 a year at Trinity. Most reporters admitted how inexact these numbers were likely to be and said that some students might pay less than the lower amount and others might pay more than the higher one. None of these estimates included the cost of private tuition, which could be as much as 50 guineas a year (private tuition was most often used only during the senior year, when students were preparing for the honours or Senate House exams). The master of Gonville and Caius told the commission that 'many Students go through their whole College course for £300 or £400, including every expense except that for private tuition.'[89] The master of St John's, Ralph Tatham, gave the royal commission somewhat higher estimates for the 'necessary expenses' from the time of entrance to graduation at his college, reminding the commissioners that college fees, tuition, and accommodation costs depended upon a student's social class and/or family wealth. He offered the following numbers: noblemen might pay between £650 and £1,400; fellow commoners between £485 and £1,050; pensioners between £355 and 630; and sizars between £220 and £280. Equivalences in 2020 pounds and dollars are listed in Table 2. This variance in fees based upon a student's social rank was also seen at Oxford.

Table 2. Estimated cost of degrees at Cambridge University.

Source	College	Date	Cost to BA	Equiv. £ in 2020	Equiv. $ in 2020
Moorman	St John's	1791	£315	£38,700	$51,600
Holmes	Jesus	1793	£300	£36,000	$48,255
Graham	Emmanuel	1849	£233	£24,700	$33,100
Graham	Pembroke	1849	£255	£27,000	$36,200
Graham	Gonville & Caius	1849	£350	£37,100	$49,700
Graham	Trinity	1849	£750	£79,500	$106,500

Moorman reports that Wordsworth's three years at Cambridge cost between £300 and £330,[90] while Holmes estimates that Jesus College cost Coleridge about £100 per annum.

The equivalents listed in the tables are based upon Measuring.Worth.com's estimates for retail prices or 'purchasing cost'; they do not, however, reflect how hard the head of a family had to work to earn that much money for his son's

---

[89] Graham, p. 148.
[90] *William Wordsworth: A Biography: Early Years 1770–1803*, p. 126.

education. For example, the average annual income for a working-class English family in the late Georgian period was £30, and £150 was thought to be enough to support a middle-class family. The listed college costs, therefore, appear to be prohibitive for any but the wealthy, the upper middle class, or students who could win substantial school exhibitions or college or university scholarships. On the other hand, a father of university-bound sons living at the same time as William Wordsworth, Oxford's Regius Professor of Civil Law, James Phillimore (1775–1855), testified to the royal commission that in his experience,

> the ordinary expenses of a University education are not excessive, nor heavier than can be defrayed by parents of moderate and limited incomes; and where diligence and learning are superadded to good conduct, there is no place where young men of moderate and limited outcomes can obtain a better position in society.[91]

The poorer sons of the clergy and gentry or the sons of tradesmen whose families were willing to take the financial risk of sending them to university could defray some of their tuition and other costs by winning school 'exhibitions'. Coleridge was awarded one of these, worth £40 annually, by Christ's Hospital. Wordsworth held two exhibitions from Hawkshead totalling approximately £20, and, by enrolling as a sizar, his fees were greatly reduced. One of his tutors, Edward Frewen, also helped him secure a Foundress Scholarship shortly after arriving at St John's.[92] At Cambridge the Rustat Scholarship offered a stipend worth £30 annually and the Chapel Clerk's Place provided a student £33 plus commons each year. As parents know today, 'commons'—or a student's daily meals for a year—is no small contribution. Coleridge won the first of these awards every year he was at Jesus College; he also secured the Chapel Clerk's stipend after narrowly losing the Craven Prize in January 1793. The stipends attached to these and other award, ranging from £10 to £20, could not, however, completely defray the cost of college.

We know that, as undergraduates, Wordsworth and Coleridge were anxious about college costs and debt. Money problems were part of the reason for Coleridge's desperate dash from Jesus College to the dragoons. Wordsworth refers in *The Prelude* to his 'fears/About my future worldly maintenance',[93] and the pressure his family placed on him about his college expenses is well documented. Nevertheless, when they had sons of their own, both men wanted them to have a university education. Coleridge was never instrumental in

---

[91] Hinds, 'Evidence', p. 232.
[92] It was a common practice to invite students to complete for scholarships or prizes *after* they had been at the university for at least a term.
[93] *Prelude*, 1805, pp. 96, 77–78, 88–89.

Educating the Romantic Poets

providing for his sons' education; that job fell to Southey, who arranged for wealthy relatives to support sending Hartley to Merton and Derwent to St John's, Cambridge. But Coleridge was proud that his sons were university men. Wordsworth consulted John Keble about finding a place for his son John at one of 'the leading Colleges' at Oxford.[94] Augustus Hare, a tutor at New College and Wordsworth admirer, volunteered to arrange the young man's admission to his college in 1823, and as no less than a gentleman commoner. His tuition would have been approximately £100 per annum. At this time, thanks to the patronage of Sir George Beaumont and the earl of Lonsdale, and his job of Distributor of Stamps for Westmoreland, Wordsworth's financial circumstances were improved.[95] The Wordsworths could live comfortably on his salary, but paying for college for his sons took a significant portion of the family's income for several years. Apparently, Wordsworth agreed with Phillimore, Copleston, and Whewell, however, that the long-term value of forming and enlarging his sons' minds and of settling them in good habits, virtue, and wisdom for a lifetime justified the price.

While these Romantic poets' sons were able to attend university, the benefits of a college education were not widely available to many others, and less privileged families had to sacrifice to give their sons this opportunity. Moreover, their son's matriculation at the universities was, more or less, a commitment to a life in the Anglican Church. Despite this 'advantage', the more lucrative church livings typically went to the sons of wealthy families with social connections, not to the poor sizars. These young men ended up as curates. The stories of poor curates who worked hard for tiny salaries to support gentleman clergy who lived comfortably on multiple livings are well known. In Southey's *Letters from England*, Don Manuel Alvarez Espriella comments on seeing servitors at Oxford, whom he describes as 'the sons of parents in low life [who are] educated for the inferior clergy'. These students, he explains, 'receive their education gratuitously, and enjoy certain pensions on condition of ... performing ... menial offices'.[96]

---

[94] Moorman, *William Wordsworth: A Biography: Later Years 1803–1850*, p. 411.
[95] The annual salary for Wordsworth's government position was £400; however, Wordsworth had to pay his staff out of that sum. The Measuring.Worth database calculates equivalences of this income for 2020 in several ways: real wage or real wealth value of that income or wealth, £26,680.00; labour earnings of that income or wealth, £317,100.00; relative income value of that income or wealth, £355,800.00; relative output value of that income or wealth, £1,738,000.00. The real wage or real wealth value measures the purchasing power of that income by its relative ability to purchase goods and services such as food, shelter, and clothing. The relative income line measures that annual salary relative to per capital GDP, which shows the economic status or relative 'prestige value' of the owners of this income because of their rank in the income distribution.
[96] Robert Southey, *Letters from England*, p. 15, Letter XXXII.

Exclusivity

Concerns about the universities' exclusivity were partly based on the costs already reported, but they were also the result of years of religious discrimination, national politics, and class attitudes. After Henry VIII founded the Church of England, Catholics were excluded from the academy. During the Civil War, Puritan scholars ousted Royalists; after the Restoration the Anglicans ejected the Puritans. Subscription to the 39 Articles became a requirement for employment and matriculation. Subscription was handled differently at the two universities in the Romantic period. In 1772, the same year that the Feathers Petition was brought before and soundly defeated in parliament, Cambridge began to require subscription only upon taking a degree, thereby making it possible for nonconforming or conscientious and/or undecided students to attend and be educated, if not credentialled. Oxford continued to require all students to subscribe upon matriculation. George Chinnery, who began his freshman year at Christ Church in 1808, wrote to his mother about the ceremony of matriculation. Prior to the event, his tutor first 'made me read the Oath that I was to take, and said, the undergraduates were to meet in the quad and to follow the procession of Grand Compounders' about to take their degree.[97] The procession included the vice chancellor, dean, sub-dean, proctors, and bachelors; all were dressed in their formal regalia. Chinnery and the other Christ Church freshmen marched to the site where the 'grand compounders' were taking their degrees and waited outside, shivering, to register their names and to pay the required fee of £2 1s. After several annoying delays, including waiting for the vice chancellor to dash to Oriel to subscribe that college's freshmen, the Christ Church students were finally allowed to pay the fee and pledge their oath of allegiance to Church and State. Returning with a little slip of paper testifying to his beliefs, Chinnery felt it was 'a terrible waste of time on a very cold and windy day'.[98]

What did subscription mean? The articles begin, of course, by asserting the authority of the Anglican Church and its bishops and other ministers. They require subscribers to profess belief in a triune God, to accept the miracles reported in the life of Jesus, to believe in original sin (an idea many broad-church clergy ignored), and to accept the roles of the scriptures and Christ in effecting man's salvation. Besides prescribing the sacraments and who might take them, the articles lay out doctrines relating to human behaviours ranging from gluttony and excess of dress to idleness and rebellion.

Dedication to subscription persisted during the Romantic period even though there was no chance that the Roman Catholic Church would ever

---

[97] Chinnery, letter of 28 January 1808.
[98] Chinnery, letter of 28 January 1808.

Educating the Romantic Poets

rise to its previous prominence in England and the old hostility between dissenters and the Anglican Church was on the wane. As matters in France became increasingly violent, however, English university leaders were troubled by the rise of Unitarian, deist, and atheistic reasoning among fellows and undergraduates, so most still supported the requirement of subscription at some point in a university student's life. At the same time, however, many also had ethical issues with requiring young men to 'yield an outward conformity to doctrines, which they may never have seriously considered, or respecting which they may afterwards entertain doubts when they have attended a course of lectures, or read up for examination on the Articles'.[99] In his 1788 pamphlet 'Thoughts on Subscription to Religious Tests, particularly that required by the University of Cambridge of Candidates for the Degree of Bachelor of Arts', William Frend asked two questions:

> Whether a young man of twenty, whose time has been fully employed in the pursuit of natural knowledge, should subscribe to the doctrines which he has never examined; [and] whether a young man of twenty who has been encouraged to exert his faculties, without restraint, in the pursuit of philosophical truth, should embrace, without hesitation, certain opinions, on which men, the most respectable for learning and wisdom, have in every age and nation been greatly divided?[100]

In 1854 the Oxford University Act finally removed religious tests for the BA; Cambridge removed them two years later.

The idea of enrolling women was not seriously considered until late in the Victorian period. Prior to then, women were occasionally allowed to attend classes, but they could not take degrees at either university. Eventually, separate women's colleges were founded: Girton (1869) and Newnham (1872) at Cambridge and Lady Margaret Hall and Somerville College (both 1879) at Oxford. Though women lived in these colleges and studied at the universities, they were not permitted to take a university degree. In 1890 Phillipa Fawcett, a Newnham student, placed above the male senior wrangler on the Cambridge mathematics tripos. Despite this, Ms Fawcett was not permitted a Cambridge diploma. It was not until the twentieth century that women were certified as holders of a university bachelor's degree. Several of the individual colleges did not admit women until the second half of the twentieth century.

Yet another issue of exclusivity had to do with social class. According to Green, during the Hanoverian period 70 per cent of all students were 'sons of country squires and parsons' or of businessmen, lawyers, physicians, politicians,

---

[99] Qtd in Hinds, 'Evidence', p. 123.
[100] Frend, *Thoughts*, p. 3.

and/or government officials.[101] Stone breaks this data down as follows: between 1781 and 1800 30 per cent of university students were 'Esquires and above', 28 per cent were 'Gentlemen', 30 per cent were sons of 'Clergymen and Doctors', and 11 per cent were 'Plebeians'.[102] This demographic was partly the result of self-selection and family tradition. Several respondents to the royal commission queries commented that they hoped distinctions of rank at the university would be abolished. Copleston recognised the problem of social snobbery at the university, admitting that 'nominal rank and precedence of the student' will be determined at college 'not by his merit, but by his standing: the habits of society, the mixed and entangled interests of life require it'.[103] Cambridge appears to have been more egalitarian. Wordsworth avers in *The Prelude* that social status was less important among students at St John's, where he and his classmates were

> ... brothers all
> In honour, as of one—community—
> Scholars and Gentlemen—where, furthermore,
> Distinction lay open to all that came
> And wealth and titles were in less esteem
> Than talents and successful industry.[104]

The Cambridge royal commissioners acknowledged, however, that class distinctions were not entirely absent at the university: 'Though sprung from different ranks, with different fortunes, different prospects ... as Members of the College, [students] meet, to a certain extent, on a footing of equality.'[105] Dr Phillimore, who took his BA degree at Christ Church in 1798 and watched as his four sons also completed degrees at his college, testified to the Oxford commissioners that

> Of all places in England, the University of Oxford is the one in which the possession of money and the display of wealth are of the least avail. Doubtless there are many Undergraduates habitually extravagant and expensive; but these are not the persons who give a tone to the general mass of society, or who rank high in the estimation of their Fellows ... and this class of Undergraduates has never acquired popularity in the University.[106]

[101] Green, 'The University and Social Life', p. 314.
[102] Stone, p. 38.
[103] Edward Copleston, p. 137.
[104] *Prelude*, 1805, p. 324, ll. 231–236.
[105] Graham, p. 16.
[106] Hinds, 'Evidence', p. 232.

Figure 14. Fellow Commoner, Emmanuel College, Cambridge, from Richard Harraden, *Costume of the various orders in the University of Cambridge* (1805).

Oxford and Cambridge in the Romantic Period

Figure 15. Nobleman, Trinity College, Cambridge, from Richard Harraden, *Costume of the various orders in the University of Cambridge* (1805).

Despite such broadmindedness, during the Hanoverian period students were still enrolled and referred to by their social status. At Oxford there were four groups: noblemen, gentlemen commoners (also called fellow commoners or upper commoners at some colleges), commoners (or foundationers), and servitors. Most of the noblemen congregated at Christ Church and Magdalen.[107] At Cambridge students were also sorted by class and ability to pay, ranging from noblemen and fellow commoners to pensioners and sizars. The sons of noblemen who went to Cambridge usually ended up at Trinity. The *Gradus Ad Cantabrigiam: Or, a Dictionary of Terms, Academical and Colloquial ...* (1803) describes noblemen and fellow commoners as 'the most shining men in the university—their gowns are richly trimmed with gold, or silver, lace ..., the tassels [on their caps] are of gold, or silver ... [and they enjoy numerous privileges] by virtue of hereditary talents instilled into their breeches' pockets'.[108] The majority of students at Cambridge were pensioners or sizars. A member of the former group is described in the *Gradus* as 'generally a person of genteel fortune, and good expectancy, who wishes to pass through the usual routine of collegiate exercises without any pecuniary emolument, without enviable distinction, or singular obsequiousness'.[109] Typically, sizars were promising students who needed reduced fees and as much scholarship support as possible; among this group numbered Newton, Paley, Wordsworth, Coleridge, and Whewell. The Cambridge *Gradus* notes that there was little distinction between pensioners and sizars, that both wore the same simpler robes, and that 'many very respectable though not opulent, families are not ashamed to enter their sons' at this rank.[110] Of the 103 students listed in the St John's roll book kept by James Wood during the years when Wordsworth was there, 13 were fellow commoners, 67 were pensioners, and 23 were sizars.[111] No noblemen were listed. All were required to wear gowns and caps that identified their social standing and students were regularly fined if they did not. Despite his pretensions of north country rusticity, Wordsworth took care to be well dressed and well coifed at Cambridge.[112] The Cambridge *Gradus* notes that gentlemen at Trinity College, Cambridge wore purple velvet gowns trimmed with gold or silver; Johnian's gowns were white silk. Byron was particularly pleased with the gold-embroidered robes he wore at Trinity.[113]

In the Romantic period noblemen not only wore the most elegant gowns but were also allowed to keep servants and were welcome at the high table

---

[107] Brockliss, p. 229.
[108] Anonymous, *Gradus ad Cantabrigiam*, pp. 62–63.
[109] Anonymous, *Gradus ad Cantabrigiam*, p. 94.
[110] Anonymous, *Gradus ad Cantabrigiam*, p. 122.
[111] Wood, 'Roll of Students', pp. unnumbered.
[112] Johnston, *The Hidden Wordsworth*, p. 121.
[113] Marchand, *Byron: A Biography*, vol. 1, p. 101.

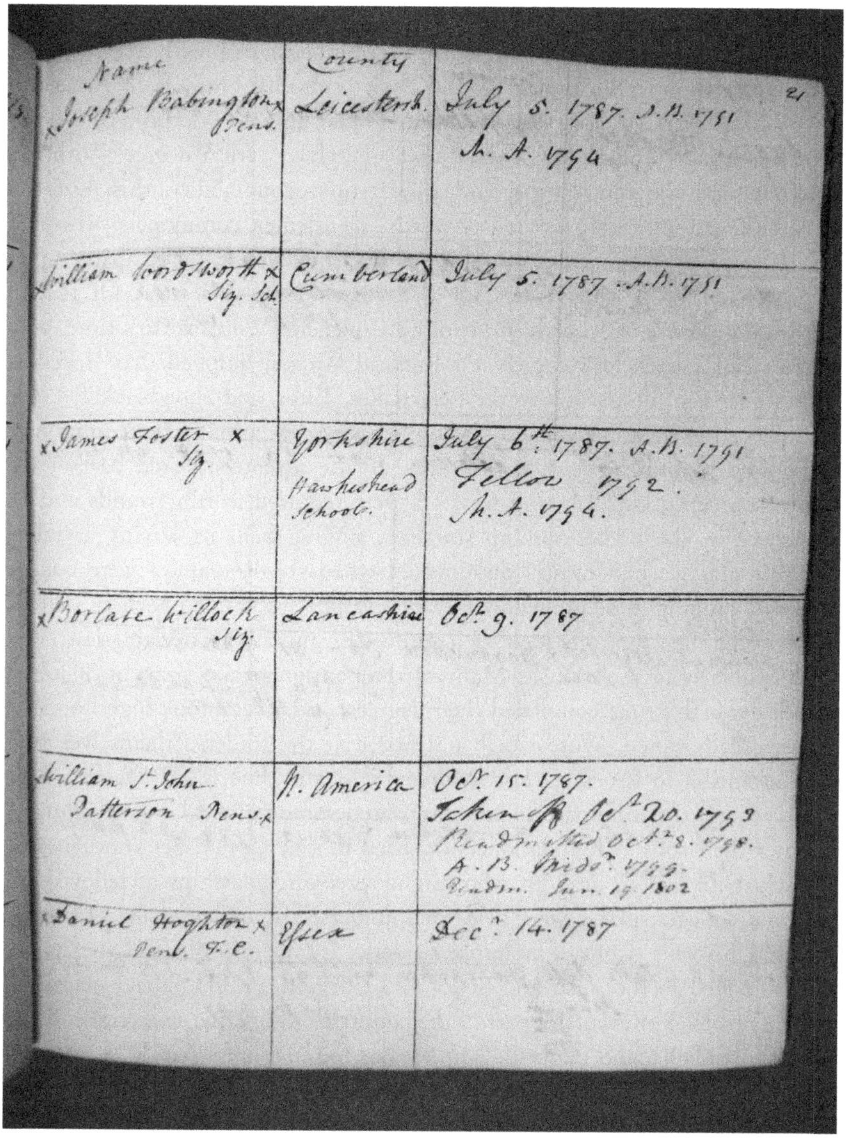

Name	County	
x Joseph Babington x Pens.	Leicestersh.	July 5. 1787. A.B. 1791 M.A. 1794
William Wordsworth x Siz. Sch.	Cumberland	July 5. 1787. A.B. 1791
x James Foster x Siz	Yorkshire Hawkshead School.	July 6th 1787. A.B. 1791 Fellow 1792. M.A. 1794.
x Borlase Willock Siz	Lancashire	Oct. 9. 1787
William St John Patterson Pens. x	N. America	Oct. 15. 1787.
x Daniel Houghton x Pens. F.C.	Essex	Dec. 14. 1787

Figure 16. Roll book of students at St John's College, Cambridge. Wordsworth's name appears on the second line. The status of the students appears as an abbreviation under their names. Wordsworth was both sizar ('siz') and scholarship student ('sch'). On this page there were two pensioners and three sizars. Reproduced by permission of the Master and Fellows of St John's College, Cambridge.

and in the senior commons with the fellows. They also occupied seats of honour in the college chapels and university church. Though noblemen and gentlemen commoners were assigned public tutors, they were often—though not always—excused from lectures. More significantly, they were not required to stand for public exams. These men rarely bothered with their studies and lived the jolly life typical of the posh fraternity brothers in American universities today. They gamed and rode horses, drank a good bit, and often neither remained long enough nor cared enough to earn a degree. With too much money, too much time, and almost no accountability, this minority caused the most trouble for college heads. Gentlemen commoners, who had the reputation of being not over-full of learning and ready to drink upon any occasion, were known at some colleges as 'Empty Bottles'. Of the 13 fellow commoners or scholars at St John's College in Wordsworth's time, only four earned a bachelor's degree. Dr Richard Watson quipped that 'a Fellow Commoner is of no use but to the Bed-maker, Tutor, and Shoe-black!!!'[114] The reading or hard-reading men at the universities were usually the commoners or pensioners and the sizars or servitors. In the seventeenth and part of the eighteenth centuries sizars and servitors were required to run errands and be of service to the higher-ranking students, ringing bells or serving at table, but this practice had mostly disappeared when the Romantics were college students. Hoping to secure fellowships or, eventually, church or school livings, these young men typically took their studies, examinations, declamations, and other scholarly tasks seriously. Many of the pensioners and sizars at St John's in Wordsworth's time completed their degrees, and several took high honours.

As already noted, Wordsworth testified that the students themselves paid little attention to issues of class. Moreover, by the time the Romantics were at university, the difference in fees motivated some practical 'gentle' families to enter their sons as foundationers or sizars to save money. Yet another issue of exclusivity had to do with who might receive scholarships or fellowships. At some colleges, places were held for founders' kin and residents of certain towns. University College preferred students from Yorkshire and the north, Exeter looked to the west, and St John's College, Cambridge held places for students from Wordsworth's part of the country.[115] Similarly, at several colleges the only students who might be admitted as foundationers had to come from certain counties or schools.

It should be no surprise that the constraints upon university enrolment incurred by social status, cost, and the religious tests reported above kept the enrolment at both universities low during the Romantic period. Fewer than 1,300 students in total were enrolled in England's universities in 1800. These numbers may have also been depressed because in that still largely agrarian nation the wealth that made university attendance possible was concentrated in the hands of little more than 10 per cent of the population. Moreover, it was

---

[114] Charles Wordsworth, p. 647, notes.
[115] Brockliss, p. 231.

generally believed that 'gentlemen' were the only men who needed or might enjoy a classical education. Additionally, the nation was at war during much of this period and some of the young men who might have gone to university had instead purchased commissions and were serving in the navy or army. In 1795 Cambridge's 17 colleges had a total of only 736 undergraduates; the combined number of fellows that year was 409. The two largest colleges in 1795 were Trinity (165 students and 67 fellows) and St John's (100 undergraduates and 62 fellows). Most of the other colleges' enrolments averaged around 30 students; the smallest college, King's, had only 12 students in 1795 (traditionally top-heavy, Kings had 59 fellows). In the first decades of the nineteenth century enrolment at Oxford ranged from as few as ten students at the smaller colleges to 100 at the largest; the ratio of students to fellows was similar to that at Cambridge. In 1800 Oxford's largest college, Christ Church, had a total of 110 students; in other years, the college had half that enrolment. In the first 13 years of the nineteenth century, only 267 new students matriculated at the entire university each year; in 1815 the number rose to 372, and thereafter continued to rise.[116] The small size of the universities during this period is worth noting, for it is a reminder of how small and closely knit the English intelligentsia was in the Romantic period. Most college men knew each other and their teachers. These young men were told that they were and came to think of themselves as the nation's future; they were chosen sons who were expected and equipped to be of service to their society.

---

[116] Hinds, pp. 17–18.

Chapter Seven

University Life

> [All members of the colleges] are subject to a code of internal laws and rules framed for the maintenance of good order and decorum and moral and religious habits ... [which are] wholesome and beneficial.
>
> Cambridge University commission

In his Preface to *The Idea of the University* Newman calls the college years 'a time of life all-important and especially favourable to mental culture'.[1] This acculturation took place in classrooms, libraries, and private study, but it was also affected by students' experiences in their college rooms and at parties, sports, meals, and jaunts into town. The effects of these extra-curricular experiences are difficult to define or measure, but they contributed then as they do now to students' developing skills, emotions, identity, and values. In the Romantic period students were required by royal statute to live and take their meals in their colleges, where they found that their lives were organised by the university calendar, its local traditions, and by a daily routine, all of which had been in place for centuries.

The academic year

Though many freshmen did not arrive in Cambridge until mid-October for the beginning of the Michaelmas term, the first event of the academic year

---

[1] Newman, p. xli.

was the opening of the Stourbridge Fair, one of the greatest Renaissance fairs in Britain. Founded in 1211 as a parish charity benefiting lepers, the fair was one of the parochial duties that still belonged to the university in the Romantic period. The vice chancellor and an entourage of college heads, doctors, canons, fellows, and students gathered at the Senate House for wine and cake and then rode in coaches to the fairgrounds to open the fair. After many of the fair's pleasures had been sampled, the university hosted a feast of oysters, beer, bread, and butter for all in attendance. A few weeks later, at the end of October, all members of the university as well as the mayor of Cambridge, two aldermen, two representatives from every nearby parish, and at least four members of parliament attended the Magna Congregatio, also called the Black Assembly, which took place at Great St Mary's Church. During this service, the senior proctor asked all students not only to keep the peace in the town and the university but also to avoid thieves, evil-doers, and those who might harbour them. The burgess's oath at this event added a pledge of fidelity to the monarch. At Oxford a similar event, the Matriculation Ceremony, took place in early October. New students, dressed in their robes, waited outside in the elements for the vice chancellor to witness their oaths of subscription to the 39 Articles of Religion. Then students processed with the dean, sub-dean, proctors, and bachelors, all dressed in their formal regalia, to the Sheldonian Theatre to be formally presented—in a Latin address—to the vice chancellor.

Once the new academic year began and all students were officially matriculated, university life was organised by terms. At Oxford the Michaelmas Term lasted until Christmas and Hilary Term lasted until Easter. The spring at Oxford was divided into two terms: the Easter or Paschal term, which lasted until May, and the Trinity term, which lasted until late June or early July. At Cambridge there were only three terms: the fall term, Michaelmas; Lenten Term, which began after Christmas and lasted until Easter; and Easter Term, which encompassed examinations and culminated with graduation in early July. The names of these terms—Michaelmas, Hilary, Lenten, Easter, or Paschal— reflect the degree to which life at both universities was governed by the Anglican Church calendar and how often students were reminded of this affiliation.

At the end of each term students took exams in their colleges. College exams, called 'Collections' at Christ Church, were designed and administered locally by the fellows and tutors of each college. They should be distinguished from university exams, which were administered in the middle and the end of a student's stay at the universities. University examinations took place at the end of the Easter term at Cambridge in the Senate House. Oxford's university exams took place at roughly the same time, at the end of the Trinity term, and were held in the Metaphysical and Music Schools in the Bodleian quadrangle. Because of the difficulty and expense of travel, some students, especially the poorer and/or hard-reading ones, elected to remain on campus during holidays

University Life

between terms. Seniors aiming for examination honours often stayed in their colleges for the entire year.[2]

Twice a year all students at both universities participated in Holy Communion services with their colleges. Just as many had done in their grammar schools, students and tutors prepared for this service in advance with study and prayer. On Ash Wednesday at Cambridge, the university assembled at Great St Mary's Church to read the Lenten Litany, which began the season of penitence and reflection. In the same space, the entire university celebrated with great festivity the end of Lent and the promise of Easter Sunday. At Oxford until 1825 the entire university gathered at the University Church of St Mary the Virgin on 10 February for a service on the feast day of St Scholastica.[3] Several weeks later came the university's celebrations of Easter Sunday and Ascension Day. Later in the spring, on the first of May, college members and city residents of Oxford gathered for May Morning, an occasion when the Magdalen College choir sang the Eucharist from the college bell tower.

In a tradition that began at Oxford in 1780, for eight successive Sundays at the end of Lent term, the Bampton Lectures were delivered at St Mary the Virgin.[4] The lectures signalled the beginning of the hard push to the university's exams. Collegiate rivalries came to a head during the seniors' examination ordeals, which lasted over a week. These students' progress and rankings were followed with great interest by their classmates and the faculty. In June at Cambridge the university ceremoniously opened another local fair at Barnwell,[5] and it added to the growing excitement about the impending university exams at the Senate House scheduled later that month. Just as at Oxford, the progress of seniors through their exams was followed with great interest by the entire university community.

The crowning event of the academic year at both universities was, of course, the degree ceremony. At Cambridge this took place in mid-July. The event began with a series of 'congregations' of college heads, doctors of the three faculties, all other university and college officials, and the students who were taking MA and BA degrees. All of these men, dressed in their full regalia, gathered ceremonially in the Senate House and again in both the Non-Regent and Regent Houses. The final ceremony certified that all students present had met the residency requirement, had passed their exams, and were of good character, after which they were awarded their degrees. One by one, in order

[2] Wordsworth spent at least one Christmas holiday at Cambridge.
[3] This service commemorated an event in 1355 when an altercation between two undergraduates and a tavern keeper grew into a two-day riot, ending with the death of 63 students and 30 townspeople.
[4] The lecturers were distinguished members of the university chosen by the college heads.
[5] This event was a combination of trade and pleasure fair.

Educating the Romantic Poets

of the esteem of their college, the seniority of their degrees, and their class rank (based on their performance on exams), the students knelt before the vice chancellor, who took each young man's hands in his and declared him admitted to the degree. After the awarding of the degrees, Cambridge's new bachelors subscribed to the 39 Articles and the vice chancellor dissolved the Congregation. All members of the university, students, friends, and family celebrated the end of the day at a fancy-dress ball. Oxford's graduation ceremony, called *Encaenia*, was a similarly grand social event, taking place in July after exams. *Encaenia* began with a procession of all college members in their regalia from their colleges to the Sheldonian Theatre, where speeches and a degree-granting spectacle similar to the one at Cambridge took place. These proceedings were punctuated by as many as three different performances of the music of Handel, ending, always, with the Hallelujah Chorus.

The college day

At both universities the college day usually began around 7 or 8 a.m. with morning prayer in the college chapels. Students breakfasted on their own in their rooms or in local coffee houses. Each weekday, between 9 a.m. and 2 p.m., students attended tutorials and studied independently. University lectures were typically delivered during this time as well. The midday meal, held in each college's great hall, might begin as early as noon or as late as 4 p.m., and was attended by students, fellows, and senior members. Classes resumed afterwards and ended with afternoon chapel services, though daily attendance at this service was not required of students. From the end of chapel until supper, which was much later in the evening, students had free time for exercise and amusements. Suppers in the hall or college buttery were not well attended; more often, students ate in their rooms.

Evenings were supposed to be spent studying and sometimes tutors superintended their charges' efforts. If exams were approaching, men aiming for honours read hard late in to the night, while less dedicated students amused themselves in town or with desultory reading, conversation, card playing, or wine or tea parties. The university statutes for Oxford decreed that students should be back in their chambers by 9 p.m.,[6] but some of the colleges were lax in applying this rule and allowed students to be out until 11 p.m. or midnight. At the designated curfew hour, the college gates were closed by the Porter. Similar rules and practices at the end of the day were in place at Cambridge. At both universities, any student who missed curfew would incur punishment, usually in the form of fines paid to the Porters. Some colleges assigned an additional written exercise due the next day.

[6] Hinds, p. 20.

University Life

Philip Yorke, who entered Cambridge in 1774 as a gentleman or fellow commoner, offers this description of a typical day at college:

Rise at 7; chapel from half past 7 till 8; 8–9, breakfast and Demosthenes by myself; 9–10, Demosthenes with Mr. Weston; 10–11, classical lecture; 11–12, Euclid; 12–1, walk and dressing time; 1–2 dinner and combination room; 2–3, friends' rooms; 3–5, correspondence or private reading; from half past 5 to 6, chapple; 6–7 visits, tea drinking; 7–9, Xenophon and mathematics; 9–11 friends' rooms or company at home. On Sunday, instead of Xenophon, Abernethy's sermons.[7]

Three decades later (just before Shelley arrived at Oxford), the young commoner George Chinnery, who was, from the first, a reading man, offers this account of his weekday routine at Christ Church:

7–8 A.M.:	Study Greek or algebra
8–9:30 A.M.:	Surplice prayers 4 or 5 times every week (if no surplice prayers, study mathematics until 10)
10 A.M.:	Breakfast
10–11 A.M.:	Work with tutor
11-Noon:	Study Blackstone
12–1:30 P.M.:	Classics
1:30–3 P.M.:	Dinner in the Hall, walk and fence or attend college divinity lecture
4–5:30 P.M.:	Learn by heart and read Le Sage or Milton or some other light reading
5:30–7 P.M.:	Dress and go to a party
7–8 P.M.:	Read classics—The *Odyssey* or Euripides or when that is done, conic sections
8–9:30 P.M.:	Write home, read German, work on theme.[8]

This schedule includes at least six hours of study each day. Christopher Wordsworth, the poet's brother, reported attending his share of wine parties as a first-year student. Later, when he was preparing for disputations and the Senate House examination in 1795, he averaged more than nine hours of study every day.[9] Though Coleridge told his family that Jesus College had no 'discipline',[10] Coleridge's daily grind as a first-year student at Jesus College

---

[7] Qtd in Winstanley, p. 226.
[8] Chinnery, letter of 4–9 November 1808.
[9] Charles Wordsworth, p. 594.
[10] CLSTC, p. 17.

Educating the Romantic Poets

was similar to Chinnery's at Christ Church. He attended chapel twice a day, studied mathematics and attended his tutor's lectures in the morning, walked in the afternoons, and spent long evenings of classical reading and translation work usually until 11 p.m. under the good influence of his schoolboy mentor and friend, Thomas Middleton, who was at Pembroke.[11] This routine was enlivened from time to time by long walks, planning a garden, playing the fiddle, attending to a pet cat, and 'taking pot-shots at the Pembroke College rats'.[12] Wordsworth describes days of 'college labours', lecturers' rooms, and examinations, marked on the quarter-hour by 'Trinity's loquacious clock'.[13] He admits that 'now and then' this labour was 'forced'; to counterbalance this work, he indulged in 'suppers, wine, and fruit' with the happy 'throng' of his classmates, for his 'heart/Was social and loved idleness and joy'.[14]

Room and board at college

Among the college students' first tasks upon arrival at university were finding, furnishing and decorating their private rooms, which were a welcome change after their communal living spaces at school. First-floor rooms cost the most; garrets were cheap. Some students paid for suites of rooms. Wordsworth's was 'in a nook obscure' above the noisy college kitchens, little more than a closet.[15] Coleridge's ground-floor room at Jesus College was a bit more spacious and had windows on two sides. Byron gloated that his rooms at Trinity were 'superexcellent';[16] situated between the rooms of his tutor and a senior fellow, they were among the best his wealthy college offered. Often with the guidance of their dean or tutors, new students purchased their own beds and bedding, tables, chairs, bookshelves, and cookery items. De Quincey listed the following room expenditures: mahogany tables and chairs, maps, wall hangings, carpets, tea services and spoons, engraved decanters, and dozens of wine glasses. At Oxford, one student reported that his room expenses included six chairs with seats of Spanish leather, a music desk, wall hangings, maps, and a wig block.[17] Students' rooms were kept tidy by paid house cleaners; their clothes were sent to a laundress. Wealthier students arranged for hot water and firewood to be delivered to their rooms each day.

The domestic life of all members of the colleges was expected to be orderly, decorous, moral, and wholesome.[18] Royal commissioners emphasised

---

[11] Holmes, p. 40.
[12] Holmes, p. 40.
[13] *Prelude*, 1805, p. 94, ll. 60–65, 51–55.
[14] *Prelude*, 1805, p. 102, l. 213; p. 94, ll. 40–41; p. 102, ll. 234–236.
[15] *Prelude*, 1805, p. 94, ll. 45–46.
[16] Marchand, *Byron: A Biography*, vol. 1, p. 102.
[17] Green, 'The University and Social Life', p. 320.
[18] Graham, p. 16.

University Life

the benefits of 'living under the same domestic rule; many of them lodged within the same walls; all assembling in the same common dining hall; associating in their course of study and in the routine of their daily habits'.[19] Living and studying in this way, the commissioners said, students are 'naturally drawn to each other by attractions of mutual kindness' and 'while particular individuals and smaller groups form for themselves their own closer intimacies and friendships, a general spirit of sympathy pervades the whole'.[20] The commission singled out 'one predominant feeling' among students in the colleges, which was 'not to do anything that tends to bring discredit on the College or [that] falls below the tone of good manners and the standard of honourable conduct'.[21] In this way, they concluded, 'social sympathy becomes auxiliary to moral discipline and academical authority'.[22]

Assembling in the common dining hall for the midday meal was an especially important daily occasion. Absence from this meal was not permitted, except for illness or special cases, and those who missed the meal without excuse were fined. Students and fellows dressed for the meal in white waistcoats, knee breeches with silver or gilt buckles, white silk stockings, and low shoes. The older members of the colleges wore wigs. Just prior to the meal, undergraduates lined up in the rooms of the college barbers to have their hair combed, curled, or powdered. Attended by all students and faculty, the meal began with a solemn grace, spoken in Latin by a senior fellow. De Quincey remarks that, along with the college chapel, the refectory hall was one of the two 'essential public suites belonging to every college'.[23]

While food at the high table could be quite fine, the food for the underclassmen, who sat according to their social rank, was unremarkable. Served by the college staff, these meals typically offered a choice of two or three 'sorts of animal food and the common vegetables'—no fish, soup, or game.[24] Wine was served at the high table. Tankards of beer were distributed down the students' tables. If a man had ordered ahead, he might have a fruit pie for dessert. Chinnery, who was accustomed to fine dining and good conversation at meals, described his first dinner in the common hall in this way:

> —the Hall itself is magnificent, but the dinner is the most unsociable thing you can conceive. The Commoners dine at one table, the gentleman-commoners at another, the students at another, the bachelors at another, the Master of Arts at another. These tables have not the least

[19] Graham, p. 16.
[20] Graham, p. 16.
[21] Graham, p. 16.
[22] Graham, p. 16.
[23] Masson, p. 48.
[24] Masson, p. 48.

Educating the Romantic Poets

communication with another: there was a leg of mutton roasted, a neck of veal with an onion sauce, and beef stakes with a brown sauce, potatoes, cabbage & turnips; every person helps himself, so that the dishes walk up and down the table in the most ridiculous manner possible. There were pies also and cheese; I eat of nothing but mutton and vegetables, the dishes themselves were ... very good, but there was no conversation; not a word was said to anybody, except to the waiters.[25]

George Gunning described being a young guest at the Trinity high table with Dr Mansel, the college master. He reported that everyone at the table was in 'great spirits' and the vice master of Trinity, Rev. Moore Meredith, 'kept the company in a roar of laughter', from 'our first assembling around the Charcoal to our quitting it after dinner'.[26]

Chinnery told his mother that students filed directly to prayers after dinner, where he was surprised to report that all students were required to dress in a surplice 'like a parson!'[27] On days with no afternoon chapel service, students and fellows usually adjourned after the midday meal to drink coffee or sherry in their respective commons rooms. Later in the evening, suppers were available in the college hall or buttery, but most students preferred to arrange for meals in their rooms. It was possible to order roasted meat or fowl from the college kitchen or local pubs to be delivered to students' rooms. Most students also had stocks of bread, butter, cheese, wine, and tea in their rooms. The grocery list of the gentleman commoner Phillip Perrin, who was at Christ Church from 1761 to 1765, indicates the sort of diet some students enjoyed at college. He lists loaf sugar, lobster, eels, eggs and toast, lamb, tarts and cream, fresh salmon, butter, fowls and gravy, puddings, duck, and many bottles of port.

Whewell echoes the commissioners' comments on communal life for university students. By eating, worshipping, and studying together, he wrote, students acquire 'a number of subjects of common interest', and in so doing are bound 'together by a tie which rarely loses its hold, or its charm, during his life'.[28] Indeed, many contemporaneous accounts praise the sense of community, college loyalty, and lifelong friendships that daily life at the colleges achieved. Wordsworth had a number of friends from the north who matriculated about the same time with him, such as John Fleming. He also made a new and lifelong friend in Robert Jones, from Wales. Wordsworth's memorable trek across Switzerland in 1790 with Jones is well known. He corresponded with Jones ever after and dedicated *Descriptive Sketches* to him in 1793, and years

---

[25] Chinnery, letter of 16 January 1808.
[26] Gunning, vol. 1, p. 111.
[27] Chinnery, letter of 16 January 1808.
[28] Whewell, p. 91.

University Life

later he and his friend contemplated another such trip to the Continent. Jones, by then a portly parish clergyman, appreciated but declined the invitation. Friends made at Cambridge stood by Coleridge during the worst of the dragoons episode. He told his brother that he received several letters from 'my friends at Cambridge—of most soothing Contents. They write me, that "with undiminish[ed] esteem and increased affection the Jesuites look forward to my return, as to that of a lost Brother"'.[29] Another famous college friendship that lasted a lifetime was that of Byron and his Trinity classmate John Cam Hobhouse.

The pleasures of sharing time, talk, and food at the university help to explain why it was not uncommon in later years for these men to gather and live together in close, college-like communities. We see examples of this congregating behaviour in the long, cohabiting visits of Wordsworth, Coleridge, Southey, Byron, and Shelley, and of many of their classmates in country house parties or European summer rentals. Holmes has attributed 'the urge to break away into some ideal, small, rural community' that runs through the history of English literature from Shelley to D. H. Lawrence to the eighteenth-century Enlightenment and associationist psychology.[30] Jessica Fay sees in these behaviours 'monastic inheritances' (see Chapter 11). It could just as easily be attributed to the communal life many of them experienced at grammar school or in university colleges.

Whewell on college life

Yet another view into the daily lived experience of Romantic-era college students is offered by William Whewell in *On the Principles of English University Education* (1837). Whewell was the master of Trinity when he published this essay and had spent almost his entire life as a student or member of a college. No doubt what he says—and leaves unsaid—was informed by those experiences and by long-standing collegiate loyalty. Whewell begins by reminding his audience that the university is charged to 'infuse a sense of moral and religious responsibility, as well as mere knowledge', and to 'form the principles of conduct as well as the intellect'.[31] The university works, he says, to 'nourish, cherish, and preserve concord, unity, peace, and mutual charity'.[32] The Trinity College rules, he asserts, call students and fellows to cultivate modesty, integrity, and 'purity of manners'.[33] He adds that students and fellows

---

[29] CLSTC, p. 73.
[30] Holmes, p. 63, footnote.
[31] Whewell, p. 81.
[32] Whewell, p. 85.
[33] Whewell, p. 83.

Educating the Romantic Poets

are expected, and directed, to behave with submission and reverence toward their superiors.[34] Whewell reports that first-year students were allowed in town only if accompanied by at least one other who would 'witness [their] proper conduct'.[35] Taking issue specifically with Cowper's suggestion in 'The Task' (1785) that college discipline was on the decline,[36] he avers that

> the great body of young Englishmen, of the condition of those who come to the Universities, conform, with a generous obedience of spirit, to rules which are the very essence of the institution in which they are placed, and of which all the better natures among them see and feel the value. I am quite persuaded that no one could become acquainted with the temper of the students of our Universities toward their College discipline, and towards those who administer it, without forming a strong affection and admiration for them.[37]

According to Whewell, the behaviours that the universities disdain are 'domestic seditions, detraction, and dissention … late revels, potations, scurrility, ribaldry, scoffs, whisperings, reproaches, and scandals'.[38] Toward the end of this essay, in a voice that seems to derive more from Victorian nationalism than Romantic rationalism, Whewell comments on the connections between the university and the homes of England and their poetry and prayers. When describing the influence of the English university upon its students, Whewell declares that the 'most decisive part of [a college student's] whole education and which forms one of the most essential parts of it [is] –namely, the feeling that he is an Englishman'.[39] This includes a student's 'knowledge of the principles by which the actions of his fellow-citizens are regulated, and by reference to which his own will be judged of'.[40] He adds that students learn 'sympathy' and 'a habit of balancing himself among … [the] impulses [of his feelings]'.

Student behaviour

Even dutiful young Englishmen under the supervision of men as idealistic as Whewell fail from time to time to balance their impulses, however. And it is likely that principled statements against domestic sedition, dissention, scurrility, and so on were necessary because from time to time students did not resist the

[34] Whewell, p. 83.
[35] Whewell, p. 84.
[36] Whewell, p. 88.
[37] Whewell, pp. 86–87.
[38] Whewell, p. 85.
[39] Whewell, p. 91.
[40] Whewell, p. 91.

University Life

temptations to amuse themselves with seditious talk, dissent, vulgarity, and so forth. Green takes a generally negative view of students' self-discipline, social conduct, and commitment to learning at late-Georgian colleges. He recounts stories of gentleman commoners' 'juvenile debauchery', drinking, and high living and cites contemporaneous complaints about others—the 'Lowngers, whose whole business is to fly from the painful task of thinking', and the more dangerous 'jolly fellows', who ridiculed 'every boy who has the folly to be sober'.[41] Christopher Wordsworth's account of social life at the universities includes a description of how one mid-eighteenth-century chancellor urged the university Senate to rouse itself from its usual non-involvement in students' daily lives to do something about their hunting, dicing, card-playing, drinking, absence from chapel services, and failure to wear the proper 'habit[s] of their degree'.[42] True to the university's hands-off notion about how to govern young 'gentlemen' and their appreciation of the human nature of undergraduates, the chancellor's efforts to interfere with college life were as unpopular with the senior members of the university as they were with students.

Southey's behaviour at Balliol and his later comments about Oxford bracket the range of student behaviours that were likely at the Romantic universities. In 1801 Southey referred to the 'soul & body-pollution of Oxford debauchery'[43] and expressed doubt that his younger brother Harry possessed the 'intellectual and moral strength' to 'resist the ruin of a University'.[44] However, Southey himself appears to have avoided debauchery and ruin, thanks, in part, to his friendship at Balliol with his sober, self-restrained, and studious friend Edmund Seward, three years his senior. Speck suggests that Seward was a 'second conscience' and sort of 'moral father' for young Southey and adds that this friendship had the effect of offsetting Southey's tendency toward 'romantic rebellion with a kind of utilitarian stoicism'.[45] Thanks to his friend's example, Southey stopped reading Rousseau and turned to Epictetus; and, thanks to his experience at Westminster, he resisted speaking out against college authorities. He did, however, spend time 'democratizing gloriously' with classmates; during a visit to a friend at Cambridge he attended Frend's trial in the vice chancellor's court.[46] Southey's letters make it clear that he spent a good bit of time at Balliol cultivating friendships, singing to the keyboard and flute music of his friends Burnett and Lightfoot, and arranging student parties.[47]

---

[41] Green, 'The University and Social Life', pp. 319–322, 336.
[42] Christopher Wordsworth, *Social Life*, pp. 67–68.
[43] CLRS, Pt 2, #564.
[44] CLRS, Pt 2, #580.
[45] Speck, pp. 29, 38.
[46] Speck, p. 40.
[47] One especially memorable party took place during university festivities staged in honour of the duke of Portland's installation as the chancellor of the university. Speck, p. 33.

Educating the Romantic Poets

Winstanley, who could be quite critical of Cambridge, claims that the 'grossly idle and dissolute were never more than a small minority of the undergraduate population'. This was because the commoners and sizars, who constituted the majority of students, 'had their way to make in the world'.[48] Judith Curthoys notes that most of the offences of Christ Church men were unremarkable: wearing improper clothing in chapel, missing mathematics lectures, being rude to senior members, or writing 'insolent' exercises.[49] At Cambridge undergraduates missed meals and chapel; they overslept and cut class; they drank too much, got loud, and sometimes came to blows or broke things. A few got into trouble with women. Compared with student life in the twenty-first century, none of the behaviours that so troubled the chancellor mentioned above or any other critics of student behaviour in the Georgian university seems particularly out-of-line for young men between the ages of 18 and 22.

Colleges managed behavioural issues in a variety of ways. Lesser offences incurred fines or writing assignments. The sequence of punishments the college head of Trinity College, Oxford, used to deal with an undergraduate with a drinking problem is illustrative. On his first instance of public drunkenness the student was required to translate an article in *The Spectator* into Latin.[50] For his second and third offences he had to translate sermons into Latin. A fourth intoxication caused him to be restricted to the college for a week, where he was also required to attend all meals and translate two sermons or recite 200 lines. On the fifth offence the college reached out to his family; after the sixth, he was rusticated for a year. Other serious infractions such as lying, cheating, or visiting prostitutes usually resulted in confinement or a year's rustication. Coleridge's experiences with prostitutes did not directly cause his leaving Cambridge, but these 'Unchastities'[51] certainly contributed to the mental state that resulted in his leaving college to enlist in the Dragoons.[52]

'Aggravated cases of immorality' or 'breaches of faith that endangered' the colleges' system of discipline, though rare, were met with expulsion.[53] Judith Curthoys cites one case that Christ Church officers called the 'most flagrant act of lewdness and immorality within the walls of college'.[54] The details of what happened and the student's name were removed from the record, but whatever he did provoked immediate expulsion. Officers of the college, however, came to his defence, citing previous good behaviour, and he was rusticated, but with a towering load of exercises to perform if he wished to

---

[48] Winstanley, p. 227.
[49] Curthoys, pp. 189–190.
[50] Green, 'The University and Social Life', p. 338, n. 1.
[51] Ashton, p. 37.
[52] They also were the subject of terrifying opium nightmares he experienced in later years.
[53] Green, 'The University and Social Life', p. 338.
[54] Curthoys, p. 188.

University Life

be reinstated. He was tasked with abridging all of Herodotus (with 'schemes and enunciations'), mastering the 5th, 6th, 11th, and 12th books of Euclid, working all the example problems in the first part of Maclaurin's Algebra, taking notes on all of St Paul's epistles and the last 100 Psalms in Hebrew (indicating that the student had been a Westminster graduate), and translating the ninth discourse of Sherlock's sermons into Latin.[55] Apparently, the young man completed this work, for he was allowed to return to the college after six months, though he was restricted to campus for three more months and his punishment announced to the entire college. After this, and upon personally asking pardon of the college officers, the student was fully reinstated, and his name and his offence were erased from the records of the episode.[56] Based on archival data, Curthoys's educated guess is that this student was Thomas Hinds, who was later made both a tutor and a rhetoric lecturer and eventually awarded a college living. In some cases, badly behaved students or those with poor academic achievement might be allowed to migrate to one of the Halls of the University. These establishments were typically more expensive than the colleges, and so offending students also paid a 'pecuniary penalty'.[57]

Related to students' behavioural indiscretions was the problem of student debt. The Oxford commissioners' report commends the university's authorities' ongoing concern and efforts to help students manage their finances, including the tradition of having tutors supervise students' spending. The commissioners observed that student debt appeared to be due most often to self-indulgence in furniture and entertainments. As is well known, Coleridge's debts due to trips to London, drinking, and 'loose sexual morality'[58] were so large when he was at college (close to £150) that he contemplated suicide. Henry Kirke White, who was a sizar at St John's in 1805, observed that there were, indeed,

> gay dissipated men [at Cambridge], who chuse to be Sizars in order that they may have more money to lavish on their pleasures. [But] our dinners and suppers cost us nothing, and if a man chuse to eat milk-breakfasts, and go without tea, he may live absolutely for nothing, for his College emoluments will cover the rest of his expenses.[59]

White himself was able to live on £15 a year.

Public concern about student debt, rowdy behaviour, and irreligion were some of the reasons cited for creating the royal commissions. However, after

---

[55] Curthoys, p. 188.
[56] Curthoys, pp. 188–189.
[57] Hinds, p. 22.
[58] Qtd in Ashton, p. 43.
[59] Robert Southey, *Remains of Henry Kirke White*, p. 181.

Educating the Romantic Poets

interviewing many students and senior members of the universities, both commissions concluded that student behaviour was not a serious problem. The commissioners did, however, encourage the universities and colleges to continue working to protect students from the temptations of 'gaming or idleness or dissipation'.[60] The Oxford report aptly summarises the universities' attitude about the 'practical difficulties' involved in managing young men:

> Students are at an age, when they cannot be subjected to the minute surveillance and rigid constraint exercised in a school, and when, on the other hand, they are not fit to be entrusted with absolute liberty and independence in acting for themselves. They are in a state of transition from the subjection of boyhood to the freedom of manhood; and no system of discipline can be properly suited to such a state unless it contains in itself a mixture of constraint and liberty; so much constraint as may guard the inexperienced against the temptation of youth and the dangers of wasteful extravagance; so much liberty, as may serve to develop the qualities of their moral character, and prepare them gradually for the weightier responsibilities and fuller freedom of afterlife.[61]

The commissioners added that learning to live freely in a collegiate system is part of the education the university supplies. The Oxford commissioners admitted, however, that 'The amount of individual freedom which we have described necessarily opens great facilities for idleness, extravagance, and dissipation' and can lead to 'lounging and indolent habits ... gambling and vice'.[62] They concluded that the best protection for college students is the 'strong and lasting' bond between them and their teachers, which causes even the 'most thoughtless Student' to take an 'interest in the credit and welfare of his college'.[63] When a longer view is taken, it seems likely that the years boys spent under the discipline of their schools readied many of them to take on the freedom as well as the academic challenges of university life. The intentionally planned stages of the Anglo-classical academy's training—first 'subjection' at school and then 'freedom' at college—seem to have had good effect on the work habits of Wordsworth, Southey, and Byron in their later lives as adult writers.

---

[60] Hinds, p. 16.
[61] Hinds, p. 16.
[62] Hinds, p. 22.
[63] Hinds, p. 22.

University Life

Advice to freshmen

Other insight into the daily life of university students in Wordsworth's and Byron's generations—and how the college experience trained students for their lives as writers—comes from a popular pamphlet *Ten Minutes Advice to Freshmen* (1785), authored by a recent graduate of Cambridge who signed himself simply 'a Questionist'. The years students spend in college, he writes, are 'as important years as any in the whole course of their lives'.[64] He notes that these years require practical knowledge and skills, so he offers advice on securing furniture, keeping out of debt, and keeping the bed-makers and coal-porter happy (give excellent, but not extravagant, tips). He urges freshmen not to fall into the trap of playing today and planning to study tomorrow. 'A lost Freshman year,' he counsels, 'is seldom recovered.'[65] Reading hard in the last year, he counsels, cannot make up for slacking in the first two.[66] He urges students to read ahead before each term begins and to study during the holidays, especially during the long Christmas break. In this way, students will be 'respected' and will find themselves 'in a fair way to gain an imminence in literature'.[67]

The Questionist offers new students the following observations about the value of their college curriculum and their tutors' teaching practices:

> I do not allow you, whatever good opinion you may have of yourself, to be a competent judge of what studies are most exactly proper for you, and what not. 'A young soldier (says an agreeable writer) must be contented to learn his exercise upon the authority of his commander, before he can be satisfied in its use in the field'. In the same manner, though you may not, at first, see the usefulness of those sciences to which you may be directed by your tutor, I would not have you think it necessary to despise them. In such a case, is it not much more probable that he should be right than you? Be not therefore discouraged but persevere; and you will find most difficulties vanish, and will be even surprised afterwards wherein their difficulty consisted. I do not mean to desire you to be a mere plodding book worm; but of this I am positively certain,—that a man who applies regularly, though but for a few hours, every day, to the studies of the University, without suffering those hours to be interrupted, will be entitled, at the three years end, to a very respectable degree. I say regularly, and without interruption.[68]

---

[64] Questionist, p. 15.
[65] Questionist, p. 44.
[66] Questionist, p. 20.
[67] Questionist, p. 44.
[68] Questionist, pp. 24–25.

Educating the Romantic Poets

He adds that freshmen should not be 'ashamed of being called a QUIZ', but that they should be 'ashamed of being a PUPPY or a BUCK, or a LOUNGER'.[69] He urges students to adhere to the 'paths of moral rectitude, to your own prudence, and to the respect due to your own character as a Gentleman'.[70]

As for time away from studies, the Questionist tells freshmen, 'If you work, you must play', and he suggests 'sociable riding or walking' and subscribing to circulating libraries or clubs. He cautions against overdoing the play, however, and urges freshmen to consider their personal economic means in choosing their company.[71] Asked about student amusements, a Pembroke student told the Oxford royal commissioners that he took his studies seriously, but 'managed thoroughly to enjoy himself throughout his academical course, frequently saw and entertained his friends at breakfast parties, went to concerts occasionally, but never boated or cricketed'.[72] He adds that he 'did not give regular wine parties, but from time to time saw friends after dinner'.[73] Christopher Wordsworth's account of social activities at the eighteenth-century universities includes party politics, clubs, bellringing, boating, shooting, football, billiards, bowls, card-playing, chess, lotteries, the Volunteer Corps, Stourbridge Fair, dramatic entertainments, and music. Chinnery's letters and other documents from the nineteenth century record most of the same student amusements at Oxford and add hunting, skating, fishing, fencing, cricket, and tennis matches. Oxford students and senior college members also enjoyed attending the Port Meadow Races. William Whewell's biographer lists sailing to Chesterton, dancing at county fairs, riding, and making rockets as other college pastimes.[74]

In the Romantic period university and colleges had not yet begun officially to sanction intercollegiate athletic competitions; indeed, some college statutes forbade any but the most gentlemanly games. So, just as the grammar school pupils had done, college students organised games and competitions themselves. Midgley reports how men from New College formed two cricket teams, one of former Eton students and the other of old Wykhamists. These teams played other colleges and athletes from the town. The Port Meadow and Bullingdon Green were popular sites for these matches. Silver trophies and gold tasselled hats were awarded at the celebratory dinners held after these events. Students also organised foot races, wrestling matches, and shooting competitions.

[69] Questionist, p. 49.
[70] Questionist, p. 50.
[71] Questionist, pp. 27, 37.
[72] Hines, p. 33.
[73] Hines, p. 33.
[74] Todhunter, p. 28.

Riding, ever a popular sport, was also common at the universities, though the university authorities frowned upon the expense of students keeping horses and complained that they too often ended their rides at ale houses. A student at Oxford reported in 1781 that in the springtime 'a large meadow adjoining to Oxford is nothing but a riding school'.[75] Students could hire horses in town; and Christ Church, New College, and Wadham all maintained their own stables for students' and faculty's horses. Informal student horse races were not uncommon, and attendance (and betting) at larger race meets at Burford, Bicester, Woodstock, and Port Meadow was popular. Fox, stag, rabbit, and badger hunting were not without their college enthusiasts. Dogs were required for these recreations, and some students kept foxhounds, greyhounds, pointers, spaniels, or terriers, though having them in college was supposed to be banned. Midgley cites frequent advertisements by students in local Oxford papers for lost canines with names such as Hector, Dido, and Grog. Violent amusements such as cockfighting and bear baiting were strongly discouraged by senior college members, but some students did find these events entertaining.

The amusements of the historic cities of Oxford and Cambridge and the readily accessible rivers and green spaces nearby were not lost on undergraduates in the Romantic period. Students and faculty enjoyed walking or bowling on the colleges' walks, lawns, and gardens.[76] The Magdalen Physic Garden, and the formally laid out gardens of Wadham, Trinity, and New College were beautiful and popular. Midgley rightly comments that the pleasant rural areas outside of town were worthy of a 'saunter'.[77] Christopher Wordsworth took note of this as well, citing a student named John Hinckesman, who wrote that

> The country hereabouts is very fertile and abounds with Wood, the chief is Elm ... . We have very fine Prospects here, they are so extensive that in some parts you may (upon ye hills especially) command 30 or 40 miles about, which makes it very agreeable upon a fine clear day, to take a view.[78]

Coleridge, Wordsworth, and Byron all report taking time to walk or ride in the green spaces outside their colleges or to swim in the Cam. In Coleridge's time, his college was surrounded by the parklike Jesus Green. In a letter to Mrs Evans, Coleridge describes the 'clear rivulet that runs thro' the grove adjacent to our College', and his pleasure in watching 'the numberless little birds—mostly singing Robins, and above all—the little lambs, each by the

---

[75] Midgley, p. 109.
[76] Only fellows, however, were allowed to walk on the lawns.
[77] Midgley, p. 91.
[78] Qtd in Christopher Wordsworth, *Scholae Academicae*, p. 318.

Educating the Romantic Poets

side of its Mother—[that] recall the most pleasing ideas of pastoral simplicity, and almost soothe one's soul into congenial innocence'.[79]

Moorman points out that alongside the mountains and lakes in Cumberland that Wordsworth knew as a boy, the fields, chalk hills, and blue sky above Cambridge also became for him a 'fruitful theatre of vision and contemplation'.[80] In Book Third of the 1805 *Prelude* he records leaving his comrades and the buildings and groves of St John's to walk 'along the fields, the level fields,/ With heaven's blue concave reared above my head'.[81] The effect upon him of these rambles was not insignificant. He explains that, though the natural world outside Cambridge was a 'change entire' from the Lake District's 'shapes sublime' with which he had been 'previously conversant', at Cambridge his mind 'seemed busier in itself than heretofore—/[and] At least I more directly recognized/My powers and habits'.[82] He continues in this vein, explaining how his college experiences, combined with ramblings at Cambridge, 'awakened, summoned, roused, [and] constrained [him]', and so he 'looked for universal things', and felt he was 'ascending now/To such community with highest truth'.[83] This statement about the value Wordsworth derived from his college days is rarely cited, but when added to other news in this book, it should help to amend the tendency of scholars to discount his education.

Along with walking in the countryside and swimming in the Isis and the Cam, Midgley reports that skiffs, gigs, cutters, canoes, and five-person wherries could and often were hired by students and faculty at Oxford. Students sailed or paddled up or downstream to inns and pubs, where they dined on fish, ham, chicken, bread and cheese, or custard and tarts, and drank wine, ale, sparkling wines, or cider.[84] Skating to these inns in winter was also popular. At Cambridge Coleridge recounted capsizing a boat; Byron recalled the boyish pleasures of diving for eggs and plates with his classmates; and at Oxford Southey finally learned to swim.

College clubs

George Chinnery's letters talk about his involvement in a college club called the One O'Clocks, 'the most magnificent in the College'.[85] When asked to join this very posh set, which gathered to 'celebrate the nativities of wise men, great authors, and philosophers' and to drink wine as often as three times a

[79] CLSTC, p. 26.
[80] *William Wordsworth: A Biography: Early Years 1770–1803*, p. 103.
[81] *Prelude*, 1805, p. 96, ll. 99–100.
[82] *Prelude*, 1805, p. 96, ll. 99–106.
[83] Prelude, 1805, p. 96, ll. 109, 115–117.
[84] Midgley, pp. 126–127.
[85] Chinnery, letter of 4 November 1808.

University Life

week, he worried because his mother considered them 'vulgar, expensive, and troublesome'.[86] Other clubs that university students enjoyed included the Constitution Club and a philosophical group called the Freecynics at Oxford. The most famous club at Oxford was the High Borlace, a Tory club to which the sons of county squires often belonged. Late in the eighteenth century, as interest in the modern sciences was growing around the country, Oxford men formed The Society for Scientific and Literary Disquisition. Meeting in members' rooms to talk and read papers, the society agreed to avoid politics and religion.[87]

Clubs at Cambridge included The Westminster, Charterhouse, The True Blue, The Speculative, the Zodiack Club, and the Old Maid's, which met at a coffee house after chapel for talks about literature. A group of politically inclined university men called The Associators met at the Tuns Tavern. Christopher Wordsworth describes a very exclusive club of wealthy Trinity men, who went so far as to create a uniform of green coats, buff vests, and knee breeches, with buttons engraved with the motto *san souci*. This group met once a week in members' rooms, to gamble at cards. They also had a monthly dinner and a posh annual gathering. Cambridge wranglers founded The Hyson Club, which was dedicated to 'drinking China tea and engaging in rational conversation'.[88] The famous Cambridge Union was formed in 1815. Byron became a part of the Whig Club at Cambridge, which provided him a posh place to explore his literary as well as political interests—and, of course, to drink and gamble. Prior to Byron's time, Wordsworth's brother Christopher and Charles Le Grice, who had been a Grecian at Christ's Hospital, founded the Literary Society. Members recited favourite Greek and Latin verses, presented papers on the state of modern poetry, and gave readings of English writers' recent works, such as the sonnets of William Lisle Bowles. The group also read and critiqued classmates' and recent graduates' work, including Wordsworth's 'Evening Walk' and Coleridge's 'To Fortune'.

Tea and wine parties

Tea and wine parties were popular among students and fellows at both universities, as were breakfast and dessert parties. Wordsworth was involved in at least one drinking party, the famous gathering in Milton's rooms at Christ's College, where he 'Poured out libations' until his 'brain reeled', and admits that he had 'Never [been] so clouded by the fumes of wine/ Before that hour, or since'.[89] His brother Christopher's infrequently kept diary describes his

---

[86] Chinnery, letter of 4 November 1808.
[87] Green, 'The University and Social Life', p. 342.
[88] Knox, *Liberal Education*, p. 216.
[89] *Prelude*, 1805, p. 106, ll. 303–307.

Educating the Romantic Poets

evening activities at Trinity for 70 days, 45 of which included attending wine or supper parties.[90] Coleridge promised his brother during his first year at Jesus College that 'I neither give nor receive invitations to wine parties because in our college there are no end to them';[91] later in his college days he broke this promise. As he left to begin his first year at Trinity, Byron asked Hanson to send him four dozen bottles each of port, sherry, claret, and Madeira.[92] Despite this purchase and his frequent boasting of drinking parties and hangovers, Byron also claimed that from time to time 'our chief beverage was soda-water'.[93] George Chinnery's mother did not mind his being involved in wine parties at Oxford, but she did object strenuously to tea parties.[94] The reason for her preference is unclear. As a sheltered 16-year-old freshman, Chinnery himself was shocked by the roaring drunken behaviour of seniors in his college.

Often the wine parties included card-playing; whist, loo, piquet, and quadrille were most popular. Card games were sometimes organised by young ladies in town. Chinnery wrote his mother about 'a local miss', who organised such parties for Christ Church men. The students' wagering and the young woman's absurd 'fawning on the Noblemen' led Dean Jackson to cancel her parties.[95] Gambling was a common amusement at the Georgian universities among not only the undergraduates but also the fellows. The Senior Commons rooms, where they kept wager books, were centres for this activity. Bets were taken on horse races, elections, and the marriage prospects of fellow colleagues. In one of his letters, young Chinnery wonders if it might be 'undecorous for men who have taken full orders in the Church to meet in this way to play for money'.[96] These relatively tame recreations were important for students, however; Chinnery tells his mother that he found it impossible to become friends with other students at college without taking part in card games, wagering of some sort, and attending tea and wine parties.

Given the range of amusements available at the Romantic university, the freedom to choose how hard one would work—explained further in subsequent chapters—the company, the beautiful and historic settings, and the emphasis upon religious matters, it would seem that life at Georgian Oxford and Cambridge was rather more agreeable than the universities' critics have maintained. Their college days would have been just as consequential for the young Romantics and their classmates as university is for students today, and perhaps more so, because the colleges were so much smaller and more

---

[90] Searby, p. 579.
[91] CLSTC, p. 18.
[92] Marchand, *Byron: A Biography*, vol. 1, p. 101.
[93] Marchand, *Byron: A Biography*, vol. 1, p. 104.
[94] Chinnery, letter of 12 November 1808.
[95] Chinnery, letter of 18 February 1810.
[96] Chinnery, letter of 5 December 1808.

intimate. While we cannot measure exactly how the Romantic writers' self-knowledge, personal beliefs, social skills, friendships, habits of reading and thought, awareness of public and private issues, and access to power were impacted by going to Oxford or Cambridge, we ought at least to begin to take more seriously the images, terms, reflections, and references in their writing and their lives that signal what they gained from and how they valued these places, people, and experiences.

Chapter Eight

The Curriculum of the English 'Confessional' University

Heroes, Shepherds, and
'Holding acquaintance with the stars'

> The university must educate not merely instruct.
>
> William Whewell

The curriculum and pedagogies of the universities in the Georgian period cannot be fully understood without reference to their classical models in the academies of Plato and Aristotle and to the universities' and colleges' medieval founding statutes. In Plato's academy, younger students studied mathematics, geometry, astronomy, music, and philosophy and the older ones—their correlative in England were the collegiate fellows—studied dialectics, epistemology, and ethics. Recalling that Aristotle framed programmes to suit individual learners' talents and his belief that higher education should last only as long as each individual student remains interested and willingly engaged, the Georgian universities were not strictly coercive nor were they determined that all students should complete degrees. English university tutors and deans considered their students 'gentlemen' and therefore accorded them the freedom due such men to make their own choices about how hard they would study. The physical side of Aristotle's programme was enacted informally by the students, who organised their own games, riding, fencing, boxing and other physical activities themselves. The university teaching schedule allowed much more time for these activities than the schools did.

The earliest Royal Letters Patent for the universities date from the time of Henry III (1216–1272). These statutes established Oxford and Cambridge as confessional institutions whose purpose was the promotion of piety as well as learning. Subsequent monarchs granted various letters and charters, the most important being The Act for the Incorporation of the Two Universities, confirmed in Elizabeth I's reign, which specified perpetual succession for the chancellors, masters, and scholars of both universities. Besides Elizabeth's act of incorporation, other documents governing the universities were Oxford's *Corpus Statutorum Universitatis Oxoniensis*, drafted by Archbishop Laud (1573–1645), and a collection of even earlier documents, Cambridge's *Statuta Antiqua*, dating from the Middle Ages, that founded individual colleges. Many of these documents were still legally in force well into the nineteenth century. As an unusual blending of Church and lay corporation, Oxford and Cambridge were granted numerous privileges by the crown and parliament. The crown gave the universities the power to confer benefices, to purchase land, and to receive property by bequest without the usual legal formalities, thereby ensuring their wealth and power for centuries. The universities were granted the sole power to confer degrees 'necessary to the attainment of many offices of honour and emolument'.[1] Hence, they were the principal route to the ministry of the established Church and to service in the court and government. Additionally, many university professorships were endowed with cathedral preferment; college heads were granted the privilege of holding church livings in absentia; and the two university presses were awarded virtual monopolies. By law a copy of every book published in the realm was to be placed in the universities' libraries.

Founding statutes—the example of Oxford

Framed in a very different time, but nevertheless legally binding, these documents made it difficult for the Georgian universities to adapt to the evolution of knowledge, particularly in the sciences, and to changes in intellectual or national culture. The Oxford Statutes, for example, spend more space detailing how students should subscribe to the articles of faith and religion, pledge their loyalty to the crown and arrange for their household servants than they do to how teaching and learning are to be managed. They did, however, enjoin the colleges to provide each student with a tutor from the time of matriculation 'until they are advanced to some degree, or, at least, have completed four years in the University'.[2] These tutors, the document specified, were to be fellows of the universities with BAs or MAs who were of 'tried virtue and learning, sincere in religion, and approved by the judgment of the head of the college'.[3] The statutes also specify that the tutor's job was to imbue scholars with 'virtuous morals, and to instruct them in approved authors, and

---

[1] Hinds, p. 3.
[2] G. R. M. Ward, p. 15.
[3] G. R. M. Ward, p. 15.

The Curriculum of the English 'Confessional' University

Figure 17. The Geological Lecture Room (located in the Ashmolean Museum), Oxford: Dr William Buckland lecturing on 15 February 1823, by Nathaniel Whittock. The Metropolitan Museum of Art.

most of all in the rudiments of religion'.[4] The statutes set up a lecturing system by 'masters' in the various 'sciences and faculties', who were charged to lecture all students of all the colleges for 45 minutes twice a week in 'a clear voice'. Among the 'sciences' to be covered in the first year were grammar (i.e. classical literature in Latin and Greek), and rhetoric, which included public speaking as well as theories of argument. In the second year and until graduation the specified subjects were logic, metaphysics, geometry, and astronomy. Lectures in music, natural philosophy, ancient history, Greek, and Hebrew were also stipulated. There was no statute requiring these 'masters' to be skilled teachers.

By the Georgian period, the college heads had done their best to bend or interpret the statutes to suit their local and historical circumstances. One of the most important results of the colleges' creativity with the statutes was their supplanting university lecturers with college tutors as the primary instructors of all undergraduates. This circumstance, too, would evolve, as

---

[4] G. R. M. Ward, p. 16.

modern revisions of the statutes governing university professorships made it more likely that professors were proven scholars whose lectures were relevant to students' courses of study. Nevertheless, as Mark Pattison (1813–1884), a fellow, tutor, and eventually rector of Lincoln College, explained to the royal commissioners, the university statutes and codes could be oppressively restrictive to academics hoping to participate in the march of knowledge and the educational needs of their times. Pattinson begged the commissioners to 'untie our hands and open our gates'.[5]

The traditional curriculum

The curriculum at Oxford and Cambridge built upon the classical language and mathematics skills and knowledge that boys had acquired in their public or grammar schools. A Cambridge tutor told an arriving freshman that in order to be ready to study at the university

> [y]ou should be able to construe the Greek Testament, anywhere, at sight, and to parse any verb. You should, also, be able to read any easy prose Greek author, as Xenophon, Lucian, Herodotus—and Homer ... . Then, all the usual common Latin schoolbooks; you should be able to read at sight—Virgil—Horace—Caesar's Commentaries—Tully's oration ... . Lastly, you should be able to write pretty correctly Latin prose, and [be familiar with] a Greek play or two ... . Now, this is the least that can be allowed to make a decent classical scholar: and, if a man be not so far proficient, he goes to College for little but to spend his money.[6]

At the universities tutors guided students through many of these same works again, but in much greater detail and more critically. They also continued schoolboys' study of mathematics and 'divinity' at both universities, though colleges varied as to which of these three areas of study they emphasised. Oxford embraced the classics and divinity, while Cambridge concentrated on mathematics; both attended to religious studies. Undergraduates at both universities were required to study in all three areas; however, students had a certain amount of freedom to choose, with the advice of their tutors, which texts they would study within each area.

The classical part of the curriculum at both universities focused on language and literature, which included history, philosophy, rhetoric, and other forms of prose, as well as verse and drama. Students read the Old and New Testaments, theology, homiletics, and texts on 'eloquence' at both universities. Attention to

---

[5] Hinds, p. 36.
[6] Qtd in Schneider, pp. 67–68.

writing and speaking forms and style were a major part of collegiate literary study. University mathematicians trained students in algebra, calculus, trigonometry, geometry, logic, and the natural sciences. The Cambridge royal commissioners' statement on the university curriculum is one of the best general explanations of the ancient rationale behind this course of study; and, at the same time, it reflects nineteenth-century beliefs about learning. 'Mathematical and Classical learning', they wrote, have 'intrinsic value [in their] acquirement' and are 'instruments of mental discipline'.[7] The knowledge of mathematics, the Commissioners explained, is above all 'practical', for it is by

> the application of mathematical principles and processes to such branches of natural philosophy as admit of this exact mode of treatment, that the noblest triumphs and most useful improvements of modern science have been achieved in mechanics, in optics, in astronomy, [and] in the exposition of the system of the world.[8]

The commissioners added that mathematical knowledge 'may be regarded as the best and most effectual exercise of the reasoning powers, habituating the mind to clearness of ideas, precision of statement, and coherence of argument'.[9] They concluded their defence of the Cambridge curriculum by explaining that

> Classical literature possesses high and peculiar recommendations. A knowledge of it is indispensable to the Student in Divinity who seeks an accurate and critical acquaintance with the books of the New Testament in their original language, and with the early monuments of Christian Theology. In a more general point of view, the spirit of the Classical authors has infused its influence into the whole range of modern literature, and their works are held in universal admiration as the noblest specimens of genius and purest models of taste, in all their varied styles.[10]

Despite these respectful words, the Cambridge commissioners recommended a 're-arrangement of the Academical system' that is more in line with the 'desire … aptitude … taste … [and] talents' of modern students.[11] They suggested curtailing the amount of time students spend in college, giving them greater freedom in choosing their courses of study, changing the examination system, and putting more emphasis upon the moral and natural sciences.

---

[7] Graham, p. 23.
[8] Graham, p. 23.
[9] Graham, pp. 23–24.
[10] Graham, pp. 23–24.
[11] Graham, p. 27.

The Oxford curriculum

In their first year Oxford students concentrated on Latin, grammar, and rhetoric. Once these skills were polished, they went on to logic and ethics, and then to Greek, Hebrew, Arabic, algebra, and geometry. If students stayed on for the MA, they studied metaphysics, astronomy, higher mathematics, optics, geography, navigation, and/or the extant natural sciences. One of the best sources of information about what students at Oxford studied in the Georgian period is the Christ Church Collections Books. These books record the titles of the texts that students chose to read for the college's term examinations. Under each student's name his progress toward degree completion is noted. These lists refute the complaint, not infrequently uttered, that Oxford was little more than a seminary for the national Church and an incubator of Tory statesmen.

When Sydney Smith, Robert Southey, Thomas Arnold, Percy Shelley, and their classmates were at Oxford, the most common prose texts at Christ Church were the history of the Greco-Persian wars by Herodotus and Thucydides's *History of the Peloponnesian War*. Herodotus's *Histories* (in Greek the title means 'research' or 'inquiry') outlines the history of Athens and tells the grand story of the conflicts between Greece, Persia, Egypt, and smaller states between the years 559 and 479 BCE. The work describes the accession and rise of Cyrus and the events of the Ionian Revolt, and ends with the defeat of Xerses by the Greeks. Thucydides's account of the great war between Athens and Sparta is valuable both as history, historiography, and political history. Besides these histories, students at Oxford were also likely to study several texts by Xenophon, including his Socratic dialogues and his history of the seven years after the Peloponnesian War. His account of Cyrus's education is a dissertation on the ideal prince and expresses Xenophon's moral and political philosophies. Plutarch's *Lives of the Greeks and Romans* was used to supplement these accounts. The biographies of men such as Pericles, Lycurgus, Alexander, Theseus, Alcibiades, and Lysander were read quite often by university students and thereby provided opportunities to study how personality and character—in real life or myth—might affect history or daily life. As an example, Lycurgus' concept of 'homoio' or equals figures prominently in Southey's and Coleridge's Pantisocracy scheme. Along with these biographies, university students in the Georgian period studied Livy's *History of Rome* and Caesar's accounts of both the Gallic war and the Roman civil war.

While they studied classical histories, Christ Church students also frequently chose to read Aristotle's *Rhetoric* for their collections. Students who chose this text had the benefit of Aristotle's instruction about the process of composition, which advises students to consider the psychology and real-world circumstances of their audience when inventing appeals, advice that Southey appears to have taken in his writing career. After Aristotle, Cicero was the rhetorician students most often chose to study. *De Officiis*, was a standard. Though his style is sometimes criticised for its use of amplification and emotion, Cicero's rhetorical treatises speak out against excessive ornamentation. A favourite rhetorical text of Oxford men was Demosthenes' 'On the Crown'. Perhaps because so many of the Christ Church students expected to serve and speak in parliament, they frequently chose to read Hermogenes, a specialist in declamatory rhetoric, who urged public speakers to aim at clarity, grandeur, beauty, rapidity, ethos, and gravity. Quintilian was often studied as well. He advises students to select topics from real life and to resist showy ornamentation. His model of the 'good man speaking well' might be taken as an early model for the Romantic idea of the Poet as a man of heightened intelligence and compassion who speaks simply and clearly and endeavours to be 'an upholder and preserver'.[12] Christ Church students in the Georgian period also frequently chose to study Aristotle's *Nicomachean Ethics* and his *Poetics*. The former of these two texts is an ideal study for young men: it investigates what makes a good life, explores the nature of human happiness, and asks how a man might live in order to find that happiness. Aristotle's answer is to be contemplative, prudent, moderate, friendly, generous, witty, and above all fair. No doubt when Romantic period college students and their tutors studied Aristotle's *Poetics*, they applied his concepts of mimesis and catharsis and his definition of tragedy to guide their study of the Greek plays that appear frequently in the Collections Book, the most popular of which were by Aeschylus, Euripides, and Sophocles.

It is worth pausing to consider the lessons Georgian college students might have learned about justice, authority, the breakdown of civil behaviour, hypocritical and/or weak men, and women's character from these works. Sophocles's *Oedipus Tyrannus*'s exploration of free will versus fate and the conflict of individuals against the state would have also been of interest to young men coming of age in the political atmosphere of the late Georgian period. The play also provides an important lesson in plot structure. Yet another popular choice for study at Christ Church was Sophocles's *Philoctetes*, which provides an unforgettable figure of romantic loneliness and suffering. Another of the most frequently chosen plays was Aeschylus's *Prometheus Vinctus*. The figure of Prometheus, who provides a sort of pagan corollary to the figure of Christ, was a favourite of the Shelleys and Byron in particular. Aeschylus's version of the Prometheus myth is different from that told in Hesiod's *Works and Days*, which college students also read. Studying both texts gave young writers an opportunity to compare how differently a story might be told. Other often-read Greek plays were Euripides's *Medea* and *Hecuba* and Sophocles's *Ajax*.

In addition to Greek tragedies, Christ Church students also read a great

---

[12] WWMW, 'Preface' to *Lyrical Ballads*, p. 606.

Educating the Romantic Poets

deal of Greek and Latin epic and lyrical verse each term. Most popular on the collections list were *The Iliad* and *The Odyssey*; Hesiod's *Works and Days*; Virgil's *Aeneid, Eclogues,* and *Georgics*; Lucretius's *De rerum natura*; and various texts by Horace. Homer's epics were already well known to most of the college men from their grammar school days. When they reread these texts in college, they turned to commentaries and attended more carefully to these writers' modes of description and their use of figurative language, foreshadowing, parallel events, digressions, and refrains. This opportunity for deeper and more thorough lessons in classical form and style was especially true for university students' study of the *Aeneid* and Virgil's *Eclogues* and *Georgics*, all of which celebrate favourite romantic themes—the natural world, the honourable work of agriculture, and living in harmony with the land. Horace stands next to Virgil as one of the most widely read Latin lyric poets, and university students regularly selected his odes, satires, and epistles for term study. The only poet Byron refers to more often than Shakespeare is Horace. Byron's 'Hints from Horace', which is adapted from the 'Epistle to Augustus', urges aspiring poets to study classical works, noting in particular that Horace will teach 'those rehearsing for the Poet's part ... the pleasing paths of song'.[13] Horace's satires are models of the skilful use of hexameter and the Alcaic and Sapphic stanza forms, and they explore one of Byron's favourite subjects—human weakness. Horace's 20 epistles, all in hexameter, address topics such as philosophy and philosophers, the advantages of country life, happiness, true independence, and the art of poetry. His odes are Latin imitations of the topics and style of Pindar and Sappho. Students often read '*Tu ne quaesieris*' ('Do not ask') and '*Nunc est bibendum*' ('Now is the time for drinking', sometimes called the 'Cleopatra Ode'). All of these texts—histories, rhetorics, plays, poems, satires, and epistles—were read in their original languages and studied in the universities not only for their content but also as models of literary and oratorical style, and of appropriate and metrical language. As such they invite review and, perhaps, new studies of classical influences upon the Romantics.

In addition to classical literature, Oxford students learned logic by spending up to five terms studying Euclid's geometry and textbooks such as Henry Aldrich's *Artis Logicae Compendium*, which is entirely in Latin and based upon Aristotle's *Organon*. These texts appear regularly on the Christ Church Collections lists. Divided into 13 books, Euclid's work begins with definitions of points, lines, angles, surfaces, and solids and then builds a complex of reasoning founded upon five axioms and five common notions. Only a compass, a straightedge, and the logic of these few axioms and common notions are needed

---

[13] Lord Byron, 'Hints from Horace' (1811), ll. 477–480. http://www.newsteadabbeybyronsociety.org/works/downloads/hints_horace.pdf. Accessed 28 June 2022.

The Curriculum of the English 'Confessional' University

to derive 465 theorems. The foundation for students' subsequent mathematical studies, Euclid's axiomatic-deductive reasoning system trained them in logical applications of facts or assumptions. Oxford men most often studied Euclid's first six books, which cover theorems, parallelograms, rectangles, incommensurables, circles, pentagons, and areas. As with the literature, Euclid was always read in its original language. The source of Aldrich's text, Aristotle's *Organon*, consists of treatises on categories, interpretation, prior and posterior analytics, topics, and sophistical refutations. For centuries, Aristotle's writing about the syllogism had been standard in the academy, though starting in the Romantic period logicians, particularly in Scotland, began to prefer the enthymeme as a more practical and fluid tool for reasoning. The English universities were slower to move past Aristotle; but it should be noted that no less a philosopher than Kant believed Aristotle's logic and discussion of the syllogism covered 'everything there was to know about logic'.[14] Students read Aldrich's rendering of the *Organon* in Latin. The introduction to the 1829 Oxford edition of Aldrich's textbook explains the purpose of teaching logic in a somewhat surprising way. Logic, Aldrich's editor writes, allows 'our souls to surrender their hidden stores: by the charms of Dialectic we may bind the Proteus within us and compel him to give true answers to our questioning. For thinking is but the converse of the soul with herself; she interrogates, and she answers, she affirms, and she denies'.[15]

The introductory matter of this textbook defends the syllogism but explains that logic's 'more valuable fruits are to be found in the training which the mind unconsciously receives, than in the conscious employment of knowledge in the formation and examination of reasoning'.[16] A text used to supplement Aldrich offers additional insights into how college teaching may have shaped Georgian students' thinking and cultural assumptions. Among other exercises, this text offers strings of statements for students to analyse, prove, or disprove, such as

> All kings should be obeyed by their subjects.
> William IV is a king.
> William IV should be obeyed by his subjects.

Or:

> All real Christians fear God.
> Those who are wicked are not real Christians.
> Those who are wicked do not live in fear of God.[17]

---

[14] Shields.
[15] Aldrich, p. xv.
[16] Aldrich, p. xxi.
[17] Anonymous, *Questions on Aldrich's Logic*, p. 42.

Educating the Romantic Poets

A third example in the exercise book no doubt brought smiles to the faces of Romantic era undergraduates. It went like this:

> Nothing is better than a virtuous life.
> Bread and cheese is better than nothing.
> Bread and cheese is better than a virtuous life.[18]

Besides logic via Euclid and Aldrich, Oxford students also studied algebra, trigonometry, and calculus, all of which show up on the Collections List. It is not insignificant that all college students, including those who became poets (or critics), had so much training in mathematics and logic.

Along with classics and mathematics, Oxford students studied 'divinity'. Members of the Georgian university community often expressed the belief that knowledge of their religion was not just a set of beliefs by which to live. They saw religion as intimately connected with history, philosophy, literature, and the progress of human thought. Hence, no system of education could be complete without it. As already noted in Chapter 5, religious study at the universities included scrutiny of the four Gospels in Greek and related scholarly commentaries. The Old Testament and Psalms were also studied, with commentaries. Various examples of Christian apologetics, such as Paley's *View of the Evidences of Christianity* (1794) and Grotius' *On the Truth of Christianity* (1627), were standard. Paley's work is a classic Georgian defence of the faith. Sections in this long work are entitled 'There is but one God', 'That God is eternal, omnipotent, omniscient, and completely good', 'That God is the cause of all things', 'Miracles', '[Miracles are] no way repugnant to reason', and 'Concerning those duties of humanity which we owe to our neighbour, though he has injured us'. Most of the second half of the work is dedicated to refuting 'pagan' religions, Judaism, and 'Mahometanism'. Paley's text walks a tricky line between contemporaneous rationalism and traditional belief: it views the Church as a human, ethical institution of great utility but it also promises a future metaphysical state of reward and punishment.[19] Though Paley takes scriptural revelation seriously in *Evidences*, his work is notable for its effort to combine historical data and human reason.

While studying these arguments, Oxford men often read books of devotion such as *The Whole Duty of Man* (1658) and Thomas A Kempis' *Imitation of Christ* (originally published in Latin 1418–1427, translated in 1653 by Benham, many hundreds of editions thereafter). College students studied Church history, the particulars of various religious controversies, and the evolution of the creeds. In a letter to his friend Charles Collins, Southey complains about

---

[18] Anonymous, *Questions on Aldrich's Logic*, p. 62.
[19] Gascoigne, p. 242.

being 'pestered' with the 'Athanasian creed & a sermon in defence of incomprehensibility' and admits to having 'lost all patience'.[20] Schoolboys had already been trained in the Anglican catechism, and upon matriculation at Oxford students had formally subscribed to the 39 Articles of Religion; but these texts, nevertheless, were reviewed and studied at the university. All students, not just those preparing for the ministry, were required to be familiar with the writings of the Church fathers, to study homiletics, and to read collections of the most respected sermons, such as those by John Tillotson, Robert South, and Francis Atterbury (1663–1732, dean of Westminster and chaplain to earls, dukes, and Charles II). Attendance at morning prayer, weekday chapel, and Sunday services, as described in Chapter 5, supported study of these texts.

Students destined for the Inns of Court might also elect to study law at Oxford. One who pursued this track was William Philip Perrin, the gentleman commoner at Christ Church from 1761 to 1765 mentioned previously, who enjoyed loaf sugar, lobster, eels, eggs and toast, tarts and cream, as well as puddings and port. His accounts and papers in the college archive include the document in Latin that he signed upon matriculation, whereby he officially subscribed to the 39 Articles, pledged his loyalty to the king, and affirmed his willingness to observe the statutes, privileges, and customs of the university. He also left behind a syllabus for 'A Course of Lectures on the Civil Law' with several related outlines and handwritten notes on Jurisprudence. Topics in this file include 'Roman or Civil Law', 'Politic Law, of Civil Government, or Sovereignty in General', and 'Public Law' relating to 'National and Territorial Rights' and 'Injuries to them redressed by War'.[21] One portion of the course includes summaries of the constitutional law of 14 nations, among them Germany, France, the Italian States, Spain, Poland, Prussia, Russia, Scotland, Ireland, and England. This course is listed as meeting from May 14 to July 2. Also in the file is a printed outline of the 'Objects of Law', which are 'Persons' and 'Things'. The headings in the section on laws regarding 'Persons' are of interest. They pertain to man's relation 'to God, to Himself, to Society' and take into account 'Life, Sex, Age, Sanity, Power (of the 'sovereign and Subject'), Liberty ('Freeman and Slave'), Country ('Citizen and Alien'), and Family ('Husband and Wife, Parent and Child, Guardian and Ward, Master and Servant, Kindred'). A 'scheme' for another course includes the topics of 'Rights of Persons and Property' and 'Private and Public Wrongs', each of which was covered by 14 to 17 lectures that convened 'exactly at Eleven in the Morning' several days each week, including Saturdays, for approximately 12 weeks between October 13 and March 26.[22]

---

[20] CLRS, Pt 1, #12.
[21] Perrin, Item #9.
[22] Perrin, Items #11 & 12.

Educating the Romantic Poets

Along with papers related to his studies of law, Perrin saved the programme of speakers at the 1763 *Encaenia*. These included the duke of Beaufort (Oriel alumnus), Lord Robert Spencer, Sir John Russell, Lord Ashbrooke, and the earl of Anglesey (all alumni of Christ Church), The Hon. Mr North (Trinity), Sir Frank Standish (Brasenose), and the principal of St Mary's Hall, along with 26 honours students from Queen's, Merton, New College, Exeter, St Mary's Hall, Magdalen, and All Souls. One of the documents Perrin also preserved is a syllabus for 'A General View of the Solar System' as taught by Pythagoras. Another is a printed 'Table of the Quantity of Air contained in the following Bodies', which used a very British sampling of 'bodies' as examples: deer's horn, oyster shell, heart of oak, mustard seed, tobacco, candle wax, Newcastle coal, coarse sugar, and hog's blood. Yet another document he saved is the syllabus for a 'Course of Mathematical Lectures and Experiments' with the headings 'Mechanicks, Opticks, Hydrostaticks, [and] Pneumatics'. These documents all help to round out the view of what students might study at Oxford in the Georgian era and suggest that the charges of narrowness or uselessness of the university curriculum were not always fair.

Two reading men at Oxford: Cyril Jackson and George Canning

Though the curriculum outlined above is based on what was taught and examined at Christ Church, it appears that most of the texts listed were standard choices at many of the other colleges at Oxford. An example of what a serious-minded undergraduate might do to earn honours from Oxford is the record of Cyril Jackson's collections at Christ Church. Jackson, who is profiled in Chapter 11, would later become the dean of his college. From 1764 to 1767 he studied and was examined on Homer's *Odyssey* (entire), Virgil's *Eclogues*, The *Aeneid* (entire), and Theocritus's *Idyllia*. He was also questioned on representative texts from Cicero, including *de Oratore*, *de Amicitia*, *Senectitutte*, and several of Cicero's political discourses such as '*Pro Ligario*', '*Pro Marcello*', '*Pro Coelio*', '*Pro Milone*', and '*Pro Archia Poeta*' (the latter of which was used to illustrate Cicero's signature five-part argument—exordium, narratio, refutation, confirmation, and peroration). In addition, Jackson read and was examined in the political histories of Sallust, who is regarded as an adept stylist and whose narratives were based on his experiences with corrupt Roman politicians and party battles.

Jackson's knowledge of the Gospels of Matthew, Mark, Luke, and John (in Greek) and of the book of Genesis and 50 psalms (in Hebrew) were all 'collected' as well. Additionally, he was queried about Grotius's *On the Truth of Christianity* (1627) and Bishop Pearson's *Exposition of the [Apostle's] Creed* (1659), which explicates each clause and is a standard Anglican work. Finally, Jackson's collections also covered six chapters of Euclid, Keil's and Worster's introductions to physics, and the logic textbooks of Aldrich and Wallis. This training was the intellectual foundation of the man who, from 1783 until 1809, was one of the storied leaders of Christ Church, Oxford's largest and most powerful college, and who supervised the learning of hundreds of young men who became actors in the Romantic public sphere.

Yet another example of an Oxford reading man is George Canning, who attended Christ Church from 1787 to 1791, the same years Wordsworth was at Cambridge. He became prime minister, and, though a satirist and critic of Southey in the *Anti-Jacobin*, in the 1820s he recognised Southey's merits as an historian and helped him obtain books for his researches. Canning's gesture is an example of how collegiate values and loyalty were inculcated at school and university and superseded political (or literary) disagreements. Canning's collections were history-heavy, well suited for a man who went on to study law, found the *Anti-Jacobin and Weekly Review*, champion Catholic emancipation and abolition, and serve in parliament as a member of Pitt's party. His collections lists begin with Herodotus's *Histories*, Thucydides's *Peloponnesian War*, and Plutarch's *Lives*. Among the lives Canning studied were those of Pericles, Alexander, Theseus, Alcibiades, Lysander, Lycurgus, Solon, Themistocles, Aristides, Cimon, Xenophon, Nicias, Artaxerxes, Agesilaus, Pelopidas, and Pyrrhus. Canning read two major texts by Xenophon, Polybius's history of the Hellenic period, ten books of the Greek historian Diodori of Sicily, Livy's *History of Rome and the Roman People*, Sallust's Roman history, Appianus's histories of the Syrian and Punic Wars, and Aeschines's oration 'Against Timarchus'. Canning was also queried over Maclaurin's Algebra, Euclidian geometry, and Aldrich's Logic. His reading in 'eloquence' included Aristotle's *Rhetoric* and orations by Cicero, Demosthenes, and Lysias. His literary examinations covered Aristotle's *Poetics*, Sophocles's *Oedipus Tyrannus* and other tragedies, Homer's *Iliad*, and *The Aeneid*. These examinations, which were both viva voce and in writing, required content knowledge and critical analysis, translations of selected passages in Greek and Latin into English, translations of English passages into Greek and Latin, and included questions about the style of some of these texts.[23] It is doubtful that any teachers of classics or the humanities today would argue that the courses of study Jackson and Canning undertook were superficial, insignificant, or 'useless'.

In contrast to these two reading men, another Christ Church student, William Gossip, may have been one of the 'honest dunces' to whom Wordsworth refers in *The Prelude*. Gossip arrived at the college in 1789, and his freshman year seems to have been fairly productive. He studied and was examined on Horace's *Epistles*, Book 3–6 of Euclid, Homer's *Iliad*, and Sophocles's *Electra*, *Ajax*, *Oedipus Tyrannus*, *Oedipus at Colonus*, and *Philoctetes*. As

---

[23] Hinds, p. 22.

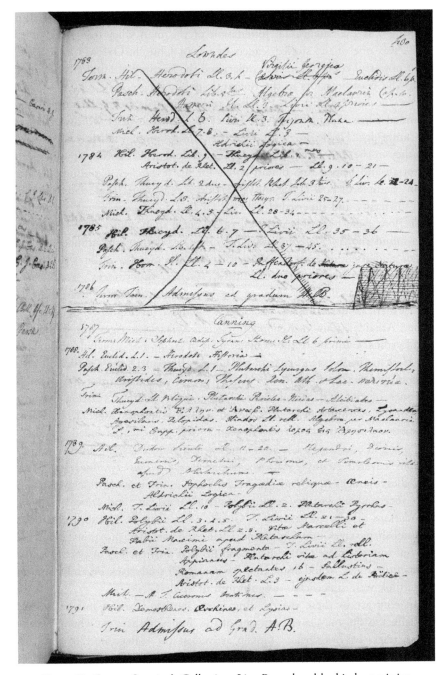

Figure 18. George Canning's Collections List. Reproduced by kind permission of Christ Church College, Oxford.

a second-year student, he studied half as many texts—*The Iliad*, Herodotus's *Histories*, trigonometry, Book 4 of Thucydides's *Peloponnesian War*, one book of Euclid, and another text the title of which was indecipherable. In his third year, Gossip continued reading Thucydides, but added only Virgil's *Georgics*, the first two books of Aristotle's *Rhetoric*, and a fourth text, the title of which is also indecipherable. His senior collections show only one text: Livy's *History of Rome and the Roman People*. There is a note at the end of this list stating he was awarded the BA, though Foster's *Alumni* suggests not. Either way, Gossip's record demonstrates how the colleges in the Georgian period made allowances for students' individual circumstances. It can be argued that Gossip's course of study was not particularly shameful for a non-reading man who was probably going to spend his life after college managing a country estate, raising a family, hunting on Wednesdays and Saturdays, and attending Anglican services on Sundays.

The Cambridge curriculum

Influenced by regard for Cambridge's favourite son, Isaac Newton, educators at Cambridge favoured mathematics over classics and divinity. Cambridge freshmen spent most of their first year building or shoring up their foundational skills in algebra, geometry, logic, trigonometry, and calculus. Some classical reading—such as Xenophon's history, works by Horace, and a Greek play— were included in the freshman course. Just as at Oxford, Cambridge students were allowed to select the texts they wished to study from the approved lists and were granted plenty of time to read independently according to their interests.[24] The theory behind Cambridge's particular emphasis on mathematics is summarised in this passage from the 1852 royal commission report:

> The mental discipline resulting from Mathematical study, is of two very distinct kinds ... Geometry and the Pure Mathematics afford perfect illustrations and examples of deductive reasoning, in which the conclusion is connected with the premises by links of argument, each susceptible of direct and absolute verification by the application of simple and easily remembered tests. If fallacy creep in, it is the Student's own fault. A given amount of steady thought will always enable him to detect and expose it. Those who have once learned what demonstrative argument really is in this school, will never feel satisfied or secure in accepting as proof any kind of general likelihood, or any argument drawn from passion, prejudice, or interest. They have learned to break up an argument into its elementary steps, and to apply, if not those exact

[24] Searby, p. 571.

Educating the Romantic Poets

tests which Mathematicians apply, at least some tests, founded on the true relations of the subject to each of them. And if they find, as they will find, in all the complicated questions of human interest to which reasoning is applied, that these tests fall far short in respect of the applicability and decisive character of what they have been accustomed to see in exact science—they will learn caution and diffidence in adhering to the conclusion. Join to this the length to which the chain of reasoning is carried—the remarkable conclusion to which it leads—the sentiment of unity and coherence in a well-constructed body of knowledge and the habit of regular study and consecutive thought requisite to impart that sentiment, and we have an account of all that is really beneficial in the deductive Mathematics in the way of mental training.[25]

Few modern university mathematicians could offer a more compelling case for why all students should study the subject.

One of Coleridge's first letters written at Cambridge describes attending 'Mathematical Lectures' once a day—Euclid and Algebra alternately—and reading maths 'three hours every day—by which means I am always considerably before the Lectures, which are very good ones'.[26] Wordsworth, on the other hand, who had been especially well trained in mathematics at Hawkshead by Cambridge graduates, found the mathematical studies in his freshman year unchallenging. His time at college did not, however, dim his enjoyment of mathematics, nor did his devotion to Euclid ever wane. As an adult he sometimes turned to its study for pleasure. Moorman points out that he borrowed figurative language from Euclid:

> While yet he lingered in the elements
> Of science, and among her simplest laws,
> His triangles, they were the stars of heaven,
> The silent stars; his altitudes the crag
> Which is the eagle's birthplace.[27]

In the Arab dream episode in *The Prelude*, Wordsworth describes the rider hurrying to save two equally precious things—not only a shell, which is a symbol of poetry, but also a stone, which represents 'geometric truth'.[28] Understanding the Cambridge curriculum and how all other learning there was founded upon mathematics gives greater force and meaning to Wordsworth's

---

[25] Graham, p. 111.
[26] CLSTC, p. 16.
[27] Qtd from 'The Pedlar' in *William Wordsworth: A Biography: Early Years 1770–1803*, p. 97.
[28] *Prelude*, 1805, p. 154, ll. 50–166.

decision to give the stone of geometry a place alongside the shell of poetry. This stone, the poem explains, 'held acquaintance with the stars, /And wedded man to man by purest bond/ Of nature, undisturbed by space or time'.[29] Moorman speculates that Wordsworth's collegiate study of the pure reason and unimpassioned truth of mathematics supplied the poet with a 'framework for the conception of the Deity'.[30] She cites the example of the 1805 *Prelude* where he describes a 'pleasure calm and deeper, a still sense/Of permanent and universal sway … [that] hath the name of God'. Indeed, much later in Wordsworth's 1850 revision of the Arab Dream passage, he describes not only the 'delight' but also the 'belief' that he gained from geometric science.[31]

Once Cambridge students' foundational mathematics skills were firmly in place, their tutors added more advanced mathematics and asked them, usually in the second year, to apply their learning to major works in astronomy, geology, and physics, often using Thomas Burnet's *Theory of the Earth* (1684). Students were also assigned John Keill's *An Examination of Dr. Burnet's Theory* (1698). Both texts combined the Cambridge Platonists programme of astronomical and geological science with Anglican readings of the Scripture, but in different ways. By assigning these works in counterpoint, tutors provided an additional intellectual challenge to their students. To round out their work in astronomy, second-year students at Cambridge studied Newtonian mechanics, statics,[32] and optics, as well as selected Greek poetry.

Topics studied by Cambridge students in the third year included further investigation of astronomy, physics, hydrostatics, and optics, and a widening list of classical texts. Keill's work was often used to launch Cambridge undergraduates' study of Newton's *Principia*. At the same time, students also read Virgil's *Georgics* and *Eclogues* and selected odes, epodes, satires, and epistles of Horace, including Epistle II.3, *Ars Poetica*. Chapter 9 describes and discusses the notes used by Wordsworth's tutor, James Wood, when he worked with students on Horace's epistles. Along with these texts, students at Cambridge read Ovid's *Fasti*, which details Roman religious practices; Caesar's commentaries; Cicero's orations and *De Officiis*; selected Roman funeral orations; the satires of Juvenal; and histories of Rome by Sallust and Livy. Greek texts included selections from Aeschylus, Euripides's (*Iphigenia in Aulis* was most frequently chosen), Sophocles's Oedipus cycle, Demosthenes's orations (including particularly 'On the Crown'), and the same texts by Hesiod, Homer, Aristotle, and Theocritus that Oxford students studied. As at Oxford, students at Cambridge studied theology, the Gospels, church

---

[29] *Prelude*, 1805, p. 156, ll. 104–106.
[30] *William Wordsworth: A Biography: Early Years 1770–1803*, p. 98.
[31] *Prelude*, 1850, p. 193, ll. 120, 132.
[32] The study of force and bodies in movement or at rest.

Educating the Romantic Poets

history, and homiletics. Paley's *Principles of Moral and Political Philosophy* (1785) became a set text at Cambridge, thanks in part to Byron's tutor at Trinity, Thomas Jones. This work moves away from a Lockean notion of government by social contract to a more utilitarian one, based 'on the will of God as collected from expediency'.[33]

Kenneth Johnston rightly comments that the ideological basis of the classical reading at Cambridge, particularly that of Livy, Tacitus, and Juvenal in Latin and of Xenophon, Thucydides, and Demosthenes in Greek, was 'thoroughly republican and anti-imperial'.[34] However, many political positions, some quite antithetical, were expressed at the university, and at times by the same person. The readiness to adapt one's thinking modelled at the university by learned men helps to explain why some of the poets who sympathised with radical views early in life eventually espoused quite conservative ones. As an example, the revered Dr Paley stood with the reformers who opposed subscription but sided with the conservatives who opposed the French notion of the rights of man; however, he also argued for the human right of resistance when government went wrong.[35] Gascoigne aptly comments that Paley's work tried 'to marry together two largely incompatible partners: an intellectual tradition which sought to reduce the nature of government and society to first principles through the use of reason, and a political and religious system which was increasingly inclined to justify itself more in terms of tradition and sentiment than reason'.[36]

Most Cambridge students also read Locke's *Essay on Human Understanding* and studied political economy and geography, which they read using contemporaneous texts in English. Wordsworth was aware of Locke's theory of the association of ideas. Johnston observes that Locke's concern about the ephemerality of early ideas 'lies immediately behind Wordsworth's desperate realisation of the need to record ... the foundations of his mental growth while he could still recall them' in 'Tintern Abbey' and *The Prelude*.[37] College examination questions also asked students to consider, for example, the powers of memory, and one even used a passage from the verse of Edward Young that explores memory and understanding.[38] Though literary study at Cambridge focused on proven models of classical literature, students were expected to be readers of English and more modern Continental literature. Term examination questions often used passages from *The Spectator* and other highbrow periodicals for translation or discussion.

[33] Qtd in Gascoigne, p. 210.
[34] Johnston, *The Hidden Wordsworth*, p. 159.
[35] Johnston, *The Hidden Wordsworth*, pp. 210–211.
[36] Gascoigne, p. 243.
[37] Johnston, *The Hidden Wordsworth*, pp. 159–160.
[38] Johnston, *The Hidden Wordsworth*, p. 160.

In addition to the Cambridge royal commission's arguments for the value of classical studies cited above, even Sidney Smith, who could be quite critical of the classical education he received at both Winchester and New College, offered grudging praise of it as well. In his review of Edgeworth's *Essays on Professional Education*, Smith admits that studying Latin and Greek teaches a student how language can be the 'vehicle of thought and passion'.[39] He adds that students benefit from experiencing the 'descriptive power' of Tacitus, the 'dignified perspicuity' of Livy, the 'simplicity' of Caesar, the 'light and heat' in Homer's verse, the 'tenderness' in works by Tibullus, the 'pathos' in Euripides's drama, and the 'natural description' used by Theocritus.[40] Smith aptly comments that classical training forms a 'person's ability to apply himself to hard intellectual work'.[41] If modern readers wish to condemn such study as boring and tedious, it is worthwhile to recall that Wordsworth himself wrote in his 'Preface' to *Lyrical Ballads* that the 'human mind is capable of being excited without the application of gross and violent stimulants', and that he found the adolescent 'thirst after outrageous stimulation' to be 'degrading'.[42] Indeed, the Georgian universities' classical pedagogies—which are the subject of the next chapter—offered precisely the type of 'long continued intercourse with the best models of composition'[43] that Wordsworth heralded in the 'Preface'. Such study not only continued to refine their knowledge of classical genres and appreciation of the effects of language but added to their already impressively stocked schoolboy memories of the sounds and sense of literary classics and further accustomed them to the 'boring but important work' necessary for the writer's life.

It should also be noted that the daily life at Cambridge and Oxford intentionally provided plenty of time for students to read according to their private interests. University students' letters and journals from the period mention the pleasures of reading and discussing Milton, Shakespeare, Chaucer, and Dante as well as poems by the contemporary authors that were regularly published in the reviews and newspapers. Coleridge's reading of Pindar (from after tea until 11 p.m. his first year) is an example of one students' private study. Christopher Wordsworth reported in his diary that his independent reading included *Paradise Lost*, Darwin's *Zoonomia*, Butler's *Anatomy of Melancholy*, Bysshe's *Art of Poetry*, and Boswell's *Life of Johnson*. Wordsworth's private study of Italian with Agostino Isola is well known,[44] as is his youthful acquaintance

---

[39] *Edinburgh Review*, 'Art. III. *Essays on Professional Education*', p. 44.
[40] *Edinburgh Review*, 'Art. III. *Essays on Professional Education*', p. 45.
[41] *Edinburgh Review*, 'Art. III. *Essays on Professional Education*', p. 44.
[42] WWMW, p. 599.
[43] WWMW, p. 614.
[44] During which time he read Boccaccio, Machiavelli, and Tasso.

Educating the Romantic Poets

with many English poets.[45] Thanks to Duncan Wu's studies of Wordsworth's reading, we know that Wordsworth not only found time to read or reread most of the English canon at Cambridge, but that he also read travel narratives and natural histories of England and Europe; Scott's *Critical Essays on Some of the Poems of Several English Poets* (1785); periodicals ranging from the *British Critic* to *The Gentleman's Magazine*; French revolutionary pamphlets, Burke, Hartley, Paine, Racine, and Daniel Webb's *Inquiry into the Beauties of Painting* (1761).

---

[45] Wu makes it clear that he read Chaucer, Shakespeare, Milton, Spenser, Thomson, Beattie, Charlotte Smith, Percy, Crabbe, Burns, and Collins as a schoolboy. The English poets he read or reread during his free time as an undergraduate at Cambridge include Moses Brown, Chaucer, Congreve, Cowley, Drayton, Drummond, Anne Finch, Langhorne, Milton, Ogilvie, Russell, Spenser, Thomson, and Young. He also read novels by Richardson and Sterne. Wu also provides a list of what Wordsworth studied at the university. See Appendix II, p. 166 f.

CHAPTER NINE

Pedagogies of Oxford and Cambridge in the Georgian Period

> When the intellect has been properly trained and formed to have a connected view or grasp of things ... in the case of most men, it makes itself felt in ... good sense, sobriety of thought, reasonableness, candour, self-command, and steadiness of view.
>
> John Henry Newman, *The Idea of the University*

University educators believed that the best way to teach college men was to allow them to be 'in great measure free agents'.[1] It was the opinion of senior members of the university that 'Compulsion [of students at college] is ridiculous'.[2] The 'active, steady, and commanding principle' they preferred in a liberal education was 'emulation'.[3] After years of school exercises, themes, memory work, and recitation, college men were assigned a tutor and given a private room. They were charged to wear academic robes, show up at dinner and chapel, and spend the rest of their time 'reading', which also meant studying. Though university professors offered lectures on a variety of subjects ranging from astronomy to theology, 'direct' teaching (Whewell's term) by college tutors, who questioned and conversed with students individually or in small groups about their reading, was the standard method. According to William Whewell, the 'main springs' that drove university learning were Englishmen's 'love of knowledge' and their 'love of distinction with the fear of disgrace'.[4]

---

[1] Whewell, p. 92.
[2] Edward Copleston, p. 137.
[3] Edward Copleston, p. 137.
[4] Whewell, p. 56.

Educating the Romantic Poets

Copleston remarks that most college men in his day were motivated by a combination of competition or emulation, professional aspiration, and the desire not to disappoint their parents. Two other motivators were cited by a Cambridge senior who had just completed his final exams; these were 'prudence, and … the respect due to your own character as a Gentleman'.[5]

According to Whewell, Cambridge's standard methods of teaching mathematics and classical languages were 'practical' because students were lectured and tutored in smaller groups, working closely with educators who were familiar with their talents, inclinations, intellectual growth, station in life, and future plans. College tutors in that period encouraged students, he said, to be actively involved in discussion and required them to produce evidence of their learning by working problems and by writing and speaking. In this process, Whewell claimed, students assimilate what they have learned and apply it, thereby developing a 'practical' habit of intellectual action. Whewell insisted that Cambridge men were trained to be problem-solvers, not pedants. Oxford's Copleston concurred, noting that the process of careful work with one's college tutor and classmates before and after 'private study' established an 'intercourse of mind, which, imperceptibly, gives a tincture even to the most thoughtless, and marks a lasting stamp on others, who are hardly conscious of the successive impulses, by which the impression is continually worn in'.[6]

The colleges' methods of instruction in classical languages and literature were built on the firm foundation laid by the grammar schools. By reading texts with which students were already familiar, parts of which they had memorised as boys, college tutors affirmed and continued to develop students' vocabularies, and skill in word choice and sentence structure, as well as their appreciation of the linguistic register, genre, style, themes, and argumentative strategies modelled in classical texts. While this careful, close-reading method limited how many texts a student was able to study during his college days and ran the risk of tedium, it made it more likely that each text would be thoroughly explored. For poets, this practice was especially useful, for it showed them how carefully crafted metrical texts were from the inside out. The Cambridge commission commended this method for another reason: it taught students about 'taste' as well as style. At the Georgian universities, having taste meant not only that a student might recognise and be familiar with well-crafted verse and prose but also that he had developed good judgement that extended to matters of 'personal conduct or social relations'.[7]

An important aspect of university pedagogies in the Georgian period was how the colleges at both Cambridge and Oxford operated as communities of

---

[5] Questionist, p. 50.
[6] Edward Copleston, p. 148.
[7] Graham, p. 58.

grown 'gentlemen', not boys. While direct instruction by college tutors and university professors was part of the university experience, so, too, was 'self-education'. Newman explains:

> there is a sort of self-education in the academic institutions of Protestant England; a characteristic tone of thought, a recognized standard of judgment is found in them, which, as developed in the individual who is submitted to it, becomes a twofold source of strength to him, both from the distinct stamp it impresses on his mind, and from the bond of union which it creates between him and others.[8]

Newman continues, saying that this is 'real teaching' and that it 'tends toward the cultivation of the intellect' and 'recognizes that knowledge is more than a sort of passive reception of scraps and details'.[9] Moreover, he asserts that self-education is usually more efficacious than listening to lectures. Operating on this belief, college tutors guided students, but left them free to work according to their own aims and individual ambitions. Given how intellectually active members of the Romantic public sphere were—Hazlitt and Brougham both characterised it as an age of curiosity, investigation, and learning—this tradition of self-education appears to have had its effects.

Teaching Horace

The example of how James Wood, a tutor at Wordsworth's college, taught Horace's 'Epistle II.1 On Popular Taste and Judgment' offers insight into how—as well as what—one influential scholar at Cambridge taught students about classical texts. This poem and two others from Horace's epistles appeared on the first college exam Wordsworth took at the end of Michaelmas in 1787, so it is likely that Wordsworth benefited from this lesson. Similar lessons were probably offered to Byron when he was at Trinity (1805–08). Wood's teaching method, as outlined in notes dated 1786 and 1808 in St John's archive, appears to be thorough, scholarly, and thought-provoking.

Horace's letter discourses on poetic taste, the role of poetry in the state, and the character and experience of the poet. Beginning with a summary of the major arguments of the epistle, Wood highlights Horace's prefatory lessons, which were that good works do not always win gratitude and that excellence often arouses envy rather than praise. Wood gives context and colour to students' experience of the text by offering historical and cultural details, such as the Romans' habit of sprinkling perfumed waters in their

---

[8] Newman, p. 111.
[9] Newman, p. 111.

Educating the Romantic Poets

theatres and the Greeks' insistence upon continuing athletic games even in wartime. He provides brief biographies of the poets Horace mentions and summarises scholarly criticism of Horace's text by Quintilian, Bentley, and Pope. Wood also comments on Horace's theory of comedy and on the relation of classical texts to the formation of taste and writing skill. He guides students' close reading, noting, for example, differences between the ceremonial style of the introduction and the ordinary, conversational style of the body of the epistle. He calls attention to issues as specific as the appropriateness of a particular metaphor, the metrical effect of certain word choices, and problems that arise in interpretation when two substantives are coupled with one verb.

In addition to these matters, Wood comments on Horace's criticism of his age's preference for 'ancient verse' over modern and invites students to consider Horace's notion that appreciation of poetry of the past is motivated 'not/ By reverence for the genius of the past/ But rather by scorn and hatred of the present'.[10] Wood's mention of this part of the epistle registers his appreciation of how Pope's translation is used to comment on attitudes about English poets (Pope's translation draws specific parallels between writers and leaders in his day and those that Horace cites). Wood's reference to Horace's friendly scoffing at the popularity of writing verse—'skilled or unskilled we all feel free to write poems'—may have been included as reference to certain contemporary English writers. If the notes were used after 1798, they might have called to mind Wordsworth's 'experiments' in the *Lyrical Ballads* or his *Poems in Two Volumes* (1807), which were criticised for ignoring classical models. Elsewhere in his notes, Wood directs students to Horace's claims that a poet might 'be of some use to his country … [by] promot[ing]/The greater good', by shaping the minds of children with 'gentle precepts'; and that poets are needed to tell stories of men 'who disciplined themselves/ Against their own capacities for anger/ Envy, savage incivility', to comfort 'the weak and helpless', and to solace 'those who are bereft and grieving'.[11] Under Wood's guidance students would also have noticed Horace's assurance that poets 'feel the listening presence of the gods' when they sing.

Clancey has traced some of the parallels between the poetic ethos of Horace and Wordsworth, and I suggest that there are also significant similarities between what Wood chose to discuss in this lecture and passages in Wordsworth's 'Preface' to *Lyrical Ballads*. For example, Wood calls attention to Horace's ideas about the poet's use to society, and Wordsworth calls the poet nothing less than 'the rock of defence of human nature; an upholder and

---

[10] Wood, 'Notes on Horace', p. 1; hereafter most page numbers are too erratic to be of use. Unless otherwise noted, quotations can be found in Book 8, between pp. 1 and 41.

[11] These are citations from the poem in Wood's notes.

preserver, carrying everywhere with him relationship and love'. Wood notes Horace's 'Experiments to see how worthily/ He could perform'; Wordsworth calls the *Lyrical Ballads* 'experiments'. The Preface and passages in 'Tintern Abbey' also echo Wood's comments on the power of poetry to calm and please and on its origins among 'the natural, innocent pleasures of country life and during the services of Religion'.[12]

Besides attending to the historical contexts and themes of literary works, as Wood did at St John's, most college tutors in the Georgian era continued to insist on the benefits of reading classical texts as examples of grammatical correctness and appropriate style. One reason was a concern many educators had (as they still do today) about students' difficulties with writing and speaking in English. In a piece for the *Edinburgh Review*, Sydney Smith explains:

> In languages so irregularly constructed as our own, [eloquence] can only be acquired, perhaps, by accustoming our thoughts to flow through purer channels [i.e., Latin and Greek verse]; in which every distinct operation of mind, or mode of thinking, has its distinct vehicle of expression; and every deviation from just order in our thought, an immediate and obvious corrective in a correspondent deviation from the established mode of speech.[13]

James Wood appears to have subscribed to this opinion; in one of his journals he wrote that 'The Romans taught their children the Latin tongue by making them read the works of their best poets. Thus, they learned the measures of their language and were early formed to correctness and elegance of stile.'[14]

College translation work

While close, critical reading of classical literature in college was a standard method used with Georgian college students, so was the practice of assigning translations.[15] Following on what students did at their public or grammar schools, tutors at the Georgian university colleges required students to translate longer and more complicated excerpts from Greek and Latin prose and verse into correct and idiomatic English. It was also common practice for tutors to ask students to recast English texts in one of the classical languages. Christopher Wordsworth records in his Trinity diary that he was assigned

---

[12] Wood, 'Notes on Horace', pp. 38–39.
[13] *Edinburgh Review*, 'Art. X', p. 430.
[14] Wood, 'Notes on Horace', pp. 38–39.
[15] See my discussion of the pedagogical value of translation exercises in Chapter 3.

Educating the Romantic Poets

translations of portions of *The Spectator* and an article from Johnson's other journal, *The Adventurer*, into Latin.[16] The passage quoted below was used on the Trinity College examinations when both Wordsworths were at Cambridge:

> How much nobler is it to place the reward of Virtue in the silent approbation of one's own breast, than in the applause of the World. Glory ought to be the consequence, not the motive of our actions; and tho' fame should sometimes happen not to attend the deed which merits it, yet it is by no means the [less] for having missed the applause it deserved. The world is apt to suspect that those who celebrate their own generous acts ... the splendour of an action which would have shone out in full lustre if related by [others] vanishes and dies away when it becomes the subject of our own applause.[17]

Coleridge was so well schooled in translation at Christ's Hospital that during his first year at Jesus College he wrote to his brother George that he imagined that, between the two of them, they could translate Anacreon 'entirely'.[18] Not infrequently, Coleridge copied excerpts of translations he was working on into his letters to George. Before his college days were over, Coleridge had become so adept that he hatched a scheme to produce and sell by subscription a volume of the best Greek and Latin lyric poems, translated and versified in English.[19] Wordsworth's early notebooks include translations from the Greek bucolic poet Moschus and sections from Horace and Virgil. Both Wordsworth's trip to France in 1791–92 and his later trip with Dorothy and Coleridge to Germany in 1798–99 were planned, at least in part, for the purpose of adding to his language skills, so he might earn money as a translator. This training helps to explain why Wordsworth describes the job of the poet as that of a translator,[20] and it helps to explain why, in later life, Wordsworth undertook translations of *The Aeneid*, Bede, and Chaucer as private, intellectual exercise.

College exercises in prose and verse

Along with writing translations for their college tutors, students at the larger colleges of the universities were required every week to compose original

---

[16] *The Adventurer* was a bi-weekly London newspaper, one of Dr Johnson's projects after *The Rambler* closed. Both journals intentionally used more elevated language than other periodicals. Christopher Wordsworth, *Social Life*, pp. 593–594.

[17] 'Trinity College Examinations', Banks, Hodson, or Challis Papers, Box 1, #30. Sutherland.

[18] CLSTC, p. 17. Some Anacreon's verse was quite erotic.

[19] CLSTC, p. 46.

[20] Preface to *Lyrical Ballads*, WWMW, p. 604.

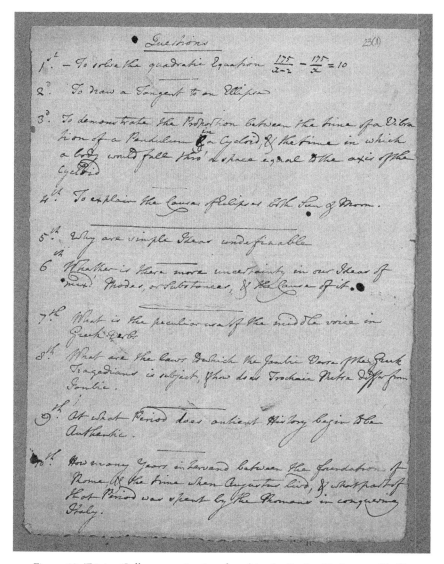

Figure 19. Trinity College examination, found in the Banks, Hodson or Challis Papers, XVIIIth Century, Box 1, Wren Library, Trinity College, Cambridge. Reproduced by permission of the Master and Fellows of Trinity College, Cambridge.

'exercises', usually two to five pages long, in prose and verse. About half of these exercises were to be written in Latin, the other in Greek and English. These exercises would be read to students' tutors, who gave oral critiques and recommendations for revision.[21] Students' compositions were read at dinner in

---

[21] Sutherland, p. 479.

Educating the Romantic Poets

the hall before the entire membership of the college. Deans and other senior members of the colleges would offer their comments then, or later in writing. Students also used these papers as entertainment in dormitories and in their literary and drinking clubs. Though Sutherland asserts that these themes were usually quite 'banal', they nevertheless 'excited a good deal of interest ... and were frequently sent home for the admiration of the [student's] family',[22] as Jeremy Bentham, Samuel Taylor Coleridge, and George Chinnery all did. Closing ceremonies at both universities featured readings of students' prize-winning compositions. In the audience were the entire university, family, friends, guests, members of parliament and, sometimes, the royal family.

Oxford's professor of poetry, Edward Copleston, as already noted, emphasised that the purpose and effects of assigning so much verse composition was not to produce great poetry but to train students' 'poetic faculty'. It would teach useful skills and habits such as 'compression without obscurity ... selecting the fittest materials, and of setting them in the nicest order'.[23] The practice also aimed at giving students 'a command of pure, terse, and polished diction'.[24] Typical university assignments included composing odes in imitation of Horace (in Latin) and 20 or more stanzas of dactylic hexameter (in Greek or English). As a student, Coleridge particularly favoured the ode form, often sending his 'Odelings' to Mary Evans.[25] Most colleges offered annual prizes specifically for verse composition. Trinity College, Cambridge, offered a series of prizes for Latin verse in lyric, heroic, and elegiac metres. The Camden Prize was awarded for the best example of Latin hexameter, and the Cambridge Chancellor's Poetry Medal was given each year to the best English ode or poem in heroic verse. The assigned topics of these poems were 'of national importance' or supported students' course of study. Copleston won a prize for an essay on 'Agriculture' in his student days and was thanked personally on behalf of the Agricultural Society by its president, Sir John Sinclair.[26] The Sapphic ode competition for the Brown Gold Medal during Coleridge's second year at Cambridge was 'The Praise of Astronomy'; this was the same term in which his class was studying the stars. In addition to prizes for original compositions, university examinations always included essay questions about poetry, such as 'What effects do Spondees produce in iambic verse?' and 'What is the difference between a common hexameter verse and a heroic hexameter?'[27]

The tradition of verse composition was the object of considerable ridicule in articles about Oxford published in 1809 and 1810 by the *Edinburgh Review*.

---

[22] Sutherland, p. 479.
[23] Edward Copleston, pp. 129–130.
[24] Edward Copleston, p. 131.
[25] CLSTC, p. 28.
[26] William James Copleston, *Memoir*, p. 5.
[27] Anonymous, 'Examination Questions in Criticism, History, Grammar', Box 1.

However, trained since boyhood to craft metrical verse almost nightly, most university students did not complain about the practice. Reflecting on his experience writing verse at Pembroke College, Samuel Johnson described himself and his classmates as 'a nest of singing birds'.[28] Coleridge's giddy pleasure in verse writing at Jesus College has already been noted. Apparently, his undergraduate poetic efforts also brought him, and probably other college students, attention from young women. Coleridge wrote to his brother George of the 'no small kudos' he earned from 'the young Belles' of Tiverton 'by complimentary effusions in the poetic Way'.[29] Comparisons of the poets' juvenilia to their writing after university make it clear that the reading, discussion, and writing practice of the Cambridge years honed Wordsworth's, Coleridge's, Southey's, and Byron's skills in handling sound, metre, and poetic conventions. Wordsworth states specifically that his time at St John's sharpened his knowledge of the 'strict laws' of metre and its historic and strategic uses.[30] It was there that he came to appreciate more fully how rhythmic language can afford pleasure and delight and where he learned how metre, by 'divesting language in a certain degree of its reality', can make the pain connected with 'pathetic situations and sentiments' more endurable.[31] *Lyrical Ballads*, created when Wordsworth and Coleridge put their two university-educated, poetic sensibilities together to address a classically educated audience, is further evidence that their composition skills and judgement were elevated by study at Cambridge.[32]

Writing in prose was also emphasised at the universities. Georgian college students were given a great deal more practice in composing arguments—and in understanding the art of argument—than most university students are today. In 1775, the new master of St John's, John Chevallier, sent out a memo that all students were to submit four themes every term to the rhetoric lecturer.[33] This amounted to 12 argumentative essays each year in addition to their tutors' usual weekly writing assignments. Examples of assigned essay prompts at Trinity included 'demonstration *a priori*' (1793), 'the difference between direct and indirect proofs' (1788), and 'Logic and Rhetoric differ in their nature and end and the means which each employs to obtain its end' (1792). Exam questions also asked students to explain Locke's idea about 'the principal Causes of the Imperfection and Abuse of Words' and to invent arguments in response to questions such as 'What is the prevailing principal of morality in

---

[28] Hill, p. 88.
[29] Holmes, p. 50.
[30] WWMW, Preface to *Lyrical Ballads*, p. 601.
[31] WWMW, Preface, pp. 609–610.
[32] Of course, time spent in nature and with Dorothy Wordsworth also contributed to that volume.
[33] Mullinger, p. 254.

Educating the Romantic Poets

Greek tragedy?' and 'What two officers in the Roman state contributed most to the destruction of Liberty?' Two other questions—'What are the distinct provinces of Faith and Reason?' and 'What is the true and adequate foundation of moral obligation?'—asked students to rehearse what they had been learning in their divinity studies. College tutors did not expect originality; they looked for good recall and a correct and readable style. Judging from the topics discussed in the journals and reviews of the period and the level of discourse in those articles, the curriculum and training in prose composition provided by the Anglo-classical academy contributed materially to the busy periodical trade in the Romantic period.

Considered from the perspective of modern composition theory and pedagogy, Georgian college tutors employed many of today's best practices in writing instruction. These included (1) making sure students accumulated a great deal of 'quality practice' (Georgian period college students wrote and spoke every week) and (2) assigning tightly structured writing tasks (all compositions were short, students were asked to summarise Sunday sermons, imitate classical writers or forms, and expand upon received arguments). These practices also include (3) being clear about the expected outcomes (verse assignments included numbers of lines, metre, forms, and writers to imitate); (4) providing 'examples or models' (most writing was undertaken only after much reading of classical models and prose assignments typically were to be short imitations of these models); and (5) specifying criteria for their evaluation (student work should be grammatically correct, idiomatic, and as close as possible to classical models. Finally, the best writing instructors also (6) give frequent, targeted feedback to individuals and groups (students read their work each week to their tutor or small group and received immediate feedback) and (7) make writing meaningful to students (their work was read in class and on many public occasions, the universities had many prize competitions for student writing, and the best writers and speakers won scholarships and fellowships).

Public speaking and argumentation

Even Sydney Smith, who complained about classical studies in the *Edinburgh Review*, recognised that public discourse was 'the principal medium of government' and that speaking skills, built from training in rhetoric and 'eloquence', were the 'most direct and honourable road to rank, power and reputation'.[34] Training in oral argument at the universities was furnished by requiring students to make and observe college declamations. At Cambridge students were required to take part in four-person debates called 'Acts and

---

[34] *Edinburgh Review*, 'Art. X', p. 430.

Opponencies' at least once a year. The tradition continued throughout the Georgian period. At the beginning of the term groups of students of similar argumentation skills and general knowledge were alerted that they had been scheduled for their Acts and Opponencies. They had to prepare to defend three specific propositions, two in mathematics and one in philosophy. The 'Act' began with a student standing up ready to defend a short Latin essay on one of the announced propositions, which was read by the moderator, a junior fellow. Mounting the rostrum, a second student delivered eight prepared arguments in syllogistic form against the proposition in Latin. The defending student replied in like form. When these two students' argument reached a point of stasis, a second opponent had to offer five arguments, and the debate proceeded in the same way until stasis was again achieved. The third opponent then took his turn, with three prepared arguments. Moderators assessed all four students' knowledge, ability to bring relevant arguments forward, tactics, and avoidance of fallacies. Apparently, in the heat of battle, students' Latin skills almost always disappointed. Winstanley has commented that rules of logic were supposed to apply, but that it was not unusual for students to 'slide into free and unconfined debate'.[35] Whewell joked about the students' bad Latin and strange renderings of syllogisms (they 'would make Aristotle stare'), but he believed that these exercises were 'well adapted to try the clearness and soundness of the mathematical ideas of the men'.[36]

Members of the colleges disagreed about the value of these disputations. Some criticised the permissive conduct of some moderators and the poor preparation of certain students. William Frend was among this group; he expressed the opinion that the acts and opponencies were worthless. Richard Watson thought they were very 'serious and solemn' and compared Cambridge's disputations favourably with those at Oxford. John Jebb believed that the disputations were 'improving' and wished only that they might be in English, not Latin. Wainwright viewed the disputations as useful because they required 'much preparatory exertion' and gave students a 'most beneficial' opportunity to participate in a 'contest of mental acuteness'.[37] According to Whewell, helpful effects of the disputations were that they produced 'sympathy of the Students in a common subject', that they 'fixed their attention on difficulties and their solutions', and that they disciplined students to 'promptness and clearness' in testifying to their new knowledge.[38] Christopher Wordsworth quotes a letter William Gooch wrote in 1790 to his parents, describing an act and opponency that suggests that students and

---

[35] Winstanley, p. 44.
[36] Winstanley, p. 47.
[37] Winstanley, pp. 46–47.
[38] Graham, p. 109.

Educating the Romantic Poets

fellows took the exercise seriously: it was 'a very capital Act, ... Abstruse and difficult as [one student's] Questions were ... his inimitable Discerning & keen Penetration were not baffled', and when the third opponent had been overcome the examiner declared *optime quidem disputasti*—'you've disputed excellently indeed'.[39] I have not found any reports about the poets' experience with acts and opponencies; but we can assume, at least, that many in their reading audience had gone through such training.

We do have evidence that some of the Romantics took part in another form of public-speaking training at the university colleges—declamation. Coleridge reported that he declaimed every term—'two spoken in a week, one English, one Latin'.[40] In the winter of 1792 he told the Evans family that his declamation on 'Posthumous Fame', spoken 'in public' had met 'with the most pointed marks of respect'.[41] In the spring of his last year at Cambridge, Coleridge was perhaps reflecting on his experience of college disputations when he wrote in a letter that he was 'fond of the subtlety of argument'.[42] In the diary he kept at Trinity, Wordsworth's brother Christopher details how the declamation process worked. Upon notice that he would soon be called to perform his declamation, he spent 'All morning ... chusing a subject, finding my opponent, going to the Dean, and procuring books &c.'[43] After this, he spent a week preparing his argument (he was to take the negative on the subject *Utrum Attici vitae ratio bonum civem deceat*), then took a draft of his argument to his tutor, who spent an hour with him working on revision. His next task was to get his argument by heart, a requirement that was not abolished until later in the Victorian period. While Christopher Wordsworth does not report how his own declamation went, he does report that one of his classmates was required to repeat his. When that student's memory failed, and he resorted to reading his argument, the dean lost his temper, called out '*descendas, descendas*', and was seconded by the vice master. The student responded with fury, came down from the dais, threw his declamation across the chapel, stalked down the chapel aisle, and threw off his gown.[44]

University examinations

Examinations were one of the most distinctive educational practices at Oxford and Cambridge. Senior members of the colleges considered the exam process not only a measure of students' learning but also a tool for building their

---

[39] Christopher Wordsworth, *Scholae Academicae*, p. 321.
[40] CLSTC, p. 17.
[41] CLSTC, p. 24.
[42] Holmes, p. 58.
[43] Christopher Wordsworth, *Social Life*, p. 588.
[44] Christopher Wordsworth, *Social Life*, pp. 588–589.

character and instilling humility. These were of two sorts: college term exams such as the collections at Christ Church, already noted, and university-wide exams. All colleges held similar exercises as a way of solidifying and measuring students' learning at the end of each term. The universities' examinations, which came at the middle and end of a student's academic career, were framed as intercollegiate competitions. Originally all of these exams were conducted orally, but during the nineteenth century college and university examiners began using written exercises, particularly for mathematical problems. After five terms of residence, students at Cambridge took the 'previous examination'. The prescribed subjects were one of the four Gospels in the original Greek, Paley's *Evidences of Christianity*, Old Testament History, a portion of one of the Greek and one of the Latin classical authors, the first and second books of Euclid, and the 'most common and useful Rules of Arithmetic'.[45]

After ten terms at Cambridge, students took the 'second' or final examination, also called the Senate House exam. Less academically inclined students (usually about two-thirds of the class) took the 'ordinary' exam. This covered half of the Acts of the Apostles and one long or two shorter New Testament epistles in Greek, a portion of the works of one of the Greek and one of the Latin authors, three of the six books of Paley's *Moral Philosophy*, the history of the Christian Church from its origins to the Council of Nice, and the history of the English Reformation. It also tested students on the general rules of arithmetic, the rudiments of algebra, the third and part of the sixth book of Euclid's *Elements*, and the elementary principles of mechanics and hydrostatics. The most ambitious and talented students—hoping to win fellowships—took a longer, more demanding series of exams—called the tripos—with especially difficult mathematics sections. These exams were an occasion of spirited intercollegiate competition that garnered much attention from all members of the colleges, young and old.

William Wordsworth read a novel when he should have been prepping for the ordinary exam and passed with a low but acceptable score. Southey and Coleridge left their university before the final exam. Wordsworth's younger brother Christopher, who wanted a clerical career and hoped to win a fellowship, took the honours exam. To be admitted to this exam, students had to have attended lectures and passed term examinations in several of the following subject areas: law, physics, moral philosophy, chemistry, anatomy, modern history, botany, geology, natural and experimental philosophy, English law, medicine, mineralogy, or political economy.[46] Additionally, they had been sorted into categories of academic merit based on their performance in college exams, the university's previous exam, and their acts and opponencies.

---

[45] Graham, p. 20.
[46] Graham, p. 21.

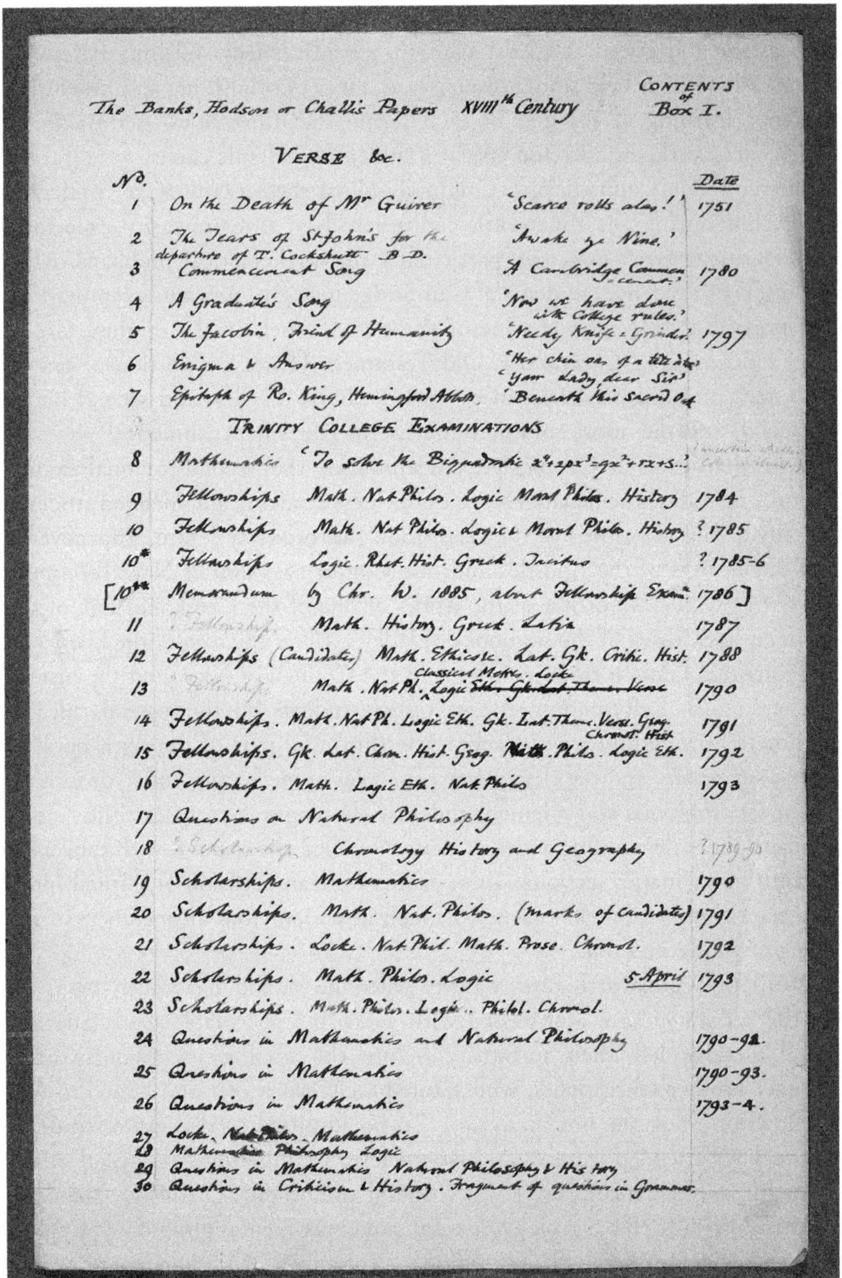

The Banks, Hodson or Challis Papers XVIIIth Century — Contents of Box I.

VERSE &c.

No.			Date
1	On the Death of Mr Guirer	'Scarce rolls alas!'	1751
2	The Tears of St John's for the departure of T. Cockshutt B.D.	'Awake ye Nine.'	
3	Commencement Song	'A Cambridge Commencement'	1780
4	A Graduate's Song	'Now we have done with College rules.'	
5	The Jacobin, Friend of Humanity	'Needy Knife-grinder'	1797
6	Enigma & Answer	'Her chin on, of a tête à tête' 'Your lady, dear Sir'	
7	Epitaph of Ro. King, Hemingford Abbots	'Beneath this sacred Oak'	

TRINITY COLLEGE EXAMINATIONS

8	Mathematics 'To solve the Biquadratic $x^4+2px^3=qx^2+rx+s$...'	
9	Fellowships Math. Nat Philos. Logic Moral Philos. History	1784
10	Fellowships Math. Nat Philos. Logic & Moral Philos. History	?1785
10*	Fellowships Logic. Rhet. Hist. Greek. Tacitus	?1785-6
[10**	Memorandum by Chr. W. 1885, about Fellowship Exam.	1786]
11	? Fellowships Math. History. Greek. Latin	1787
12	Fellowships (Candidates) Math. Ethics etc. Lat. Gk. Critic. Hist.	1788
13	? Fellowships Math. Nat Ph. Classical Metres. Logic	1790
14	Fellowships. Math. Nat Ph. Logic Eth. Gk. Lat. Theme. Verse. Geog. Chronol. Hist	1791
15	Fellowships. Gk. Lat. Chron. Hist. Geog. Math. Philos. Logic Eth.	1792
16	Fellowships. Math. Logic Eth. Nat Philos	1793
17	Questions on Natural Philosophy	
18	? Scholarships Chronology History and Geography	?1789-90
19	Scholarships. Mathematics	1790
20	Scholarships. Math. Nat. Philos. (marks of candidates)	1791
21	Scholarships. Locke. Nat Phil. Math. Prose. Chronol.	1792
22	Scholarships. Math. Philos. Logic 5 April	1793
23	Scholarships. Math. Philos. Logic.. Philol. Chronol.	
24	Questions in Mathematics and Natural Philosophy	1790-92.
25	Questions in Mathematics	1790-93.
26	Questions in Mathematics	1793-4.
27	Locke, ~~Nat Philos.~~ Mathematics	
28	Mathematics Philosophy Logic	
29	Questions in Mathematics Natural Philosophy & History	
30	Questions in Criticism & History. Fragment of questions in Grammar.	

Figure 20. Table of Contents of Banks, Hodson or Challis Papers, XVIIIth Century, Box I, Wren Library, Trinity College, Cambridge. Reproduced by permission of the Master and Fellows of Trinity College, Cambridge.

Christopher Wordsworth recorded in his diary that he studied for almost ten hours every day from 7 September 1795 until the exam period in early January 1796, with only one holiday, 17 December, Commemoration Day. Expecting to be first wrangler, young Wordsworth was devastated when he learned he had been judged to be only tenth wrangler. This placement, however, suggests how talented and hardworking his classmates were.

The traditions of these exams are worth noting. All senior students at Cambridge gathered at the Senate House at around 7.30 a.m. on 'Examination Monday' with their college 'Fathers'—usually recent BAs and junior fellows appointed as guides, coaches, and advocates for the students. Promptly at 8 a.m. the first round of written exams began. Students ranking high in their class were given harder problems and directed to sit by a window to solve them—hence the name 'window problems'. At 9 a.m. the students bundled their papers, turned them in to the fellows appointed as moderators, and left for breakfast. Thirty minutes later, students returned and took more written exams or did window problems until 11 a.m., when the Senate House was cleared yet again. At 1 p.m. they returned, did more problems until 3 p.m., took a half-hour break, and began a fourth round, working until 5 p.m.

The ordinary students were done for the day, but the top ones taking the Mathematical tripos went to the moderators' rooms at 7 p.m., where they continued to solve problems until 9 p.m., when they were given fruit, sweets, wine, and tea. 'Examination Tuesday and Wednesday' continued in a similar fashion. Student rankings—the brackets—were revised after each round of exams and published at 9 a.m., 11 a.m., 3 p.m., and 5 p.m. In 1779 a fourth day of exams was added and in 1808 a fifth. In some years, the schedule of examination days was modified to make Wednesday a day of rest. By the fourth day, the contenders for top honours had been identified. Any competitor who disagreed with his ranking could challenge the student ahead of him. For this process, moderators called in proctors and distinguished MAs. James Wood of St John's and Isaac Milner of Queens' were often commissioned for this duty.

During the first three days, while the ordinary students were taking their exams, the better students—the honours candidates—were examined in Euclid's *Elements*, algebra, plane trigonometry, conic sections, statics, dynamics, hydrostatics, optics, and astronomy. After the week described above, the honours candidates were given a week to eight days off before beginning a second round of examinations. In this round, students were tested on the higher parts of abstract mathematics, several branches of natural philosophy, Paley's *Moral Philosophy*, the New Testament, and ecclesiastical history. At the conclusion of these examinations, candidates were arranged into three classes in the order of their merit—wranglers, senior optimes, and junior optimes—and their names were published. The top twelve students were 'wranglers', and,

Educating the Romantic Poets

upon the announcement of these placements, all undergraduates took part 'in the rejoicings of the successful candidates', which included dining out no fewer than three times in the following week.[47]

Years after he took his own exams, when Christopher Wordsworth was master of Trinity and serving a term as vice chancellor of the university, he created another university-wide examination, the classical tripos. It was a suitable contribution for the brother of the poet. The examination was voluntary and, like the mathematic tripos, the ordeal took many days. This exam required students to translate selections from the Greek and Latin writers into English, to answer questions about those passages, to translate selections of English prose and verse into Greek and Latin prose and verse, and to answer questions about ancient history. The names of the classical students and their placement on these exams were made public, and the top ten also won the coveted title of 'wrangler' and—as the mathematics wranglers did—brought honour to their college. The Cambridge royal commissioners considered this scheme of examinations in both classics and mathematics a 'judicious plan, equally adapted to strengthen the mental power by wholesome discipline, and to give coherence and solidity, and consequently, real value to, the acquisition of knowledge'.[48]

At Oxford the university administered an examination similar to Cambridge's previous exam after students' second year. If they passed, students were admitted to the title of *Sophista Generalis*. This exam was less about competition and ranking the colleges than the final exams were; rather, the goal was to determine if a student had 'an accurate grammatical acquaintance with the structure' of Latin and Greek.[49] Greek authors used in these exams included Xenophon, Homer, Herodotus, Demosthenes, and the dramatists; Latin authors were Virgil, Horace, Sallust, Livy, and Cicero. Students' knowledge of logic and geometry was also tested. Copleston explains that students taking these examinations were questioned in groups of eight, with several juniors attending as observers.

Oxford also administered a series of university-wide final exams for all seniors. Two kinds were offered—the ordinary exam, which was given to less talented or motivated students, and the honours exam, or schools exam, similar to the Cambridge Senate House exam or tripos. The schools exam was also a route to fellowships and careers in the Church or university. The literary texts covered in Oxford's ordinary examination included four plays by Euripides, four or five books of Herodotus, six books of Livy, and half of

---

[47] Christopher Wordsworth, *Social Life*, pp. 594–595.
[48] Graham, p. 22.
[49] Edward Copleston, p. 130.

Horace, along with four books of Euclid or Aldrich's *Compendium of Logic*.[50] Students taking this exam were required to translate a passage from English into Latin, to construe any passage from the four Gospels (in Greek), to repeat the 39 Articles, to illustrate them orally with examples from the Scriptures, and to answer questions on Old and New Testament history. The mathematics sections of the ordinary examination focused primarily on geometry. The Oxford royal commission admitted that, compared with the expectations of hard-reading men, the attainments required of the college's ordinary students on this exam were not great, and it was possible to pass them with only a 'meagre' knowledge of literature and logic and only 'very slight' linguistic skill.[51] However, the commissioners also expressed the belief that, even though the stringency of some of the ordinary exams varied and allowances were made for less able or ambitious students, those who chose to be serious could achieve, through 'deep and independent study' for these exams, 'an intimate acquaintance with the Latin poets' and with other classical literature on the standard of 'Porson or Elmsley'.[52]

Oxford's honours examinations covered *Literae Humaniores* and mathematics. Because of the length and stringency of these exams, usually less than a fifth of the undergraduate students at Oxford took them. Passing these exams, however, was compulsory for any student wishing to secure a fellowship, and most senior members of the university—fellows, tutors, masters, and many other office holders—had done so. Though there was a university honours exam in mathematics during the Georgian period, Oxford men were usually more interested in competing for honours in classics and religion. Copleston reports that on the first day of the examination week students were asked to construe a passage in the Greek Testament and to answer questions to determine if they 'had a proper view of the Christian scheme, and of the outline of sacred history'.[53] Students were also expected to 'give some account of the evidences of Christianity' to show their acquaintance with the 39 Articles and related commentaries. Testing for knowledge of logic, rhetoric, and ethics came next, using treatises such as Aristotle's *Organon* and Cicero's *De Officiis*. According to Copleston, the questions were calculated to bring 'into play all the energies of the intellect, and for trying, not merely the diligence of the scholar, but the habit of discrimination which he has formed, the general accuracy of his thoughts, and the force and vigour of his mind'.[54] The Oxford royal commission report noted that the reading list for the honours exam in some

---

[50] Hinds, p. 60.
[51] Hinds, p. 62.
[52] Hinds, p. 62. Elmsley remained a close friend of Southey until his death.
[53] Edward Copleston, p. 140.
[54] Edward Copleston, p. 141.

years included as many as 20 classical authors. Sir William Hamilton's list of texts for his exam was so long that it took an extra day to finish questioning him over all of them.[55] The honours exam's 'circle of subjects' between 1807 and 1825 included Homer, Demosthenes, Cicero, Lucretius, Terence, Plutarch, Longinus, and Quintilian. By 1850 the list ranged between 12 and 14 authors, arranged as follows:

> (1) in Philosophy,—Aristotle's Ethics, with his Rhetoric or Politics, two or three Dialogues of Plato, Butler's Analogy or his sermons.
> (2) in Ancient History,—Herodotus, Thucydides, the 1st or 2nd Decade of Livy, the Annals or the Histories of Tacitus.
> (3) in Poetry,—Aeschylus, Sophocles, Aristophanes, Virgil, Horace, and Juvenal.

This examination lasted for several days, and, while the mathematics portions were conducted in writing, the classics and religion portions were viva voce and quite public. In 1808 George Chinnery wrote home about Robert Peel's university examination, for which he won a double first. It took place in a room that was 'as full as it could hold':

> I among the rest of our ChCh men went to hear Peel's examination yesterday, which even all the Out College men confessed to be the most splendid thing they ever had heard. He was equally perfect in Divinity, Ethics, Politics, Logic, Classics, and Mathematics, and in each of these he is superior to any man who has yet appeared in the schools. When he had been examined in Ethics, the examining masters said to him, 'really, Sir, you have answer'd every question in so comprehensive and masterly a manner that it were needless for us to trouble you any further'. His construing was equal to a composition; when I come home, I shall give you an idea of it. When his examination on Newton and other branches of the mathematics was over, the examining masters told him that he had read them with no common degree of attention, that he had brought up more than any man ever did, and that they hoped his example would be followed by others.[56]

After the honours examinations, the public posting of student rankings was a major moment of celebration across the university. Just as was the case with the Cambridge Wranglers, the top few Oxford students who earned 'firsts' not only heaped honour on their college but also carried this personal distinction

---

[55] Brockliss, p. 238.
[56] Chinnery, letter of 20 November 1809.

throughout their lives. Significantly, it was the view of the Oxford commissioners that this examination quite literally determined 'the literary character of Oxford'.[57] It also contributed to the literary character of the Romantic and early Victorian public spheres and to the taste of many in the reading audience.

Even the writers who did not shine academically—or who did not take these exams or complete their degrees—recognised that the learning, skills, and acquaintances they acquired at their university were important to them, and as adults they often mentioned their affiliation with their college on the title pages of their publications. During their years at Oxford and Cambridge young men became familiar with the *lingua franca* of western culture and politics and with the traditions of the English Church. At the universities students became conversant with Western literary traditions and had the opportunity to become skilled readers and critics of poetry. They learned to 'stand up' and compete, to think on their feet, and take criticism. Many improved their writing, speaking, and argument skills; and, thanks to their identities as matriculants at one of these great universities, they stood at the doorway of the English Republic of Letters, ready and welcome to walk through if they so chose. The scholars who brought them to that point in their lives—the college deans, fellows, and tutors—are the subject of the next chapter.

---

[57] Hinds, p. 63.

Chapter Ten

The Educators of Oxford and Cambridge in the Georgian Period

Human champions [in the] church militant of knowledge.

Thomas De Quincey

By the Georgian period, teaching at the universities had evolved into a 'mixed voluntary and compulsory system'.[1] Students were required to meet with their tutors daily. College tutors worked one-on-one or with small groups to make sure that students understood their term assignments in classics, math, and theology. University professors delivered high-level lectures in their areas of speciality. These events were open to all university students and faculty; however, students were not usually required to attend. Finally, private tutors resided in both Oxford and Cambridge and could be hired by students wanting further assistance, mainly struggling undergraduates or seniors who aspired to top academic honours.

By statute, tutors were college fellows and 'virtuous men'; their charge was to teach the approved authors and the rudiments of religion. Though the stereotype of the college tutor has been that of a bored 'clerical celibate'[2] who was merely marking time until one of his college's church livings became available and he could marry and leave Oxford, in most cases these men were good scholars and teachers. Winstanley explains the 'exacting and various' duties of a tutor: 'He was expected to be the guide, friend, and guardian of his pupils as well as their instructor. He had not only to teach them, correct their

---

[1] Graham, p. 77.
[2] Briggs, p. 142.

misdemeanours, and enforce discipline; he had to play the far more difficult part of the friendly adviser whose counsel is sought and valued.'[3]

The Oxford commissioners, who were otherwise rather critical of the university, confirmed the value of college tutors and noted that they typically formed early, strong, and lasting bonds with their students such that even the 'most thoughtless' student took an 'interest in the credit and welfare of his college'.[4] Tutors had good reason to work hard and well, for their individual acclaim as teachers and the success of their students on examinations affected the reputation, enrolments, and income of their colleges. Not without some irony, Thomas De Quincey called them 'human champions [in the] church militant of knowledge'.[5]

Tutors' tasks included planning students' reading, holding classes each week, coaching students individually on their reading, and assigning and assessing papers and verses. They prepared students for and scheduled their exams and communicated with the examiners to be sure students were tested according to their reading, readiness, and ability. Tutors also scheduled and helped students prepare for their acts and opponencies, declamations, and verse recitations.[6] It was the tutor's business to ensure not only that students completed assignments but that they also attended class and chapel, took their meals, were inside the walls before the college gates were closed at night, and were clean, healthy, and properly dressed. Some arranged students' travel. Green cites an occasion when an Oxford tutor arranged a student's marriage.[7] If an undergraduate failed to pay his college bills or got into debt with local tradesmen, it was the tutor who was called to account. He was a busy man. As an example, when Copleston was a tutor at Oriel, along with his teaching, he took his turn as college preacher, proctored exams, advocated successfully for reform of university examinations, served as the captain of the college's military volunteers (who were called up during the French invasion scare), and was an active scholar.

Brockliss takes a more negative view, describing tutors as 'hired wage slaves' who were 'socially inferior to many of their charges, and with few disciplinary weapons' at hand.[8] Winstanley admits that at some of the smaller or poorer colleges tutors were 'inferior men'.[9] The Oxford commission report, however, asserts that tutors at the larger colleges—those that most of the Romantic writers attended—were men of excellent learning and character. Some had

---

[3] Winstanley, p. 270.
[4] Hinds, p. 22.
[5] Masson, p. 18.
[6] Winstanley, p. 44.
[7] Green, 'The University and Social Life', p. 329, n. 5.
[8] Brockliss, p. 259.
[9] Winstanley, p. 30.

been sizars or pensioners, but almost all had also been honours graduates or wranglers, a status that was of highest regard in the academic community. They had been nominated for the job by their peers and approved by the college head. Moreover, because many had recently been undergraduates themselves, tutors understood the kinds of study habits required by the university curriculum and were well aware of the temptations of college life. Oxford's Benjamin Jowett, who was a tutor at Balliol in the 1830s and 1840s, explained to the royal commissioners that the most critical duty of the tutors was to improve students' composition skills in Latin, Greek, and English so they would be ready for higher studies with university professors.[10] He counselled the commissioners against meddling with the tutorial system for it was 'a great good' and allowed instructors 'more time for personal acquaintance with [their] pupils' and was 'closely connected with the peculiarity of the English Universities as an assemblage of Colleges'.[11]

Tutors were usually assigned between four and 12 undergraduates. When Wordsworth was at St John's, each year a *Lector principalis* and a *Lector Graecus in Aula* were chosen to head a team that included four *Lectores Mathematici* and four *Lectores matutine*. This is a ratio of one teacher to every ten students. Cambridge's college tutors were also charged to be Catechists and Praelectors of Greek, Latin, and logic. Speaking for University College, Oxford, A. P. Stanley reported to the royal commissioners that his college employed three tutors and one mathematics lecturer for 51 undergraduates. Balliol reported having 70 students who were provided with three tutors, an assistant tutor, a mathematical lecturer, and a catechetical lecturer.

Though the public and grammar schools did their best to launch students' language and reasoning skills, not all who arrived at the universities were ready for the work. Sometimes the universities accepted younger students; Bentham was enrolled at Queen's College at the age of 13. Chinnery was 16 when he matriculated at Christ Church. Hence, tutors often faced the challenge of teaching students with a wide range of abilities and very different levels of maturity. To manage this state of affairs, the fellows and tutors typically interviewed new students and sorted them according to their 'abilities, quickness, and mental habits'.[12] At Christ Church Dean Jackson himself talked with new students and assessed their preparation, aptitude, and expectations. He assigned tutors that were most likely to be able to address each student's circumstances. Copleston believed this method of individual instruction was better 'than any other system', and he adds that the tutor–student relationship not only awakened undergraduates to

---

[10] Hinds, 'Evidence', p. 37.
[11] Hinds, 'Evidence', p. 37.
[12] Edward Copleston, p. 146.

'emulation' but also inspired the *tutor* to 'vivacity [like that] of a public speaker addressing an audience'.[13]

The close tutorial relationship also went a long way toward curbing students' tendency to bad behaviour. The intimacy of the student–tutor relationship did not, however, prevent tutors from disciplining students from time to time. 'Literary impositions' and fines were the first two orders of punishment.[14] These were usually imposed for missing chapel, coming in late, or not wearing robes and proper hats or caps at appointed times. Green retells the story of a student who had the bad luck of vomiting in the Sheldonian during the Oxford *Encaenia*. His tutor required him to translate Pope's 'Pastorals' into Latin hexameters before leaving for the summer holiday.[15] To protect tutors, who were required to cover students' debts, some colleges would not allow indebted students to depart for the summer until their accounts were settled. Tutors were also the authors of testimonials of good behaviour for students seeking ordination. On at least one occasion James Wood held back a testimonial for one of his students. Regarding the management of student behaviour, the Cambridge commission report notes that

> [t]here are other modes, which though they do not admit of very accurate description, are too important to be omitted in the consideration of the subject of discipline. Frequent personal intercourse between the tutor and the Pupil, the consciousness of the Student that he is living under the immediate observation of many persons senior to himself, who have successfully passed the same period of academical probation before him, membership of one common society, associating together at the hours of meals, of instruction and of prayer, are beyond doubt most effective instruments for good in the discipline of an University Education conducted on the Collegiate system.[16]

Tutors all received stipends as fellows, lived in college rooms, and were provided with commons. They also collected instructional fees from undergraduates directly. The amount of the tutorial fees varied. In most cases, fees were set by the university on a sliding scale, depending upon the college's reputation and students' circumstances. At Cambridge in 1802, one account records that tutorial fees for the year were £30 for noblemen, £15 for gentlemen or fellow commoners, and £6 for scholars (also called sizars). A fee table printed in the Oxford commission report lists college tutorial fees as £16 per annum;

---

[13] Edward Copleston, p. 146.
[14] Hinds, p. 21.
[15] Green, 'The University and Social Life', p. 345.
[16] Graham, p. 146.

however, elsewhere the commissioners record that noblemen paid 45 guineas, gentleman commoners paid 30 guineas, and that commoners paid 12 guineas per annum.[17] At some colleges pensioners and sizars were not required to pay their tutors at all. The following resolution illustrates how one college dealt with an occasion in which a student was behaving badly:

> Whereas Coleridge is still in arrears with his Tutors and has been absent for some time from the College (where we know not), it is ordered by the Master and Fellows that his name be taken off the boards on the 14th day of June next, unless cause be shown to the contrary, or some one of the Fellows declares himself willing to be his Tutor before that time, and that his present Tutors do endeavour to inform him of this order.[18]

Nevertheless, Winstanley asserts that the job of tutor was usually 'remunerative' and that it was also 'influential, and of considerable interest' for the tutors themselves. He attests that 'it gave much of what men most desire' and that it could lead to the 'crown of an academic career'—a college mastership.[19] Such was the case with most of the men who became college deans—James Wood of St John's, Isaac Milner of Queens', and William Whewell of Trinity.

The excerpts from James Wood's teaching, discussed in Chapter 8, describe how carefully he guided students' studies and exams when he was a tutor, and they make it clear that he appreciated high-quality academic work. His tutorial efforts were often required even before classes began. His papers describe his efforts to find students suitable rooms and to help them buy furniture. Once the term began, Wood informed parents about their sons' behaviour and health. He regularly sent them bills for their sons' expenses in town and upon receipt of those funds he paid the local tradespeople. When students left the college without paying their bills, he covered their debts and informed their families. He spent more than ten years trying to recover a substantial debt owed him by one of Lord Lowther's wards. In Wood's letter book for the year 1802 is a note that William Wordsworth, who graduated in 1791, still owed him £10.

Of 78 letters in another of Wood's letter books, kept when he was a tutor, 37 attend specifically to students' studies, ten relate to their expenses, five deal with housing situations for students, another five refer to behaviour or discipline matters, 12 pertain to academic or church jobs for college fellows, six are about scholarly matters of personal interest to Wood, and three are courtesy notes. Wood reminded students of the residence requirements for their degrees, arranged for and communicated with private tutors, and wrote

---

[17] It is a sign of the value appertaining to these services that costs were listed in guineas.
[18] Resolution of Jesus College, dated 6 April 1795. This was a year after Coleridge left.
[19] Winstanley, pp. 267, 276.

Educating the Romantic Poets

recommendations for students who hoped to be called to the bar or who were competing for lectureships, fellowships, or church livings. He endeavoured to assist one worried mother in locating her son's lost books and silver spoons. Another mother begged him to protect her son from his father's wrath, and on several occasions he was commissioned to inform students of deaths in their families. In the midst of all these jobs, Wood also communicated with other scholars about their publications, sermons, and lectures and kept up with his own preaching duties and scholarly work.

Specific examples of Wood's communications with parents include the following: 'Under no circumstances should [your son] be allowed to take lodging in town during the vacation instead of staying in his college rooms [because he will] be idle and expansive and may incur censure.'[20] Your son 'did not gain much credit at his exams, [he attended to the classical subjects, but] has given up all thought of distinguishing himself in Math and Natural Philosophy ... [He is, however,] regular in his conduct and does not outrun his allowance'.[21] Wood informed one father that his son's conduct was 'highly gratifying and [that] he passed an excellent examination'.[22] To the father of two St John's students Wood wrote, 'Your son Henry is almost as great a favourite as Edward.'[23] Along with sending a hefty bill to another parent for his son's debts, Wood told the father that if his son 'intends to return next term, [it must be] with different ideas of expenses and better resolutions of application'.[24]

Quick to praise students for working hard at their studies, Wood was concerned when they did not. He was pleased to inform students of their academic awards and medals and regularly reminded them of the necessity to read for their exams during their Christmas and Easter holidays. From the nature of these letters and others available in the archives, it appears that Wood was a serious and humane educator and a careful mentor who expected and encouraged but did not compel his students to apply themselves. Wordsworth hardly mentions him or his other tutor, Edward Frewen, in his writing. Given Wordsworth's ambivalence about entering the Church and his decision not to stand for mathematical tripos, it is likely that both tutors simply followed the collegiate custom of not coercing reluctant or uncommitted students. Their seeming neglect did, however, give him space and time to read and think for himself.

Also part of the Georgian academic scene were private tutors, many of whom were, or had been, college fellows. Their services benefited first-year students

---

[20] Wood, 'Letter Books', MI/3, p. 31.
[21] Wood, 'Letter Books', MI/3, p. 33.
[22] Wood, 'Letter Books', MI/3, p. 41.
[23] Wood, 'Letter Books', MI/3, p. 41.
[24] Wood, 'Letter Books', MI/3, p. 43.

who did not have the benefit of a public- or grammar-school education. Dean Jackson suggested this to George Chinnery after interviewing the 16-year-old upon his arrival at Christ Church. Young Chinnery employed Charles Lloyd for several years and records paying him £25 per annum. Seniors aiming to earn fellowships often employed private tutors to help them prepare for the Senate House or Schools examinations. Both the Oxford and Cambridge commissions estimate that private tutors for these seniors typically cost £50 a year. The hiring and methods of private tutors were issues at the late Hanoverian universities. The cost was a concern, but college officials were more troubled because they believed that private tutors replaced 'real' learning with cramming and memory tricks. Whewell explains,

> When a man gives his mind to any subject of study on account of a genuine wish to understand it, he follows its reasonings with care and thought, ponders over its difficulties, and is not satisfied till all is clear to his mental vision. On the other hand, when he studies for an examination only, he does not wish to understand, but to appear to understand; he cares not for unsolved difficulties in his mind.[25]

Once the examination is over, Whewell says, whatever was 'learned' is forgotten and students 'relapse into comparative apathy and obliviousness'.[26]

The Oxford royal commissioners had much to say about both college and private tutors. They note upfront the obvious 'good effects produced by the tutorial system on the discipline of the place', but qualify this statement by adding '[as long as tutors act] with zeal and judgment, and the Pupil answers his care by confidence and respect'.[27] The commission recognised that having a personal relationship with one's tutor enhanced the value of his teaching, but added that 'the disadvantages of the system are greater still'.[28] Referring to a list supplied by Mark Pattison (1813–1884), a tutor and the sub-rector of Lincoln College, the commissioners outlined the 'Causes of the disrepute of the College tutor'.[29] The first was that some college tutors were simply bad teachers. Some were not expert in the disciplines. Others were indifferent about the job of teaching because they simply took the position while waiting for a church living. Still others were charged with being too tolerant of idle students. In response to the first two criticisms, Winstanley points out tutors who did not feel competent to teach a particular subject regularly arranged for an assistant

---

[25] Whewell, p. 56.
[26] Whewell, p. 57.
[27] Hinds, p. 87.
[28] Hinds, p. 87.
[29] Hinds, 'Evidence', p. 45.

tutor to take his place. Regarding the fourth complaint, Winstanley admits that some tutors interfered 'too little rather than two much' in their students' daily lives; yet he adds that in general 'tutors took a greater interest in their pupils than is commonly supposed' by critics of the university and some even demonstrated 'tutorial zeal'.[30]

Other defenders of the system noted that college heads asked tutors to take on 'too many classes ... too many pupils' and 'to teach too great a variety of subjects'.[31] Deans also were guilty at times of admitting ill-prepared students who lowered the general tone of instruction. Even though Pattinson registered his criticisms of the system with the commissioners, he also testified that pedagogical theory and his own experience supported tutoring as the truest and best 'instrument of instruction'.[32] He added that professors' lectures might supply students with 'current information', but tutors discipline the faculties, and their catechetical and Socratic methods are preferred because they 'throw the work upon the student himself'.[33] Though Whewell complained to the Cambridge royal commission about private tutors, he strongly supported college tutors and averred that any changes to the existing system would be unfortunate. The Cambridge commissioners cite testimony of several other high-ranking college members who also approved of tutorial instruction, as well as of one who noted that 'the benefits derived by the Student from receiving instruction, often of the highest quality, from the same persons whom he is accustomed to respect as the superintendent of his moral conduct, his friend and adviser, are too great to allow' any change to the existing tutorial system.[34]

Several students living in the Georgian period have left accounts of their experiences with tutors. In 1776 Philip Yorke wrote to his guardian about the 'real intellectual excitement' he felt at Cambridge during his tutorials on astronomy and optics with Isaac Milner.[35] Coleridge reported that his tutor at Jesus College, John Plampin, treated him 'with exceeding and most delicate kindness'.[36] It was Plampin who reached out to Coleridge's brother George during the dragoons episode. He helped to bring his errant student back to Cambridge and secured £70 from the allowances Coleridge had earned from Christ's Hospital, from the Rustat Scholarship, and from other funds to help Coleridge discharge his college debts.[37] De Quincey asserts that his university's

---

[30] Winstanley, p. 272.
[31] Hinds, 'Evidence', p. 48.
[32] Hinds, 'Evidence', p. 45.
[33] Hinds, 'Evidence', pp. 45, 48.
[34] Whewell, p. 77.
[35] Searby, pp. 559–560.
[36] Holmes, p. 59.
[37] CLSTC, p. 64, n. 1.

The Educators of Oxford and Cambridge in the Georgian Period

tutors were 'the best qualified amongst those of its senior members', and were given the job only after 'careful selection, trial, and probation'.[38] College tutors, he said, were not 'poor mercenary haberdashers of knowledge' but 'independent and liberal teachers'.[39] The teaching of Wordsworth's nephew John Wordsworth when he was a tutor at Trinity has been described as careful and erudite. Undergraduates clamoured to be assigned to him.

George Chinnery's descriptions of his tutors at Christ Church testify to their good faith efforts. His first tutor settled him in his rooms, showed him where his tutorials would take place, gave him a list of local tradespeople who might help him furnish his rooms, collected £12.10 caution money, and made sure he knew when and where to attend chapel.[40] He also helped Chinnery with his subscription to the 39 Articles. His next tutor, chosen by Dean Jackson himself and arranged privately, was Lloyd. He helped Chinnery shore up his Latin and Greek skills. He worked with the lad on his themes, praised his progress, and supported his industry.[41] Eventually Chinnery had several college tutors, with whom he met every day. He described how Mr Goodenough helped him prepare for a lecture on Aristotle's *Rhetoric*: he advised Chinnery first to construe a large passage of the text and then to make extracts of examples that illustrated each of Aristotle's rules.[42] Rather 'pleased with this idea', Chinnery found that it made the assignment 'more practicably useful' and helped him follow the lecture.[43] After Chinnery returned from the lecture, Goodenough reviewed what the lad had learned, asking clarifying questions. In several other letters Chinnery told his mother that his tutors were quite helpful in steering his reading and that they praised him amply when he did well. Later, when he won the cherished Newdigate Prize for poetry, he wrote his mother that his tutors delighted almost as much as he did in this success.

University professors

One of the most misunderstood and confusing traditions at the English universities in the Romantic period is that of the university professors. As already noted, tutors employed by the colleges carried most of the teaching load. As if living on a separate planet, professors employed by the university offered lectures according to their own interests or the charges of their endowment. Their discourses were primarily for the fellows; undergraduates were not required to attend their lectures. The total number of professorships

---

[38] Masson, p. 30.
[39] Masson, p. 31.
[40] Chinnery, letter of 16 January 1808.
[41] Chinnery, letter of 12 February 1808, and several scattered mentioned later.
[42] Chinnery, letter of 6 February 1810.
[43] Chinnery, letter of 6 February 1810.

in existence at Oxford and Cambridge during the Georgian period was just under 30. Many of these were founded in the sixteenth century and most were dedicated to theology, classics, mathematics, and astronomy. In the eighteenth century Cambridge added chairs in chemistry, botany, and geology. Oxford created a chair of poetry in 1708, a sign of how highly valued this literary genre was at the university. In 1724, Robert Walpole endorsed King George I's creation of endowed chairs in modern history at both universities. These professors were to be skilled in modern languages and destined for international diplomacy.[44] In 1755 Oxford established the Vinerian Professorship of Law. The Norrisian Professorship of Revealed Religion (f. 1777) and the Jacksonian Professorship of Natural Philosophy (f. 1782) followed thereafter. All told, at least 16 of the 29 professorships were in fields that might be termed 'useful', such as law, modern history, modern languages, medicine, and the emerging natural sciences. Most of these professorships were life-long appointments, and they were well endowed, with stipends ranging from £300 to £500. The position typically required the delivery of lectures for members of all colleges, and, remarkably, along with their stipends, professors collected admission fees for their lectures, ranging from three to six guineas per person. Professorial stipends and fees, when combined with the church livings that were usually attached to the professorships, and collegiate emoluments, meant that some professors earned over £1,000 a year.

For centuries in England, the highest academic degree, Doctor of Divinity and title of 'doctor', was reserved for the clergy, civil law, and medicine, though most professors of Greek and Hebrew were also Doctors of Divinity. It was entirely acceptable in the Georgian period for professors in the other fields to be MAs. Added to this, most of the natural sciences were still in the early stages of development as academic disciplines and had not yet established expert standards or credentials for these fields beyond that of the MA. The professors of botany, experimental philosophy, astronomy, and mathematics were almost without exception MAs. At Cambridge the same pattern can be observed: professional and classical subjects were taught by Doctors and almost all of the professors of chemistry, astronomy, experimental philosophy, modern history, geology, and geometry were MAs; a few had earned no more than the BA.

What counted as qualifying knowledge for some of the professorships has also confused modern academics. Most Romanticists are familiar with Richard Watson's election to the professorship of chemistry, a field in which he had very little expert knowledge. At that time, however, the field of chemistry was so new that it was almost entirely the invention of 'gentleman amateurs'. Thus, Watson's lack of training was not as surprising then as it is today. To Watson's credit, after nine years of self-directed study, home experiments (some of which

---

[44] Sutherland, p. 474.

proved quite disastrous), and teaching, he published five volumes of *Chemical Essays* (1781–87). Though his work is looked upon now as little more than good reporting of others' research, rather than ground-breaking scholarship, the top chemist of the day, Humphry Davy (also largely self-educated), approved of his work at the time.[45]

In some cases, the statutory provisions for the method of selecting professors led to the elevation of less qualified men. For example, The Lady Margaret Professor of Divinity at Oxford could only be chosen by former students holding the bachelor of divinity. The students' choice sometimes ended up being their favourite person, not necessarily the best scholar.[46] Some professors had to be chosen by the Convocation of all living fellows. In such cases, 'the electing body [was] so large, so fluctuating', that it was quite 'liable to heterogeneous influences, local, personal, collegiate, political and theological'.[47] Several other professorships, such as those of natural philosophy, moral philosophy, and Arabic, were chosen by the vice chancellor and only two or three other college heads.[48] On the occasions when these men had little personal knowledge relating to a particular professorship's field they were susceptible to local politics or favouritism. Another troubling example is the fact that from 1673 to 1829 the chair of moral philosophy at Oxford was automatically given to the senior proctor, regardless of his academic speciality.[49] The original reasoning for this practice was that the proctor's job, by statute, was supervision of students' moral lives; therefore, given their general university training and clerical status, these men should have been well equipped for this position. However, the job was often treated rather cavalierly. By the Georgian period a few professorships had devolved into mere sinecures. Others, such as the Lady Margaret Professorship of Divinity at Cambridge and some of the Regius Professorships, were treated as rewards to senior fellows who had performed years of civic, college, or Church service. A few of the men who held professorships that specified teaching and scholarly duties simply ignored the statutes, and their colleagues at the university looked the other way. This practice, however, was discouraged during the Georgian period.

Yet another complaint about some professors was that their statutory duties were no longer needed. Cambridge's Lady Margaret Professorship of Divinity (f. 1502) and the Regius Professor of Divinity (f. 1540) were originally charged with one task only: to give public readings of important Latin theological texts. When these statutes were written, these works were few and prohibitively expensive.

---

[45] Winstanley, p. 145.
[46] Hinds, p. 105.
[47] Graham, p. 104.
[48] Graham, p. 105.
[49] Graham, p. 105.

Educating the Romantic Poets

As a result, the professors served an important purpose. By the Georgian period printed texts had become more common and affordable, making readings of this sort unnecessary. The professors' statutory duties, however, had never been altered. In the case of the Lady Margaret professorship the founders were long-since dead and no surviving heirs were available to consult about changing the professorships' statutes. Professorships established by the crown were also very difficult to amend, so in many cases the universities simply let these positions devolve into sinecures, with nothing but a few perfunctory public appearances. This situation led to the infamous 'wall lectures' in which these men spoke to empty rooms because they were legally bound to do so.

The most legitimate complaints about university professors had to do with whether or not students benefited from their efforts. Despite the students' generally good knowledge of classical languages, lectures in Latin were not always the best way to make difficult subjects clear. Added to this, students were not permitted to ask questions during lectures. Undergraduates who had become used to the more informal tutorials found this style of teaching frustrating. Another issue was the fact that professors were not required to coordinate the topics of their lectures with the texts and subjects students' were reading for their examinations. Practical college men had little time to spend on any subjects for which they would not be held responsible. Because tutors also had a stake in their charges' performances on these exams, they often discouraged students from attending university lectures unless a particular professor was especially talented or was lecturing on a topic directly relevant to the examinations. The Cambridge University commission report explains:

> when a course of reading is once marked out by a tutor, to whose guidance a student submits himself, he can rarely venture with safety to depart from it; for if the principles of reasoning upon which the fundamental propositions are based, or the order of succession in which they are taken is materially different with different teachers, a student, who attempts to follow more than one of them, will very generally end in understanding none of them completely.[50]

A closer look at selected university professors in the Georgian period

Despite these complaints, Winstanley reports that by the time the Romantics were at university 'at least some professors were conscientious teachers, and a few were great scholars'.[51] He is right; at least 20 are cited as such in the *Dictionary*

---

[50] Graham, p. 173.
[51] Winstanley, p. 179.

of National Biography.[52] Given how small these institutions were, the number of distinguished professors is noteworthy. All of these men were honours graduates, fellows, and tutors before they became chaired professors, so their influence began long before they were elevated to professorships. Among the Georgian period professors who should be recognised by modern scholars as worthy practitioners was Herbert Marsh (1757–1839), the Lady Margaret Reader in Divinity at Cambridge from 1807 to 1839. As a professor he did not simply read old Latin books to his colleagues and students as his position required; instead, he delivered two lectures each week in English on topics such as the Ante-Nicene Fathers, liturgies of the Church of England, pastoral theology, and the duties of the parish priest. Besides being one of the first to lecture in English, he also instituted more liberal and theorised biblical criticism. Because over a third of the students at the university expected to enter the ministry, these topics were particularly useful to them. Moreover, Marsh's lectures were so compelling and popular—students are reported to have listened to him 'with rapture'—that he was required to hold them in Great St Mary's church.[53]

John Kaye (1783–1853), the young master of Christ's College, was also the Regius Professor of Divinity at Cambridge from 1816 to 1827. His discourses on topics such as early church history, Justin Martyr, Clement of Alexandria, and the Council of Nicæa were well attended, thanks to the quality of his scholarship and his pleasing style of speaking. Kaye is also notable for the educational activities he undertook in his capacity as a clergyman. As bishop of Bristol and Lincoln he established schools, reintroduced catechising at these schools, and insisted that all candidates for holy orders in his see should pass the theological examination of the University of Cambridge, which for years had been only voluntary. Both Marsh and Kaye presided every other Thursday over disputation exercises and delivered Latin determinations upon the subjects the students debated. They helped with theological examinations and the awarding of doctoral degrees as well and participated in selecting the winners of scholarships and prizes such as the Craven, Browne, Battie, and Chancellor's medals.[54]

At Cambridge, one of the most notable university professors, a man from humble beginnings, was the 'amiable' Samuel Vince, FRS (1749–1821, see

---

[52] At Oxford these included Thomas Hornsby (1733–1810); Thomas Winstanley (1749–1823); Edward Copleston (1776–1849); Thomas Gaisford (1779–1855); Charles Lloyd (1784–1829); and John Keble (1792–1866). At Cambridge this group was even larger and included Francis John Hyde Wollaston (1731–1815); John Hey (1734–1815); Samuel Vince (1749–1821); Isaac Milner (1750–1829); Herbert Marsh (1757–1839); William Farish (1759–1837); William Lax (1761–1836); John Kaye (1783–1853); Adam Sedgwick (1785–1873); Charles Babbage (1791–1871); and William Whewell (1794–1866).

[53] Venables.

[54] Graham, pp. 46–48, see also the *Historical Register of Cambridge* and the *DNB*.

Figure 21). Vince was the son of a bricklayer who was sent to St Paul's School and then to Gonville and Caius in 1771 as a sizar. He earned his MA at Sidney Sussex and was ordained. In 1780 his paper 'Principles of Progressive and Rotatory Motion' won the Copley medal, the Royal Society's oldest and most prestigious award, given each year for the most important scientific discovery or for the greatest contribution made by experiment. In 1785 Vince undertook an involved course of experiments on frictions; later he focused upon fluids and refraction, which were the topics of his three Bakerian Lectures at the Royal Society. In 1796 Cambridge named him the Plumian Professor of Astronomy and Experimental Philosophy, a role charged with presenting the principal points of current solar, lunar, and planetary theories and with teaching courses in astronomy, optics, trigonometry, mechanics, statics, hydrostatics, magnetics, pneumatics and other related subjects. From 1797 to 1808 Vince brought out the three volumes of his *A Complete System of Astronomy*, which, according to John Playfair, 'marked a great epoch in astronomical science'.[55] Ironically, Playfair's article was published in the *Edinburgh Review* of June 1809, the same year that the *Review* began launching its attacks on the universities for teaching useless subjects. Between 1814 and 1823 Vince brought out and enlarged a second edition of his *Complete System*. These volumes solidified Vince's monumental reputation.[56] Several of his works, including one he co-authored with James Wood, of St John's, were used as textbooks and ran through many editions. Though primarily honoured as a man of science, Vince also published well-received theological works, among which were his defence of miracles, *The Credibility of Christianity Vindicated, in Answer to Mr. Hume's Objections* (1798, 1809), declared by *The British Critic* to be a 'Masterful example of Christian argument'.[57] In 1807 he published *A Confutation of Atheism from the Laws of Heavenly Bodies*.[58]

William Whewell, the defender and interpreter of the universities quoted so often in this book, was another student who rose from humble beginnings to become an important scholar and academic leader. He entered Trinity as a sizar in 1812. As an undergraduate he excelled at mathematics but also won both the Latin declamation prize and the Chancellor's Medal for his epic poem 'Boadicea'.[59] He won a fellowship at Trinity and became a mathematical lecturer and assistant tutor for his college. As an educator he encouraged active-learning and problem solving and was concerned about students' reasoning processes and moral development. In 1820 he was elected

[55] Qtd in Clerke.
[56] Clerke.
[57] Anonymous, 'Review of the Credibility of Christianity Vindicated', p. 258.
[58] After his death, his son published *Observations on Deism* (1845), based on extracts from several of his father's manuscripts.
[59] *DNB*, vol. 28, p. 1366.

Figure 21. Astronomy and mathematics: Samuel Vince reading in his rooms at Sidney Sussex College, Cambridge, by the light of a shaded lamp. Aquatint by F. Jukes with engraving by J. K. Baldrey after R. C. Chilton, c.1784. Wellcome Collection. Public Domain Mark.

a fellow of the Royal Society; three years later, he was made head tutor at Trinity. The Geological Society initiated him in 1827; he would later serve as its president. After tutoring and performing other college duties for Trinity, he won the university chair in mineralogy in 1828, which he held until 1832. In 1838 Whewell became a noticeably active professor of moral philosophy.

Whewell appears to have been a model of intellectual curiosity and broad scholarly activity. He travelled in France to study church and abbey architecture. He participated in geology field trips with George Biddell Airy in Cornwall and with Adam Sedgwick in the Lake District, where he was introduced to William Wordsworth. He met often with Analytical Society members, including John Herschel, Charles Babbage, and George Peacock, to discuss calculus, geometry, and algebra as both a theorist and an educator. He helped to found and was an early president of the British Association for the Advancement of Science. Admired and consulted throughout his career at Cambridge as a teacher, leader, and scholar, Whewell is cited by the *Stanford Encyclopedia of Philosophy* as one of the most important thinkers of his age.[60] He delivered between 12 and 20 lectures during the ten-week terms at Cambridge and published over 140 books, articles, scientific papers, society reports, reviews, and translations. Whewell's most important scientific studies were of tides, but he wrote in many fields, including mineralogy, geology, astronomy, mathematics, mechanics, natural theology, moral philosophy, political philosophy, education, architecture, and the history and philosophy of the physical sciences. He also published translations of Greek philosophy and German poetry.

Georgian Oxford also had professors who deserve modern scholarly respect. One of these is Thomas Hornsby (1733–1810). A fellow of Corpus Christi, in 1763 he was named to the Savilian Chair of Astronomy,[61] tasked with giving a yearly course of lectures while helping to plan, build, and equip the Radcliffe Observatory. In 1782 he was elected the Sedleian Professor of Natural Philosophy, whereupon he turned his attention almost entirely to professorial duties. His lectures on experimental philosophy were widely praised. Thomas Winstanley (1749–1823), who was chosen as the Camden Professor of Ancient History in 1790, was elected seven years later to also be principal of St Alban Hall. A respected classical scholar, Winstanley was also a student of modern languages. He worked on Aristotle's *Poetics* and published an edition, *Aristotelous peri poiētikēs*, in Greek along with a Latin version, *Aristotelis de poetica liber* (1780). These volumes included criticism and scholarly notes and were standard textbooks at the university for decades. He also collected, edited, and in 1802 published the writings of Daniel Webb (1719–1798), a contemporary and a very popular theorist of the visual arts. The collection, which was titled *Miscellanies*, included Webb's *Remarks on the Beauties of Poetry* (1762, 1764) and *Observations on the Correspondence between Poetry and Music* (1769). No recent scholarship has been published on the relation of Webb's poetics to the Romantics, but because of Winstanley's prominence at Oxford it is likely that Webb's ideas circulated among undergraduates during the years that Smith, Canning, Southey, Arnold, and Shelley, and were there. Duncan Wu reports that Wordsworth read Webb's *Inquiry into the Beauties of Painting* when he was at St John's.

A third professor at Georgian Oxford worthy of mention is Thomas Gaisford (1779–1855), who served as a tutor and public examiner at Christ Church for a decade, and was named Regius Professor of Greek in 1812. For the next 20 years he devoted himself to scholarly matters. He was a curator of the Bodleian Library and a delegate to the Oxford University Press. In the latter

---

[60] See their article about him for a complete list of his publications.

[61] It is worth noting that the committee that selects the Savilian Professor includes the president of the Royal Society, the university chancellor, the astronomer royal, and the director of the Radcliffe Observatory.

capacity Gaisford helped raise the standards of the press, hired important scholars as editors, and commissioned a ground-breaking series on English history. Gaisford's own scholarly efforts were extensive. His early work was on Cicero, including an edition of the *Tusculan Disputations* (1805), followed by work on *De Oratore* and *De Natura Deorum*. His editions of Euripides's plays earned him an international reputation. Other works followed, one on the minor Greek poets as well as editions of Herodotus and Sophocles. His two lexicographical editions, the *Lexicon of Suidas* and the *Etymologicon Magnum*, were heralded as important and lasting contributions to Greek scholarship. He also published on the ecclesiastical writers and patristic literature. Thirty-three major works (some of them multivolume) are listed for Gaisford in the *Dictionary of National Biography*. Much of this work was accomplished while he was also the dean of Christ Church. In 1856, the year after the professor's death, the university founded the Gaisford prizes for Greek compositions in prose or verse in his honour.

Besides their scholarly activities, not a few university professors were devoted educators. Kaye and Whewell have already been mentioned; Dr Abraham Robertson DD also deserves such note. Robertson, of Christ Church, followed Hornsby as the Savilian Professor of Astronomy; among his other duties was delivering two 45-minute lectures each week. Robertson's reputation among students was excellent, and George Chinnery wrote to his mother that he 'rejoices most amazingly' in expectation of Robertson's coming lectures on Newton. He described visiting Robertson at his home—Robertson was a married man and lived in town—where they had a long conversation about Newton. Robertson read Chinnery the prospectus for his course and advised him to study the beginning of the *Principia* on his own before the lectures began.[62] Chinnery followed his advice and read the work in Latin with his private tutor, Lloyd. After the first lecture Chinnery wrote again, saying that Robertson's lecture style was '1,000,000,000 times better than Lloyd's'.[63] The *Dictionary of National Biography* reports that Robertson 'was always anxious to encourage his pupils'; Chinnery noted that he would often go back and explain confusing bits, something not all lecturing professors were expected to do.

The responsibilities of chaired professors in the Georgian period included other important services to the university community, among them preaching in the Sunday services at the university church. In many cases these sermons were timely and important statements on theological or ecclesiastical issues of the day and had the effect of arousing, guiding, or redirecting the universities' and/or the national Church's thought and practice. They were sometimes used to critique or urge reform of the universities. The texts of these sermons were

---

[62] Chinnery, letter of 4 February 1810.
[63] Chinnery, letter of 18 February 1810.

Educating the Romantic Poets

published by the university presses and distributed throughout the country and students were often tasked with studying them in print. Most professors served, as Marsh and Kaye did, as moderators at students' term disputations. Winstanley asserts that moderating was an important teaching role, for the professors' summative comments were often thorough, always learned, and usually quite instructive to all in attendance.[64] Other professorial duties, such as committee work, were also expected, and when these committees involved issues such as reform of the examinations that work was of great significance to the entire university.

To conclude, the system in the Georgian universities whereby undergraduates worked closely with college and private tutors, studied independently, and had the opportunity to attend discourses by university professors appears to have been more effective and engaging than many of its critics have maintained. Instruction was individualised and active. Because of the 'confessional' mission of these universities, college educators were also responsible for students' manners, morals, and religious lives. Newman claimed that, as a result of observing and working so closely with such men in this system, students came to apprehend

> the great outlines of knowledge, the principles on which it rests, the scale of its parts, its lights and its shades, its great points and its little ... [and that they formed] a habit of mind which lasts through life, of which the attributes are freedom, equitableness, calmness, moderation, and wisdom; or what [might be called] a philosophical habit.[65]

---

[64] Winstanley, pp. 105–106.
[65] Newman, p. 76.

Chapter Eleven

Leadership at Oxford and Cambridge

MAGNUS his ample front sublime up rears:
Placed on his chair of state, he seems a god.

'Thoughts suggested by a College Examination', Byron

National power and the English universities

The universities' involvement in Church and court politics, which were still so closely connected in the Romantic period, along with their many privileges and great wealth, meant that members of the greater colleges enjoyed a species of national influence that their students could not possibly ignore. Brockliss's account of Oxford's governance and the 'frequent bursts of state interference in both universities' affairs' between 1770 and 1850 is a valuable digest and should be of interest for Romanticists who study political matters.[1] So, too, are Gascoigne's much more detailed discussions in *Cambridge in the Age of the Enlightenment* (1989) and *Science, religion, and politics from the Restoration to the French Revolution* (1989). Though generalisations always have many exceptions, in the Romantic period Oxford was a Tory stronghold; Cambridge was home to many Whigs. For much of the late eighteenth century, academic issues—examinations, standards for honours and fellowships, student behaviour, university sermons, and college livings—were discussed at both universities in a relatively peaceable, scholarly way. When Wordsworth first arrived at Cambridge in 1787, the colleges were increasingly meritocratic

---

[1] Brockliss, pp. 143–158.

Anglican communities, where latitudinarians and 'enlightened', empiricist scholars (deists and Unitarians) resided side by side along with evangelicals. By the time Coleridge and Southey arrived at their colleges (Coleridge started at Jesus College in October 1791; Southey arrived at Balliol in January 1793), life at the universities—especially at Cambridge—would become much more tempestuous, thanks to events in France.

A distinguishing aspect of the experience at Georgian Oxford and Cambridge is how close students were to the powerful men who were active in these matters. The chancellors at both universities were great men of court; a number of professors held bishoprics and sat in the House of Lords. Both universities elected their own members of the House of Commons; and more than half of the men who served in parliament had been trained at Oxford or Cambridge; some had even been fellows or tutors. MPs, ministers, and members of the royal family were often visitors. Moreover, the small size, residential life, formal midday meals, and church and chapel requirements meant that university students were well acquainted with classmates, had speaking acquaintance with many fellows and deans, and had many opportunities to witness how educated adults exercised local and national leadership.

Added to these advantages, the label of being an Oxford or Cambridge man, no matter how junior, was respectfully acknowledged around the country. Indeed, years spent at one of these universities conferred upon students, even those who did not take degrees, automatic public distinction, which contributed to their intellectual self-confidence and added authority to their projects. The curriculum, pedagogies, traditions, and examples of the men who worked at these universities taught students that words and rational argument and action were powerful and that they were expected to serve the nation that had educated them. It is no wonder, then, that Wordsworth wrote in 'Salisbury Plain' that the labours and 'gentle words' of 'the sage' might assuage 'benighted mortals' and that 'Heroes of Truth' possessed 'the race of Reason' which could crush 'Oppressors' and end 'foul Error's monster race'.[2]

University chancellors

The honorary heads of the two universities were the chancellors, chosen for their 'exalted rank and honourable name'.[3] Every chancellor at both universities during the Romantic period had been educated in the Anglo-classical academy. As peers or members of the royal family, the chancellors represented the universities in the House of Lords. Non-resident, unpaid, and appointed for life, chancellors were charged to summon the congregation, admit candidates to degrees, see

[2] WWMW, p. 28, ll. 510–514, 541–545.
[3] Graham, p. 3.

that the officers of the university performed their duties, and preside over festive events such as commencement. They typically added their voices to those of deans to help college men secure church livings, headmasterships, deanships, and bishoprics, and they were expected to give substantial annual prizes out of their own pockets to worthy undergraduates students. At Cambridge, the chancellor from 1768 to 1811 was the duke of Grafton. A former Whig prime minister, he opposed subscription, became a Unitarian, and stopped attending most events at the university after 1792. From 1811 to 1834 the chancellor of Cambridge was the duke of Gloucester and Edinburgh, the nephew and son-in-law of George III. Though not particularly active politically,[4] he did take a stand against the slave trade. In the Victorian period, the job of chancellor was held consecutively by the marquess of Camden, a staunch anti-Catholic; the duke of Northumberland, a Tory church-builder; and Prince Albert.

Between 1772 and 1792 the chancellor of Oxford was Lord North, the man who ran the war with the American colonies. The duke of Portland, signatory of the Treaty of Paris and notable for his restraint in applying the sedition and treason laws, served from 1792 until 1809. He was followed by Lord Grenville, known for his efforts to crush English radicalism. His ministry of all the talents did, however, end the slave trade. After Grenville, the duke of Wellington served as chancellor from 1832 to 1852. The effect upon students and faculty of having men of such national prominence—and such antithetical views—placed as the nominal heads of their universities, attending important academic assemblies and representing them in London, would not have been insignificant. Universities also had visitors, men from the court serving on behalf of the crown. From time to time, they stood in final authority over the universities and inserted royal prerogative into local university matters.

Parliamentary representation of the universities

As already noted, many members of parliament were university men.[5] Until 1950, both Oxford and Cambridge also elected two members to the House of Commons. Deans and professors who held bishoprics sat in the House of Lords as well. By granting the universities such representation, the commonwealth signalled not only its recognition of their vast holdings of land around the country but also its respect for their intellectual property. The burgesses from Oxford and Cambridge were expected to 'make learned contributions to discussion of national affairs'.[6] Edmund Burke argued that members from the

---

[4] His nickname at court was 'silly Billy'.
[5] Green, 'The University and Social Life', p. 358.
[6] Meisel, A Magnificent Fungus on the Political Tree', p. 116.

Educating the Romantic Poets

universities could 'virtually' represent the entire nation.[7] Lyon Playfair, who eventually stood for two universities—Edinburgh and St Andrews—argued that plural representation for university graduates was reasonable because 'the culture and even the material interests of the nation' depended upon them.[8]

At Oxford, representation of the university was a coveted honour and seat for life reserved for 'that good old sort ... an independent country gentleman a true friend to Church and King, unconnected with any party, of a good old family'.[9] Among the university's MPs were Sir William Dolben, a champion of parliamentary reform and abolition; Sir William Scott, FRS, a jurist specialising in maritime and international law; Charles Abbot, 1st Baron Colchester, FRS, a Vinerian Scholar and barrister who also advocated for parliamentary reform; and Sir Robert Peel. The list of men who represented Cambridge in parliament during the Romantic period includes Charles Manners, 4th duke of Rutland, a close friend of Pitt, who urged reconciliation with the American colonists; Sir James Mansfield, a member of the Fox–North coalition, noted for his quick temper and service as a trial judge; William Pitt, the Younger; George Henry FitzRoy, 4th duke of Grafton, an abolitionist, who supported anti-Catholic measures for the university but fought for other reforms; and Henry Petty-Fitzmaurice, 3rd marquess of Lansdowne, a champion of Catholic emancipation. Half of these men hailed from Wordsworth's and Byron's colleges.

Vice chancellors

The most influential position at both universities was that of vice chancellor. These men were heads of colleges who were elected by the Cambridge Senate or the Oxford Convocation, the legislative bodies of the two universities, which were composed of all senior members and fellows. Their term of service was two years at Cambridge and up to four at Oxford. The position was a routine, rotating responsibility of all the colleges' heads. However, 'objectionable or obnoxious individuals' could be prevented from election to the position, and any college head who felt unable or unwilling to serve his turn would be excused.[10] The vice chancellors were the first point of contact between the chancellor and the university's MPs. The primary responsibilities of this office were to make sure university officers did their duty and, with the advice of the Hebdomadal Board or the Council and the consent of the full Convocation or Senate, to enact new statutes for the 'advancement of learning and the

---

[7] Meisel, 'A Magnificent Fungus on the Political Tree', p. 135.
[8] Meisel, p. 134.
[9] Qtd in Thorne, p. 68.
[10] Hinds, p. 9.

Leadership at Oxford and Cambridge

maintenance of order'.[11] Vice chancellors called and presided over all Convocation or Senate meetings and had the power of veto. They made decisions about university scholarships and prizes and, in consultation with deans and canons, they made final decisions about conferring degrees.

It was the vice chancellors' charge as well 'to repress offences against order, morals, and religion' and to punish 'transgressors of the Statutes or of good order and discipline'.[12] Vice chancellors at both Cambridge and Oxford acted as judges and magistrates in their cities and presided over lawsuits and personal pleas of university men and employees. They were empowered to execute statutes of the realm. Vice chancellors also had the right to grant and revoke licences for local wine-sellers, ale houses, and theatres and to prohibit students from dealing with local tradesmen. Winstanley describes the job of the vice chancellor as that of a 'chairman, not a dictator',[13] and neither of the two royal commissions took serious issue with the duties and performance of the universities' vice chancellors. At Oxford an annual stipend of £200 was attached the office; at Cambridge a similar practice was in effect through the nineteenth century.

College heads

The men most directly responsible for administration, academic standards, community-building, and discipline at Oxford and Cambridge were the individual college heads, whose titles might be dean, master, rector, president, provost, or warden. Typically, a college was run by the dean with the support of up to eight senior fellows, called canons. Deans held their positions for decades; their times of service most often ended only with debilitating illness or death. They were permitted to accept preferments, to marry, and to receive a larger share of the college rents. They and their wives entertained almost every week and their homes were the hubs of social life at Oxford and Cambridge. At both universities, deans officiated at statutory feasts and hosted annual celebrations honouring new fellows and new graduates.

A college official testifying before the Oxford commission explained that most deans were elected by colleges because of their past service, skill in managing 'finance, property, and discipline; or from social merits calculated to govern and harmonize the society'.[14] Two college heads were royal appointments—the dean of Christ Church and the master of Trinity College, Cambridge. The bishops of Ely, who founded Peterhouse and Jesus College, appointed masters of those colleges. The heirs of Thomas Audley (1488–1544),

---

[11] Graham, p. 4.
[12] Hinds, p. 19; Graham, p. 4.
[13] Winstanley, p. 25.
[14] Graham, p. 12.

Educating the Romantic Poets

the founder of Magdalene College, Cambridge, had the right to appoint the master of that college. While the job description of the college heads quoted above does not mention excellence as a scholar or teacher, evidence from the writing and careers of college heads in the Georgian period suggests that commitment to scholarship and teaching went without saying. Most college heads had been wranglers or honours graduates, had served as tutors and college preachers, and had at least a modest record of publication. Winstanley describes deans as 'constitutional monarchs', and, as the details below make clear, they were busy men.[15] Incomes reported for deans ranged from £600 to over £1,000 per annum.

Deans were expected to reside in the college from October to July, to take their turn preaching in the college chapel and university church, and to conduct Holy Communion. They chose which students would be admitted and assigned college rooms and tutors. It was their duty to speak with new students and with any undergraduates who stood out for academic excellence, leadership ability, family difficulties, or bad behaviour. With the assistance of tutors, deans scheduled college examinations and disputations and observed or officiated at these events. Additionally, they made the final decisions about which students earned college exhibitions or scholarships. With the advice of the president of the Society of Fellows, college heads supervised fellows, awarded college livings, and helped to find them positions of public or church service. When placing fellows in church livings, masters negotiated their employment details, including the number of services each clergyman would conduct, how often he might be absent from his parish, and if he could hire a curate. Some of the larger colleges had advisory relationships with selected grammar schools; the deans corresponded with those schools' headmasters and deputised fellows to serve as school visitors. With the approval of the fellows, deans sometimes contributed college funds to increase the incomes of vicars and curates, to build and support schools, and to repair or build churches or other structures in regions where the college owned property.

Besides these duties, deans managed the holdings and assets of their colleges, which included dormitories, the chapel, great hall, library, buttery, kitchens, breweries, income-producing properties, endowments, investments, and church and school livings. The wealth coming from college properties funded all college members and provided student scholarships. Some of the wealthiest colleges—such as St John's and Trinity at Cambridge and Christ Church and Balliol at Oxford—held properties and livings in almost every county in the country. When queried by the royal commissioners about revenues and fiscal management, the master of Pembroke offered the following general information about his college's income and expenditures:

---

[15] Winstanley, p. 277.

Gross income from lands	£5,420
Gross income from houses	£378
Gross income from tithe rents charges	£3,009
Gross income from investments	£2,468
Gross income from student rooms and fees	£737
Total gross income	£12,012
Deductions for taxes, repairs, insurance, etc.	£2,004
Clear net income	£10,008

When James Wood assumed the duties of master of St John's in 1815, he oversaw vast properties and 42 church livings in counties ranging from Devon to Kent and from the Isle of Wight to Yorkshire. The deans of Christ Church and Trinity managed similar portfolios. Consequently, the larger colleges and their leaders played a significant role in the national economy, as long as it remained land based. One of Wood's dealings with college assets was the swap of a parcel of land in town with another college in order to expand the St John's grounds. On another occasion, he was called to mediate a controversy over tithing that had arisen between the clergyman holding one of the college's church livings and his parishioners.

The royal commission report on Oxford expresses a rather negative view of college heads, perhaps out of frustration with their reluctance to be forthcoming with the information the commissioners sought and with their resistance to outside interference and suggested 'improvements'. At least one of the professors who testified to the Oxford commission, H. H. Vaughan, fellow of Oriel and Regius Professor of Modern History, was quite critical of Oxford's college heads, and the commission quotes him at length. Vaughan complained that college deans were simply good managers with good connections, not important scholars, and were not directly or even closely connected with instruction at the university.[16] Details from biographies, memoirs, periodical articles, and surviving letters at both Oxford and Cambridge paint a more complimentary picture of college heads, many of whom had been respected tutors and/or scholars.

Given how small the colleges were in the Romantic period and how involved deans were in the daily life of their colleges, their actions and beliefs were more apparent to students than they typically are today. When Wordsworth was at St John's, the masters of his college were John Chevallier (1775 to 1789) and William Craven (1789 to 1815). Chevallier, who has been described as 'mild ... humane, generous, and learned', had been a tutor before earning

---

[16] Hinds, p. 12.

his Doctor of Divinity.[17] He took steps to maintain St John's reputation as a hard-reading college and was particularly interested in students' writing and rhetorical skills. It was he who required all undergraduates to write 12 additional essays in Latin each year. During Chevallier's time as master, Johnians regularly numbered among the university's wranglers and prize men, and junior and senior members of the St John's community were at peace, even while problems were on the rise at Jesus College (see below). William Craven came into the master's chair in the middle of Wordsworth's time at St John's. As an undergraduate, Craven had been a 4th wrangler and winner of the First Chancellor's Medal and the Members' Latin Essay Prize. He had served his college as steward, president of the Society of Fellows, and bursar. He also held two professorships of Arabic, the Adams and Almoner chairs; but Winstanley believes that he was a mere amateur in the language and that the positions were sinecures.[18] Details of Craven's management or leadership skills have not survived, which suggests that there were no important controversies during his time in office. He has been described as worthy, unselfish, uncomplicated, and unostentatious by both Winstanley and Mullinger. Distinguished as a 'Christian without guile', he delivered sermons between 1760 and 1804 at the college, at Great St Mary's, and in parishes around Cambridge; these were collected and published in his lifetime.[19] In 1796 Craven published a well-regarded sermon on charity, and two years later he released portions of a scholarly study of *The Jewish and Christian Dispensations Compared with Other Institutions*, which includes a discussion of 'Religious Systems of the Learned', 'Jewish Governments', 'Moses the Law-Giver', the 'History and Prophetical Writings of the Jews', and several chapters on messianic prophecies. It seems doubtful that he would have been one of the 'Presidents and Deans' that Wordsworth criticises in *The Prelude*.[20] Given the importance of sermons in the university churches, of church history in the collegiate curriculum and in Wordsworth's later writing, and the popularity of sermon-reading among the public, Craven's sermons may be worthy of attention by scholars.

The careful, scholarly tutor of mathematics and classics discussed in Chapters 8 and 9, James Wood, BA, MA, BD, DD, and FRS, became the master of St John's in 1815 and served until 1839. The son of poor Lancashire weavers, Wood entered St John's as a sizar. Wood's poverty and dedication to his studies dictated that, during his first four years at St John's, he never left the college, even for holidays. He took his degree in 1782, as senior wrangler

---

[17] Mullinger, p. 254.
[18] Winstanley, pp. 136–137.
[19] Prior to his service as dean, he published *Sermons on the Evidence of a Future State of Rewards and Punishments arising from a view of our Nation and Condition* (1775, 1783).
[20] *Prelude*, 1805, p. 112, l. 421; 1850, p. 113, l. 413.

and first Smith's prizeman, and was immediately named a fellow. He tutored for many years, including the entire time that Wordsworth was at the college. In 1791 he was elected junior proctor and from 1802 to 1815 he served as the president of the Society of Fellows. Considered one of the best mathematicians in the university, Wood was often called upon to moderate at the university's Senate House exams. His four-volume *Principles of Mathematics and Natural Philosophy* (1795–99), co-written with Samuel Vince, was designed to aid students who intended to take the tripos examination. It went through several editions. Another of Wood's academic contributions, *Elements of Algebra*, was reprinted 16 times from 1795 to 1861. Textbooks on mechanics, optics, and astronomy followed. The entry for Wood in *The Dictionary of National Biography* notes that his 'equable temper and firm, courteous manner made him the ideal ruler of a college'. He was also praised for his 'high personal character, great natural ability, sound judgment, moderation, [and] forbearance'. Wood gave St John's close to £50,000 during his lifetime and, on his death, the college gained his extensive personal library, which included mathematics texts in English, French, and German; classical, religious, and literary texts; and a copy of Percy Shelley's 'On the Necessity of Atheism'. During the periods of Craven's and Wood's leadership, enrolment at St John's was always high.

The master of Jesus College when Coleridge was there was Dr William Pearce. He served from 1789 to 1820 and, like Wood, he was respected and well liked by senior members. As a result he was chosen to be vice chancellor several times. A man of some means, in 1796 he contributed a valuable altar piece painted by Jouvenet for its chapel renovation.[21] It was Pearce who recognised Coleridge's talents and awarded him the Chapel Clerk's Place when he lost the Brown Medal by the slimmest of margins in 1793. Pearce's response to Coleridge's dragoons escapade was appropriately balanced: he supported his tutor Plampin's efforts to get the truant back to the college in time to take his annual scholarship examination and then confined him to the campus.[22] Holmes reports that Coleridge sometimes conversed with Pearce about his dreams of Pantisocracy.[23] Despite the controversy caused by the religious reformism of William Frend, Pearce kept up his acquaintance with this junior fellow and allowed him to remain a resident until the Jesus fellows and the vice chancellor's court ruled against him.

Among the college deans at Oxford in the Romantic period was John Davey, a Blundell divinity scholar who was appointed master of Balliol in 1785. Blundell immediately began poaching promising young fellows from other colleges: the first were John Parsons from Wadham and George Powell

[21] Dyer, vol. 2, p. 90.
[22] Holmes, p. 59.
[23] Holmes, p. 77.

from Brasenose. Among his other contributions to the university were improved finances and a building fund, thanks to a coal-mining venture on the college's property at Long Benton. Davey also began the move to fully competitive admissions. He reduced the privileges of fellow commoners and after 1796 admitted only those who qualified for study. John Parsons lived up to the promise that Davey saw in him and became master in 1798. *The Dictionary of National Biography* quotes a contemporary who described Parsons as 'a second founder of his college, a reformer of the abuses of the university, an enforcer of its discipline, an able champion of its privileges, and a main pillar of its reputation'. The article adds that Parsons had 'vigorous colloquial powers' and was lively and witty when conversing with congenial companions, but that in general society, with students, he was grave and reserved. When Southey was an undergraduate and Parsons was a junior fellow, the two were well acquainted. Upon reading that Parsons had been made college master in 1798, Southey told a friend that it was 'an event by which I think the College must be benefitted. I was glad to see they had made so good a choice.'[24] As master, Parsons helped to write the new University Examination Statute of 1800 and brought more distinguished fellows into the college; within a decade Balliol men were regularly earning firsts in the Schools examinations.

Christ Church's Dean Jackson and Trinity's Master Mansel

The careers of the heads of the largest and most influential colleges in the Georgian period—Christ Church and Trinity College, Cambridge—provide additional evidence about the culture and communities at the universities in the late Georgian period and how training at these institutions may have affected the lives and work of writers and readers of the period. Cyril Jackson, the dean of Christ Church from 1783 to 1809, was educated at Manchester Grammar School and Westminster before matriculating at Oxford in 1764 as a commoner. As already noted, Jackson was a hard-reading prizeman. After taking his BA he was ordained, spent five years as a private tutor to the two eldest sons of George III, earned the degrees of MA, BD, and DD, and served as a preacher at Lincoln's Inn and canon at Christ Church. In 1783, upon the advice of the prime minister, the duke of Portland, the king appointed Jackson—then only 37—to be the dean of the college. A clever politician, Jackson maintained political friendships with Portland, William Pitt, Lord Auckland, and Charles Abbott. His 'backstairs influence' helped to launch the careers of numerous Christ Church men.

Though busy with politics and running the largest of Oxford's colleges, Jackson often took time to talk with students and to follow their academic progress. Though he had no room for him, Jackson took the time to visit with

---

[24] CLRS, Pt 2, #359.

young De Quincey when he was seeking a place at Christ Church. Jackson interviewed young George Chinnery in 1808 upon his arrival as a 16-year-old freshman and met with the young man's parents. Noting that Chinnery's father expected his son to have a public life like his own at the Treasury, Jackson grilled the young man on his mathematical skills and counselled him to learn to do maths in his head. This, the dean explained, would impress people in the government. Upon discerning that even though Chinnery knew several modern languages, his Greek was not up to Christ Church standards, Jackson declared with grand humour that 'I, my magnanimous Self' would arrange for a private tutor.[25] Jackson instructed Chinnery to come to visit him at the dean's lodge from time to time, so that he might check on his progress. Chinnery did so, and on one of these occasions the dean spent more than two hours with the young man. He discoursed, Chinnery says,

> on the points of similarity & difference between vulgar and decimal fractions, on the practical uses of both and what deficiencies in calculation brought on the invention of the latter. He really gave me a lecture, and from the regularity in the reasoning, the clearness of his expression, and his unimpeded flow of words you really would have supposed that he had prepared beforehand.[26]

A regular practice at many of the colleges was for students to read their compositions in the hall at the midday meal. Jackson would listen, collect their papers, and make comments on their writing and oral performance. Almost every evening Jackson had lively dinners for tutors and other fellows, and every year he took the most promising Christ Church undergraduates with him on his travels around the realm. It is no surprise that Jackson provoked many opinions or that many of his idiosyncrasies lived after him. Ward's account of his life in the *Oxford Dictionary of National Biography* reports that Lord Holland thought Jackson was a 'worshipper of rank' and that the earl of Dudley called him a 'mountebank'. Bishop Reginald Heber described Jackson's leadership as an 'absolute monarchy of the most ultra-oriental character'.[27] After visiting with Chinnery's parents, Jackson told the freshman that parental visits 'only seem to disturb', and he desired particularly that Mrs Chinnery should not come again to the college.[28] Throughout his time as dean, Jackson vocally opposed admitting Catholics and dissenters. A champion of serious academic work for all students, he urged Peel, who was already one of the

---

[25] Chinnery, letter of 25 January 1808.
[26] Chinnery, letter of 27 January 1808.
[27] W. R. Ward.
[28] Chinnery, letter of 10 February 1808.

most brilliant and dedicated students in Christ Church's history, to 'work very hard, & unremittingly—work like a Tigur, or like a Dragon, if Dragons work more & harder than Tygurs'.[29] Recognising the need to reform the university's examinations, Jackson joined in the effort to make them more accurate in assessing students' learning. Jackson also made sure that the new exams—for both ordinary and honours students—included specific questions about the 39 Articles. Students were asked not only to recite the language of several important articles but also to cite the biblical authority for each. Among the students at Christ Church when Jackson served as dean were most of Robert Southey's friends from Westminster, Monk Lewis, three future prime ministers, three future governors of India, a future chancellor of the exchequer, and one of the founders of the British Association for the Advancement of Science.

William Lort Mansel, master of Trinity College, Cambridge
A man of very different temperament and reputation was William Lort Mansel, the master of Trinity from 1798 to 1820. Entering the college in 1770 as a pensioner, Mansel was not a particularly brilliant undergraduate; he took his BA in 1774 but does not appear on the lists that year of wranglers, senior optimes, or even junior optimes. By 1775, however, he was elected junior fellow. In 1777 he attained the degree of MA; his fellowship was made permanent, and he worked in various capacities at the college for the next ten years, as *sublector secundus, lector linguae Latinae, lector primaries, lector lingua Græcæ,* junior dean, and catechist. Students ranging from sizars to the duke of Gloucester admired and liked him. Mansel was elected public orator in 1788. He left the college in 1789 to take a nearby living in Chesterton and marry Isabella Hagerston, the daughter of a local solicitor. During his marriage, Mansel maintained his connection with the university as public orator and university preacher and participated in college and county politics. Though he would later show tolerance for religious differences, during the Frend trial Mansel stood with the trinitarians. Mansel also maintained friendships with Pitt, who had been at Pembroke when Mansel was a junior fellow, and with Spencer Perceval, who had been his student.

In 1798, the same year that Wordsworth's brother Christopher was elected a fellow at Trinity, Perceval and the duke of Gloucester petitioned Pitt to arrange Mansel's appointment as master of the college. An honorary Doctor of Divinity was quickly awarded to Mansel, and he became the master of Cambridge's largest and most prestigious college, serving until his death in 1820. Disappointed that he had not been considered for the post, Isaac Milner of Queens' took it upon himself to inform the king that fellows and students of Trinity were rather too liberal in general and were not enthusiastic about

---

[29] W. R. Ward.

subscription. Subsequently, the royal documents of Mansel's appointment included the following directive: 'Restore discipline in that great seminary, and a more correct attachment to the Church of England and the British Constitution than the young men educated there have for some time been supposed to possess'.[30] Like Jackson at Christ Church, Mansel spent a great deal of time with students and colleagues. The master's lodge at Trinity was where kings, queens, princes, and judges were entertained whenever they visited the university.[31] Warm-hearted, easily amused, and famously witty, Mansel has also been described as 'afraid of nothing and of no one'.[32] When a local mob was threatening to break down the Trinity gates after a run-in with a group of students, Mansel went outside and, as horrified fellows looked on, began talking with the 'crowd of roughs'.[33] He was able 'by his eloquence or powers of persuasion' to induce them to disperse quietly, and they were 'so pleased by his bravery that they cheered him heartily as they went off'. As master, Mansel was known to treat men fairly, regardless of their political or religious beliefs. When the enthusiastic evangelism of two local clergymen, Charles Simeon and Robert Hall, became a cause of concern for college heads and university proctors, Mansel defended them.

In 1803 Mansel's personal world was shattered. His beloved wife died and his eldest son, a 13-year-old midshipman in the Royal Navy, was taken prisoner by a French gun brig. The boy remained in a French prison for five years. At the prison the French established a school for the younger prisoners, and Mansel regularly sent money to pay for the boy's education and maintenance, 'exactly as if he had voluntarily placed him there'.[34] A group of officers and young Mansel escaped in the winter of 1808. Hiding for three months in woods, ditches, marshes, and haylofts, and travelling at night, the youngster finally made it home in March 1809. Upon his arrival at Cambridge the town rang church bells and fired cannons for two days in the family's honour.[35] After a short visit at home, Midshipman Mansel insisted upon returning to the navy; within a year, still weak from his imprisonment, he died at sea. The same year Mansel lost his son, his friend Perceval arranged his appointment as bishop of Bristol. Never one for formality, Mansel raised eyebrows among the clergy when he chose not to wear a wig at the 'kissing of the hand' ceremony to which all new bishops must submit and which Mansel appears to have thought a rather silly exercise. As bishop, Mansel visited his diocese often. Records of only three sermons survive, however. He was known to be

---

[30] Mansel, p. 11.
[31] Dyer, vol. 2, p. 329.
[32] Mansel, p. 12.
[33] Mansel, p. 13.
[34] Mansel, p. 17.
[35] Mansel, pp. 18–22.

Educating the Romantic Poets

a student of modern languages and literature, especially French and Italian, and he corresponded with various literary and educational figures of the day.[36] Among his correspondence are letters from George Crabbe and Hannah More.

When Wordsworth and Coleridge were at Cambridge Mansel was serving either as public orator or preacher in the university church and, no doubt, they would have heard him speak. Byron and his friends Edward Long, William Bankes, John Cam Hobhouse, and Charles Matthews were all at Trinity when he was master. One Trinity alumnus described 'enchanted evenings ... spent in the [Master's] little library in which our souls [were] riveted to [Mansel's]'.[37] Another former student commented on Mansel's having 'the best principles ... and the fortitude to maintain them'.[38] He often took time to write to students both in triumph and in sorrow. Several letters of thanks for the eloquence and kindness of his letters survive. Byron admired Mansel's sense of humour and portrays him as the 'sublime' and godlike Magnus in 'Thoughts suggested by a College Examination':

> High in the midst, surrounded by his peers,
> MAGNUS his ample front sublime up rears:
> Placed on his chair of state, he seems a god.
> While Sophs and Freshmen tremble at his nod.

The Mansel memoir includes a note in which Byron insists that

> [n]o reflection is here intended against the person mentioned under the name of Magnus. Indeed, such an attempt could only recoil upon myself, as the gentleman is now as much distinguished by his eloquence, and the dignified propriety with which he fills his situation, as he was in former days for wit and conviviality.[39]

Letters written upon Mansel's death describe him as a 'noble character ... who [had] religion and learning', 'good humour ... and ... vivacity', but who also respected 'order and discipline'.[40] One former student wrote to a Trinity fellow that he believed that

> we may go far and near ... and find and keep many friends of talent, of spirit, and of heart, but never shall we find a man in whom shall

---

[36] Mansel, p. 49.
[37] Mansel, pp. 159–160.
[38] Mansel, p. 37.
[39] Mansel, p. 23.
[40] Mansel, pp. 137, 159.

be united that brilliancy of genius, that elegance of manners, and that warmth of affection which we have found and enjoyed in Bishop Mansel.[41]

Mansel was a part, the student continued, of a 'golden time' at Trinity and Cambridge. Besides Byron and his circle, other men of letters who were at Trinity when Mansel was master were Francis Wrangham and Thomas Babington Macaulay. So, too, were three future prime ministers, two future chancellors of the exchequer, William Whewell, Adam Sedgwick, Charles Babbage, George Biddell Airy, and George Peacock.

Christopher Wordsworth, master of Trinity College

Following Mansel as master of Trinity was William Wordsworth's youngest brother, Christopher. He served from 1820 until his resignation in 1841 owing to ill health. A much more willing and diligent student than his brother William, Christopher Wordsworth was tenth wrangler in 1796 and earned a fellowship in 1798. In 1799 he took his MA. While he waited for a church living, so he could marry Charles Lloyd's sister, Priscilla, he remained at Cambridge as private tutor to Charles Manners-Sutton. When Manners-Sutton's father became archbishop of Canterbury in 1805, Wordsworth was recruited as his domestic chaplain at Lambeth. During the next several years Christopher Wordsworth collected lucrative church livings in Kent, Essex, and Suffolk. His residence at Lambeth gave him access to an excellent library, and in 1810 he published his six-volume *Ecclesiastical Biography; or Lives of Eminent Men, Connected with the History of Religion in England; from the Commencement of the Reformation to the Revolution*. During this time, he also joined the Anglican philanthropist Joshua Watson and others who were building Waterloo churches. They founded the National Society for Promoting the Education of the Poor in the Principles of the Established Church in England and Wales. In 1817, when the younger Manners-Sutton became Speaker of the House, Wordsworth was named chaplain to the House. Three years later the archbishop and his son arranged his royal appointment as master of Trinity.

One of Christopher Wordsworth's most lasting accomplishments for the college was building the New Court, for which he hired William Wilkins, architect of the National Gallery and University College London. Not only did he establish the already mentioned classical tripos, but he also created prizes for compositions in Latin hexameters, elegiacs, and alcaics. Twice during his time as master Wordsworth was elected vice chancellor (in 1820–21 and 1826–27). His *Ecclesiastical Biography* was an important accomplishment; his building projects were impressive, as were his efforts to support the humanities,

---

[41] Mansel, p. 159.

but he was not regarded as a particularly successful college dean. His high Toryism, piety, and rigidity about college rules, along with his reserved and somewhat reclusive temperament, in contrast to Mansel's, did not make him popular with students. Even his older brother regretted his 'coldness' and reluctance to give the family much of his time during visits—'not more I think than twenty minutes at the very utmost when I saw him in town'.[42] He battled with students over chapel attendance. In reaction, students created the Society for the Prevention of Cruelty to Undergraduates and collected and published data about the chapel attendance of fellows. Even when Christopher Wordsworth was generous—for example, when he reinstated the Union Debating Society, which proctors had closed down—most students tended to be unappreciative. His handling of the Connop Thirlwall affair in 1834 did not help his reputation. That year a decree allowing dissenters to take university degrees provoked a flurry of pamphlet-writing. Thirlwall, a fellow, argued that the colleges of Cambridge were no longer merely seminaries of the established church and criticised the colleges' requiring divinity lectures and compulsory chapel. Wordsworth asked Thirlwall to resign. The younger members of the college urged him to stay; but Thirlwall resigned, nevertheless.

The first time Wordsworth returned to Cambridge after leaving in 1791 was to visit his brother at the master's lodge. Whenever he returned to the university thereafter, he stayed with Christopher, who often invited undergraduates to the lodge to visit with the poet. According to Moorman, the poet truly enjoyed these evenings, and Trinity became 'the nursery of Wordsworth's fame at Cambridge'.[43] Among the Cambridge students who gathered to hear the poet were John Moultrie, Arthur Hallam, Richard Monckton Milnes, and Richard Trench. In 1829 Trinity students arranged a Cambridge Union debate to decide which Cambridge poet—Wordsworth or Byron—was more revered. That year Byron won, but over the coming decades, Wordsworth increasingly became the favourite. Mary Wordsworth wrote that her husband was 'in such great request always at Cambridge' and that it was 'marvellous to see how a man of sixty can walk, talk, and enjoy himself with more spirit than the youngest of them'.[44] The time Wordsworth spent talking with Cambridge undergraduates and fellows on these visits may have contributed to his belief in the teaching function of poets. It was also during one of these visits to Cambridge that Wordsworth began his *Ecclesiastical Sketches*, which are both a companion piece in verse to his brother's monumental *Ecclesiastical Biography* and the fullest announcement of the retrospective and explicitly Anglican/nationalist turn Wordsworth chose to take in his later career. Among these sonnets are

---

[42] Qtd in Moorman, *William Wordsworth: A Biography: Later Years 1803–1850*, p. 424.
[43] *William Wordsworth: A Biography: Later Years 1803–1850*, p. 328.
[44] Qtd in *William Wordsworth: A Biography: Later Years 1803–1850*, p. 329.

tributes to his brother's work building Waterloo churches and to King's College Chapel—that 'immense/And glorious Work of fine intelligence'.[45] This volume might be profitably studied in the context of and as if in conversation with his brother's career and church biographies.

College fellows

College fellows in the Georgian period have been much maligned, but my research suggests that many were more productive and useful to the university than their critics have charged. The best of the college heads noted above, tutors, professors, and men as different as the evangelical Charles Simeon and the classicist Richard Porson, were all fellows. Schneider calls the group of fellows that were coming up at Cambridge in the 1770s and 1780s 'philosophes'. Many were liberal-minded Whigs who were interested in rationalising religion, reforming academic procedures, and realising, if possible, the positive benefits of events in France. Among these were John Jebb, Richard Watson, Gilbert Wakefield, Robert Tyrwhitt, William Frend, and William Paley. The colleges considered the Society of Fellows to be essential members of the university community. The founders' purposes in creating fellowships were to give young scholars 'freedom from necessary employment, … constant intercourse with a learned body, and the liberty of admission into an extensive public library'.[46] The Oxford commission explains that the founders believed it was the 'duty of the fellow' to continue to learn and to complement his undergraduate studies with more work 'in one of the Superior Faculties, generally that of Theology' and to diligently 'attend Public Lectures, and the frequent performance of Exercises in the Schools of the University'.[47] Among other requirements, fellows of Christ Church who were working toward the MA were expected to declaim in the hall twice a week and to write six lectures on Aristotle. Christ Church fellows with the MA were required to dispute every Friday in Latin and to lecture twice a week. All members of the colleges were expected, as the Oxford commissioners rather quaintly put it, to 'learn something new every day'.[48]

Both royal commission reports stress the importance of fellows in the life of the university. The Oxford report explains that 'from this body of men' will come 'all the studying and all the educating power of the university—all the professors, all the tutors, all those who pursue learning for its own sake, and beyond the needs of practical life'.[49] The Cambridge report declares that the

---

[45] WWPW, p. 354, Sonnet XLIII, ll. 4–5.
[46] Heberden, p. 47.
[47] Hinds, p. 134, 140.
[48] Hinds, p. 138.
[49] Hinds, p. 149.

fellows are 'the chief source of life and vigor to the whole academical system'.[50] It adds that a college fellowship is for students 'the chief motive to exertion and the great reward of successful industry and talent'.[51] Indeed, most reading students considered a fellowship to be 'the crown of all earthly things'.[52] Besides being steps on the ladder for young men who wished for a career of university teaching and preaching, a fellowship also put a young man in line for a church or public school living, where he might have his own establishment and a wife and family. Resident fellows typically fell into two categories: more mature members, who were active scholars, chaired professors, canons and administrators, and younger members, who were teaching, studying, and waiting for a college living elsewhere or promotion within the college.

In most cases, college fellows were chosen from the latest crop of bachelors. Patrons, kin, and friends among the senior fellows could influence these choices. This is why Wordsworth's family was so confident that he could succeed to his uncle's fellowship at St John's. Preference was, of course, given to those who had earned high marks on the university tripos or honours examinations and on subsequent fellowship exams in the colleges. Some fellowships required specific knowledge. Gonville and Caius looked for men with skill in dialectics, while Trinity Hall looked for aptitude and knowledge of civil law. Some fellowships were reserved for candidates from certain schools or counties. Some specified that the candidate had to have held his degree for a certain number of years. Others were available only to students of the law or of medicine; many were reserved for students of theology who intended to take clerical orders. Some colleges had specific age requirements—24 for lay fellowships and 30 for clerical ones were common. Most colleges also required fellows to select and move on to a profession within a specified amount of time, vacating their fellowship for the next worthy scholar. At Trinity, fellows were expected to vacate within seven years; at St John's within six. If a junior fellow landed an ecclesiastical preferment or was given or inherited income double the value of a junior fellowship on a seven year's average, then he was required to vacate his fellowship.[53] The requirement of residence varied from college to college; usually less than half of a college's fellows were in residence. Celibacy was expected of all resident fellows, and most fellowships had to be surrendered if a man wished to marry.

Colleges worked to keep their fellowships filled. Some appointed new fellows within a month of the occurrence of a vacancy; the larger colleges at Cambridge held election once a year. All required examination. Though

---

[50] Graham, p. 156.
[51] Graham, p. 156.
[52] Graham, p. 228.
[53] Graham, p. 171.

Leadership at Oxford and Cambridge

fellowship examinations were sometimes carelessly conducted, after controversies about them swirled in the 1780s most exams were rigorous, including a long written section and an oral examination by the college head and a group of senior fellows. Even before the reforms, some fellowship exams were gruelling. Winstanley records Richard Cumberland's description of his exam at Trinity in 1752. The candidates were called one by one and asked to account for their entire academic career at Cambridge in 'the several branches of philosophy'.[54] After having their collegiate learning thoroughly probed by the college dean, who took 'nothing upon trust', the candidates were asked leading questions about what they had been reading in addition to assigned texts. They were required to give 'a summary account of the several great empires of the ancient world, the periods when they flourished, their extent when at the summit of their power, the causes of their declension, and dates of their extinction'.[55] Next, each candidate was seated alone in a room where he was given a page of Greek to translate into Latin or English as quickly as possible. Finally, he was given topics upon which he was to compose a prose theme and an original verse, 'impromptu' and 'with dispatch', in Latin.[56] The fellowship exam at Trinity College, Cambridge in 1788 asked candidates to solve a series of higher level mathematical problems, to translate passages in both Greek and Latin, to explain how to read and scan classical verse, to write a discourse explaining the differences between physics, metaphysics, and ethics, and to answer this query: 'What were the leading principles which distinguished the principal sects of the Greek philosophers—such as the Pythagoreans, the Platonists, the Stoics, the Epicureans, the Pyrrhonists?' The final phase of this exam required candidates to write impromptu essays and poems in Latin.

An alumnus's winning a fellowship was an occasion of celebration for all members of his college. George Chinnery described one such 'delightful event' to his mother, explaining that the selection of two of his college's graduates as fellows of All Souls 'reflects great credit on CHCH'.[57] Upon hearing the news, the Christ Church cathedral bells rang and 'all the College was rushing to the rooms of the new fellows to felicitate them upon the promotion'.[58] Years of hard reading and excellent university exams—double firsts or honours as a wrangler—prepared men for the fellowship exams. Of the 356 fellows named at Cambridge in the Georgian period, 310 (87 per cent) had been wranglers and prize winners. Along with the honour, the income from fellowships could be well worth the trouble, especially for poorer students. Over the centuries,

---

[54] Winstanley, p. 239.
[55] Winstanley, p. 239.
[56] Winstanley, p. 239.
[57] Chinnery, letter of 4 November 1808.
[58] Chinnery, letter of 4 November 1808.

Educating the Romantic Poets

thanks to various royal and aristocratic endowments and dividends from college lands, the wealthier colleges offered fellows stipends ranging from £75 at Balliol in 1775 to £100 at University College in 1782. In 1800 the stipend for a fellow at All Souls was £124.[59] Fellows might hold their position for life, if they stayed at their college and performed teaching, preaching, and administrative duties, some of which were quite lucrative. The attractions of fellowship also included room and board, a place at the high table, access to the best libraries in the land, connections that advanced careers, and lifelong friendships. Fellows were allowed to absent themselves from the college for nine weeks each year.

Social life for fellows was not too different from that of undergraduates, though meals and rooms were finer. Fellows were expected to attend chapel and dress for dinner. They were free to visit taverns as well as coffee houses; many belonged to clubs. They recreated as the undergraduates did—walking, riding, swimming, and fishing, though usually with a bit more dignity. In the senior common rooms they followed parliamentary debates and national news, played cards and chess, and drank wine and whiskey. All contributed to the well-stocked liquor cabinets of their common rooms. In 1811 the fellows of Oriel consumed 1,470 bottles of port, 171 of sherry, 48 of madeira, and various quantities of gin, rum, and punch.[60] Betting books were kept in the common rooms, where fellows recorded wagers on the success of bills in parliament, the progress of military campaigns, the outcomes of elections, winners of horse races, and even certain colleagues' likelihood of marriage. After fellows left the college many returned on Sunday evenings to dine at the high table. At King's College, this was called the Samaritan Supper; at St John's, it was the Curate's Club; and at Christ's College it was The Apostolic. According to Gunning, these dinners could be rather large, as most of the rectors and curates of the churches within ten miles of Cambridge were university men. They could also be boisterous.

At Cambridge most colleges also extended the title of preachership to fellows. At larger colleges, such as Trinity and St John's, at least one-fourth of the fellows held preacherships. College preachers were responsible for delivering learned sermons and catechistical lectures both in their college and in the community, for encouraging the scholarly efforts of other fellows and students, and for monitoring the 'righteousness' of all.[61] Fellows who took college preacherships were expected to be good biblical scholars, excellent orators, and teachers. However, between the Restoration and 1786, when reforms were finally put into place, Cambridge preacherships were carelessly managed and sometimes bestowed

[59] Sutherland and Mitchell, pp. 238–239.
[60] Green, 'The University and Social Life', p. 347.
[61] Smith, pp. 47–50.

Figure 22. All Souls College, Oxford: cloisters and chapel. Line engraving by J. Le Keux after F. Mackenzie. Wellcome Collection. Public Domain Mark.

upon undistinguished senior fellows. Among the college preachers in Gunning's time at the university were individuals whom he described as a gourmand, a ladies' man, and a madman. Yet another made lewd advances upon the master's wife.[62] Stories such as these fuelled a public perception that fellows were unproductive scholars, lukewarm clergymen, and freeloaders. John Duncombe's poem 'An Evening Contemplation in a College, being a Parody on the "Elegy in a Country Churchyard",' added to these perceptions:

> The peaceful fellows of the college sleep.
> The tinkling bell proclaiming early pray'rs,
> The noisy servants rattling o'er their head,
> The calls of business, and domestic cares,
> Ne'er rouze these sleepers from their downy bed.
> No chatt'ring females crowd their social fire,
> No dread have they of discord and of strife;
> Unknown the names of husband and of sire,
> Unfelt the plagues of matrimonial life.

[62] Smith, p. 68.

> Oft have they bask'd along the sunny walls,
> Oft have the benches bow'd beneath their weight:
> How jocund are their looks when dinner calls!
> How smoke the cutlets on their crowded plate!
> O let not Temp'rance too-disdainful hear
> How long our feasts, how long our dinners last;
> Nor let the fair with a contemptuous sneer
> On these unmarry'd men reflections cast!
> … These sons of Science shine in black alone.
> … But Science now has fill'd their vacant mind
> With Rome's rich spoils and Truth's exalted views;
> Fir'd them with transports of a nobler kind,
> And bade them slight all females—but the Muse.[63]

In 'Thoughts Suggested by a College Examination', Byron describes fellows variously as dull, ill-mannered, vain, sad, tedious, bigoted, and ambitious. Winstanley, too, notes fellows' reputation as unproductive scholars and bad-mannered drinkers. He adds, however, that it is likely that the fellows' shortcomings were exaggerated and that 'scandals [make] better copy than tales of edification'.[64]

During the years when the Romantics were undergraduates, Oxford was taking steps to raise its standards for fellowships and to liven up their intellectual life. Oriel and Balliol led the way. Southey recalled looking with admiration upon Thomas Howe, a fellow at Balliol, as he declaimed against the war with France, praised America, and asserted the right of every country to model its own form of government.[65] Oriel's provost John Eveleigh and his successor Copleston maintained high standards for their fellowships. As noted, Balliol's Davey and Parsons took pains to recruit highly qualified fellows, even stealing them from other colleges. Among the more notable fellows of Oxford during this time were Thomas Arnold and John Henry Newman. Whewell defended the Cambridge fellows, noting their important service of administering and moderating college examinations. This was no small job, as all students were examined orally and in writing three times a year. Fellows, he explained, not only checked the 'caprice and carelessness' of students but also strengthened the 'hands of the teaching body, since they appear as an independent class, sanctioning the studies and instructions of the teachers, and keeping up an acquaintance with their literary and scientific pursuits'.[66]

---

[63] Duncombe, pp. 6–8, ll. 16–32, 36, 49–52.
[64] Winstanley, p. 258.
[65] Charles Cuthbert Southey, p. 215.
[66] Whewell, p. 63.

Leadership at Oxford and Cambridge

Whewell maintained that fellows contributed to the 'general cultivation of the mind' at the colleges and were examples for the undergraduates of men who actively kept 'their hold on science and literature, and [continued] to acquaint themselves with the highest point that knowledge has reached'.[67] By the time many of the Romantics and most of the young Victorians got to Cambridge, fellowships went to reputable scholars and teachers such as William Frend, James Wood, Adam Sedgwick, Joseph Romilly, and William Whewell himself. The life of Thomas Jones (1756–1807)—a fellow Byron knew well—suggests that the poet's negative comments about fellows cited above were probably made in jest.

A graduate of Shrewsbury, Jones migrated from St John's to Trinity College in 1777. While he and Herbert Marsh of St John's were anxiously preparing to compete for honours on the tripos exams, Jones generously tutored Marsh throughout their senior year. Jones became first Smith's prizeman and senior wrangler, Marsh was second Smith's prizeman and second wrangler, and the men became lifelong friends. Jones was selected as a fellow at Trinity in 1781. Five years later he was among the group of angry junior fellows who protested the mismanagement of the fellowship election of 1786 and petitioned college leaders to make these exams impregnable to abuse. He served as junior dean from 1787 to 1789 and as head mathematics tutor from 1787 to 1807, when Byron was in residence. The poet George Dyer identified Jones as 'one of the most eminent tutors in the university', adding that he was 'a man of strict principle' who 'sedulously ... and affectionately devoted himself to the improvement of his pupils in the higher sciences'.[68] His lessons were described as clear and methodical, and he has been credited with raising academic standards and morale at his college.[69]

Jones was one of the fellows who stood by his former student, William Frend, during his trial in the vice chancellor's court. Among his many students were Queen Victoria's Lord Melbourne, two chancellors of the exchequer, the geologist Adam Sedgewick, Byron, and Hobhouse. Jones was conscientious to the end of his days. Though well acquainted with Byron's 'tumultuous passions',[70] in early 1807, the last year of Jones's life, he patiently fulfilled his tutorial duty to his erstwhile charge. At that time Byron was deeply in debt and depressed; he was bouncing between Southwell and London and revising *Poems on Various Occasions*. Jones wrote to Byron, requesting him to return to the university. Byron sent Jones a snappish (and inaccurate) reply, saying he

---

[67] Whewell, p. 63.
[68] Dyer, vol. 2, p. 320.
[69] In 1791, after two undergraduates from Pembroke were involved in a fatal duel, Jones preached a memorable 'sermon on Dueling' at the university church.
[70] Marchand, *A Biography*, vol. 1, p. 131.

had done absolutely no academic study at Trinity and that he had few friends there.[71] But, soon thereafter, Byron returned to Trinity in high spirits, larking about with his friends Hobhouse and Matthews.

The careers of two other fellows, John Hailstone (1759–1847) and John Tweddle (1769–1799), argue against the bad reputation of this cohort of university men. Hailstone had been a second wrangler at Trinity and second Smith's prizeman in 1782. After election as a fellow, he became senior bursar and in 1788 was appointed Woodwardian Professor of Geology. Hailstone travelled throughout England and the Continent on fieldwork and contributed significantly to the Cambridge geology museum. He was elected FRS, was a founding member of the Geology Society, and published widely. Upon retirement, he became involved in promoting the education of the poor in his home county. Moore recalled Byron's mentioning him as one of the men he respected most at Cambridge. Tweddle, a fellow of Trinity, was a classics scholar who won more prizes than any other individual in the history of the college, including all of the Browne's prizes for Greek ode, Latin ode, Greek epigram, and Latin epigram several years in succession as an undergraduate and bachelor's prizes in 1791 and 1792.[72] Dyer praises the 'elegance' of his compositions, and his college proudly published all of his award-winning poems. As an undergraduate, and then as a fellow, Tweddle was a staunch supporter of Frend. He left the university without taking orders to study law and died aged 30 while travelling in Athens. Both men embodied Whewell's portrait of the ideal fellow.

William Frend, fellow, tutor, religious radical

The story of the short but remarkable university career of William Frend (1757–1841), of Jesus College, rounds out this discussion of college fellows during the Romantic period.[73] Frend was one of the most admired of the philosophes, but his choice in the years between 1788 and 1793 to mount an unflinching campaign to abolish subscription, to end the 'superstition' of the trinity, and to turn the behaviour of the clergy towards humbler and more Christlike ministry brought his academic career to an end. This episode illustrates the complicated political climate at 'whiggish' Cambridge when Wordsworth and Coleridge were students there and provides context for some of their early 'radical' verse. Frend's education began at the Anglo-classical King's School in Canterbury. At 17 he was sent to Canada by his wealthy

---

[71] Marchand, *A Biography*, vol. 1, p. 126.
[72] Dyer, vol. 2, p. 321.
[73] See Kenneth Johnston's chapter '"Frend of Jesus, friend of the Devil": William Frend (1757–1841)' in *Usual Suspects* for a spritely account of Frend's valiant but ultimately frustrated efforts to reform the university and the church.

Leadership at Oxford and Cambridge

wine merchant father to prepare for the family business. While there he was recruited briefly by the British army to fight against the American colonists. Frend returned to England determined to enter the Anglican ministry. He matriculated at Christ's College, Cambridge in 1775, where his tutor was William Paley. A hard-reading man from the beginning, Frend took his BA in 1780 as both a second wrangler and Smith's prizeman and was soon after named a fellow. By 1783 he was ordained and awarded two nearby parishes, Long Stanton and Madingley. At the latter of these, with the help of the local squire's daughter, he started a Sunday School. Frend was a Hebraist, and his scholarly work led him to question the Anglican doctrine of the trinity. Despite these sentiments, in 1786 Frend was elected tutor at Jesus College and, owing to his 'open, cheerful disposition',[74] he soon became an admired teacher, with a large following of Cambridge undergraduates. Among his close companions and supporters in the university and town were Robert Tyrwhitt (1735–1817), Robert Robinson (1735–1790), and George Dyer (1755–1841).[75] Tyrwhitt had resigned his fellowship and did not teach, but he remained an active Hebrew scholar at Jesus College, took his turn doing duty in the university church, and quietly kept his Unitarian opinions to himself. Robinson was a local preacher and self-educated scholar, who was head of the St Andrew's Baptist congregation in Cambridge. His sermons were popular in Cambridge, and it is possible that Wordsworth attended some of them. A tireless religious reformer, friend of liberty, and abolitionist, Robinson was the founder of the Cambridge Constitutional Information Society. The third member of this group was Dyer, from Emmanuel College, who became friends with Wordsworth and Coleridge in London. Among his works were several volumes of poetry, *Complaints of the Poor People of England* (1793), and *History of the University and College of Cambridge* (1814).[76] This group, with the support of Joseph Johnson, saw to it that at least one of the local Cambridge bookstores maintained shelves for works by deists and Unitarians, and made sure that these 'heretical' volumes were 'put in the way of Students'.[77]

During Wordsworth's first year at St John's, 1787, Frend was speaking publicly about religious freedom at the university. At the same time, however, a group of the university's top mathematicians, who were also evangelicals, were becoming stridently hostile to any talk of academic, religious, or political reform. This group was led by Isaac Milner, who would become President of Queens' in 1788; Henry Coulthurst, fellow of Sidney Sussex; and William

---

[74] Qtd in Frida Knight, p. 70.
[75] See Roe, *Wordsworth and Coleridge*, pp. 90–96 for more on these men.
[76] In the chapter on Jesus College, Dyer does not mention the Frend affair, nor does he say anything in the Queens' College chapter about Frend's nemesis, Milner.
[77] Frida Knight, p. 99.

Farish, mathematics tutor at Magdalene. When, in December 1787, yet another 'grace' or formal proposal to end subscription was summarily rejected with no discussion by the Senate, Frend lost all patience. He wrote the first of three notorious pamphlets, *Thoughts on Subscription to Religious Tests Particularly that required by the University of Cambridge, of Candidates for the Degree of Bachelor of Arts, in a Letter to the Rev. H. W. Coulthurst, B.D.* (1788). Joseph Johnson published the pamphlet, which required a second edition shortly thereafter. As the title makes clear, the pamphlet is a letter to Coulthurst, who had delivered a commencement oration 'with unbecoming virulence and asperity of language' condemning the anti-subscription grace. Frend's pamphlet begins with a history of the violence committed by men in the name of religion. After which he declares:

> But let not the philosopher, nor the man of feeling and honour associate together the history of the church and of Jesus. The mild and amiable founder of Christianity taught mankind to be good and to be happy: the church, in every part of the world, endeavours to enslave mankind, to make men hypocrites and knaves.[78]

Elsewhere in *Thought on Subscription* Frend scorns 'prelates' for their 'secret love of arbitrary power' and praises instead the 'humble curate and the benevolent pastor' who 'preach a better doctrine than the church has given them'.[79] He condemns the church as an institution because: 'it has always been unfriendly to the civil liberty, the domestic comfort, the moral and literary improvement of man: as a Christian, I abhor it, because it is entirely repugnant to the conduct and express command of our Lord and Saviour Jesus Christ.'[80] Frend calls required subscription a 'violation of honour' and questions the judgement of educators who require young men to make so serious a commitment. Because the university properly requires a remarkable 'degree of assiduity and diligence' from students as they prepare for 'an examination not to be paralleled perhaps in Europe', Frend argues, it is virtually impossible for them to give 'divinity' the attention a 'subject of such high importance demands'.[81] Frend's argument against subscription was based not only on principles of personal freedom and sound pedagogy but also on his belief that articles two, five, and eight supporting the trinity are unscriptural. His attack on these articles cites passages from the Old Testament and from the Gospels of John and Matthew. He even adds a long footnote 'for the sake of

---

[78] Frend, *Thoughts*, p. iv.
[79] Frend, *Thoughts*, p. v.
[80] Frend, *Thoughts*, p. vi.
[81] Frend, *Thoughts*, p. 4.

Leadership at Oxford and Cambridge

junior students' that explains the leading features of 'the sects now prevailing in the nation'—Unitarians, trinitarians, Athanasians, Arians, and Socinians.[82]

At first authorities took no action to censure Frend, and the college allowed him to retain his fellowship, perhaps because his wealthy and influential friend Tyrwhitt (who had just recently funded restoration of the college chapel) stood by him. Frend was also championed by several other respected fellows at Jesus, and by Jones at Trinity. John Hammond, a fellow from Queens', stood up for Frend against Isaac Milner. Undergraduates admired Frend's courageous activism. They read and discussed his pamphlet, which is not only clearly argued but also punctuated by Frend's deep religious conviction; they began to consider him a hero. In the fateful summer of 1789 he travelled to Germany, Belgium, and France. He did not, however, go to Paris. During his travels he met and talked with Joseph Priestley and was deeply moved by what he and his travelling companions saw and discussed during the trip. Upon his return to the university Frend resigned his two livings and withdrew from the Anglican Church. Even then, he was allowed to remain a tutor, fellow, and steward at Jesus College. Just a stone's throw away from Jesus College, Wordsworth was at Cambridge during most of this time, so we can assume that he was aware of Frend's activities.[83] Whether or not he knew about Frend's trip prior to taking his own to the Continent in 1790 is unclear.

Shortly after these resignations, Frend published *An Address to the Members of the Church of England, and to Protestant Trinitarians in General, exhorting them to turn from the false worship of Three Persons, to the worship of the One True God* (1789). This pamphlet reiterates and further develops his earlier his claim that there is no scriptural support for the trinity.[84] Against his opponents' charge that jettisoning the trinity would upend the Anglican Church and with it 'the benefit of social worship', Frend replies that 'social worship is a very desirable thing; but for the sake of social worship, I cannot worship an idol'.[85] Finally, he calls his readers '[f]rom false objects of worship to the worship of the living God' and exhorts them to 'forsake the temples where they have set up other objects of worship'.[86] This pamphlet provoked Jesus's master, Dr Richard Beadon, who retired later that year, to remove Frend from his college tutorship and to forbid undergraduates from contracting with Frend for private tutoring. Frend was, however, allowed to retain his fellowship.

Frends' allies in Cambridge and London counselled him to stand strong, and he gamely appealed to the master and to the university visitor in London.

---

[82] Frend, *Thoughts*, pp. 25–26, n. *.
[83] Coleridge and Southey were not yet at university during this part of Frend's story.
[84] Frend, *An Address*, p. 8.
[85] Frend, *An Address*, p. 9.
[86] Frend, *An Address*, pp. 9–10.

Educating the Romantic Poets

Both officials, however, rejected his appeal.[87] Frend responded by publishing a statement in four London papers along with Beadon's and the visitor's replies to his appeal. In London Theophilus Lindsey, the founder of the Essex Street Unitarian Chapel, shared these publications and Frend's pamphlets with the radical community and Dr Priestley, who sent letters of encouragement. Junior fellows and many undergraduates also rallied around Frend. By this time, Coleridge had arrived for the Michaelmas term and, though Frend was not permitted to be his tutor, he was, nevertheless, a presence at the college. Coleridge mentions him in a letter to his brother in the new year, saying 'Mr. Frend's company is by no means invidious. On the contrary, Pierce himself [the new college Master] is very intimate with him.'[88] In the next sentence Coleridge adds, 'Tho' I am not an *Alderman*, I have yet *prudence* enough to *respect* that *gluttony of Faith* waggishly yclept Orthodoxy.' Frend was banned from addressing the university, but he continued speaking in private homes and local halls.

Throughout 1792 Pearce allowed Frend to continue as a residential fellow. When war with France commenced in 1793, Frend was further aroused by that conflict, particularly by the taxation it required, and the hardships that it inflicted on England's working people. His response was to publish *Peace and Union recommended to the associated bodies of Republicans and Anti-Republicans* (1793). This document begins by declaring that the threats from France cannot be forgotten, but that neither can the plight of England's unenfranchised poor. Claiming that America and France had erected in their constitutions 'much nobler edifices' than England's, he asserts that 'our government is susceptible of improvement … for the benefit of the community at large without injuring a single individual'.[89] He specifically urges shortening the duration of parliaments and expanding the franchise and right to hold office. He calls for greater equality and clarity in the laws, the abolition of entails, and revision of the 'cruel and oppressive' game laws.[90] He also argues for revision of the poor laws and related legislation so that a 'labouring man' could earn 'sufficient wages to enable him to bring up a numerous family and to lay by something for his support in the decline of life'.[91] Finally, he urges governments to pay less attention to 'the maintenance and support of the corinthian capitals of society' and more to the 'comfort and welfare of the most numerous and important part of the community'.[92] All of these arguments might have found support among the university leaders had they

[87] Gascoigne, p. 228.
[88] CLSTC, p. 20. Coleridge misspells Pearce's name.
[89] Frend, *Peace*, p. 5.
[90] Frend, *Peace*, p. 18.
[91] Frend, *Peace*, pp. 19–20.
[92] Frend, *Peace*, p. 21.

been made in less turbulent times, but when Frend also argued that there was no longer a need for a national church he had crossed one too many lines. Shortly after *Peace and Union* began to circulate, the senior fellows of Jesus College passed a resolution condemning Frend and forwarded them to the vice chancellor and the bishop of Ely.[93]

It was Frend's bad luck that Isaac Milner, the ambitious, evangelical master of Queens' College, was taking his turn as the vice chancellor of the university in 1793. Outraged by *Peace and Union*, he called Frend before the vice chancellor's court for having 'Jacobin and infidel principles'. Under Milner's hand, the university's official actions were arbitrary, secretive, and grossly unfair. Specific charges against which Frend might defend himself were not published. Due process was rarely in force, and Milner kept postponing meetings so that Frend could not talk with his accusers. According to Gunning, Milner and his allies were more interested in posturing for an anxious national audience, parliament, and the king than they were in justice, much less academic freedom. Throughout the ordeal and during the trial, when it finally began, Frend's self-defence was dignified, eloquent, and rational. He accurately cited statutory support for his actions, invoked the standard of academic freedom, and reminded the court how many senior members of the university— including the divinity professor, Bishop Watson—had once or even still held many of his same views. Undergraduates attended his trial and argued about the case late into the night. Those who had supported him before—Tyrwhitt, Jones, and Lambert—continued to do so; but when the month-long trial was over at the end of May 1793, the university banished Frend, and by a small majority the Jesus fellows voted to expel him from the college as well.

Milner smugly warned those who continued to support Frend that the university 'would not suffer the sacred and venerable institutions of the Established Church to be derided and insulted … at a time when a profane and licentious spirit of infidelity and irreligion makes rapid advance and threatens the destruction of our ecclesiastical fabric'.[94] Milner also used the occasion to brag to Wilberforce and his powerful friends at court that he had 'exerted every nerve to crush that Monster', the 'school of Jacobinism' at the university.[95] In truth, Frend's issues were more theological than political, but by linking them to issues of national security during a crisis of alarm Milner—the evangelical—was able to prevail against 'rational religion'. Because Milner's construction of the debate prevailed, dissenting campaigns in the last decades of the eighteenth century at Cambridge hurt the university's national reputation for a time. At Oxford, no such campaigns took place; the effects of the

---

[93] Roe, *Wordsworth and Coleridge*, p. 102.
[94] Qtd in Gascoigne, p. 232.
[95] Gascoigne, p. 233.

Educating the Romantic Poets

American rebellion, the rising up of English working people, the French Revolution, and war forced Oxford, already firmly attached to the doctrines of the Established Church, into an 'unshakeable' alliance with the government.[96]

Frend's courage, his eloquence, and the reasoning of his arguments, however, were inspirational to impressionable and sympathetic students such as Coleridge, who were in residence at the time. Though Wordsworth left before Frend's trial and banishment, no Cambridge man moving about in London, as Wordsworth did after graduation, could have missed the news of his case. In London after his graduation, Wordsworth was more than once a guest in the exiled Frend's home. It was through Frend that he first met Godwin. Portions of 'Salisbury Plain', written in 1793, appear to reflect his knowledge of Frend's story and writing, for it archly denounces arbitrary authority and explores some of the very same issues that Frend addressed in *Peace and Union*: poverty, inequality, oppression, and bad laws. Similarly, both texts oppose the war with France, in part because of its effect upon the poor. Roe has already pointed out that Wordsworth's 'Salisbury Plain' and some of the *Lyrical Ballads* express the same 'sympathetic identification' with outcasts and the poor that Frend and other rational radicals used in their protests.[97] Certainly the range of religious opinions Wordsworth explores throughout his career, starting with his early, almost pantheistic writing and going through *The Excursion* to *Ecclesiastical Sketches*, show the effects of acquaintance with Frend's arguments, which may have contributed to the religious confusion he expresses in Book Tenth of *The Prelude*. There, he attests that after 'dragging all passions, notions, shapes of faith,/ Like culprits to the bar ... now believing,/ Now disbelieving, endlessly perplexed/' and seeking in this effort the 'ground/ Of moral obligation', he finally 'lost all feeling of conviction, and, in fine,/ Sick, wearied out with contrarieties,/ Yielded up moral questions in despair'.[98]

Coleridge arrived at Cambridge late in Frend's story, but he entered Jesus College with a keen interest in theological matters. Impressed with Frend's intelligence, passion, and arguments, he attended his trial, recited to gathered students what he heard said on both sides, and embraced many of Frend's unitarian arguments. As is well known, Coleridge's lectures and writings between 1794 and 1805, before he experienced his reconversion to the established trinitarian church in Malta, echo many of Frend's and other dissenters' claims about society, government, and religious belief. During this time, Southey's Oxford was relatively quiet politically, but he had already had occasion to challenge religious and academic authority at Westminster. In No. V of *The Flagellant* he had called on 'all doctors, reverends, and plain

---

[96] Gascoigne, p. 188.
[97] Roe, *Wordsworth and Coleridge*, p. 132.
[98] *Prelude*, 1805, p. 406, ll. 889–900.

masters' to recognise that 'there is but one God'.[99] The letters Southey wrote after Vincent expelled him show that he had already decided for himself that 'church and state are rotten at the heart' and 'deserved to be cast down'.[100] He even travelled to Cambridge in 1793 to watch part of Frend's trial. Inspired in part by their university experiences and Frend's arguments and activism, when these two undergraduates met in the summer of 1794 they excitedly and idealistically rehearsed many of Frend's ideas and explored republicanism, free thought, and Unitarianism for themselves. Together they dreamed of Pantisocracy and imagined a life of aspheterism. Both young men were also building their literary portfolios. Southey had completed most of *Joan of Arc*. He had also written *The Botany Bay Eclogues*. He and Lovell finished *Poems by Bion and Moschus*, and he was working on the verse tragedy of Wat Tyler. Between 1789 and 1794 Coleridge had composed sonnets such as 'To the Autumn Moon', 'Pain', 'On Quitting School for College', Genevieve', and 'To the River Otter'. He had produced an award-winning 25-stanza ode on the slave trade, 'Monody on the Death of Chatterton', and 'Songs of the Pixies', with its interesting prose preface. He had published 'To Fortune' in the *Morning Chronicle* and began keeping his famous notebooks. In no less than two days, the two new friends co-wrote their dramatic poem *The Fall of Robespierre*, which was published by the *Cambridge Intelligencer*, the same periodical that had published Frend's documents and story. There can be little doubt that Roe is right to say that Frend provided these idealistic undergraduates a radical model with whom they could identify.[101] But, perhaps more significantly, the Frend affair had given Southey and Coleridge the final reason they needed to quit their universities. Southey badly wanted to get married. Coleridge found college life too expensive and full of temptations he rightly feared. Both recognised in their openness to Frend's Unitarian arguments that they could not in good conscience become Anglican clergymen. With that realisation, they found honourable grounds for leaving their universities. It is noteworthy, however, that though this affair led to their rejection of Cambridge and Oxford, their subsequent writing careers showed they were moulded by the social, religious, and educational training they received there and that in later years they both recognised the value of these institutions. In 1820, seven years after being named poet laureate, Southey returned to Oxford to receive an honorary degree (along with Wellington). He dined with the vice chancellor at Brasenose and was feted at a dinner at Balliol. Coleridge returned to Jesus in 1833 for the meeting of the British Association for the Advancement of Science and spent much of his later career as a freelance educator. By their middle age, both

---

[99] Robert Southey, 'No. V', pp. 88–89.
[100] CLRS, Pt 1, #12.
[101] Roe, *Wordsworth and Coleridge*, p. 35.

Educating the Romantic Poets

men, and Wordsworth too, had come to appreciate what they had learned at their universities. Moreover, they demonstrated in all that they published how well trained they had been both there and at their grammar schools for the writerly lives they chose.

Chapter Twelve

Conclusions

... and we will teach them how.

William Wordsworth, *The Prelude*

The question that launched this book is 'Why did so many writers of true importance and originality emerge in the Romantic period?' It seemed obvious to me that their formal schooling must have had something to do with this, but for two centuries scholars and historians have dismissed as ineffective and retrograde the grammar schools and colleges of Oxford and Cambridge that these writers attended. It is true that these institutions excluded women and the working classes, that they were expensive and classist, and that they did not teach all of the 'modern' subjects. Boys were caned, a few headmasters were tyrannical, and some university educators were lazy and/or bibulous. Nevertheless, writers trained in these schools were some of the most skilled, innovative, and productive in English literary history. As I studied the curriculum, pedagogies, routines, and lives of the men who worked in the Anglo-classical academy, it became clear that the criticisms trumpeted so memorably in the nineteenth century by the *Edinburgh Review* and by most commentators ever since were hardly the whole story of education in these institutions. While there can be no doubt that the Anglo-classical educators and their programme were not without flaws, much of what they taught and asked students to do was effective, especially for that of poets. Indeed, young men wanting to become writers in Georgian England and who had the privilege of being trained in the Anglo-classical academy had many more opportunities than most modern students do to build the literary knowledge and compositions skills that can lead to successful writing careers.

Among the learning outcomes this programme made possible were rich Latinate vocabularies, powerful and well-stocked memories, polished grammar and sentence skills, familiarity with a wide range of literary genres and models, appreciation of the uses and power of prosody, and years of experience putting pen to paper. Anglo-classical pedagogies trained students to endure the 'boring but important work' that writing always involves. Most noteworthy is how carefully students were asked, from their earliest school days, to hear the melodies and rhythms of language and to craft metrical verse. By the time these young men left university they were well on their way towards the Gladwellian marker of 10,000 hours of practice necessary to achieve expertise.[1] I suspect, as well, that by teaching classical fables and myth the schools spurred boy's fancy; and that by inviting older students to consider metaphysical beliefs sanctioned by the Anglican church their imaginative faculty was stimulated. Finally, being members, however briefly, of the Anglo-classical academy and the Republic of Letters over which it held sway was an internationally respected credential, the possession of which imparted a measure of confidence and even audacity that not a few young Romantic writers displayed.

The experience of living and learning in the little worlds of the Georgian boarding schools and university colleges explains another phenomenon of Romantic literary history—the tendency of writers to gather as adults in small coenobitic communities where they talked, read, and wrote together. These 'monastic' gatherings—of Wordsworth and Coleridge in their great decade from 1797 to 1807, of Byron and Shelley during their European travels, and of the 'Lakers' from time to time later in life—generated some of the most important literary works of the era. Jessica Fay has identified 'monastic inheritances' in Wordsworth's poetry from 1806 to 1822 and asserts that these writings demonstrate a persistent response 'to the cultural and material remains—the routines and structure, the landscapes and architecture—of the monastic system'.[2] She further argues that 'such sites become palimpsests of collective identity; centuries of worship in these places produces a spiritual legacy that is inherited and enriched by successive generations and that creates a sense of local attachment and transhistorical community'.[3] With similar confidence, I can assert that the 'monastic remains' evident in Wordsworth's and other Romantics' work are also legacies of years spent in Anglo-classical boarding schools and colleges at Oxford and Cambridge. Thomas Arnold explains the effect of this experience:

> There is ... something very ennobling in being connected with an establishment at once ancient and magnificent, where all about us, and

---

[1] Popularised in Gladwell's *Outliers, the Story of Success*.
[2] Fay, p. 3.
[3] Fay, p. 2.

Conclusions

all the associations belonging to the objects around us, should be great, splendid, and elevating. What an individual ought and often does derive from the feeling that he is born of an old and illustrious race, from being familiar from his childhood with the walls and trees which speak of the past no less than of the present and make both full of images of greatness; this, in an inferior degree, belongs to every member of an ancient and celebrated place of education.[4]

Yet another contribution to the writing careers of the Romantic age was the way in which these schools and university colleges provided a unique period of safety and relative quiet for the young Romantics. They continued training them according to classical and Anglican orthodoxies while the larger world was reeling into political and religious upheavals and large-scale war. The dynamic tensions of these contrary factors—orthodoxy and its opposites; peace and turbulence—help to explain how these two generations of writers developed their sometimes contradictory political views, when they developed them, and why certain poets entertained ambitions to be labourers toward a day of firmer trust. In particular, the older Romantics' turn to Anglican apologetics and English nationalism, which so annoyed Byron and Shelley and which has seemed so uninteresting to modern critics, might now be seen as less of a disappointing defection from more idealistic philosophies. It seems more like a genuine response to a long-established cultural through-line of nineteenth-century English life, one into which they had been carefully initiated at school and university. The longer-lived Romantics' religiously conservative turn was also an understandable response to personal tragedies and midlife responsibilities. Moreover, as Fulford has pointed out, it was also a calculated, practical move on the part of serious, professional writers to both revise their public reputations and adapt to the literary marketplace.

An important by-product of the Anglo-classical academic tradition that should not be ignored was its provision of an audience that was well trained as knowledgeable and careful readers of verse. Many of the men who consumed writing in English in the Romantic period were very familiar with classical and biblical literature and had been taught certain long-accepted standards and expectations of poetry, history, philosophy, and drama. Wordsworth and Coleridge acknowledged as much when they felt it necessary to write a preface explaining the reasoning behind their 'experiments' in *Lyrical Ballads*. Later in life, rather than working against that current, Wordsworth endeavoured to accommodate the enduring taste of these readers using classical forms, Latinate diction, more conservative topics, and 'a tougher, more stoical, more traditional style'.[5] Hence,

---

[4] Qtd in Stanley, vol. 1, pp. 95–96.
[5] Fulford, *Wordsworth's Poetry*, p. 1.

275

Educating the Romantic Poets

he turned from lyrics to dialogues, narrative and epic forms, inscriptions, and memorial verse. That the three longest-living male poets—Coleridge, Southey, and Wordsworth—crafted verse, essays, histories, and Christian apologetics in forms that were more familiar and likely to please this audience was not necessarily an abandonment of their early ambitions. They were still 'men speaking to men' who embraced a duty to give 'immediate pleasure to a human Being possessed of that information which may be expected from him'.[6] Abandoning the audacious ambition of binding 'together by passion and knowledge the vast empire of human society', they chose instead to 'teach' and 'instruct' their readers.[7] Older, battered by life and public opinion, they recognised more realistically what they could 'expect' from their audience. Recalling the principle of *kairos* from their early rhetoric training, they published more dignified and impersonal works that still offered 'Redemption' and 'Reconciliation' but that did so by invoking the audience's English history and alliance with the 'true Religion' of the national church.[8] The result was works such as *The Excursion, Ecclesiastical Sketches, Sir Thomas More: Or, Colloquies on the Progress and Prospects of Society, The Book of the Church, Aids to Reflection,* and *On the Constitution of Church and State*. Understanding these writers' education, and that of many in their audience, helps to explain this turn and these works and invites more enthusiastic scholarly investigation of them. Fulford has started this effort, showing how Wordsworth's later works were still remarkably innovative and founded on the 'historicization and monumentalization of art'.[9] He quotes these remarkable lines to illustrate this point:

> And thus a Structure potent to enchain
> The eye of Wonder rose in this fair Isle;
> Not built with calculations nice and vain
> But in mysterious Nature's boldest style,
> Yet orderly as some basaltic Pile
> That steadfastly repels the fretful main.[10]

Besides the Romantics' remarkable training in verse composition, a practice that would eventually be abandoned in the Victorian period,[11] two other

[6] WWMW, Preface to *Lyrical Ballads*, pp. 603, 605.
[7] WWMW, Preface to *Lyrical Ballads*, p. 606.
[8] CLSTC, IV, pp. 574–575.
[9] Fulford, *Wordsworth's Poetry*, p. 238.
[10] Jackson, *Sonnet Series*.
[11] In the nineteenth century schools and universities began moving classics and poetry instruction aside to make space for modern subjects, especially the natural sciences. A study of the effects of these changes upon Victorian literature is beyond the scope of this book.

Conclusions

aspects of Anglo-classical education stand out. The first is the dailiness of religious life at both the schools and colleges and how familiar students were with scripture. This phenomenon helps to explain certain Romantics' turn toward religious conviction and conservative politics. As David Craig has argued with regard to Southey,[12] and Ryan has explained generally with regard to the Romantics' 'reformation', religion is a key to the inward consistency of many Romantic poets' thought. The information in this book about Coleridge's language training, daily prayer in school and college, and study of theology and church history should be especially helpful for Coleridge scholars. It supplies further support, for example, of Jeffrey Barbeau's claim in *Coleridge, the Bible, and Religion* (2008) that 'Coleridge was among the most knowledgeable biblical scholars in all of England during the early nineteenth century'; and it also supports his claim that Coleridge's lifetime of theological studies—including Latin, Greek, and Hebrew—proves that he was more focused and methodical than his poetical endeavours have led most scholars to believe.[13] The regimen of daily life in the Anglo-classical academy, where students spent time every day with clergymen, praying and studying church history and scripture, also adds important contexts and colour to Wordsworth's concept of the poet as pastor in his early poetry and to his playing the role of history teacher and advocate of the Anglican community in his later sonnet sequences, such as *Ecclesiastical Sketches*. Pairing this educational history with what we have already learned about Wordsworth's sonnets in studies by Fay, Frey, Easterlin, and Tomko can add even more to our understanding of Wordsworth's mature thought and aesthetics.[14] It is my hope that this book might also spark new research into the original texts, schoolbooks, sermons, commentaries, and devotional works that the Romantics read in their schools and universities. Studies of the clergymen who taught there, the architecture of the chapels in which they worshipped there, and the music they heard or sang in services are also areas ripe for more study by literary scholars of the period.

Finally, the story told here is a reminder that the teaching profession in the Romantics' day, allied as it was in the period with the national Church, was more widely respected than it is in modern times. This helps to explain why the Romantics often figured the poet as an educator and behaved as such in their own lives. The account in this book of how the Anglo-classical academies functioned to keep youngsters steady and focused on their learning in that most revolutionary of times helps to explain why many in Wordsworth's and Byron's generations manifested an enduring interest in education for the good not only of their own children but also of the nation. Their advocacy of national

---

[12] Craig, p. 205.
[13] Barbeau, *Religion in Romantic England*, p. 161. See also King.
[14] See Frey; Easterlin; Tomko.

education and the educative impulse in so many of their published works was, of course, fed by the Enlightenment and the expectations all had of the rising modern sciences, but it was also fostered by the grammar schools' and colleges' ancient traditions and practices that honoured learning and literature. The satire of Byron, the journalism of Coleridge and Southey, the histories of Southey, Wordsworth's *Excursion*, and the writings of women such as Mary Wollstonecraft and Mary Shelley, who knew about, but were excluded from, the Anglo-classical academy, all spoke of or advocated education. Moreover, many of these writers assumed the role of teacher or tutor and leaned into the work of guiding their readers and the nation as their own clergyman–teachers had done. Finally, it is no accident that Wordsworth concludes *The Prelude* with educative promises. Indeed, given the nature of his academic training, Wordsworth's famous declarations at the conclusion of *The Prelude* take on new meaning as well.[15] Saying that he and Coleridge find 'solace in what they have learnt to know',[16] he vows to work towards the 'deliverance' of people whom he fears are once again sinking into 'servitude'. These two friends are, he says, 'Prophets of Nature', who have been 'sanctified' in this role by their ability to 'reason' and by their 'faith'.[17] Finally, he vows that 'we will teach' others to love 'what we have loved', and

> Instruct them how the mind of man becomes
> A thousand times more beautiful than the earth
> On which he dwells ...
> ... [and] is itself
> Of quality and fabric more divine.[18]

Alongside these lines' oft-noticed respect for the natural world and claim to vatic authority lie quietly but unmistakably the lessons of the Anglo-classical education that both men received, with its daily emphasis upon faith as well as reason and their memories of the benevolent, uplifting, and empowering roles their teachers played in shaping their lives. Above all, it was in that academy that they first recognised 'the inherent and indestructible qualities of the human mind'.[19]

---

[15] In the 1805 edition he writes that that 'solace' is found in the knowledge 'which we have', p. 482, l. 436. In 1850 he acknowledges the agency of his teachers using the word 'learnt', p. 483, l. 440.

[16] *Prelude*, 1850, p. 483, ll. 445, 437.

[17] *Prelude*, 1850, p. 483, ll. 446, 447–448. In the 1805 edition he writes 'reason and truth', p. 482, l. 444.

[18] *Prelude*, 1850, p. 483, ll. 440–456.

[19] WWMW, Preface to *LB*, p. 600.

Works Cited

Adams, Matthew. *Teaching Classics in English Schools, 1500–1840*. Cambridge Scholars Publishing, 2015.
Aldrich, H. *The Rudiments of the Art of Logic with Explanatory Notes to Which Are Added Questions for Examination*. A new edition edited by J. Vincent. 1823.
Allan, George A. T. *Christ's Hospital*. Ian Allan Ltd, 1949.
Allen, Guy. 'The "Good Enough" Teacher and the Authentic Student'. *Pedagogy of Becoming*, edited by John Mills, Rodopi, 2002, pp. 143–176.
Allestree, Richard (attributed to). *The Whole Duty of Man*. R. Norton, 1682.
Anonymous. *An Introduction to Construing and Parsing of Latin Adapted to the Eton Grammar*. Wrexham, 1800.
—. 'Article I. *Reflexions on the Decline of Science in England, and on Some of Its Causes*. By Charles Babbage, Esq. Lucasian Professor of Mathematics at the University of Cambridge'. *Quarterly Review*, vol. 42, no. 86, 1830, pp. 305–342.
—. *Appendix to the Eton Latin Grammar*. J. Hamilton and Co., 1797.
—. 'Examination Questions in Criticism and History 1–66 and Grammar'. The Banks, Hudson, and Challis Papers, XVIII Century (1791–1793). Wren Library, Trinity College, Cambridge University.
—. *Gradus At Cantabrigiam: Or, a Dictionary of Terms, Academical and Colloquial, Or Cant, Which Are Used at the University of Cambridge …* W. J. and J. Richardson, 1803.
—. 'The King of Clubs:—an Account of the Proceedings Which Led to the Publication of "the Etonian"'. *The Etonian*, vol. 1, no. 1, 1820, pp. 3–31.
— *Preces Quotidianae in Usum Scholar Collegii Regalis Apud Etonam*. Thomas Pote, 1769 (originally 1444).
—. *Questions on Aldrich's Logic with Reference to the Most Popular Treatises*. 2nd ed., 1836.

—. 'Review of *The Credibility of Christianity Vindicated, In Answer to Mr. Hume's Objections*'. *The British Critic*, vol. 12, 1798.

—. 'St. Paul's Appositions'. *The Universal Magazine of Knowledge and Pleasure*, 17 March 1768.

Arnold, Thomas. *Sermons*. B. Fellows, 1834.

Ashton, Rosemary. *The Life of Samuel Taylor Coleridge: A Critical Biography*. Blackwell, 1996, 1997.

Austen, Jane. *Persuasion*. Norton Critical Edition, W. W. Norton & Company, 2013.

Babbage, Charles. *Reflections on the Decline of Science in England and on Some of Its Causes*. Augustus M. Kelley Publishers, 1830.

Barbeau, Jeffrey, editor. *The Cambridge Companion to British Romanticism and Religion*. Cambridge University Press, 2021.

—. *Coleridge, The Bible, and Religion*. Palgrave Macmillan, 2008.

—. *Religion in Romantic England: An Anthology of Primary Sources*. Baylor University Press, 2018.

Beattie, James. *Essays on Poetry and Music, as They Affect the Mind; On Laughter and Ludicrous Composition; And on the Utility of Classical Learning*. William Creech, 1776.

Bettelheim, Bruno. *A Good Enough Parent*. Thames & Hudson, 1987.

Birch, Dinah. *Our Victorian Education*. Blackwell, 2007.

Bowen, James. 'Education, Ideology and the Ruling Class: Hellenism and English Public Schools in the Nineteenth Century'. *Rediscovering Hellenism: The Hellenic Inheritance and the English Imagination*, edited by G. W. Clarke, Cambridge University Press, 1989, pp. 161–185.

Briggs, Asa. 'Oxford and its Critics'. *The History of the University of Oxford*, vol. 6, Nineteenth-Century Oxford. Part 1, edited by M. G. Brock and M. C. Curthoys, Oxford University Press, 1997, pp. 134–145.

Brock, M. G., and M. C. Curthoys, editors. *The History of the University of Oxford*, vol. 7, Nineteenth-Century Oxford. Part 1. Clarendon Press, 1998.

—. *The History of the University of Oxford*, vol. 7, Nineteenth-Century Oxford. Part 2. Clarendon Press, 2000.

Brockliss, I. W. B. *The University of Oxford: A History*. Oxford University Press, 2016.

Brown, Peter C., Henry L. Roediger III, and Mark McDaniel. *Make It Stick: The Science of Successful Learning*. Harvard University Press, 2014.

Butler, Marilyn. *Romantics, Rebels and Reactionaries: English Literature and Its Background 1760–1830*. Oxford University Press, 1985.

Byron, Lord. 'Harrow on the Hill, Lines Written beneath an Elm in the Churchyard of Harrow'. https://www.bartleby.com/270/1/190.html. Accessed 4 April 2023.

—. *Hours of Idleness*. *The Works of Lord Byron*, vol. 5. Murray, 1831.

Carlisle, Nicholas. *A Concise Description of the Endowed Grammar Schools of England and Wales*. 2 vols. Baldwin, Craddock, and Joy, 1818.

Chandos, John. *Boys Together: English Public Schools 1800–1864*. Hutchinson and Co., 1984.

Chapman, George. *A Treatise on Education, with a Sketch of the Author's Method*. 3rd, enlarged ed., London, 1784.

Chinnery, George. 'The Correspondence of G. R. Chinnery'. Christ Church College Archives, Oxford, 1808–11. MA xlviii.a.42a-55.

Clancey, Richard. *Wordsworth's Classical Undersong: Education, Rhetoric, and Poetic Truth*. St Martin's Press, Palgrave, 2000.

Clarke, M. L. *Classical Education in Britain 1500–1900*. Cambridge University Press, 1959.

Clerke, Agnes Mary. 'Samuel Vince'. *Dictionary of National Biography*. England, Smith and Elder, 1885–1900.

Coleridge, Edward. 'Autobiography, Comments Upon His Life at Eton College'. Eton College Archives, British Library Manuscript Collection (Add MS 47555 NRA 20966), 1876.

Coleridge, Samuel Taylor. 'Biographia Literaria'. *Samuel Taylor Coleridge*, edited by H. J. Jackson, Oxford University Press, 1985, pp. 155–482.

Copleston, Edward. *A Reply to the Calumnies against Oxford by the Edinburgh Review Containing an Account of the Studies Pursued at That University*. For the Author, 1810.

Copleston, William James. *Memoir of Edward Copleston, D.D. Bishop of Llandaff with Selections from His Diary and Correspondence, Etc.* John W. Parker and Son, 1851.

Cowie, Leonard W. 'Charles Simeon'. *Dictionary of National Biography*, vol. 18. England, Smith Elder, 1903, pp. 255–257.

Cozolino, Louis. *The Social Neuroscience of Education: Optimizing Attachment and Learning in the Classroom*. W. W. Norton, 2013.

Craig, David. *Robert Southey and Romantic Apostasy: Political Argument in Britain, 1780–1840*. Boydell Press, 2007.

Croft, George. *A Plan of Education Delineated and Vindicated: To Which Are Added a Letter to a Young Gentleman Designed for the University and for Holy Orders. And a Short Dissertation Upon the Stated Provision and Reasonable Expectations of Publick Teachers*. Wolverhampton, 1784.

Cummings, Brian, editor. *The Book of Common Prayer: The Texts of 1549, 1559, and 1662*. Oxford University Press, 2011.

Curran, Stuart. *Poetic Form and British Romanticism*. Oxford University Press, 1986.

Curthoys, Judith. *The Cardinal's College: Christ Church, Chapter and Verse*. Profile Books, 2012.

Curtis, Jared, editor. *The Fenwick Notes of William Wordsworth*. Bristol Classic Press, 1993.

Darwall-Smith, Robin, and Peregrine Horder, editors. *The Unloved Century: Georgian Oxford Reassessed*. Oxford University Press, 2022.

Davey, Natalie. 'The Good Enough Teacher'. *The Journal of the Assembly for Expanded Perspectives on Learning*, vol. 25, no. 7, 2020, pp. 157–172.

Davies, Horton. *Worship and Theology in England from Watts and Wesley to Martineau, 1690–1900*. Princeton University Press, 1961.

Deboo, James. *The Anglican Wordsworth: Broadening a Religious Tradition*. University of Lancaster Press, 2005.

De Selincourt, Ernest, editor. *The Letters of William and Dorothy Wordsworth: The Later Years*. Clarendon, 1939.

De Selincourt, Ernest, and Mary Moorman, editors. *The Letters of William and Dorothy Wordsworth: The Middle Years. Part I: 1806–1811*. 2nd ed., Clarendon, 1969–1970.

Dictionary of National Biography. England, Smith Elder, 1903.

Douglas, Wallace W. 'Review: *Wordsworth's Cambridge Education* by Ben Ross Schneider'. *The Journal of English and Germanic Philology*, vol. 58, no. 2, 1959, pp. 302–304.

Duguid, Timothy. *Metrical Psalmody in Print and Practice: English 'Singing Psalms' and Scottish 'Psalm Buiks' C. 1547–1640*. Ashgate, 2014.

Duncombe, John. *An Evening Contemplation in a College, Being a Parody on the 'Elegy in a Country Churchyard'*. Dodridge, 1753.

Dyer, George. *History of the University and Colleges of Cambridge Including Notices Relating to the Founders and Eminent Men*. 2 vols. Longman, Hurst, Rees, Orme, and Brown, 1814.

Easterlin, Nancy. *Wordsworth and the Question of Romantic Religion*. Bucknell University Press, 1998.

Edinburgh Review. 'Art. I. *Traite de Mechanique Celeste*. Par P. S. La Place, Membre de l'Institute National de France, et du Bureau des Longitudes. Paris'. *Edinburgh Review*, vol. 11, no. 22, 1808, pp. 249–284.

—. 'Art. III. A Latin Grammar for Use at Westminster School'. *Edinburgh Review*, vol. 53, no. 105, 1831, pp. 64–82.

—. 'Art. III. *Essays on Professional Education* by R. L. Edgeworth, Esq., F.R.S'. *Edinburgh Review*, vol. 15, no. 29, 1809–10, pp. 40–53.

—. 'Art. III. *The Proposals for Founding an University in London Considered*. By an Oxonian'. *Edinburgh Review*, vol. 42, no. 84, 1825, pp. 346–367.

—. 'Art. III. The Public Schools of England—Eton'. *Edinburgh Review*, vol. 51, no. 101, 1830, pp. 65–80.

—. 'Art. III. The Public Schools of England—Westminster and Eton'. *Edinburgh Review*, vol. 53, no. 105, 1831, pp. 64–82.

—. 'Art. VI. Addenda ad Corpus Statutorum Universitatis Oxoniensis'. *Edinburgh Review*, vol. 53, no. 106, 1831, pp. 384–427.

—. 'Art. VII. A Reply to the Calumnies of the *Edinburgh Review* against Oxford; Containing an Account of the Studies Pursued in That University'. *Edinburgh Review*, vol. 16, no. 31, 1810, pp. 158–187.

—. 'Art. X. *Strabonis Rerum Geographicarum Libri XVII &C juxta Ed Amstelodamensem. Codicum MSS. Collationem, Annotationes, Tabulas Geographicas Adjecit Thomas Falconer olim e Coll. Aenei Nasi, Oxon*'. *Edinburgh Review*, vol. 14, no. 28, 1809, pp. 429–441.

—. 'Article III. *Remarks on the System of Education in Public Schools*'. *Edinburgh Review*, vol. 16, no. 32, 1810, pp. 326–334.

—. 'Article VI. 1. *Addenda Ad Corpus Statutorum Universitatis Oxoniensis*. 2. *The Oxford University Calendar, for 1829*'. *Edinburgh Review*, vol. 53, no. 106, 1831, pp. 384–427.

—. 'Article VII. *Thoughts on the Study of Mathematics as a Part of a Liberal Education. By the Rev. William Whewell, M.A. Fellow and Tutor of Trinity College, Cambridge*'. *Edinburgh Review*, vol. 62, no. 126, 1836, pp. 409–455.

—. 'Article IX. *The Legality of the Present Academical System of the University of Oxford. Asserted against the New Calumnies of the Edinburgh Review. By a Member of Convocation*'. *Edinburgh Review*, vol. 54, no. 108, 1831, pp. 478–504.

Elledge, Paul. *Lord Byron at Harrow School*. Johns Hopkins University Press, 2000.

Falkus, Malcolm. 'Fagging and Boy Government'. *The World of the Public School*, edited by G. M., Fraser, Weidenfeld & Nicholson Ltd, 1977, pp. 56–78.

Fay, Jessica. *Wordsworth's Monastic Inheritance: Poetry, Place, and the Sense of Community*. Oxford University Press, 2018.

Fraser, G. M., editor. *The World of the Public School*. Weidenfeld & Nicholson Ltd, 1977.

Frend, William. *An Address to the Members of the Church of England, and to Protestant Trinitarians in General, Exhorting Them to Turn from the False Worship of Three Persons to the Worship of the One True God*. Joseph Johnson, 1788.

—. *Peace and Union Recommended to the Associated Bodies of Republicans and Anti-Republicans*. For the Author, 1793.

—. *Thoughts on Subscription to Religious Tests Particularly That Required by the University of Cambridge*. Joseph Johnson, 1788.

Frey, Anne. *British State Romanticism: Authorship, Agency, and Bureaucratic Nationalism*. Stanford University Press, 2010.

Fulford, Timothy. *The Late Poetry of the Lake Poets: Romanticism Revised*. Cambridge University Press, 2013.

—. *Wordsworth's Poetry, 1815–1845*. University of Pennsylvania Press, 2019.

Fulford, Timothy, and Lynda Pratt, editors. *Robert Southey: Later Poetical Works 1811–1832*. Pickering and Chatto, 2012.

Fulford, Tim, Ian Packer, and Lynda Pratt. 'The Collected Letters of Robert Southey, Part Five: 1816–1818'. 2016. http://romantic-circles.org/editions/southey_letters/Part_Five/index.html. Accessed 4 April 2023.

Gascoigne, John. *Cambridge in the Age of the Enlightenment: Science, Religion and Politics from the Restoration to the French Revolution*. Cambridge University Press, 1989.

Gates, Barbara T. 'Wordsworth's Mirror of Morality: Distortions of Church History'. *The Wordsworth Circle*, vol. 12, no. 2, 1981, pp. 129–132.

Gill, Stephen. *William Wordsworth: A Life*. 2nd ed., Oxford University Press, 2020.

—, editor. *William Wordsworth: The Major Works*. Oxford University Press, 1984.

Gladwell, Malcolm. *Outliers: The Story of Success*. Little, Brown and Company, 2008.

Goldhill, Simon. 'Cultural History and Aesthetics: Why Kant Is No Place to Start Reception Studies'. *Theorizing Performance: Greek Drama, Cultural History and Critical Practice*, edited by E. Hall and S. Harrop, Duckworth, 2010, pp. 56–70.

—. *The Poet's Voice: Essays on Poetics and Greek Literature*. Cambridge University Press, 2011.

—. *Victorian Culture and Classical Antiquity: Art, Opera, Fiction, and the Proclamation of Modernity*. Princeton University Press, 2011.

Graham, John, George Peacock, John Herschel, John Romilly, and Adam Sedgwick. *Cambridge University Commission. Report of Her Majesty's Commissioners Appointed to Inquire into the State, Discipline, Studies, and Revenues of the University and Colleges of Cambridge: Together with the Evidence, and an Appendix*. W. Clowes and Sons, 1852.

Grant, William. 'Letters from Rugby School'. Temple Reading Room, Rugby School, 1791–96.

Graver, Bruce. 'Classical Inheritances'. *Romanticism: An Oxford Guide*, edited by Nicholas Roe, Oxford University Press, 2005, pp. 38–48.

—. '"Honourable Toil", the Georgic Ethic of "Prelude I"'. *Studies in Philology*, vol. 92, no. 3, 1995, pp. 346–360.

—. 'Wordsworth and the Language of Epic: The Translation of the *Aeneid*'. *Studies in Philology*, vol. 83, no. 3, 1986, pp. 261–285.

—. 'Wordsworth's Georgic Beginnings'. *Texas Studies in Literature and Language*, vol. 33, no. 2, 1991, pp. 137–159.

—. 'Wordsworth's Translations from Latin Poetry'. PhD thesis, University of North Carolina, 1983.

Green, V. H. H. 'Religion in the Colleges 1715–1800'. *The History of the University of Oxford*, vol. 5, The Eighteenth Century, edited by L. S. Sutherland and L. G. Mitchell, Clarendon, 1986, pp. 425–467.

—. 'The University and Social Life'. In *The History of the University of Oxford*, vol. 5, The Eighteenth Century, edited by L. S. Sutherland and L. G. Mitchell, Clarendon, 1986, pp. 309–358.

Gregory, Jeremy. 'The Prayer Book and the Parish Church: From the Restoration to the Oxford Movement'. *The Oxford Guide to the Book of Common Prayer*, edited by Charles Heffling and Cynthia Shattuck, Oxford University Press, 2006, pp. 93–105.

Griggs, Earl Leslie, editor. *Collected Letters of Samuel Taylor Coleridge*, vol. 1, 1785–1800. Clarendon, 1956.

Grildrig, Solomon. *The Miniature, a Periodical Paper*. Windsor, 1802.

Gunning, Henry. *Reminiscences of the University, Town, and County of Cambridge, from the Year 1780*. George Bell, 1854.

Hainton, Raymonde, and Godfrey Hainton. *The Unknown Coleridge: The Life and Times of Derwent Coleridge 1800–1883*. Janus Publishing Co., 1996.

Hall, E., and S. Harrop, editors. *Theorizing Performance: Greek Drama, Cultural History and Critical Practice*. Duckworth, 2010.

Halmi, Nicholas, P. Magnuson, and Raimonda Modiano, editors. *Coleridge's Poetry and Prose*. W. W. Norton & Company, 2004.

Hans, Nicholas. *New Trends in Education in the Eighteenth Century*. Routledge and Kegan Paul, 1951, 1966.

Hawtrey, Edward Craven. *Sermons and Lectures Delivered in the Eton College Chapel: In the Years 1848–1849*. Kessinger Legacy Reprints, 1849 (reprint 2010).

Hazlitt, William. *The Spirit of the Age*. Project Gutenberg, 2004. https://www.gutenberg.org/cache/epub/11068/pg11068.html. Accessed 4 April 2023.

Heath, Chip, and Dan Heath. *The Power of Moments*. Simon and Schuster, 2017.

Heberden, William. *Strictures Upon the Discipline of the University of Cambridge, Addressed to the Senate*. W. H. Lunn, 1792, 1794.

Hefling, Charles, and Cynthia Shattuck, editors. *The Oxford Guide to the Book of Common Prayer*. Oxford University Press, 2006.

Heinzelman, Kurt. 'Roman Georgic in the Georgian Age: A Theory of Romantic Genre'. *Texas Studies in Literature and Language*, vol. 33, no. 2, 1991, pp. 182–214.

Heywood, James, editor. *Oxford University Statutes Translated in 1843 by the Late G. R. M. Ward*. William Pickering, 1851.

Hill, George Birkbeck, editor. *Boswell's Life of Samuel Johnson*. 6 vols, vol. 1. Bigelow, Brown, and Co., 1799.

Hinds, Stanley, Archibald C. Tait, Francis Jeune, Henry G. Liddell, John L. Dampier, Baden Powell, and George Henry Sacheverell Johnson. *Oxford University Commission. Report of Her Majesty's Commissioners Appointed to Inquire into the State, Discipline, Studies, and Revenues of the University and Colleges of Oxford: Together with the Evidence, and an Appendix*. W. Clowes and Son, 1852.

Hiscock, Matthew. 'Reception Theory, New Humanism, and T. S. Eliot'. *Classical Receptions Journal*, vol. 12, no. 3, 2020, pp. 323–339.

Holmes, Richard. *Shelley: The Pursuit*. Weidenfeld and Nicholson, 1974.

Hopkins, David, and Charles Martindale, editors. *The Oxford History of Classical Reception in English Literature*, vol. 3, 1660–1790. Oxford University Press, 2012.

Howe, Emily, Henrietta McBurney, and David Park. *The Wall Paintings of Eton College*. Scala Arts and Heritage Publishers, 2012.

Hutchinson, Thomas, editor. *The Poetical Works of Wordsworth: With Introduction and Notes*. New edition, revised by Ernest De Selincourt. Oxford University Press, 1974 [1904].

Jackson, Geoffrey, editor. *Sonnet Series and Itinerary Poems, 1820–1845 by William Wordsworth*. Cornell University Press, 2004.

Jackson, H. L., editor. *Samuel Taylor Coleridge*. Oxford University Press, 1985.

Jeffrey, Francis. 'Art. I. *The Excursion* Being a Portion of *the Recluse* a Poem by William Wordsworth'. *Edinburgh Review*, no. 47, November 1814, pp. 1–30.

—. 'Art. I. *Madoc, a Poem: In Two Parts*. By Robert Southey'. *Edinburgh Review*, vol. 7, no. 13, 1805–10, pp. 1–21.

—. 'Art. VIII. *Thalaba, the Destroyer: A Metrical Romance* by Robert Southey'. *Edinburgh Review*, vol. 1, no. 1, 1802–10, pp. 63–83.

—. 'Art. XIV. *Poems, in Two Volumes*. By William Wordsworth, Author of the *Lyrical Ballads*'. *Edinburgh Review*, vol. 11, no. 21, 1807–10, pp. 214–231.

Johnston, Kenneth R. *The Hidden Wordsworth: Poet, Lover, Rebel, Spy*. Norton, 1998.

—. *Usual Suspects: Pitt's Reign of Alarm and the Lost Generation of the 1790s*. Oxford University Press, 2013.

Kempis, Thomas à. *Imitation of Christ*. Translated by William Benham. 1653.

Ken, Bishop Thomas. *Manual of Prayers for the Use of the Scholars of Winchester College*. London, 1675.

King, Joshua. 'Chapter 1. Coleridge's *Aids to Reflection*. The Clerisy and a National Spiritual Republic of Letters'. *Imagined Spiritual Communities in Britain's Age of Print*. Ohio State University Press, 2015, pp. 21–56.

Knight, Frida. *University Rebel: The Life of William Frend (1757–1841)*. Victor Gollancz Ltd, 1971.

Knight, William, editor. *The Poetical Works of William Wordsworth*, vol. 5. Macmillan and Co., 1896.

Knox, Vicesimus. *Essays, Moral and Literary by Vicesimus Knox, D.D. ... in Two Volumes*, vol. 1. 14th edn. Dilly, 1823.

—. *Liberal Education: Or, a Practical Treatise on the Methods of Acquiring Useful and Polite Learning*. C. Dilly 1781.

Koelb, Janice Hewlett. *The Poetics of Description: Imagined Places in European Literature*. Palgrave Macmillan, 2006.

Lang, James M. *Small Teaching: Everyday Lessons from the Science of Learning*. Josscy-Bass, 2016.

Lawson, John, and Harold Silver. *A Social History of Education in England*. Methuen, 1973.

Leach, Arthur Francis. *A History of Winchester College*. Duckworth and Co., 1899.

Leedham-Green, Elisabeth. *A Concise History of the University of Cambridge*. Cambridge University Press, 1996.

Lily, William. *A Short Introduction of Grammar Generally to Be Used ... For the Bringing up All Those That Intend to Attain to the Knowledge of the Latin Tongue*. S. Buckley and T. Longman, 1797.

Mackenzie, R. J. 'Public Schools in the Olden Time'. *Littell's Living Age*, vol. 178, no. 2304, 25 August 1888, #2, pp. 495–502.

McGann, J., editor. *Lord Byron: The Complete Works*, vol. 5, *Don Juan*. Clarendon Press, 2008.

—, editor. *Lord Byron: The Major Works including* Don Juan *and* Childe Harold's Pilgrimage. Oxford University Press, 2008.

Mansel, William Lort. 'Memoir and Correspondence of William Lort Mansel'. Wren Library, Trinity College, Cambridge, 1820–21.

Marchand, Leslie A. *Byron: A Biography*. 3 vols. Alfred A. Knopf, 1957.

—, editor. *Byron's Letters and Journals*. 12 vols. Harvard University Press, 1973.

Martindale, Charles. 'Performance, Reception, Aesthetics: Why Reception Studies Need Kant'. *Theorizing Performance: Greek Drama, Cultural History and Critical Practice*, edited by E. Hall and S. Harrop, Duckworth, 2010, pp. 71–84.

Masson, David, editor. *The Collected Writings of Thomas De Quincey*. 14 vols, vol. 10. Black, 1890.

Maxwell-Lyte, H. C. *A History of Eton College 1440–1884*. Macmillan and Co., 1889.

Mayhew, Matthew, Alyssa Rockenbach, Nicholas Bowman, Tricia Seifert, and Gregory Wolniak, with Ernest Pascarella and Patrick Terenzini. *How College Affects Students: 21st Century Evidence That Higher Education Works*, vol. 3. Jossey-Bass, 2016.

The Microcosm, a Periodical Work. Knight, 1786.

Midgley, Graham. *University Life in Eighteenth-Century Oxford*. Yale University Press, 1996.

Milner, John. *An Abstract of Latin Syntax; … To Which Is Added, Prosody, or, the Art of Latin Poetry … for the Use of Schools*. 1743.

Moberly, George. *Sermons, Preached at Winchester College. Second Series. With a Preface on 'Fagging'*. Francis & John Rivington, 1848.

Moore, Thomas. *Letters and Journals of Lord Byron with Notices of His Life*. Spottiswoode, 1830.

Moorman, Mary T. *William Wordsworth: A Biography: Early Years, 1770–1803*. Clarendon, 1957.

—. *William Wordsworth: A Biography: Later Years, 1803–1850*. Clarendon Press, 1965.

Morell, Thomas. *Exempla Minora: Or, New English Examples to Be Rendered into Latin Adapted to the Rules of the Latin Grammar*. T. Pote, 1794.

Morgan, Nathaniel. *Grammaticae Quaestiones: Or a Grammatical Examination, by Question Only: For the Use of Schools; Particularly Those Where the Eton Grammar Is Taught*. S. Hazard, 1794.

Morgan, Victor, Christopher Brooke, and Roger Highfield. *A History of the University of Cambridge 1546–1750*. Cambridge University Press, 2004.

Mullinger, James Bass. *St. John's College*. F. E. Robinson & Co., 1901.

Napleton, John. *Advice to a Student in the University, Concerning the Qualifications and Duties of a Minister of the Gospel in the Church of England*. Fletcher and Hanwell, 1795.

Newbery, John. *Poetry Made Familiar and Easy and Embellished with a Great Variety of Epigrams, Epitaphs, Songs, Odes, Pastorals, & from the Best Authors*. 4th ed., T. Carnan and F. Newbery, 1776.

Newlyn, Lucy. *William and Dorothy Wordsworth: All in Each Other*. Oxford University Press, 2013.

Newman, John Henry. *The Idea of a University Defined and Illustrated*. University of Notre Dame Press, 1852.

Newsome, David. *Godliness and Good Learning*. Cassell and Co., 1961.

Ogilvie, R. M. *Latin and Greek: A History of the Influence of the Classics on English Life from 1600 to 1918*. Archon Books, 1969.

Paley, William. *Natural Theology, or Evidence of the Existence and Attributes of the Deity Collected from the Appearances of Nature*. 7th ed., R. Faulder, 1802, 1804.

—. *The Principles of Moral and Political Philosophy*. Cambridge, 1785.

—. *View of the Evidences of Christianity*. Cambridge, 1794.

Parkin, George R. *Edward Thring, Headmaster of Uppingham School; Life, Diary, Letters*. MacMillan, 1900.

Parsons, Jed. 'A New Approach to the Saturnian Verse and Its Relation to Latin Prosody'. *Transactions of the American Philosophical Association*, vol. 129, 1999, pp. 117–137.

Peck, Tracy. 'Notes on Latin Quantity'. *Transactions of the American Philological Assocation*, vol. 13, 1882, pp. 50–59.

Perrin, William Philip. 'Accounts and Papers of William Philip Perrin'. Christ Church College, Oxford, 1761–65.

Pratt, Lynda, Tim Fulford, and Ian Packer. *The Collected Letters of Robert Southey*. 2009. https://romantic-circles.org/editions/southey_letters. Accessed 4 April 2023.

Priestley, Joseph. *An Essay on a Course of Liberal Education for Civil and Active Life*. London, 1765.

Prins, Yopie. 'Historical Poetics, Dysprosody, and the Science of English Verse'. *PMLA* New Lyric Studies, vol. 123, no. 1, 2008, pp. 129–234.

—. 'Metrical Translation: Nineteenth-Century Homers and the Hexameter Mania'. *Nation, Language and the Ethics of Translation*, edited by Sandra and Michael Wood Berman, Princeton University Press, 2005, pp. 229–256.

Quennell, Peter, editor. *Byron – A Self-Portrait: Letters and Diaries 1798 to 1824*. 2 vols. John Murray, 1950.

Questionist. *Ten Minutes Advice to Freshmen*. J. Archdeacon, Printer to the University, 1785.

Reed, Mark L. *Wordsworth: The Chronology of the Early Years 1770–1799*. Harvard University Press, 1967.

Reiman, Donald, and Sharon Powers, editors. *Shelley's Poetry and Prose*. W. W. Norton & Company, 1977.

Richardson, Alan. *Literature, Education, and Romanticism: Reading as Social Practice, 1780–1832*. Cambridge University Press, 2004.

Robinson, Jeffrey. *Poetic Innovation in Wordsworth 1825–1833: Fibres of These Thoughts*. Anthem Press, 2019.

Roe, Nicholas, editor. *Romanticism: An Oxford Guide*. Oxford University Press, 2005.

—. *Wordsworth and Coleridge: The Radical Years*. 2nd ed., Oxford University Press, 2018.

Ross, Catherine. 'Coleridge's "Eolian Harp"'. *The Explicator*, vol. 60, no. 1, 2002, pp. 17–20.

—. '"Restore Me to Reality": Revisiting the Figure of Pensive Sara in Coleridge's "Eolian Harp"'. *The Coleridge Bulletin* New Series, vol. 23, Winter 2004, pp. 74–82.

Rothblatt, Sheldon. *The Revolution of the Dons: Cambridge and Society in Victorian England*. Cambridge University Press, 1968.

—. *Tradition and Change in English Liberal Education: An Essay in History and Culture*. Faber and Faber, 1976.

Rugby Magazine. 'On Composition'. *Rugby Magazine*, vol. 1, no. 1, 1835, pp. 64–67.

—. 'On the Method of Translation Employed in Rugby School'. *Rugby Magazine*, vol. 1, no. 1, 1835, pp. 29–34.

—. 'The Rugby Debating Society'. *Rugby Magazine*, vol. 2, no. 3, 1836, pp. 230–233.

—. 'School a Little World'. *Rugby Magazine*, vol. 1, no. 2, 1835, pp. 95–105.

—. 'School Society'. *Rugby Magazine*, vol. 1, no. 3, pp. 207–215.

—. 'Some Remarks on the Study of the Classics'. *Rugby Magazine*, vol. 4, no. 4, 1835, pp. 358–370.

Ryan, Robert M. *The Romantic Reformation: Religious Politics and English Literature, 1789–1824*. Cambridge University Press, 1997.

St Clair, William. *The Reading Nation in the Romantic Period*. Cambridge University Press, 2004.

Sargeaunt, John. *Annals of Westminster School*. Methuen, 1898.

Schneider, Ben Ross. *Wordsworth's Cambridge Education*. Cambridge University Press, 1957.

Searby, Peter. *A History of the University of Cambridge*, vol. 3, 1750–1870. Cambridge University Press, 1997.

Shields, Chrispher. 'Aristotle'. *The Stanford Encyclopedia of Philosophy*, edited by Edward N. Zalta. https://plato.stanford.edu/entries/aristotle/. Accessed 4 April 2023.

Simon, Brian. *Studies in the History of Education 1780–1870*. Lawrence & Wishart, 1960.

Slinn, Sara. *The Education of the Anglican Clergy 1780–1839*. Boydell Press, 2017.

Smith, Jonathan. 'The Preachers of Trinity College, Cambridge, 1552–1860: The Use and Abuse of a College Office'. *History of Universities*, edited by Mordechai Feingold, Oxford University Press, 2005, pp. 47–75.

Snyder, Laura J. 'William Whewell'. *Stanford Encyclopedia of Philosophy*, edited by Edward N. Zalta. https://plato.stanford.edu/entries/whewell/. Accessed 4 April 2023.

Southey, Charles Cuthbert, editor. *The Life and Correspondence of Robert Southey*. 6 vols, vol. 1. Longman, Brown, Green, and Longmans, 1849.

Southey, Robert. *Letters from England: By Don Manuel Alvarez Espriella. Translated from the Spanish*. Longman, Hurst, Rees and Orme, 1808.

—. 'No. V'. *The Flagellant*, vol. 1, 29 March 1792, pp. 75–89.

—. editor. *The Remains of Henry Kirke White, of Nottingham, Late of St John's College, Cambridge; with an Account of His Life*. Vernor, Hood, and Sharpe, 1807.

Speck, W. A. *Robert Southey: Entire Man of Letters*. Yale University Press, 2006.

Stephen, Leslie. 'William Whewell'. *Dictionary of National Biography*, vol. 28. England, Smith Elder, 1903, pp. 1365–1374.

Stanley, Arthur P. *The Life and Correspondence of Dr. Arnold*. 2 vols. Ward Lock, 1844.

Stanwood, Paul G. 'The Prayer Book as Literature'. *The Oxford Guide to the Book of Common Prayer*, edited by Charles Hefling, Oxford University Press, 2006, pp. 140–149.

Stevenson, William. *Remarks on the Very Inferior Utility of Classical Learning*. London, 1796.

Stone, Lawrence. 'Literacy and Education in England 1640–1900'. *Past and Present*, vol. 42, 1969, pp. 69–139.

Storey, Mark. *Robert Southey: A Life*. Oxford University Press, 1997.

Storr, Anthony. 'The Individual and the Group'. *The World of the Public School*, edited by G. M. Fraser, Weidenfeld & Nicholson Ltd, 1977, pp. 97–110.

Sutherland, L. S. 'The Curriculum'. *The History of the University of Oxford*, edited by L. S. Sutherland and L. G. Mitchell, Clarendon, 1986, pp. 469–491.

Sutherland, L. S. and L. G. Mitchell, editors. *The History of the University of Oxford*, vol. 5, The Eighteenth Century. Oxford University Press, 1986.

Tatham, Edward. *Oxonia Purgata: A Series of Addresses on the New Discipline*. Oxford, 1807.

Taunton, Lord Henry, *et al.* 'Report of the Commission'. *Schools Inquiry Commission*, London, 1868, pp. 1–661.

Temperley, Nicholas. *The Music of the English Parish Church*. 2 vols, vol. 1. Cambridge University Press, 1979.

Thompson, T. W. *Wordsworth's Hawkshead*. Oxford University Press, 1970.

Thorne, R. G. 'Cambridge University'. *The History of Parliament: The House of Commons 1790–1820*, vol. 1, edited by R. G. Thorne, Boydell & Brewer, 1986, pp. 62–63.

Todhunter, Isaac. *William Whewell: An Account of His Writings, with Selections From His Literary and Scientific Correspondence*. Macmillan and Company, 1876.

Tomko, Michael. 'Superstition, the National Imaginary, and Religious Politics in Wordsworth's "Ecclesiastical Sketches"'. *The Wordsworth Circle*, vol. 39, no. 1/2, 2008, pp. 16–19.

Touchstone, Timothy. 'Prefatory Address'. *The Trifler*, vol. 1, no. 1, 31 May 1788, pp. 1–10.

—. 'Simplicity in Poetry'. *The Trifler*, vol. 1, no. 35, 24 January 1789, pp. 447–469.

Toynbee, William, editor. *The Diaries of William Charles Macready 1833–1851*. Putnam, 1912.

'Trinity College Examinations, Banks, Hodson or Challis Papers XVIIIth Century, Box 1, #30'. Wren Library, Trinity College, Cambridge, 1784–94.

Tyerman, Christopher. *A History of Harrow School 1324–1991*. Oxford University Press, 2000.

Ulmer, William A. *The Christian Wordsworth, 1798–1805: New Perspectives in Critical Thinking*. State University of New York Press, 2001.

Vance, Norman, and Jennifer Wallace. *The Oxford History of Classical Reception in English Literature*, vol. 4, 1790–1890. Oxford University Press, 2015.

Venables, E. 'Herbert Marsh'. *Dictionary of National Biography*, vol. 12. England, Smith Elder, 1903, pp. 1096–1100.

Vincent, William. *A Defence of Public Education*. 3rd ed., London, 1802.

—. 'A Discourse Addressed to the People of Great Britain', edited by The Society for Preserving Liberty and Property Against Republicans and Levellers. London, 1792.

Walker, Micah. 'Psalms, Hymns, and Spiritual Songs: The Influence of Sacred Music in Early British Romantic Poets'. MA thesis, The University of Texas at Tyler, 2020, pp. 1–52.

Ward, G. R. M. *Oxford University Statutes*. William Pickering, 1845.

Ward, W. R. 'Cyril Jackson (1746–1819)'. *Dictionary of National Biography*, vol. 10. England, Smith Elder, 1903, pp. 525–527.

Warwick, Andrew. *Masters of Theory: Cambridge and the Rise of Mathematical Physics*. The University of Chicago Press, 2003.

Whewell, William. *On the Principles of English University Education*. John W. Parker, 1837.

Willis, Judy, and Malana Willis. *Research-Based Strategies to Ignite Student Learning*. Revised and expanded edition, ASCD, 2020.

Winnicott, D. W. *The Child, the Family, and the Outside World*. Penguin, 1991.

Winstanley, D. A. *Unreformed Cambridge*. Cambridge University Press, 1935.

Wood, James. 'Letter Books of James Woods, Tutor and Master, St. John's College, Cambridge'. St John's College Archive, Cambridge, 1808–36.

—. 'Notes on Horace, Sjar/1/3/Wood/I, Box 3, Book 8'. Papers of James Wood, School of Pythagoras, St John's College Archive, Cambridge, 1786–1839.

—. 'Roll of Students at St John's College'. St John's College Archive, Cambridge, 1791.

Wordsworth, Charles. *Annals of My Early Life, 1806–1846: With Occasional Compositions in Latin and English Verse*. 2 vols. London, 1891–93.

Wordsworth, Christopher. *Memoirs of William Wordsworth, Poet-Laureate, D. C. L.* 2 vols. Ticknor, Reed, and Fields, 1851.

—. *Scholae Academicae. Some Account of Studies at the English Universities in the Eighteenth Century*. Augustus M. Kelley Publishers, 1877, 1969.

—. *Social Life at the English Universities in the Eighteenth Century*. Deighton, Bell, and Co., 1874.

Wordsworth, Jonathan, M. H. Abrams, and Stephen Gill, editors. *The Prelude 1799, 1805, 1850*. W. W. Norton, 1979.

Wordsworth, William, *The Complete Poetical Works of William Wordsworth, in Ten Volumes*. Vol. 1: Early Poems. Cosimo Inc., 2008 [1904].

Wordsworth, William, and Dorothy Wordsworth. *The Letters of William and Dorothy Wordsworth: The Middle Years*. 2 vols. Clarendon Press, 1937.

—. *The Letters of William and Dorothy Wordsworth: The Later Years*. 3 vols. Clarendon Press, 1939.

Wright, J. M. F. *Alma Mater: Or, Seven Years at the University of Cambridge. By a Trinity-Man*. 2 vols. Black, Young, and Young, 1827.

Wright, Luke S. H. *Samuel Taylor Coleridge and the Anglican Church*. University of Notre Dame Press, 2010.

Wu, Duncan. *Wordsworth's Reading 1770–1799*. Cambridge University Press, 1993.

Wu, Duncan. *Wordsworth's Reading 1800–1815*. Cambridge University Press, 1995.

Xu, Hongxia. 'The Poet as Teacher: Wordsworth's Practical and Poetic Engagement with Education'. Unpublished PhD thesis, University of Edinburgh, 2013.

Index

Acts and Opponencies 213–216, 224
   see also declamations, orations, public speaking, recitation
The Adventurer 208n16
Aeschines and works by *see* classical writers, texts
Aeschylus and works by *see* classical writers, texts
Aikin, John 86
Airy, John Biddle *see* universities, professors
Akenside, Mark 86
Aldrich, Henry 191–192, 195
Aldrich's *Compendium of Logic* 190–192, 195, 219
algebra 88, 143, 165, 173, 187–188, 192, 195, 197–198, 215, 217, 237, 249
All Souls College *see* universities, colleges of Oxford
American
   colonies, colonists 243–244, 265
   revolution, rebellion 2, 12, 270
   universities 158
Analytic Review 7
anatomy 7, 139, 215
Anglican Church 7, 29, 97–102, 111n39, 123, 127, 150–152, 162, 167, 274

Anglican orthodoxy 3, 6, 124–126, 268, 275–276
Annual Register 86
Anti-Jacobin, or, Weekly Examiner 7, 10, 37, 195
apologetics 25, 116, 192, 275–276
Appianus *see* classical writers, texts
Arabic 53, 188, 233, 248
architecture 114, 126, 238, 274, 277
argument 74, 82n37, 185, 187, 194, 197, 211–214, 221, 236, 242
Aristophanes *see* classical writers, texts
Aristotle and works by *see* classical writers, texts
arithmetic 88, 215
Arnold, Thomas *see* grammar and public schools, headmasters
Assessment 89–95
Astronomy 9, 88, 183, 185, 187–188, 199, 203, 210, 217, 230, 232, 236–239, 249
Athenaeum 38
audience 8, 39, 65, 67, 89, 92, 107, 115, 121, 124, 126–128, 169, 188, 210–211, 214, 221, 226, 269, 275–276
Austin, Gilbert 135
   Chironomia 135

293

Educating the Romantic Poets

Babbage, Charles *see* university, professors
Bacon, Francis 86, 87n54, 135
Balliol College *see* universities, colleges of Oxford
Banks, Hodson, or Challis papers, Trinity College, Cambridge 208n17, 209fig19, 216fig20
Banks, Joseph 10n15, 25
Barbeau, Jeffrey 120n89, 277n13
Bath Grammar School *see* grammar and public schools
Baxter, Richard, hymnodist 114
Beadon, Richard *see* universities, college heads
Beattie, James 49–50, 58, 71, 86, 202n45
  Essays on Poetry and Music 49n3, 58
Beaumont, Sir George 8, 25, 125, 150
Beddoes, Thomas *see* universities, professors 11n15
Bede 79, 208
behaviour of pupils or students, social behaviour 2, 9, 12,32, 48n97, 54, 72, 86, 90, 111, 134, 147, 169, 170–174, 180, 189, 226–227, 241, 246, 264
Bentham, Jeremy 10, 111, 210, 225
Bentley, Samuel 3, 38, 87n54, 206
Bentley's *Dissertation on Phalaris* 87n54
Bentley's Miscellany 38
Berkeley, George 135
Bible *see* scripture
billiards 176
Blackstone, Sir William 11n17, 86–87n54, 135, 165
Blair, Hugh 86–87n54, 135
Blake, William 3, 129
boating 5, 176, 178

Book of Common Prayer 7, 102, 107, 109, 111, 115n51, 116
  see also Anglican Church
botany 215, 232
Bowles, William Lisle 7, 10, 104, 179
bowls, bowling 176
boxing 183
Brasenose College *see* universities, colleges of Oxford
British Association for the Advancement of Science 237, 252, 271
The British Critic 7, 202, 236
The British Review 38
Brougham, Henry 10, 13, 205
bullying 16, 47–48
Burke, Edmund 7, 43n71, 86–87n54, 202, 243
Burns, Robert 3, 86, 202n45
Butler, Dr George *see* grammar and public schools, headmasters
Butler, Joseph 220
  Analogy of Religion 220
Butler, Marilyn 1–2
Butler, Samuel *see* grammar and public schools, headmasters
Byron, Lord George Gordon
  on education, his educational experiences 4, 6–7, 10, 12, 20, 23n62, 27, 35, 39–41, 44, 46, 53, 61, 77–78, 81, 86, 100, 122n86, 134–137, 156, 166, 169, 175, 177–180, 200, 205, 241, 244, 254–256, 262–264, 277
  as a poet or writer 2, 9, 20, 31, 35, 37, 40n61, 53, 78, 115, 118, 174, 189–190, 211, 274–275, 278
  and religion 9n14, 100, 104, 114–115, 121–122
  works by
    Beppo 86
    The Bride of Abydos 41

294

Cain 41, 122n86
Childe Harold 37
The Corsair 86
Don Juan 20, 122
Fugitive Pieces 136
The Giaour 41
'Harrow on the Hill' 100
Hours of Idleness 78, 136
Manfred 41, 86, 122
Poems on Various Occasions 132, 136, 263

Caesar *see* classical writers, texts
calculus 143, 187, 192, 197, 237
Callimachus *see* classical writers, texts
Cambridge *see* universities
Cambridge Platonists 199, 259
Canning, George 10, 11n17, 27, 36n39, 37–38, 194–196, 238
canons, of the church, university 93, 117, 250
cards, card games 164, 171, 176, 179–180, 26
chancellors *see* universities
Charterhouse *see* grammar and public schools
Chatterton, Thomas 7, 86, 271
Chaucer, Geoffrey 86, 201, 202n45, 208
chemistry 7, 139, 143, 215, 232
chess 176, 260
Chevallier, John *see* universities, college heads
children 11, 13, 16, 20n54, 21, 25n71, 33, 41, 51, 53, 57–58, 99, 113, 124, 127, 206–207, 277
 see also families
 brains, cognitive development 51, 82
 gender identity 47
 parents' plans for, expectations of sons 12, 14, 19, 30, 41, 53–54, 107, 125, 147, 153, 149–153, 156, 158–159, 228

children's books 20
 see also schoolbooks
Christ Church College *see* universities, colleges of Oxford
Christ's Hospital School *see* grammar and public schools
church architecture 114, 126, 237, 274, 277
Church of England *see* Anglican Church
church music, choirs, metrical psalms 114–115, 120, 127, 163, 277
Church of St Mary the Virgin, Oxford 102, 103fig12, 163
Cicero and works by *see* classical writers, works
Clancey, Richard 20, 72n8, 206
Clare, John 3
Clarkson, Thomas 7, 19
classical writers, texts studied in the schools and university colleges
 Aeshines 195
  Against Timarchus 19, 195
 Aeschylus 73, 84, 189, 199, 220
  Prometheus Vinctus 61, 189
 Apollonius of Rhodes 84, 85fig7
 Appianus 195
 Aristophanes 220
 Aristotle 20, 74, 137–138, 141, 183, 188–189, 190–191, 195, 197, 199, 213, 220, 231, 238, 257
  Ethics 220
  Nicomachean Ethics 189
  Organon 190, 219
  Poetics 189, 195, 238
  Rhetoric 197, 220, 231
 Caesar 7, 73, 86, 135, 186, 201
 Callimachus 23, 73
 Catullus 61, 74, 78
 Cicero 43, 54, 72–74, 77, 83–84, 90, 135, 139, 186, 189, 194–195, 199, 218–220, 239
  De Amicitia 72, 194

De Officiis 72, 189, 199, 219
De Oratore 194, 239
'Pro Archia Poeta' 194
'Pro Coelio' 194
'Pro Ligario' 194
'Pro Marcello' 194
'Pro Milone' 194
Senectitutte 194
Tusculan Disputations 239
Demosthenes 7, 73, 84, 135, 165, 189, 195, 200, 218, 220
'On the Crown' 189, 199
Diodori of Sicily 195
Epictetus 73, 139, 171
Euclid 7, 73, 89, 132, 165, 173, 190–192, 194–195, 197–198, 215, 217, 219
Euripides 61, 73, 165, 189, 199, 201, 218, 239
Alcestis 61
Iphigenia at Aulis 199
Medea 189
Hecuba 189
Herodotus 43, 73, 84–85, 90, 173, 186, 188, 195–197, 218, 218, 220, 239
Histories 188
Hesiod 7, 23, 73, 189–190, 199
Works and Days 73, 189–190
Homer 7, 22, 33, 39, 57, 60, 74, 78, 86n54, 90, 186, 199, 201, 218, 220
Iliad 60n39, 73, 86, 190, 195–197
Odyssey 73, 165, 190, 194
Horace 7, 10, 20, 23, 64–65, 90, 186, 190, 195, 197, 199, 205–208, 210, 218–220
Ars Poetica 199
Epistles 195
Nunc est bibendum 190
Tu ne quaesieris 190
Isocrates 74

Juvenal 61, 73, 85, 199–200, 220
Livy 72–73, 78, 85, 90, 188, 195, 197, 199, 200–201, 218, 220
History of Rome and the Roman People 188, 195, 197
Longinus 73, 220
Lucan 22, 61, 186
Lucian 43, 73, 186
Lucretius 74, 190, 220
De rerum natura 190
Lysias 86, 195
Moschus 208, 271
Ovid 7, 22, 54n15, 71–72, 85, 199, 214
Fasti 199
Metamorphoses 54, 72
Tristia 72
Persius 73
Phaedrus 54, 71
Pindar 7, 73, 190, 201
Plato 139, 183, 199, 220
Plantonists, classical 259
Pliny 90
Plutarch 43, 73, 188, 195, 220
Lives of the Greeks and Romans 188
Polybius 195
Quintilian 23, 72, 74–75, 135, 189, 206, 220
Institutes of Oratory 74
Sallust 72, 86, 135, 194–195, 199, 218
Sappho 73, 190
Seneca 43, 139
Sophocles 85, 90, 189, 199, 220, 239
Ajax 189, 195
Electra 195
Oedipus at Colonus 195
Oedipus Tyrannus 189, 195
Philoctetes 189, 195
Strabo 135, 140
Tacitus 73, 84–85, 132, 200, 201, 220

Index

Terence 74, 86, 220
Theocritus 73, 90, 199, 201
Thucydides 7, 73, 78, 84–85, 90, 188, 195, 197, 200, 220
  Peloponnesian War 73, 188, 195–197
Tibullus 201
Virgil 7, 22, 33, 61, 72, 74, 78, 83, 90, 186, 190, 194–195, 197, 199, 208, 218
  The Aeneid 60, 72, 78, 190, 194–195, 208
  Eclogues 190, 199
  Georgics 22, 61, 72, 83n39, 190, 197, 199
Xenophon 73, 90, 139, 165, 186, 188, 195, 200, 218
clergy, clergymen, pastors xiv, 5, 11, 13n27, 17, 54, 110, 116, 121, 125, 134, 149–151, 153, 232, 253, 261, 264, 266, 271, 277
clubs 147, 176, 178–179, 210, 260
Coleridge, Derwent 88, 150
Coleridge, Edward 31–32, 55, 61
Coleridge, George 131, 230, 268
Coleridge, Hartley 150
Coleridge, John Taylor 10, 112
Coleridge, Samuel Taylor
  on education, educational experiences 6–7, 10, 12, 30, 51, 53, 61, 73–74, 82, 89, 108, 131, 134, 148–150, 156, 165–166, 169, 172–173, 177–178, 180, 188, 198, 201, 208, 210–211, 214, 215, 227, 230, 242, 249, 254, 264, 267n83, 268, 270–271, 277–278
  and memory 60–62
  and Pantisocracy 24, 123, 132, 188, 249, 271
  as a poet or writer 2, 7–8, 24–25, 37, 51, 112n41, 115, 123, 125, 129, 169, 179, 208, 210–211, 264–265, 271, 274–276, 278
  and religion 7–8, 99, 108, 110, 114n49, 123, 277
  and translation 51, 78–79, 208
  Works by
    Aids to Reflection 7, 276
    Biographia Literaria 60–61, 73, 79
    On the Constitution of Church and State 276
    Religious Musings 123
    'Rime of the Ancient Mariner' 115
college fellows *see* universities
college heads *see* universities
communion 104, 111, 127, 163, 246
composers, hymnodists, music editors
  Attwood, Thomas 115
  Cooke, Benjamin 115
  Cotterhill, Thomas 10
  Croft, William 115
  Handel, George Frederick 115, 164
  Purcell, Henry 115
  Wesley, Charles 10
  Whitfield, John Clark 10
composition, compositions, composition instruction, writing xiv, 3, 5, 16, 22, 49–96, 116, 119, 127, 129, 188, 201, 225, 225, 209–212, 220, 225, 239, 251, 255, 264, 273, 276
  see also themes and essays, verse composition
confirmation 111, 127
continental teaching 2, 12, 14, 140
Cooke, John, Christ Church chaplain 119
Coote, Charles editor, *Critical Review* 38
Copleston, Edward, Oxford Professor of Poetry *see* universities, professors
Cotterhill, Thomas 10
Cowper, William 10, 33, 114, 170

297

The Task 81, 1 70
'Tirocinium' 33
Crabbe, George 10
Craig, David 277
cricket 5, 31, 34, 45, 176
Curthoys, Judith 172
The Critical Review 7, 38

dame schools 3
Dante 86, 201
Darwin, Erasmus 10, 30, 86n54
Daventry Academy 139
Davy, John *see* universities, college heads
debating societies 5, 9–10, 35, 37, 256
debts of college students 108, 133, 173, 226–268, 230
   see also university, costs
declamations 10, 75, 77, 84, 131, 158, 212, 214, 224, 236
   see also eloquence, public speaking, orations, acts and opponencies
deists, deism 7, 99, 116, 121, 152, 242, 236n58, 265
Demosthenes and works by *see* classical writers, texts
De Quincey, Thomas 10, 53, 146–147, 166–167, 223–224, 230, 251
devotional works 109, 118, 277
devotions 33, 67
dialogues 54, 55, 67, 73, 94, 188, 220, 276
   see also various classical writers, texts
Diodori of Sicily *see* classical writers, texts
dissent, dissenters, dissenting academies 3, 7, 12–15, 18, 66, 119, 123, 137n32, 138–139, 152, 170–171, 251, 256, 269–270
'divinity' as a course of study, and doctors of 4, 117, 118n64, 120, 122n86, 124, 165, 186–187, 192, 197, 212, 220, 232–233, 235, 248–249, 252, 256, 266, 269
drama, dramatists 5, 7, 9, 61, 66n69, 186, 201, 218, 275
   see also individual classical writers
dramatic entertainment 5, 37n44, 75–77, 176
drink, drinking, wine, port, etc. 12, 17, 19, 36n40, 47, 134, 140, 158, 162, 164–168, 171–173, 176, 178–180, 190, 193, 210, 217, 245, 260
Drury, Henry *see* grammar and public schools, schoolmasters
Drury, Dr James *see* grammar and public schools, headmasters
Dumfries Grammar school *see* grammar and public schools
Dyer, George 10, 61, 63n55, 263, 265
   Complaints of the Poor People of England (1793) 265
   History of the University and College of Cambridge (1814) 265

Easterlin, Nancy 277
Edinburgh Annual Register 7
The Edinburgh Review 10, 12–13, 27, 38, 44–46, 53n13, 56, 58, 81, 138–141, 201n39–41, 207, 210, 212, 236, 273
Edinburgh University 140, 244
education, opinions or beliefs about 1–8, 13–21, 23–25, 27–29, 43, 62, 68–69, 88, 98, 117, 120–126, 132–135, 138–144, 170, 174, 183, 188, 192, 200–201, 203, 205, 226, 276–278
   advocacy of, defenders of 24, 141, 230, 264, 278
      see also Royal Commission Reports
   critics of *see The Edinburgh Review*, Priestley, Sydney Smith, Stevenson

history of 11–22, 29n6, 54, 56, 142, 200, 183
  see also grammar and public schools, founders, founding principles; universities, founding statutes
elegy 8, 16, 33, 64, 77, 81, 90, 210, 255, 261
Elledge, Paul 20, 31, 35, 76
eloquence 135, 186, 195, 207, 212, 253–254, 270
Ely, Bishop of, Cathedral 61, 245, 269
Encaenia see universities
enlightenment 25, 116, 169, 241, 278
epic 8, 22, 64, 66, 72, 190, 236, 276
  see also specific titles
Equiano, Olaudah 3
ethics 183, 188–189, 219–220, 259
Eton College *see* grammar and public schools
Euclid *see* classical writers, texts
Euripides and works by *see* classical writers, texts
European Magazine 38, 86
evangelical/s 99, 112, 257 269
Everleigh, John *see* universities, college heads
examinations 10, 14, 90, 136, 138, 145, 158, 162, 166, 188, 195, 208, 210, 215–221, 224, 229, 234–235, 240–241, 246, 250, 252, 258, 262
  see also universities, examinations
Exeter College *see* universities, colleges of Oxford

faith 24, 75, 83, 94, 97, 109–110, 112–113, 116–121, 124–125, 127, 129, 172, 184, 192, 212, 268, 270, 278
  see also Anglican church, devotions, lessons in the faith
family, families 9, 12, 14, 17, 25, 37n43, 53, 62, 72, 110, 117, 124–125, 131, 146, 148–150, 153, 156, 158, 164, 172, 193, 210, 227
  fathers 7, 41, 107
  mothers 54, 102, 124, 231, 239, 259, 228
  George Chinnery's mother 108, 151, 168, 179–180
  parents 9, 14, 16–17, 27, 30, 41, 53, 60, 75–76, 86, 92, 119, 127, 147, 149, 150, 204, 213, 227–228, 251
  sons *see* children, parents' expectations for
Farish, William *see* universities, college heads
Farnaby's Rhetoric 74
Fay, Jessica 128, 169, 274, 277
fellows see universities, fellows and fellowships
fencing 176, 183
Fielding, Henry 86
fishing 34, 176, 260
football 176
French Revolution 2, 7, 73, 123, 241, 270
Frend, William *see* universities, tutors
Frere, John Hookham 36n39
Frewen, Edward *see* universities, tutors
Frey, Ann 277
Fulford, Tim 24, 62, 121, 124, 126–129, 275–176
Fysshe Palmer, Thomas 72

Gaisford, Thomas *see* university professors
gambling, betting 19, 47, 174, 177, 180, 260
games, including cricket games, tennis games, card games 5, 9, 13, 28, 31, 34, 45, 176, 180, 183, 206
Gentleman's Magazine 7, 38, 202
geography, maps 62, 88–90, 140, 188, 200

299

Educating the Romantic Poets

geology 7, 199, 215, 232, 237–238, 264
geometry 88–89, 133, 143–144, 183, 185, 187–188, 190, 195, 197, 199, 218–219, 232, 237
Gibbon, Edward 10, 87n54, 117
Gifford, William 1
Gill, Stephen 124, 126, 128
Gilpin, William 10
Girton College *see* universities, colleges of Cambridge
Gladwell, Malcolm 22, 274
Godwin, Mary *see* Shelley, Mary
Godwin, William 3, 7, 270
Goldsmith, Oliver 86–87
Goodenough, Edmund *see* universities, tutors
grammar 5, 7, 30, 49–58, 60, 63–4, 67, 77–78, 88, 91, 97n1, 138, 185, 188, 274
grammar and public schools 10–11, 13, 13n24n27, 15–16, 27, 29–30, 33, 39–40, 44, 47–48, 56n23, 57–58, 60, 63n55, 74–75, 79, 88, 92, 128, 137, 139, 169, 229, 258
  boarding, boarding houses, boarding pupils xiv, 28, 30, 32–34, 39, 47–48, 99, 123, 274
  chapel xiii, 92, 99, 100, 102
    see also Anglican Church, church architecture
  communion, eucharist 104, 111, 127
  confirmation 111, 127
  critics of 3, 12, 47, 58
  debating societies 5, 9–10, 35, 37
  declamations 10, 75, 77, 84
  dramatic entertainment 5, 37n44, 75–77, 176
  fagging, forced service 5, 27–28, 32, 39, 43–47, 158
  food, meals 5, 32–33, 45
  founders, founding principles 29–30

headmasters and schoolmasters 4, 12, 13n27, 16–17, 20–21, 25–27, 30n12, 31–33, 41, 43, 45–46, 48, 58, 60, 74–76, 89, 91, 93, 106–107, 132, 169, 174
  see also clergymen
  Arnold, Thomas, Rugby 28, 36, 47, 56, 58, 60, 61, 73, 81–83, 88, 90, 104, 107, 110, 112, 116, 188, 238, 262, 274
  Bowman, Thomas, Hawkshead 8
  Boyer, James, Christ's Hospital 74, 89
  Butler, George, Harrow 40–41
  Butler, Samuel, Shrewsbury 32, 46
  Chapman, George, Dumfries Grammar School, Scotland 60, 89
  Collis, J. D., King Edward VI Grammar School 146–147
  Drury, Henry, Harrow 40, 100
  Drury, James, Harrow 6, 20, 61n40, 107
  Goodall, Joseph, Eton 82
  Goodenough, Edmund, Westminster 44
  Hawtrey, Edward Craven, Eton 48n97
  Keate, John, Eton 82, 89–90
  Knox, Vicesimus, Tonbridge Grammar School 10n15, 29, 30n9, 51, 54, 58, 60–61, 71, 72n9, 79, 81–83, 85, 89, 97, 137
    Essays, Moral and Literary 29
    Liberal Education: Or, a Practical Treatise on the Methods of Acquiring Useful and Polite Learning 137

300

Lily, William, St. Paul's 54n17, 56–58
Moberly, George, Winchester 48, 107
Russell, Dr., Charterhouse 46
Taylor, William, Hawkshead 8, 31, 69, 81
Vincent, William, Westminster 43, 62, 74–75, 108, 132
Warner, John, Charterhouse 63n5
leaving books 87–88
lessons in the faith 116–121
music, musical entertainment 5, 23, 106, 110–111, 114–115, 120, 129
pedagogies and subjects taught
  astronomy 88, 183
  composition xiv, 3, 5, 16, 22, 49–69
  geography 62, 82, 88–90
  history (church, classical, military) 5, 33, 62, 73, 75, 86–89, 97, 116–117
  language and literature 6, 30, 36, 39, 58, 61, 67–68, 71–74
    see also classical writers/texts
    etymology 50
    grammar 5, 7, 30, 49–58, 60, 63–64, 67, 77–78, 88, 91, 97n1, 138, 185, 188, 274
    Greek 3, 5, 7, 9, 33, 53, 57–58, 63, 73, 76, 81–82, 85, 89–92, 94, 116
    Hebrew 53, 93n6, 116–117
    Latin 5, 7, 9–11, 14, 33, 40, 50–58, 59fig4, 60, 63–65, 72, 74–75, 77–85, 89–94
    orthography 50
    prosody, metre 4–5, 22–23, 50, 57, 63–68, 79, 93, 115, 140, 274
    see also pedagogies, prosody
    syntax 49–50, 55, 64, 67, 79
  rhetoric and oratory 74–96
    see also pedagogies
  translation 4, 16, 22, 51, 77–82, 85, 88, 90
  mathematics (arithmetic, geometry, algebra) 4, 6–7, 14, 73, 88–89
  memory work 7, 22, 31, 47, 51, 55, 58–62, 75, 203
  religion *see* Anglican Church, 'divinity', faith, sermons, prayer and worship services
play, games, amusement 31, 33–39
  see debating societies, specific sports, school magazines
prayer and worship services 9, 31, 94, 98–99, 102–113, 116, 120, 122, 124, 163–165, 193, 226, 277
  evening prayer, vespers 31, 103, 106, 109
  morning prayer, matins 31, 102–104, 107, 164, 193
  Sundays 106–110
prefects, praeposters 28, 31, 41n64, 45, 47–48, 89, 106
prizes, honours books 76–77, 81–82, 84, 85fig7, 87n31, 93
punishment 12, 17, 32n16, 40–44, 47, 75, 108, 164, 173, 192, 226
routines 27–48
schools
  Bath Grammar School 64
  Charterhouse 46, 63n55, 110n33, 199

Christ's Hospital School 10, 15, 24, 29, 36, 74–75, 99, 101fig11, 123, 149, 179, 208, 230
Dumfries Grammar School 92
Eton College xiii–vi, 10–12, 15, 28, 30–39, 45, 50, 54–57, 63, 72, 77, 79–80, 89, 94, 104, 106, 122–123, 176
　Eton College Chapel 100fig10
　Eton Latin Grammar 50
　Gradus as Parnassus 80fig6
　King's Scholars 55, 91, 93
　Preces Quotidianae 105fig13
　Speech Day Programme 76fig5
Harrow School 6, 10, 15–16, 20, 31–35, 40, 45–46, 61, 76, 81, 86, 100, 107, 122, 134–136
Hawkshead Grammar School 6, 8, 10, 17, 20, 21n58, 23n62, 24, 29n6, 30–31, 33–34, 49, 68, 73, 86, 87fig8, 93, 99, 124, 149, 198
Heversham Grammar School 97n1
King Edward VI Grammar School 147
Manchester Grammar School 250
Merchant Taylor School 44
Rugby School xiii–xvi, 28, 32–37, 51, 71, 73, 78, 81–82, 84–85, 88, 90, 93, 97, 107
St Paul's School 29n6, 38, 44, 53, 56, 75, 77, 84, 92, 104, 236
Shrewsbury School 32, 46, 263
Tonbridge Grammar School 29, 85, 137
Westminster School xiii–xiv, 5, 10, 12, 13n24, 15, 24, 34, 37n44, 38, 40, 42fig2, 43–44, 53, 56, 62, 64–66, 74–75, 77–78, 81, 90–93, 99–100, 108, 116–117, 125, 132, 171, 173, 179, 193, 250, 252, 270
　'Helps to the Challenge' 5, 90–99
Winchester College xiii–xiv, 11–12, 28fig1, 29, 33–34, 40–41, 48, 60, 75, 77, 81, 84, 85fig7, 92–94, 104–105, 107, 116, 139–140, 201
Graver, Bruce 72n6, 78, 79n25, 83
Gray, Thomas 86
Great St Mary's Church, Cambridge 102, 137, 162–163, 235
Greece 87fig8, 88, 188
　Athens 89, 188, 264
　Sparta 41–42, 89, 188
Greek language or literature 3, 5, 7, 9, 33, 53, 57–58, 61, 63, 73, 76, 81–82, 85, 89–94, 110, 112, 116–117, 127, 133, 135–137, 140, 144, 165, 179, 185–201, 207–210, 212, 215, 218–219, 225, 231–232, 238–239, 259, 264, 277
Grotius 43, 75, 116–117, 192, 194
　De veritate religionis Christianae (On the Truth of Christianity) 116, 192, 194

habit/s of study, of behaviour 4, 32, 43, 49–50, 71, 81, 83, 88, 98, 107, 120, 139–140, 142–144, 147, 150, 153, 161, 167, 170, 181, 198, 204, 210, 219, 225, 240
Hailstone, John *see* universities, college heads
Hallam, Henry 10–11n15
Hamilton, William 10–11n15
handball 31, 34

Index

Harrow School *see* grammar and public schools
Hartley, David 10n15, 202
Hawkshead School *see* grammar and public schools
Hazlitt, William 3, 23, 205
Hebrew 53, 93n6, 116–117, 173, 185, 188, 194, 232, 265, 277
Herodotus and works by *see* classical writers, texts
Herschel, John 10, 237
Hesiod and works by *see* classical writers, texts
Heversham Grammar School *see* grammar and public schools
hexameter 23, 51, 64, 72, 81, 90, 190, 210
see also metre
Hey, John *see* universities, college heads
Hinchcliffe, John *see* universities, college heads
history as a school or university subject 9, 15, 18, 21–22, 26, 33, 62–63, 73, 75, 86–89, 97, 102, 116–117, 121, 124, 126–128, 138–139, 185–186, 188, 192, 195, 197, 200, 210n27, 215, 217–220, 232, 235, 238–239, 247–248, 255, 265, 275, 277–278
Hobhouse, John Cam 122n86, 136, 169, 254, 263–264
Homer and works by *see* classical writers, texts
homiletics 113, 117, 120, 186, 193, 200
see also sermons
Hooker, Richard 135
Horace and works by *see* classical writers, texts
Hornsby, Thomas *see* universities, professors
horses, horse riding, horse racing 18, 34, 135, 147, 158, 176–177, 180, 183, 260

Hume, David 86–87n54, 135, 236
Hunt, Leigh 10, 61
hunting 3 4, 134, 147, 171, 176–177, 197
hydrostatics 199, 215, 217, 236
hymns, hymnody 8, 10, 103–104, 112, 114, 115n51, 123n88
see also composers

idleness 47, 107, 131, 151, 166, 174
imitation/s and models 3–4, 37–38, 66, 68, 72, 77–79, 84, 108, 183, 187, 190, 200–201, 206, 210, 212, 274
immorality, lewdness, 'domestic seditions' 170, 172, 261
see also vice
Inns of Court 193
inscriptions 81, 124, 127–128, 276
Isocrates *see* classical writers, texts

Jackson, Cyril *see* universities, college heads
Jebb, John 136, 213, 257
Jeffrey, Francis 10, 65–67, 128
Jerram, Charles 112
Jesus College, Cambridge *see* universities, Cambridge colleges
Johnson, Joseph 265–266
Johnson, Samuel 10n15, 86, 86n54, 201, 211
Johnston, Kenneth 13n28, 72, 200
Jones, Robert 168–169, 269
Jones, Stephen, editor, *The European Magazine* 38
Jones, Thomas *see* universities, tutors
Jowett, Benjamin *see* universities, tutors
Juvenal *see* classical writers, texts

kairos 75, 276
Kaye, John, master and professor *see* universities, college heads and professors

303

Keate, John *see* grammar and public schools, headmasters
Keats, John 3, 39
Keble, John *see* universities, professors
Ken, Bishop Thomas 105, 115n51
  Manual of Prayers for the Use of the Scholars of Winchester College (1675) 104
King Edward VI Grammar School *see* grammar and public schools
King James Bible 7
Kings' College *see* universities, colleges of Oxford
Knox, Vicesimus and works by *see* grammar and public schools

Lady Margaret Hall *see* universities, colleges of Oxford
Lamb, Charles 10, 11n15, 56n23, 61
Langhorne, John 86, 202n45
Latin language and literature, Latinate diction 5, 7, 9–11, 14, 21, 33, 40, 50–65, 74–85, 89–94, 104–106, 116, 127, 131, 135, 140, 144, 162, 167, 172–173, 179, 185–186, 188, 190–195, 200–201, 207–210, 213–215, 218–219, 225–226, 231, 233–239, 248, 255, 257, 259, 264, 275–277
  see also Rome, Roman literature
law, canon law, civil law as course of study, legal scholars 11, 29, 139, 193, 195, 215, 232, 244, 258
Lax, William *see* universities, college heads
Lewis, Monk 10, 30, 61, 252
libraries 84n46, 86–88, 161, 176, 184, 238, 246, 249, 254–255, 260
Lincoln College *see* universities, colleges of Oxford
literature, literary studies *see* classical writers, texts, grammar and public schools, pedagogies, universities

Livy and works by *see* classical writers, texts
Lloyd, Charles *see* universities, college professors, tutors
Locke, John 86–87n54, 135, 142, 211
  Essay on Human Understanding 200
Lockhart, John Gibson 10
Logic 9, 74, 137, 140, 142, 185, 187–188, 190–192, 195, 197, 211, 213, 218–220, 225
London 7, 12–13, 18, 29, 49, 75, 92, 99, 137–138, 173, 243, 255, 263, 265, 267–268, 270
The London Magazine 7
The Looker On 38
Lucan *see* classical writers, texts
Lucian *see* classical writers, texts
Lucretius and works by *see* classical writers, texts
Lysias *see* classical writers, texts

Macaulay, Thomas Babington 10, 255
Maclaurin's Algebra 173, 195
Magdalen College *see* universities, colleges of Oxford
Malthus, Thomas 10n15
Manchester Grammar School *see* grammar and public schools
Mansel, William Lort *see* universities, college heads
Marsh, Herbert *see* universities, professors
mathematics 2, 4, 6, 9, 14, 97, 112, 134, 136, 141, 143, 145, 152, 165–166, 172, 183, 186–188, 192, 197–199, 204, 213, 215, 217–220, 225, 232, 236, 238, 248–249, 263, 266
  see also calculus, geometry, trigonometry
matins *see* Anglican Church
Maxwell, James Clerk 2

Index

Maxwell-Lyte, Henry Churchill 15, 85
  A History of Eton College 1440–1884 15
mechanics 139, 144,187, 199, 215, 236, 238, 249
  see also physics
medicine, as a course of study 215, 232, 258
memorials, memorial verse 62, 102, 124, 128, 276
memory, memory work, uses of 7, 22, 31, 47, 50–51, 55–62, 74–75, 78, 86, 116, 120, 139, 200, 203, 214, 229
Merivale, Charles 60, 61n40
Merton College *see* universities, colleges of Oxford
metaphysics 183, 188, 259
  see also philosophy
metre, prosody, and instruction about 4–5, 22–23, 51–52, 57, 63–65, 67–68, 72, 81, 90, 93, 115, 140, 190, 210–212, 226, 255, 274
  see also pentameter, hexameter, tetrameter
metrical psalms 115, 127
Milner, Isaac *see* universities, college heads, professors, tutors
Milner, John 64
  An Abstract of Latin Syntax…to which is Added, Prosody, Or, The Art of Latin Poetry … for the Use of Schools 64
Milton, John 7, 43, 74, 81, 84, 86, 127, 142, 165, 179, 201
mineralogy 215, 237–238
models *see* imitation
monasteries, monastic, monks, coenobitic 12, 18, 43, 94, 123, 128, 169, 274
Monthly Magazine 7
moral philosophy 138, 215, 217, 233, 237–238
  see also philosophy
The Morning Chronicle 7, 271

The Morning Post 7
Moschus *see* classical writers, texts
music, musical entertainment, church music 5, 22–23, 30, 49n3, 58, 60–61, 63–64, 94, 102, 106, 110–111, 114–115, 120, 126, 129, 162, 164, 166, 171, 176, 183, 185, 277
  see also hymns and hymnody, metrical psalms, composers

Napleton, John 119–120
  Advice to a Student in the University, Concerning the Qualifications and Duties of a Minister of the Gospel in the Church of England 119
Napoleonic war 2, 34, 38, 40, 44, 73, 86, 159, 262, 268, 270, 275
nation, the English 4, 25, 8sn35, 125, 141, 144, 146, 152, 158–159, 242, 244, 248n19, 267, 277–278
national church 12, 98, 188, 169, 276–277
  see also Anglican Church
national education 13, 278
nationalism 170, 275
natural philosophy *see* science
National Society for Promoting the Education of the Poor in the Principles of the Established Church in England and Wales 255
natural theology 99, 117, 136, 238
nature 1, 19, 21, 38, 39, 69, 72, 79, 109, 125–126, 139–140, 199, 278
navigation 188
New College *see* universities, colleges of Oxford
Newnham College *see* universities, Cambridge colleges
Newton, Isaac 7, 86, 86–87n54, 135, 156, 197, 220, 239
Newton, John hymnodist 114
Nichols, John Bowyer 38

305

odes 5, 8, 34n23, 36, 65, 73, 94, 124, 134, 190, 199, 210, 264, 271
Olney hymns 114
optics 187–188, 199, 217, 230, 236, 249
orations 74, 77, 86, 92, 94, 186, 195, 199, 266
  see also Acts and Opponencies, public speaking
oratory 71, 74–75, 108
Oriel College see universities, colleges of Oxford
orthodox, orthodoxy 268
  see also Anglican Church
Ovid and works by see classical writers, texts
Oxford University see universities

Paine, Thomas 7, 202
Paley, William 7, 10, 86–87n54, 99, 117, 135–136, 156, 192, 200, 257, 265
  Natural Theology, or Evidences of the Existence and Attributes of the Deity (1802) 99, 117, 215
  Principles of Moral and Political Philosophy (1785) 99, 136, 200, 215, 217
  View of the Evidence of Christianity (1794) 136, 215, 248n19
Pantisocracy 24, 123, 132, 188, 249, 271
parents see families
Parsons, John see universities, college heads
pastor see Anglican clergy
Pattison, Mark see universities, college heads, tutors
Peacock, George 10–11n15, 237, 255
Pearce, William see universities, college heads
pedagogy, pedagogies 2–4, 207n15, 19, 25–26, 29, 58, 62, 77, 140, 145, 183, 201, 212, 203–221, 230, 242, 266, 273–274
  see also grammar and public schools, pedagogy, universities, pedagogies, and specific topics such as argument, assessment, composition, examinations, grammar, memory work, recitation, rhetoric, *progymnastmata*, public speaking, themes or essays, translation
Peel, Robert 11n17, 220, 244, 251
The Peloponnesian War 73, 188, 195, 197
Pembroke College see universities, colleges of Oxford
pentameter 23, 64, 68, 81, 93
  see also metre
Percy, Thomas 10, 86, 202n45
periodicals and journals 2, 37n44, 65, 86, 201–202, 207–208, 212, 278
  see also individual journals by title
Peterhouse College see universities, colleges of Cambridge
philosophy, moral 5, 9, 29, 37, 83, 99, 136, 138, 183, 186, 190, 192, 200, 213, 215, 217, 220, 233, 237–238, 259, 275
  see also metaphysics
physics 1–2, 9, 195, 199, 215, 259
  see also mechanics, optics
Pitt, William the Younger 11n17, 244, 250, 252
Plampin, John see universities, tutors
Plato see classical writers, texts
play, and amusement 31, 33–39, 142, 176, 178–180, 219
  see also clubs and specific sports
Plutarch and works by see classical writers, texts
poet, the 8, 19–21, 25, 37, 39, 49, 62, 78–79, 82n35, 84, 114, 115n57, 125, 129, 133, 189, 190, 199,

Index

205–206, 208, 218, 238, 256, 263, 271, 277
poetry and verse, early experiences of, reading of, instruction, beliefs about 2–9, 19–20, 23, 30–31, 36–38, 40n61, 51–53, 56, 58, 60–69, 72, 74–75, 77–85, 93–95, 116, 124, 126–129, 131, 135, 170, 179, 189–190, 199, 200–201, 204–212, 218, 220–221, 232, 238–239, 259, 274–277
politics, political beliefs, political economy, political history, political philosophy, reform 2, 6, 18–20, 22, 25, 36, 48, 86, 99, 121, 123–124, 129, 136, 140, 142, 144, 151, 176, 179, 188–189, 194–195, 200, 215, 220–221, 233, 238, 241, 243n6, 250, 252–253, 264–265, 269, 275, 277
Polybius *see* classical writers, texts
Pope, Alexander 81, 83, 86, 136, 206
Third Moral Epistle 81
prayer and worship services 9, 31, 94, 98–99, 102–113, 116, 120, 122, 124, 163–165, 193, 226, 277
   communion, eucharist 104, 111, 127, 163, 246
   confirmation 111, 127
   daily prayer 277
   evening prayer, vespers 31, 103, 106, 109
   morning prayer, matins 31 102–104, 107, 164, 193
Price, Richard 7
Priestley, Joseph 75, 138–139, 267–268
Essay on a Course of Liberal Education, For Civil and Active Life (1764, 1788) 138
prime ministers 11n17
private academies 3, 14–15
private tutors 15, 89, 140, 146, 148, 223, 227–230, 239–240, 250–251, 255, 267
prizes, school and university 76–77, 81–82, 82n35, 84, 93, 149, 149n92, 210, 212, 231, 235–236, 243, 245, 248, 255, 259, 264
   Battie Medal, Cambridge 235
   Browne prizes for Greek ode, Latin ode, Greek epigram, Latin epigram, Cambridge 264
   Cambridge Chancellor's Prize, English ode or poem in heroic verse 210, 236, 248
   Camden Prize, Latin hexameter, Cambridge 210
   Craven Prize, classics, Cambridge 149
   English Prose Prize, Winchester 84, 85fig7
   Essay prize, contemporaneous topics, Oxford 82n35, 210
   First Chancellor's Medal, Cambridge 248
   Gaisford prizes for Greek compositions in prose or verse, Oxford 239
   headmasters' prizes 77
   Latin Declamation Prize, Cambridge 236
   Newdigate Prize, for poetry, Oxford 231
   Oxford essay prize (contemporaneous topic) 82n35, 210
   St John's Members' Latin Essay Prize 248
   university fellows' prizes for schoolboys 77
proctor/s 107, 151, 162, 233, 249, 253, 256
see also prefects
professional education 12n20, 140–141, 201, 204, 232

307

professionalism of writing 275
progymnasmata 120, 82–83
prosody 4–5, 22–23, 51, 57, 63–69, 140, 274
  see also meter
  romantic era critics and classical prosody 65–69
pubs, taverns, ale houses 47, 136, 163n3, 168, 177–179, 245
public figures who attended Anglo-classical academies 10–11
public schools *see* grammar and public schools
public service 25, 68, 102, 107, 123, 159, 184, 233, 244–246
public speaking and argument 6, 60, 77, 92, 185, 212–214
  see also oratory, orations, acts and opponencies
punishment 12, 17, 32n16, 40–44, 47, 75, 108, 164, 173, 192, 226

The Quarterly Review 10, 37, 61n40, 141
Queen's College *see* universities, colleges of Oxford
Quintilian and works by *see* classical writers, texts

recitation 4, 16, 27, 31, 51, 54–55, 60 1,77, 91–93, 104, 116, 172, 179, 203, 252, 270
  see also memory, memory work
religion 2–3, 88, 94, 97–129, 135, 141, 162, 173, 179, 184–185, 192–193, 207, 219–220, 223, 232, 241, 245, 254–255, 257, 266, 269, 276–277
  see also Anglican Church
Report of the Schools Commission (1868) 14, 47, 56n23
republic of letters 7, 68, 140, 221, 274
Reynolds, John Hamilton 38

Reynolds, Sir Joshua 3, 86–87n54
rhetoric 9, 74–77, 135, 137–138, 141–142, 185–186, 188–189, 195, 197, 211–212, 219–220, 231, 276
riots, school rebellions 17, 40–41, 46, 151, 163n3
Roberts, William 38
Robertson, Dr Abraham *see* universities, professors
Robinson, Robert 265
Roget, Mark Peter 10–11n15
Rome, Roman literature 3, 7, 63, 73, 188, 193–195, 197, 199, 212
  see also Latin
routines, at schools 31–33
rowing 34, 45
royal family 9, 77, 210, 242
Royal University Commission Reports xiii, 2, 14, 117, 145–149, 153, 161, 166–168, 173–174, 176, 186–187, 197, 204, 218–219, 221, 224–225, 227, 229–230, 234, 246–247, 257
Rugby School *see* grammar and public schools
Ryan, Robert 277

St Andrew's University, Scotland 137n32, 140, 244
St Ann's College *see* universities, colleges of Oxford
St Hugh's College *see* universities, colleges of Oxford
St John's College, Cambridge *see* universities
St Paul's School *see* grammar and public schools
Sallust *see* classical writers, texts
satire 9, 22, 61, 73, 81, 93, 132, 190, 199, 278
school books 55, 186, 277
  The Accidence, or, First Rudiments of the Latin Tongue, for the Use of Youth 56n23

college textbooks xiii, 142, 190, 195, 236, 238, 249
An English Introduction to the Latin Tongue, for the Use of the Lower Forms in Westminster-School (1732) 56n23
Exempla Minora: Or, New English Examples to be Rendered into Latin adapted to the Rules of the Grammaticae Quaestiones: Or a Grammatical Examination by Question Only 57
The Greek Examiner 57
An Introduction to Construing and Parsing of Latin Adapted to the Eton *Grammar* 57
Latin Grammar, by Thomas Morell (1703–1784) 55
A Plan of Education Delineated and Vindicated (1784) 83
Poetry Made Familiar and Easy 79
A Short Introduction of Grammar Compiled and Set Forth for the Bringing up of All Those That Intend to Attain the Knowledge of the Latin Tongue (1728) 57
A Treatise on Education, with a Sketch of the Author's Method (1773, 1784), George Chapman 60
school magazines 35–39
　Christ's Hospital's *Album* 36
　The Etonian 36–37, 61n45, 46, 82, 94
　The Flagellant 29, 37, 75, 132, 270
　The Microcosm 36–37, 38n47, 48
　The Miniature 36
　Rugby Magazine 36, 82
　Westminster *Trifler* 36, 38–39
schoolmasters *see* grammar and public schools
science, experimental, modern, natural, and as a method or field of study 6, 12, 15, 25–26, 35, 49, 68, 74, 88, 97, 113, 138, 141, 185, 187, 198–199, 217, 228, 232–233, 236–238, 241, 249, 252, 262–263, 271
　see also natural philosophy
Scotland, Scottish schools and universities 3, 10, 12–14, 49n3, 56n23, 60, 137n32, 138, 140, 191, 193
Scott, Sir Walter 135
scripture 277
　Gospels 74, 94, 116–117, 192, 194, 199, 215, 259, 266
　New Testament 54, 90, 109, 111, 116, 119, 187, 215, 217, 219
　Old Testament 53, 75, 109, 117, 192, 215, 266
　Psalms 5, 74, 94, 104–106, 109, 115–117, 119, 127, 173, 192, 194
　Septuagint 93
Sedgewick, Adam *see* universities, college heads
Seneca *see* classical writers, texts
Sermons xiii, 33, 47–48, 66, 87n54, 99, 107–108, 113, 116–119, 137, 165, 172–173, 193, 212, 220, 228, 239, 241, 248, 253, 260, 265, 277
sexual behaviour 19, 47–48, 172–173
Simeon, Charles 113–114, 119, 253, 257
Shelley, Mary 2, 278
Shelley, Percy Bysshe
　adult reading programme 24
　on education, educational experiences 10, 12, 28, 30, 33, 35, 39, 44, 46, 53, 57, 61, 76fig5, 77, 79, 80fig6, 188, 238
　and memory training 61
　as a poet, writer 2, 9, 30, 53, 129, 169, 274
　and religion 9, 106, 122–123, 126, 129, 249, 275
　works by

309

Educating the Romantic Poets

'Defence of Poetry' 129n117
'The Necessity of Atheism' 122, 249
Sheridan, Richard 135
shooting 176
Shrewsbury School *see* grammar and public schools
skating 34, 176, 178
Smith, Adam 10, 86, 87n54
Smith, Charlotte 86, 202n45
Smith, Robert 'Bobus' 36n39
Smith, Sydney 10, 84, 85fig7, 104, 139–140, 188, 207, 212, 25
Somerville College *see* universities, colleges of Oxford
the sonnet, sonnets 34, 36–37, 61, 68, 85, 93–94, 101n14, 102n15, 106, 108, 114, 121, 124, 126, 127–128, 179, 256, 257n45, 271, 276n10, 277
Sophocles and works by *see* classical writers, texts
South, Dr Robert 117, 193
Southey, Robert
  on education, educational experience 10, 12, 24, 29–30, 37, 39, 42–44, 46–47, 53, 61, 64–65, 75, 81, 91n64, 110, 120, 132–133, 134, 150, 171, 178, 188, 215, 219n52, 238, 242, 250, 252, 262, 267, 270–271
  and memory 61
  and Pantisocracy 24, 123, 132, 188, 249, 271
  as a poet, writer 2, 7–8, 24–5, 37, 53–54, 65–67, 75, 81, 150, 169, 174, 188–189, 195, 211, 271, 276, 278
  and religion 8, 25n71, 43, 65, 75, 108, 110, 120–121, 125, 132, 192–193, 276–277
  and translation 79
  works by

The Book of the Church 8, 25, 79, 276
The Fall of Robespierre 271
The Flagellant 29, 36n40, 37, 42, 75, 132, 270
Joan of Arc 44, 271
Letters from England 133, 150
Sir Thomas More: Or, Colloquies on the Progress and Prospects of Society 8, 25, 276
Thalaba 65–67
The Spectator 37, 86, 90, 172, 200, 208
speech/es, speech days 20, 23, 28, 31, 35–36, 50, 75–77, 86–87, 92, 95, 164, 207
Spenser, Edmund 7, 86, 94, 202n45
sports 3, 19, 28, 31, 34, 48, 161, 177
  see also shooting, fencing, hunting, tennis, cricket, riding, rowing
statics 217, 199, 236
Stevenson, William 138–139
Stoics, stoicism 45, 73, 171, 259
Strabo *see* classical writers, texts
subjects, skills, genres taught in the Anglo-classical academy *see* grammar and public schools, subjects; universities, pedagogies, subjects; also individual items such as calculus, classical writers, texts, composition, memory, epic, ode
subscription to the 39 Articles of Religion 7, 86, 113, 136, 138, 151–152, 162, 200, 231, 243, 253, 164, 266
Sunday schools 3, 13, 15
Swift, Jonathan 86
swimming 18, 34, 178, 260

Tacitus *see* classical writers, texts
taste 3–4, 38, 44, 50–51, 58, 66, 78, 83, 124, 128, 140, 143, 147, 187, 204–206, 221, 275

310

Index

Tatham, Edward *see* universities, college heads
Tatham, Ralph *see* universities, college heads
tea parties 19, 164–165, 179–180
teaching, teaching methods, teaching professional *see esp* Chapter Three (49–70), Chapter Four (71–96), and Chapter Nine (203–21); 3–4, xiii–xiv, 2–4, 9, 13n28, 14, 16–18, 21–22, 24–26, 32, 52fig3, 57, 71, 73, 82–83, 98–99, 116, 120, 123, 137, 140, 142–144, 175, 183–84, 191, 277
   see also pedagogy
technical schools 15
tennis 45, 176
tetrameter *see* metre
Thelwall, John 3, 72
themes or essays, assigned 6, 9, 30, 47, 67, 84–85, 89–90, 108, 116, 203, 210–211, 231
   see also composition
Theocritus *see* classical writers, texts
theology 33, 60, 97, 99, 116–117, 122, 136, 138, 186–187, 199, 203, 223, 232, 235, 238, 257–258, 277
   see also Anglican Church, Anglican orthodoxy, lessons in the faith
Thomson, William 2, 7, 86, 202n45
Thucydides and works by *see* classical writers, texts
Tillotson, John Archbishop of Canterbury 117, 135, 193
The Times 7
Tomko, Michael 277
Tonbridge Grammar School *see* grammar and public schools
Tooke, John Horne 10n15
translation, instruction about 4, 16, 22, 51, 73, 77–79, 82, 85, 88, 90, 140, 166, 200, 207–208
trigonometry 187, 192, 197, 217, 236

Trinity College, Cambridge *see* universities, colleges of Cambridge
Trinity College, Oxford *see* universities, colleges of Oxford
tutors *see* universities, tutors
Tyrwhitt, Robert, Fellow Jesus College 265, 267, 269

Unitarian, Unitarians, Unitarianism 7, 44, 75, 99, 110, 112–113, 118, 123, 136–138, 152, 242–243, 265, 267–268, 270–271
universities
  academic year 161–164
    Cambridge terms: Michaelmas, Lenten, Easter 162 ff
    Oxford terms: Michaelmas, Hilary, Easter or Paschal, Trinity 162 ff
  'Advice to Freshmen' 173
  chapel and Sunday services see Chapter Five, 97–130, 164–166, 167–168, 171–172, 179, 193, 203, 224, 226, 231, 242, 246, 256, 260
  chapels 100, 102, 114, 120, 149, 157, 164, 257, 267, 277
  clubs 178–179
  college day 164–166
  college life 169–170
  colleges of Cambridge
    Girton 13n30, 152
    Jesus 5–6, 12–13, 113, 123, 131–132, 148–149, 165–166, 180, 208, 211, 227n18, 230, 242, 245, 248–249
    Newnham 13n30, 152
    Peterhouse 136, 245
    St John's xviii–iv, 93, 112, 124, 133, 137–138, 156, 157fig16, 158–159, 173, 178, 205, 211, 217, 228, 246–249, 258, 263
    Trinity xiii–iv, 6, 12, 19, 49, 61n43, 63n55, 93, 97, 98n1,

311

104, 110n35, 114, 134–137, 143, 148, 155–156, 159, 166, 168–169, 179–180, 200, 205, 207–211, 214, 216fig20, 218, 227, 231, 236–237, 145–147, 250, 252–267

colleges of Oxford
All Souls 194, 259, 261fig 22
Balliol xviii–vi, 44, 132, 138, 171, 225, 142, 246, 249–250, 260, 262, 271
Brasenose 1, 12, 194, 250, 271
Christ Church xiii–iv, 12, 38, 43–44, 53n12, 82n35, 92–93, 99, 104, 108, 112, 114, 117, 119, 132, 134, 138, 151, 153, 156, 159, 162, 165–166, 168, 172, 177, 180, 188–190, 193–196, 215, 225, 229, 231, 238–239, 245–247, 250–252, 257, 259
Exeter 158, 194
Kings' College xiv, 11n18, 29n6, 93, 101, 113–114, 257, 260
Lady Margaret Hall 13n30, 152
Lincoln 25, 112, 118n64, 137, 229, 235, 250
Magdalen 112, 114, 156, 163, 177, 194
Merton 112, 150, 194
New College 11n18, 29n6, 93, 114, 140, 150, 176–177, 194, 202
Oriel College 49, 118n64, 138, 141, 147, 151, 194, 224, 247, 260, 262
Pembroke 100, 112, 146–148, 166, 176, 211, 246, 252, 263n69
Queen's 111, 225
St Anne's 13n30, 152
St Hugh's 13n30, 152

Somerville 13n30, 152
Trinity 144, 172, 177, 194
University College 12, 146, 158, 225, 260
Wadham 177, 249
commons 149, 226
commons hall, commons rooms 112, 115, 157, 167, 168, 180, 260
communion, eucharist 111, 163, 246
confirmation 111, 127
cost 13, 131, 146–150
critics of 3, 12, 47–48, 136
Edgeworth, Richard Lovell 140
Essays on Professional Education 140
Edinburgh Review 81, 139–141
Jebb, John 136, 137n32, 213, 257
Lofft, Capel 136
Priestley, Joseph 138–139, 267–268
Smith, Sydney 140
Stevenson, William 138–139
curriculum, traditional 186–187
Cambridge 197–202
see also individual subjects, texts, and skills such as apologetics, law, classical writers, texts, composition
Oxford 188–194
see also individual subjects, texts, and skills such as apologetics, law, classical writers, texts, composition
debating societies 256
defenders 141–144
degree ceremony, commencement or graduation 162–164, 243, 266

Index

degrees
    bachelors, BA degree 10, 117, 132, 134, 136, 146–148, 151–152, 158, 162–164, 167, 175, 188, 197, 232–233, 258
    doctor, degree of, DD, doctor of Divinity 43, 66, 118n64, 162–163, 232, 252, 270
    MA degree 136, 163, 188, 219–220, 232, 257
dramatic entertainment 176
Encaenia 115, 164, 194, 226
exclusivity 151–159
fellows, fellowships 7, 9, 12, 18, 82, 92, 107, 110–112, 118n64, 136–137, 147, 152–153, 157, 159, 162, 164, 167–169, 177n76, 179–180, 183–184, 214–216, 219, 221, 223, 225–258, 231, 233, 235–236, 242, 244–246, 248–253, 256–269
food 162, 166–168, 193, 217
founding statutes 184–186
great hall 164–165, 167–168, 210, 246, 251, 257
honours 19, 117, 148, 158, 163–164, 194, 215, 217, 218–220, 223, 225, 235, 241, 246, 252, 258–259, 263
informal religious gatherings 112–114
leadership
    chancellors 171–172, 238n61, 242–243
    canons 117, 162, 250
    college heads, position of (also referred to as dean, proctor, warden, master) 29n6, 43, 56, 61n40, 93, 104, 138, 151, 162, 166, 180, 193–194, 214, 225, 229, 231, 239, 245–246, 250–256, 259, 263
    see also clergymen

Beadon, Richard, Jesus College 247–248, 267–268
Chevallier, John, St John's Cambridge 211
Davey, John, Balliol 249–250, 262
Everleigh, John, Oriel 118n64, 138
Hinchcliffe, John, Trinity Cambridge 137
Jackson, Cyril, Christ Church 138, 180, 194–195, 225, 229, 231, 250–253
Kaye, John, Christ's College, Cambridge 235, 239–240
Mansel, William Lort, Trinity Cambridge 6, 135–136, 168, 252–255
Milner, Isaac, Queens' 112, 217, 227, 230, 252, 265, 267, 269
Parsons, John, Balliol 138, 249–250, 262
Pattison, Mark, Lincoln College 186, 229
Pearce, William, Jesus College 249, 268
Tatham, Edward, Lincoln College 118n64, 137–138, 148
Tatham, Ralph, St John's 148
Whewell, William, Trinity Cambridge 97–98n1
Wood, James, St John's 156, 199, 217, 226–227, 236, 247–248
Elements of Algebra 249
Principles of Mathematics and Natural Philosophy, 4 vols (1795–99) 249

313

Wordsworth, Christopher,
Trinity Cambridge 18–19,
103–104, 110n35, 113,
124, 165, 171, 179, 201,
207, 214–215, 217–218,
252, 255–256
  sub-dean 108, 151
  vice chancellor 98n1, 107–108,
    151, 162, 164, 218, 233,
    244–205, 269, 271
lessons in the faith 116–121
members of parliament
  standing for the university
  243–244
music, musical entertainment 162,
  164, 166, 171, 176, 183, 185,
  277
pedagogies and subjects taught
  203–221
  argument, public speaking
    212–214, 251
  Acts and Opponencies 213–216,
    224
    see also declamations,
      orations, public speaking,
      recitation
  declamation 214
  composition, writing, exercises
    in prose and verse 4, 6, 10,
    143, 172, 187–188, 201,
    204, 207–212, 220, 239,
    248, 251, 255, 262, 264,
    273, 276
    see also themes and essays,
      verse composition
  discussion, questioning 4, 7,
    22, 112–113, 120, 194, 200,
    203–204, 211, 118, 95, 220,
    229–231
  examinations 195, 200,
    208–212, 214–221
    Cambridge Senate House
      exam, tripos 5, 148, 152,
      163, 165, 215, 217–218,
    228–229, 249, 255, 258,
      263
    Cambridge term exams 162,
      166, 208, 210, 215
    Oxford Collections xiii, 162,
      188–190, 192–197, 215
    Oxford honours examination
      215, 218–220, 258
    Oxford 'ordinary
      examination' 215,
      218–219
    Previous Exam 215, 218
    Window problems 217
  lectures 9, 12, 19n50, 117–118,
    143, 152, 158, 163–164,
    166, 185–186, 193–194,
    198, 203, 205, 215, 223,
    230–232, 234–236,
    238–239, 256–257, 260
  private study 161, 165, 201,
    204, 208
  private tutors 15, 89, 140,
    146, 148, 223, 227–230,
    239–240, 250, 255,
    267
  reading, study 6–7, 165–166,
    171, 175, 194–198, 200–201,
    203–207, 219, 224, 227,
    231, 234, 252–252
    see also classical writers,
      texts; subjects of study
  'self-education' 205
  translation 166, 200,
    206–208
prayer 9, 31, 94, 98–99, 102–113,
  116, 120, 122, 124, 163–165,
  193, 226, 277
  daily prayer 277
  evening prayer, vespers 103,
    106, 109
  morning prayer, matins 31,
    102–104, 107, 164, 193
preachership 260
prizemen

Index

Oxford 'firsts' 10, 117, 248, 250, 259
Cambridge wranglers 10, 41n62, 97, 136, 152, 179, 217–218, 220, 225, 246, 248, 252, 255, 159, 263–265
prizes 82n35, 149, 210, 212, 231, 235–236, 239, 243, 245, 248, 255, 259, 264
    Battie Medal (classics), Cambridge 235
    Browne Prizes (Greek ode, Latin ode, Greek epigram, Latin epigram), Cambridge 264
    Cambridge Chancellor's Prize (English ode or poem in heroic verse) 210, 236
    Camden Prize (Latin hexameter), Cambridge 210
    Chancellor's Gold Medal (poetry), Cambridge 248
    Craven Prize (classics) 149
    Gaisford Prizes (Greek compositions in prose or verse), Oxford 239
    Latin Declamation Prize, Cambridge 236
    Newdigate Prize (poetry), Oxford 231
    Oxford essay prize (contemporaneous topic) 82n35, 210
    St John's Members' Latin Essay Prize 248
professors 9, 19, 81, 107, 141, 144–145, 147, 149, 186, 203, 210, 223, 225, 230–240, 242–243, 247, 257–258, 262, 269
    see also clergymen
    Airy, John Biddle (Cambridge) 237, 255
    Babbage, Charles (Cambridge) 11n15, 235n52, 237, 255
    Beddoes, Thomas (Oxford) 11n15
    Copleston, Edward (Oxford) 81, 82n35, 141–144, 146–147, 150, 153, 204, 210, 218–219, 224–226, 235n52, 262
    Farish, William (Cambridge) 235n52, 266
    Gaisford, Thomas (Oxford) 235n52, 238–239
    Hailstone, John (Cambridge) 135, 264
    Hey, John (Cambridge) 235n52
    Hornsby, Thomas (Oxford) 235n52, 238–239
    Kaye, John (Cambridge) 235n52, 235, 239–240
    Keble, John (Oxford) 19, 102, 112, 150, 235n52
    Lax, William (Cambridge) 235n52
    Lloyd, Charles (Oxford) 229, 231, 255, 235n52, 239
    Marsh, Herbert (Cambridge) 235n52, 240, 263
    Milner, Isaac (Cambridge) 112, 217, 227, 230, 235n52, 252, 265, 267, 269
    Robertson, Dr Abraham (Oxford) 239
    Sedgwick, Adam (Cambridge) 235n52, 255, 263
    Vince, Samuel (Cambridge) 235n52, 235–237, 237fig21

315

Principles of Mathematics and Natural Philosophy, 4 vols (1795–99) 249
Watson, Richard 158, 213, 232, 257, 269
Whewell, William (Cambridge) 235n52, 237–238, 97–98, 113, 141, 143–144, 156, 168–170, 176, 183, 203–204, 213, 217, 229–230, 235n52, 236–239, 255, 262–264
Winstanley, Thomas (Oxford) 235n52
Wollaston, John Hyde (Cambridge) 235n52
Wood, James (Cambridge) see college heads, tutors
public speaking and argumentation 212–214
punishments 108, 164, 172–173, 226, 249
reading men 158, 194–197, 219
room and board 166–169
Royal Universities Commissions Reports xiii, 2, 144–149, 152, 161, 166–167, 197, 204, 219, 224, 226, 229–230, 234, 245, 247, 257
scholarships, exhibitions 82, 93, 131–132, 147, 149, 156, 157fig16, 158, 212, 230, 235, 245–246, 249
social life 171
subjects of study *see* individual topics such as algebra, apologetics, Arabic, argument, botany, calculus, classical writers and texts, 'divinity', drama, elegy, epic, ethics, geography, geology, geometry, grammar, Greek, Hebrew, history (church, classical, military), homiletics, hydrostatics, Latin, law, logic, mathematics, mechanics, medicine, metaphysics, metre, mineralogy, moral philosophy, music, natural science/natural philosophy/natural theology, navigation, odes, optic, oratory, philosophy, physics, poetry, politics, prosody, public speaking, rhetoric, satire, scripture, statics, theology, trigonometry
subscription to the 39 Articles 7, 86, 113, 136, 138, 151–152, 162, 200, 231, 243, 253, 164, 266
Sundays 106–110
student behaviour 108, 164, 170–178, 212, 224, 226, 256
see also clubs, tea and wine parties, hunting, etc.
student categories/class/descriptors
commoner 165, 168, 193, 227, 250
fellow commoner 148, 154fig14, 158, 165
gentleman commoner 110, 150, 227
nobleman 110, 134, 136, 148, 155fig15, 156–157, 180, 226–227
pensioner 148, 252, 156, 225, 227
sizar 19, 148–150, 156–158, 172–173, 225, 226–227, 236, 248, 252
tea and wine parties 165, 179–181
tutors, tutorial duties xiii, 4, 9, 24–25, 107, 135, 143–144, 147, 149, 157, 162–164, 166, 173, 175, 183–186, 189, 199, 203–239, 212, 219, 223–231, 234–235, 242, 246–247, 251, 257, 263

Index

see also clergymen
Frend, William, Jesus College, Cambridge 5, 13, 18, 72, 113–114, 123, 131, 138, 152, 213, 249, 252, 257, 263–272
Frewen, Edward, St. John's College, Cambridge 149
Goodenough, Edmund, Christ Church, Oxford 231
Jones, Thomas, Trinity College, Cambridge 5, 137, 200, 263, 267, 269
Jowett, Benjamin, Balliol, Oxford 225
Lloyd, Charles, Christ Church, Oxford 229, 231, 235n52, 239
Milner, Isaac, Queens' College, College Cambridge 227
Pattison, Mark, Lincoln College, Oxford 229
Plampin, John, Jesus College, Cambridge 230
Whewell, William, Trinity College Cambridge 227
Wood, James St. John's College, Cambridge 205, 207, 227–228, 263
Wordsworth, John, Trinity 231
wranglers, first prize men 10, 41n62, 97, 136, 152, 179, 217–218, 220, 225, 246, 248, 252, 255, 159, 263–265

University College *see* universities, colleges of Oxford
University College London 12–13, 255

verse composition 10, 16, 63–64, 67–68, 79, 81–82, 85, 90, 116, 210, 224, 276
vespers *see* prayers
vice 13, 16, 47, 69, 84, 174
vice chancellors *see* universities, leadership
Victorian Period, Victorian xiv, 2, 17, 21–22, 31, 73, 104, 107, 114, 115n51, 152, 170, 214, 221, 243, 276
Vince, Samuel *see* universities, professors
Vincent, Dr William *see* grammar and public schools, headmasters
Virgil and works by *see* classical writers, texts

Wadham College *see* universities, colleges of Oxford
walking 18, 176–178, 260
Walpole, Horace 10, 30, 86
Walpole, Robert 232
Warton, Thomas 10, 86
Warwick, Andrew 1–2
 Masters of Theory: Cambridge and the Rise of Mathematical Physics 1–2
Watson, Richard *see* universities, professors
Webb, Daniel 238
 Inquiry into the Beauties of Painting (1761) 202
 Observations on the Correspondence between Poetry and Music (1769) 238
 Miscellanies (1762) 238
 Remarks on the Beauties of Poetry (1764) 238
Wesley, Charles 10
Wesley, John 10n15
Wesley's 'Holy Club' 112
Wesley's hymns 114–115
Westminster School *see* grammar and public schools

317

Educating the Romantic Poets

Westminster *Trifler* 38
Whately, Richard 10–11n15
Whewell, William *see* universities, college heads, defenders, professors, tutors
Whitfield, John Clark 10
The Whole Duty of Man 33, 109, 116, 192
Wilberforce, William 7, 10, 86–87n54, 112–113, 269
Williams, Helen Maria 61, 86
Wilson, John 10
Winchester College *see* grammar and public schools
Winstanley, Thomas *see* universities, college heads
Wollaston, John Hyde *see* universities, college heads
Wollstonecraft, Mary 7, 278
women, girls 3, 6, 12, 14–15, 19, 20n54, 62, 128, 152, 172, 211, 273
    exclusion from classical education 273, 278
    writings by 278
Wood, James *see* universities, college heads, tutors
Wordsworth, Catherine 124
Wordsworth, Christopher, brother *see* universities, college heads
Wordsworth, Christopher, nephew 18, 171, 177, 179, 213–214, 163
Wordsworth, Dorothy 62, 208, 211n32
Wordsworth, John, brother 124
Wordsworth, John, nephew *see* universities, tutors
Wordsworth, John, son 150
Wordsworth, Mary 102, 256
Wordsworth, Thomas 124
Wordsworth, William
    on education, educational experiences 1–2, 6, 8, 12, 19–21, 23–25, 30, 34, 49n3, 53, 54n15, 61, 68–69, 73, 87–89, 110n33, 125, 133–134, 149–150, 153, 156–158, 166, 168–169, 178–179, 195, 198–202, 205, 208, 211, 215, 225, 227–228, 238, 241, 244, 247–249, 254, 265, 267, 271–272
    and memory 34, 61–62, 200, 125–128, 201, 276
    as a poet, writer, on poets 2, 8, 17, 23–25, 78, 83, 108–109, 174, 200, 206–207, 242, 273–278
    and religion 79, 81, 98–99, 101–103, 106, 110, 114, 124–129, 228, 265
    return to Cambridge 256–257
    works by
        Ecclesiastical Sketches 7, 68, 79, 98, 101–102, 106, 114, 121, 124, 126–128, 217, 239, 255–256, 258, 269, 270, 276–277
        The Excursion 1, 3, 20, 65n64, 124–126, 128, 270, 276, 278
        Lyrical Ballads 2–3, 8, 24, 67, 112n41, 126, 189n12, 201, 206–208, 211m, 270, 275
        Poems in Two Volumes 65, 678, 112n41, 128, 206
        The Prelude 6, 12, 16, 19–20, 34, 109, 126, 133, 149, 153, 178, 195, 198–200, 248, 270, 273, 278
working classes, exclusion from education 12, 20n54, 149, 268, 270, 273
wrangler *see* universities
wrestling 34, 176
writing, writing instruction *see* composition

Yorke, Philip 165, 230

Xenophon *see* classical writers, texts

Printed and bound by CPI Group (UK) Ltd, Croydon, CR0 4YY
30/06/2024
14521515-0002